W9-CFA-208

DISCARDED
Goshen Public Library

THE ★★★ Federal Investigators

THE ★★★ Federal Investigators

Miriam Ottenberg

Englewood Cliffs, N.J.
PRENTICE-HALL, INC.

Library of Congress Catalog Card Number: 62-17427

Printed in the United States of America
31387-T

The cases related in this book are true but in the interest of national security, confidentiality of records, safeguarding the anonymity of undercover agents and protecting the innocent, certain names and other identifying details have been altered in a few chapters.

DEDICATION

To my father, who gave me faith in justice, and to my mother, who taught me to fight for it.

ACKNOWLEDGMENTS

To all the government officials, the public information officers and the Federal investigators themselves, who gave me their generous assistance in the preparation of this book, I want to express my sincere thanks.

Foreword

A frequent after-work pastime in Washington is talking about the importance and excitement of one's job. Yet a substantial number of federal employees, whose work is honestly important and usually exciting, cannot indulge in such shop-talk. They probably don't mind. Not being able to talk shop, even with their wives, is a minor burden compared with posing as a spy, living the life of a "junkie," or protecting the safety of thousands of airplane passengers. More important, the basic attitude of these men—Federal investigators—is to do their jobs and let the results speak for themselves.

Unfortunately, it doesn't always work that way. The Federal investigator rarely is credited in the newspaper stories about the arrest of a stock swindler or the seizure of rotten food. Sometimes even his agency is not identified. The importance of the Federal investigator to the health and safety of our country—in fields ranging from espionage to orange juice—is not widely enough recognized.

By providing this careful appraisal of the agencies' responsibilities and some vivid illustrations of how those responsibilities are met, Miriam Ottenberg has done a great service, both to the agencies and to the American public. It is doubly appropriate that she be the author of such a book. She writes well and knowledgeably, after years of covering these agencies for The Washington *Evening Star*, and she herself is an outstanding investigator. Her investigative abilities are evidenced not only by a Pulitzer Prize, but also other journalistic honors. She also has won the respect of the investigators about whom she writes—and whom she often assists with the results of her own digging for the facts.

Such investigative reporting—the sometimes plodding, sometimes dangerous search for the truth—is one of the highest aspects both of the newspaper profession and of the Federal investigator. Such a book is needed and I am pleased it was written. I am even happier that it was written by Miriam Ottenberg.

ROBERT F. KENNEDY,
Attorney General of the United States

CONTENTS

Foreword by Robert F. Kennedy vii

A More Perfect Union: An Introduction xi

Part I: ESTABLISHING JUSTICE

Chapter 1 Pattern for Espionage—Federal Bureau of Investigation 3

Part II: THE COMMON DEFENSE

2 A Diplomat Named Scarbeck—State Department's Office of Security 25

3 The Black Marketeers—The Army Criminal Investigation Division 48

4 The Case of the Lonely Sailor—Office of Naval Intelligence 62

5 Across the Barbed Wire—Air Force Office of Special Investigations 77

Part III: THE GENERAL WELFARE

6 The Clue On the Tape—Civil Aeronautics Board 97

7 The Guterma Affair—Securities and Exchange Commission 116

8 What Happened to the *Steelhead?*—Coast Guard 135
9 The Smuggling Ambassador—Federal Bureau of Narcotics 150
10 The Orange Juice Conspiracy—Food and Drug Administration 169
11 Man On a Tightrope—Alcohol and Tobacco Tax Division, Internal Revenue Service 191

Part IV: DOMESTIC TRANQUILITY

12 The Fall of Joe Adonis—Immigration and Naturalization Service 213
13 The Security Risk—Civil Service Commission 230
14 The Richmond Caper—Internal Revenue's Intelligence Division 249
15 The Girl With the Counterfeit Checks—Secret Service 272
16 The Gun Runers—Customs Agency Service 289
17 Dollars for the Chinese Reds—Postal Inspection Service 309

The Blessings of Liberty: A Conclusion 333
Appendix: Other Agencies 337
Index 344

A More Perfect Union: An Introduction

You may never meet an investigator for the United States government, but you are safer, more comfortable, more secure because thousands of Federal agents labor unceasingly in the background of American life.

Take an average day. You turn on your radio to catch the morning news. The words come through without jamming, without interference, because the "kilocycle cops" of the Federal Communications Commission patrol the air waves.

You reach for your vitamin pill and sit down to breakfast. Both the food and the pill are pure and what they claim to be because inspectors and chemical detectives of the Food and Drug Administration make sure that food processing plants are clean and that the words on the label of the pill bottle are true.

You open your morning mail. There's a check in one envelope, but it arrived safely; for that, you can thank the Postal Inspection Service.

You send your children to school, knowing with more confidence than you used to feel that no kidnapper is going to snatch your child, and that marihuana peddlers now run a real risk of capture whenever they offer children what look like harmless cigarettes but are anything but harmless. The agents of the Federal Bureau of Investigation and the Federal Bureau of Narcotics both have a share in protecting your child.

You scan the advertisements for shopping tips with reasonable assurance that the claims of the nation-wide products are not false or misleading. The Federal Trade Commission investigators see to that.

You go to work under the protection of many Federal investigators. There's the wage-and-hour investigator to make sure your employer doesn't work you 12 hours for eight hours' pay. If you're a union man, there's a labor-management compliance officer on the lookout to prevent a union boss from abusing your confidence or misusing your dues. If you're the employer, the same investigator or an FBI agent checks any attempt to force you to pay tribute for labor peace. If you're a small businessman, the Federal Trade Commission investigators are there to protect you from unfair competition or the squeeze act from the big combines. If you're a manufacturer, the agents of the Bureau of Customs guard you against having to compete with foreign products smuggled into the country or sneaked in with false evaluations.

This may be the day you decide to buy some stocks. You can invest more safely than your father did because investigators of the Securities and Exchange Commission make sure that stock prices aren't being manipulated and that you know the truth about the stocks you buy.

You may have to make a hurry-up trip to another city. You can also fly more safely than your father did because the air safety investigators of the Civil Aeronautics Board find the causes of past crashes and make sure the fatal defects are corrected.

Before the day ends, you may be handed some cash. You don't even bother to examine the bills to see if they're genuine, thanks to the Secret Service agents' unceasing war against the counterfeiters.

And all this time, other agents at home and overseas are laboring in the open and in secret to guard you against spies and saboteurs, against fraud and corruption, against Communist minions and master criminals.

What we take for granted now as our due in a free country has been built laboriously over nearly two centuries, beginning with the mandates of the Constitution.

In the preamble to the Constitution, the founding fathers stated their aspirations in broad terms. They didn't write law into the preamble but purpose—their purpose of establishing a more perfect union within the framework of a Constitution flexible enough to stand the test of time and provide for the unseen future.

To Congress, they granted the authority to make the laws; to the President and his executive departments, the authority to carry them out; and to the courts, the authority to make certain that what the Congress legislated and the President ordered would fit within the bounds of the Constitution. As the Congress made the laws for the country and the President executed them, there followed the need for investigators to assure that the laws were properly administered and enforced.

Sometimes, the executive departments have found a need for investigators ahead of Congressional authorization and looked to their Constitutional authority to appoint them. Sometimes, a law has been on the books for decades before the need for specialized investigators became apparent.

And sometimes, many times, the courts have used their Constitutional authority to curb the investigators, making their tasks more difficult. On occasion, after the court has spoken, Congress has reentered the picture to draft a law meeting the court's objections and trying to restore the delicate balance between the rights of the individual and the rights of law-abiding society.

The Supreme Court, however, has not always been restrictive to investigative needs. In 1819, the high court's decision in the landmark case of McCulloch versus Maryland laid the groundwork for the investigation of crime in the course of collecting taxes. The court in effect ruled that if the end be legitimate and within the scope of the Constitution, all appropriate means to achieve that end which are not prohibited by law may Constitutionally be employed. As recently as 1937, that Supreme Court decision was quoted by a lower court in ruling that Alcohol and Tobacco Tax investigators had a right to demand reports on sugar sales in their efforts to locate moonshiners.

Congress has used its taxing power under the Constitution and this broad interpretation by the Supreme Court to create such crime-hunting Treasury agencies as the Alcohol and Tobacco Tax Division and the Bureau of Narcotics. Congress also went after gambling originally by requiring gamblers to pay a tax on their profits. The act didn't add greatly to the nation's revenue because the gamblers shied away from publicly identifying themselves as such, but then they could be tracked down as Federal law violators.

Another power granted Congress under the Constitution which puts Federal investigators on the job is the right of Congress to regulate interstate and foreign commerce. Under that power, Congress created the Federal Trade Commission, with investigators looking into monopolies and unfair business practices interstate, and passed the Fair Labor Standards Act under which wage-and-hour investigators cover companies whose goods and services cross state lines. It was under the same power that Congress recently handed the FBI the job of enforcing a package of racket-busting laws, including one banning interstate travel in aid of racketeering enterprises.

In creating new tasks for Federal investigators, Congress has done a lot of investigating on its own. Ever since 1792, Congressional investigators have been probing for weaknesses in the executive machinery and plugging loopholes in the law.

The sordid revelations of influence-peddling and tax-fixing aired on Capitol Hill in 1951 prompted President Truman to reorganize the Bureau of Internal Revenue and create another investigative unit within it—the Inspection Service. Its 500 investigators rout out the favor seekers and those who would bribe the public's servants to shave their taxes.

The Labor Department's recently established Bureau of Labor-Management Reports with its corps of compliance officers stemmed from the exposé of labor racketeering by Chairman McClellan's Senate Select Committee on Improper Activities in the Labor or Management Field. The former chief counsel of that committee is now the Attorney General of the United States, Robert F. Kennedy.

Frequently, the President rather than Congress has taken the initiative in calling attention to the need to protect the public from some profound abuse. As a college professor, Woodrow Wilson had lectured his classes on the problems of big business combining to restrain trade. When he became president, he gave the same lecture to Congress and the Federal Trade Commission was established to move against unfair methods of competition.

Most of the Federal agencies using investigators to enforce their laws were spawned by twentieth century problems, but some investigators can trace their predecessors back to the birth of the Republic—or even earlier. Benjamin Franklin, who can easily be classified as the first Federal investigator, was investigating mail thefts in colonial times.

The history of the Federal investigative power closely parallels the nation's growth and the problems that went along with it. The basic needs of the new nation, the westward expansion, the transcontinental railroad, the booms and the depressions, fast and faster transportation bringing the rest of the world closer, the rising social consciousness, radio and television, the natural and man-made disasters, the farm-to-city movement, the changing face of crime—all these have shared in creating the demand for Federal watchdogs.

The first Federal investigators drew their authority directly from the Constitution itself. The founding fathers, recognizing the mails as the lifeline between the scattered colonies, directed Congress to establish post offices and post riders. Inevitably, postal agents were needed to make sure the mail went through. The authors of the Constitution had to meet another urgent demand of the infant nation—import duties to finance the government. So customs agents emerged to detect and prevent smuggling and other devices to cheat the government out of the funds it needed to survive. The Constitution also recognized that the nation needed a system of currency its people could trust. It gave Congress the power to coin money, set its value and punish counterfeiters—a precaution that took on added significance when the thieves started turning out phony bills. Thus, the Secret Service was born to carry out another mandate of the founding fathers.

Until the close of the nineteenth century, however, the Federal guardians of the public welfare as visualized in the preamble to the Constitution still represented only a handful of investigators in the Treasury and Post Office Departments. Inevitably, their duties were much broader than their original missions for lack of other Federal enforcers. The Secret Service alone carried out assignments now performed by half a dozen different agencies. The needs were there, but neither Congress nor the Chief Executive had gotten around to meeting them.

In the first half of this century, Congress made up for lost time. The public—or some vocal segment of it—demanded protection and Federal investigators were required to provide it. So, as the population burgeoned and unregulated business boomed, as inventions created both new promise and new problems, as crime and subversion threatened domestic tranquillity, Congress went about the business of fulfilling the purposes implied in the preamble. And where the President and his executive departments could move without specific Congressional approval, they moved.

The processing of food had shifted from the family kitchen to the factories, then unregulated, unclean and unsafe. Out of the public outcries came the pure food and drug investigators. Land thieves preying on the opening West and big business trusts stifling the economy in the east prompted President Theodore Roosevelt's outraged demands for a Bureau of Investigation, forerunner of today's FBI. That new invention—radio—spurred Congress to require radio equipment on sea-going passenger vessels and inspectors to enforce the law. World War I forced the nation's leaders to look for the first time at outside threats requiring the talents of investigators to track down spies, saboteurs and subversives. The war had another effect—increased taxes with their built-in incentive to evade. So investigators were mobilized to go after the tax evaders and a new weapon was forged against criminals who could be brought to justice no other way—the tax-dodging overlords of crime.

The gaudy Twenties gave way to the problem-ridden Thirties and

Congress was jolted into giving the Federal government powers implied but not specifically spelled out in the Constitution. More Federal laws, by this time, meant more Federal investigators to enforce them.

So Federal agents moved onto the farms, into the dust bowls, down the mine shafts, into the factories. Attorneys and accountants doubling as investigators probed the world of securities to guard against another stock-market crash. Air safety investigators invented new techniques to ward off other kinds of crashes. Wage-and-hour investigators started bringing businessmen into line with laws putting a floor under wages and a ceiling over hours.

Congress had met the major crime threats of the lawless Prohibition Era by giving the FBI more laws to enforce, but the post-Prohibition years brought new faces, new techniques, new sources of profit to the high command of crime and Congress created new Federal agencies for the counterattack.

In the uneasy peace after World War II, other threats emerged to jeopardize the nation's security. At home, investigators were mobilized in the Immigration and Naturalization Service to search for the evidence needed to deport the foreign-born Communists infiltrating the country's key industries. Abroad, the hush-hush corps of the Central Intelligence Agency went into action to find out about Communist tactics.

Today, more than 20,000 Federal investigators carry out the purposes expressed and implied in the preamble to the Constitution. Along with those whose prime function is investigating, other Federal officers operate along similar lines as inspectors, analysts, examiners, compliance officers—all doing a job for the people under Congressional mandate.

Almost every Federal agency has some form of investigative unit from the Interior Department's Fish and Wildlife Service, whose men go undercover to infiltrate gangs of commercial duck hunters, to the Atomic Energy Commission's Compliance Division with its responsibility for protecting the public against radiation hazards. Some agencies simply have small units to protect their own security. Others are clearly dedicated to some area of Federal law enforcement. The Treasury Department alone has six services going after criminals and would-be criminals via its authority over money and taxes. In peacetime, its jurisdiction includes the Coast Guard with its intelligence and marine inspection forces.

Since the investigative arms of Federal agencies were born out of necessity and matured under additional missions, there is no one pattern or official table of organization applying to them all. The framework chosen to present the agencies here stemmed from the author's analysis of their prime duties and how they fit into the grand design of the founding fathers.

The Federal force of investigators continues to grow, but unlike other countries, we have never had a national police force and no one wants it now. The basic responsibility for law enforcement as well as for many other forms of public protection still rests with the states. Then, why does the roll of Federal investigators go up? The answers are many and complex.

First, crime crosses state lines. Even the most well-intentioned local officer can't cope with the syndicates conducting an interstate business via the mails, planes, automobiles and telephones. The same is true of many individual criminals. A bandit can rob a bank in New York before noon and be hidden out in San Francisco before nightfall. A confidence man in Chicago can swindle a victim in Miami without leaving the side of his telephone. Only Federal officers have the right to follow both crime and criminal across state lines.

Second, local law enforcement officers rely on the FBI's central storehouse of fingerprints, the use of its crime laboratories, the training it provides through its police academy, the exchange of information. They rely on other Federal agencies, too, to help them solve cases with skilled manpower, technical equipment and tips. A Federal charge may assure a much longer sentence than a state charge—and Congress has had that very fact in mind in specifying severe penalties for Federal violations that closely parallel state crimes.

Third, there are some communities in this country where local law enforcement is so lax that big-time criminals move in. If anybody is going to get them there, it's got to be the Federal agents.

Aside from crime, uniform laws and enforcement are needed in many areas of public protection where a product or a service covers many states. You can't have different laws in every state crossed by an airplane in a single day. You can't have different labelling or standards of purity for products distributed nation-wide or different state laws covering national advertising. As these products and services cross the country only the Federal investigators can pick up violations anywhere along the line.

Then, too, the states and their people look to the Federal government and its investigators to protect their interests against the common enemies—the smugglers, the counterfeiters, the spies and subversives, the dope traffickers and the inanimate killers in airplane defects and mislabelled medicines.

Considering the extent of their responsibilities, the size of most Federal investigative units is surprisingly small. What they lack in size, however, they make up in the concentrated intensity of their efforts and—for most investigators—a working day that never ends.

The Treasury Department, for one, makes no bones about telling prospective agents what is required of them. After warning the applicants that they must be proficient marksmen, may have to go undercover and live with criminals for long periods, the Treasury announcement adds: "Performance of these duties may require work at irregular hours, involve personal risks, exposure to all kinds of weather, arduous physical exertion under rigorous and unusual environmental conditions and considerable travel."

The long roll of dead and injured Treasury agents indicates that the government's carefully-couched warning is sheer understatement. If they're still game after that outline of their duties, the Treasury agents and their counterparts in other investigative agencies are given other warnings once they make the team.

These FBI rules are typical: The agent can't take a drink on duty, of course, but he's got to stay sober off-duty, too, because he's always subject to call. He cannot use a government car except for official business. He cannot use duress in dealing with any person under investigation, regardless of how recalcitrant the person may be. He cannot disclose information to any unauthorized person, including his wife. He cannot accept rewards in any form, he must pay his taxes and meet all his other financial obligations and he must not lose government property.

In other words, he has to be a model citizen, a man above reproach.

On the surface, the investigators spread across more than a score of Federal agencies don't fit a pattern. The FBI agent in his conservative suit and snap-brim hat looks nothing like the narcotics agent whose slick hoodlum air serves both as disguise and protection when he goes undercover. The gray-haired Food and Drug inspector who takes samples to be tested bears no resemblance to his colleagues in the same agency who pose as truck drivers to track down distributors of "pep pills." The pilot turned investigator to find out why planes crash comes from a different background than the accountant turned investigator who wades through countless records to turn up a stock fraud or a tax dodge.

And yet, they all have much in common—the same patience, the same persistence, the same dogged drive to find the one elusive but conclusive clue.

During my years as a crime reporter, I've come to know many

of these Federal agents. I've met more in the course of developing the cases presented here. Watching them, talking with them, the same thought has often crossed my mind. These are the kind of men you'd like to have as next-door neighbors. They are mature, disciplined, above average in intelligence and devoted family men.

Perhaps their strong attachment to their wives and children stems from the risks they face so often. Life and all its good things becomes more precious when death or crippling injury may lie around the next corner.

Then, too, they are forced to be away from their families at frequent intervals. They never know when they'll be called away from home to stay a day, a week, a month or more. An air safety investigator doesn't know when a plane is going to crash. An FBI agent never knows when a bank may be robbed or a child kidnapped. A narcotics agent may be tapped at any time for a year's undercover assignment. A Secret Service agent goes at a moment's notice on the merest hint of a threat on the President's life.

And the wives of these agents often don't know where they're going, how long they'll be away—or why.

"Nicky," ace undercoverman for the Secret Service whose story is told here in the case of "The Girl with the Counterfeit Checks," has never told his wife that he goes undercover on his trips out of town. After many years of married life, she still thinks he's got a safe desk job and he takes considerable pains to keep it that way. He doesn't want her to worry about him, which is one of several reasons why his real name doesn't appear in this book.

The wife of Customs Agent Wallace D. Shanley wasn't aware of his intricate maneuvers with "The Gun Runners" until a truckload of guns was stored in the garage of the Shanley home. Internal Revenue Agent Sidney Macauley slipped across Richmond occasionally to spend a night at home during "The Richmond Caper" but, as far as his wife knew, he was out of town the rest of the time.

The Federal agents go through rigorous training to prepare them for their assignments. Usually, although not always, they have the equipment they need to compete with the well-equipped criminals. They are supervised and directed, but many times they are alone at the moment of decision and then they've got the loneliest job in the world.

These, then, are the men you will meet—family men, most of them college-trained, using their brains instead of their fists, ploughing through snow and swamp to plane crashes, facing the twin hazards of recognition and betrayal every time they go undercover, risking death from ambush and forever walking the narrow path of justice as laid down by the courts.

They are the men chosen by your government to protect you—the Federal investigators.

Part I ★

ESTABLISHING JUSTICE

1 ★★★

Federal Bureau of Investigation

Throughout the land, a disciplined corps of some 6,000 Federal agents is routing out the nation's enemies—foreign and domestic.

It's the mission of these government men to see that fugitive criminals have no place to hide, that the innocent are protected and the guilty pursued, that local law enforcement is bolstered and Federal law enforcement is effective.

Their job and their numbers continue to grow because whenever Congress passes a criminal law without specifying which Federal agents should investigate violations, the task automatically falls on them. They are the special agents of the Federal Bureau of Investigation, the investigative arm of the Justice Department.

Because Congress and successive Presidents have wanted it that way, they are now charged with investigating more than 165 Federal matters ranging from anti-trust violations and auto theft to sabotage and sedition. Their responsibility often begins when the crime or criminal crosses state lines. It ends when they present their package of evidence. Once they find the truth, the criminal usually knows he's beaten. In more than 90 per cent of the cases, when the FBI investigates, the offender pleads guilty.

Through scientific crime detection the men of the FBI have located a murderer through a handful of dust and identified an extortionist through the perforated edge of a postage stamp. By March of 1962 they had solved all but three of the 647 major kidnappings they investigated over three decades, including a kidnap-murder unraveled by examining two million samples of handwriting. They have established the innocence of the falsely accused from a man serving a 35-year prison term to one facing mob violence as the killer of three women.

They combed the country for prisoner-of-war victims of Japanese torture in World War II and made a case of treason against a Japanese-American whose sadism had added to the prison nightmare. Their Disaster Squad travelled to Belgium to identify 38 of the 49 American victims of the crash that killed the United States skating team, despite the apparent hopelessness of the task in the mass of charred and crushed bodies. (The other American victims had been identified by Belgian authorities from personal effects.)

They found the traitors who gave the Soviet Union America's most precious secret—the atom bomb. And they regularly weed out the Soviet representatives who come here under cover of diplomacy to spy for their Communist masters.

But the FBI's role in the nation's protection extends beyond enforcing its pack of criminal laws and Presidential directives. Acutely aware that the tentacles of organized crime, once concentrated in the cities, now reach into the smallest communities, the FBI has pioneered in uniting all law enforcement agencies against their common enemy—the forces of crime. This cooperative effort is based on the principle that no single law enforcement agency—not even the FBI—can go it alone against today's enemies of society.

So, the FBI, through its crime laboratories and fingerprint repository, helps local law enforcement solve crimes and locate criminals. The FBI's National Academy and the instructors it sends to local police schools help develop career police forces dedicated to high principles of justice under the Constitution. The FBI's crime conferences in local communities alert civic leaders and businessmen as well as police and prosecutors to methods of coping with pressing criminal problems. The criminal information it channels to other law enforcement agencies—numbering over 100,000 items in a recent 12-month period—not only leads to the solution of specific crimes but tips off communities when big-time racketeers come to town.

The FBI's monthly Law Enforcement Bulletin keeps the law men current on the latest gambits of the criminals and the latest techniques for circumventing them. Finally, its annual compilation of crime reports from police forces throughout the country gives local law enforcement agencies—and their communities—an up-to-date reading of crime in their home towns and throughout the nation.

The FBI appeals directly to the people to share in the fight against crime through its "Ten Most Wanted Fugitives" program and its thousands of "wanted" circulars. And the people regularly respond with the tips that put more bandits and killers out of circulation. Between March, 1950, when the program started, and March, 1962, a total of 154 of the "most wanted" fugitives were located, 63 of them on the basis of tips furnished by citizens who recognized the fugitives from wanted posters or widespread publicity in news media.

The FBI is unique in many things, its size, the range of its investigative responsibilities, its national popularity. It's also unique among government agencies in getting all the money it requests from Congress. As the House Appropriations Committee phrased it in giving the FBI the $127,216,000 it requested to operate during the 1962 fiscal year:

"The confidence which the Committee has in the Federal Bureau of Investigation under the highly capable and efficient leadership of Director J. Edgar Hoover is best illustrated by the fact that this is the tenth consecutive year that not one penny of the funds he has requested of the Committee has been denied . . ."

It wasn't that way for the FBI under its original management. In fact, it had fallen into disrepute by the time J. Edgar Hoover took command.

The FBI had its beginnings on July 26, 1908, two months after Congress forbade the Justice Department and all other executive agencies outside the Treasury to use Secret Service agents for their investigations. President Theodore Roosevelt, who had been borrowing Secret Service agents in his campaign to clean up land thievery in the West and big-business trusts in the East, and had stepped on some Congressional toes in the process, was outraged at Congress for striking this low blow at Federal law enforcement. He counterattacked by ordering the Attorney General to establish an investigative force within the Justice Department. It was soon called the Bureau of Investigation.

In its early years, it was inept, ineffective and dominated by politics. Its agents were appointed not on what they knew but whom they knew. Untrained and undisciplined, they were ill-prepared for the role expected of them in World War I. As a result, German saboteurs dynamited vital installations and German espionage rings faced little interference. The Bureau's Justice Department bosses encouraged the support of vigilantes, thus causing the bureau to sink even lower in public esteem. It fell to its lowest point when it was swept by the backwash of the "Teapot Dome" scandal in the Harding Administration.

President Coolidge, determined to cure the fever of corruption in government, brought in Harlan Fiske Stone as Attorney General. Later to be Chief Justice of the United States, the new Attorney General moved cautiously but quickly. Within a few weeks, he had accepted the resignation of William J. Burns as director of the Bureau of Investigation. When he looked around for a successor, Herbert Hoover, then Secretary of Commerce, suggested he would find the man he sought within the bureau itself—a man of the same surname but no relation.

J. Edgar Hoover was then the 29-year-old assistant director of the bureau. When the Attorney General offered him the job of acting director, young Hoover set certain conditions for accepting. He wanted assurance that the bureau would be divorced from politics and relieved of political hacks, that appointments of agents would be based on merit and promotions on proven ability. In giving him that assurance, Attorney General Stone did more at a single stroke for law enforcement than his predecessors had done over more than a dozen years.

When Hoover became director in 1924, the bureau had few criminal laws to enforce, including the "white slave act" which outlawed taking women across state lines for immoral purposes and the Dyer Act making it a crime to take a stolen car across state lines. Since the agents otherwise spent their time investigating civil matters for the Attorney General, they were known as "briefcase agents." They had no authority to carry a gun or make an arrest.

It was just as well their powers were limited because they hadn't been trained for anything more. Hoover saw to it that they got training. He established discipline and stern rules of personal conduct. He turned a deaf ear on politicians demanding favored treatment for their protégés and patiently weeded out the misfits. In their place, he put a different breed—young men trained in the law or accounting.

A wave of lawlessness was sweeping the country, but the FBI didn't become directly involved in it until the kidnapping of Charles A. Lindbergh's baby jolted Congress into passing the Federal kidnapping law in 1932. Like so many criminal laws to follow, the responsibility for going after kidnappers who took their victims across state lines was handed to the FBI. It was a kidnapper who tagged FBI agents with a nickname that caught the popular fancy in 1933. When the agents closed in on "Machine Gun" Kelly, he cried: "Don't shoot, G-Men!" The term, short for government men, stuck through the lawless years.

Those were the days when the killer breed of bank robbers was terrorizing communities, particularly in the Midwest. The Dillinger gang, the Barker-Karpis mob, "Baby Face" Nelson, "Pretty Boy" Floyd and Frank Nash were cutting a swath of looted banks and dead policemen. Congress reacted with a package of crime laws, turning the FBI loose on bank robbers and extortionists, giving agents permission to carry firearms and make arrests, clearing the way for the FBI to aid the states by pursuing major criminals across state lines.

The 1934 crime package put FBI agents on the firing line and some of them died shooting it out with experienced killers. "Baby Face" Nelson had already killed one FBI agent when two others encountered him and his cronies on an Illinois highway. Nelson shot them both but, mortally wounded, they kept on firing. Nelson died with them.

Another agent was killed in what came to be known as the "Kansas City Massacre." A band of Frank Nash's cronies made a daring attempt to rescue him as he was being escorted from the Kansas City railroad station. In the fusillade of machine gun fire, an FBI agent was killed, along with an Oklahoma police chief, two Kansas City detectives and Nash himself, and two FBI agents were wounded. "Pretty Boy" Floyd was one of the assassins who escaped. When he was killed 16 months later, shooting it out with FBI agents, a silver half-dollar with ten notches was found in his pocket. It was believed to be his count of the murders he had committed.

Congress did what it could to stem the tide of death by making it a Federal crime to assault or kill an FBI agent. The FBI itself responded to the death-dealing bandits by training its agents to become expert marksmen.

By the end of the Thirties, the FBI had killed off or sent to prison and the execution chamber most of the kidnap and bank robbery gangs of the day. As it gained the upper hand over the machine-gun mobsters, however, another threat to the nation's security emerged.

By a secret memorandum on June 26, 1939, and a public directive three months later, President Franklin D. Roosevelt instructed the FBI to take charge of investigations dealing with espionage, counterespionage, sabotage, subversive activities and violations of neutrality laws.

The FBI had to look to both left and right to guard the nation from totalitarian assaults. The Germans were planting the seeds of sedition among those who took advantage of America's desire to stay out of war by organizing, preaching Nazi hate doctrines, and raising their arms in the Nazi-Fascist salute. At the same time, the Communists were expanding their Moscow-trained nucleus of agents into cells penetrating both government and industry.

The Presidential directive gave specific authority to FBI investigations that had been going on for years under the broad cloak of various anti-subversive laws. Hoover had been aware of the Communist goal of world domination since the Twenties and of the Nazi threat since Hitler's rise to power in the Thirties. As a result, his agents knew whom to watch when the President issued his first directive in 1939, reiterated by subsequent Presidential orders in 1943 and 1950.

By correlating intelligence data flowing from many sources, by sending agents on secret missions into Latin America to block enemy efforts to use our neighbors as relay points for supplying submarines and spies, the FBI played a major role in warding off the sabotage that had plagued the nation in World War I. It tracked down the eight Nazi saboteurs who were landed in this country by submarine and brought them to justice. It located several espionage rings before they could get going. And, despite the Soviet switch from enemy to friend, it kept a wary eye on Communists of both the home-grown and foreign variety.

This proved a wise precaution as the hot war with Germany was succeeded by the cold war with the Communists. When the reality of the Communist threat became more pronounced and charges of "Reds in government" promoted public hysteria, President Harry Truman set up orderly standards to determine the loyalty of government employees. At first, the full weight of loyalty investigations fell on the FBI, complicated by a series of Congressional enactments directing the FBI to investigate all employees hired by the Atomic Energy Commission and other agencies involved in the national security. In 1952, however, when the burden of Federal employee investigations was obviously draining FBI manpower needed elsewhere, Congress shifted the primary responsibility to the Civil Service Commission. The FBI continued to be responsible for checking Federal employees through its identification division and investigative files and making full investigations when the initial inquiries turned up any information revealing possible disloyalty.

The FBI agents have gone into the full loyalty investigations with an acute awareness that a man's reputation is at stake and there can be no margin for error. In distinguishing fact from rumor, the FBI investigations have often proved the innocence of government employees who emerged as the victims of spite and smear charges.

For the FBI, the potential threat posed by Communist adherents in government was followed by the reality of Communists stealing the nation's most precious secret—the making of the atomic bomb. The FBI's investigation first pinpointed Klaus Fuchs, German-born British scientist who had worked on atomic development in this country. The trail of treachery led from him to Harry Gold, an American chemist to whom Klaus had turned over atomic secrets; to David Greenglass, an ex-Army sergeant who had served at the Los Alamos, N.M., nuclear establishment, and finally to Julius and Ethel Rosenberg, who were convicted and executed for the crime of putting the secret of the atomic bomb in the hands of the Russians.

The execution of the Rosenbergs only spurred the Russians to send their own emissaries on espionage missions. One of them was Col. Rudolf Abel, a Soviet master spy using all the tricks of the trade from slit coins and cuff-links for concealing coded microfilms to "drops" where messages could be cached in the cracks of park steps. Arrested in 1957, Abel was sentenced to 30 years in prison but, in February, 1962, he was sent back to Russia in exchange for Francis Gary Powers, the American U-2 pilot captured by the Soviets.

The Communists have also used their diplomats for espionage as well as to tangle Americans in the Soviet web. These diplomats are not sent to American prisons after the FBI pinpoints their activities. Instead, the United States Government evicts them. In the dozen years since 1950, more than a score of Soviet bloc nationals have been forced to go home because of spying activities proved by the FBI.

During the same period, the FBI has responded to Congressional mandates by rounding up more than 100 top level and secondary leaders of the Communist Party in America whose activities indicated their goal was the overthrow of the American form of government.

The post-war surge of Communist activity was matched by an equally serious surge of major crime. The decade of the Fifties began with the biggest cash robbery in the nation's history on January 17, 1950, when a gang of men invaded the theoretically impregnable fortress of the Brinks money storehouse in Boston and walked out with over $1,218,000 in cash. So cleverly was the crime executed that the FBI spent years running down false trails to dead ends. Nearly six years later—only a matter of days before the men would have been forever safe from prosecution because of the statute of limitations—the FBI turned over the solved case to the state of Massachusetts. Eight men were sent to prison for life.

One of the most intensive manhunts in modern law enforcement history also was launched early in the decade when a kidnap-killer named William Edward Cook, Jr., went on a rampage through the Southwest. By the time the FBI was called in on January 4, 1951, the authorities feared that Cook was responsible for the disappearance of an Illinois family named Mosser whose abandoned car was found on an Oklahoma road with six exploded cartridge cases on the floor and several blood-splattered bullets in the upholstery.

On the basis of a sales receipt for a gun found in a car Cook had stolen earlier, FBI agents traced the gun to its original owner in Texas and dug around his farm until they found two .32 caliber shells which matched those found in the Mosser car. To corroborate the link between Cook and the Mosser family's disappearance, FBI agents traced the cancellation stamp of a cigarette package to a Winthrop, Ark., cafe. There, the proprietor and three customers identified photographs of Mr. and Mrs. Mosser and their three children and Cook as the party who had stopped in for a snack on New Year's Day.

Two days after the FBI search began, Cook struck again in California. Tracing his movements, agents found he had kidnapped a deputy sheriff, left him bound on a lonely road, made off with his car and abandoned it, killed the driver of another car, abandoned that one and, at last reports, was believed to have kidnapped two men who failed to return from a hunting trip in their red car.

The FBI saturated the area with wanted flyers, printing some in Spanish for Mexican distribution and even dropping wanted notices from helicopters. Posses of law men searched the area of mountain and desert over a wide sweep of the Mexican border, looking for Cook and the red car.

On January 13, exactly a week after the FBI launched its massive manhunt, the clue of the red car paid off. It was spotted outside a Mexican cafe where Cook, still holding his two hostages, surrendered without a fight. Two days later, the search for the Mosser family ended when their five bodies were found in an abandoned mine shaft near Joplin, Mo. On December 12, 1952, Cook was executed at San Quentin.

Within a little more than a year, two more kidnap-killers ended their careers in a gas chamber. On September 28, 1953, Carl Austin Hall and Bonnie Heady took six-year-old Bobby Greenlease, Jr., from his school in Kansas City, Mo., by faking a story that the boy's mother had suffered a heart attack. They killed the child almost immediately, but kept alive the family's hopes of his safe return with a cruel series of letters and telephone calls until they collected $600,000 in ransom money. Less than two days after the pay-off, they were arrested by local police on a tip from a cab driver. The child's body was found, but only part of the loot was turned over to the FBI. Several years later, the FBI was still picking up Greenlease bills—the tainted proceeds from the death of a small boy.

A different kind of kidnapping in the Fifties led FBI agents to tangle with the hooded and robed terrorists of the Ku Klux Klan in a North Carolina county. A woman and a boarder in her home had been seized in the night by white-robed men, taken across the line into South Carolina and flogged unmercifully. In the next three months, the Klansmen rode again and again until 15 floggings had been reported, and men dared not venture out after dark unarmed. The Klansmen had taken an oath of secrecy and their relatives and friends in the tightly-knit community wouldn't talk to outsiders.

Slowly and persistently, however, the FBI pierced the web of secrecy. They located some residents who had no sympathy with the Klan doings and protected those who would talk by questioning those who wouldn't, so the Klan had no idea of their progress. The Klansmen got their answer on February 16, 1952, when the agents made simultaneous arrests of the ten men who had taken part in the first floggings. With their conviction, the Klan's reign of terror in Columbus County, N.C., came to an end.

The rate of bank robberies climbed through the Fifties, and the FBI fought to stem the tide as amateurs with nervous trigger fingers and hardened criminals with submachine guns threatened, terrorized, kidnapped and sometimes murdered bank employes.

Another decades-old crime problem, auto theft, took on new dimensions. Gangs of professional auto thieves organized to transport quantities of stolen cars. In one case, they tied up with previously legitimate used car firms to dispose of "hot" cars through altered serial and motor numbers and counterfeit documents. The trail of those cars led as far as Kuwait, an Arabian sheikhdom on the Persian Gulf. The FBI investigation of that ring netted ten conspirators and located more than 160 cars valued at over a quarter of a million dollars.

In the 1960's, both interstate auto theft and bank robberies reached new highs—but so did the rate of convictions.

Meanwhile, in the past few years, a number of new duties have been laid at the door of the FBI. In 1959, Congress extended the FBI's investigative role in labor-management relations to include embezzlement of union funds, extortionate picketing and threats and violence against union members.

In 1960, Congress broadened the FBI's responsibility to investigate alleged violations of civil rights, including the right of equal protection under the law and the right to vote as well as to have the vote properly counted. The 1960 Civil Rights Act covered interstate transportation of explosives with intent to damage property, obstruction of Federal court orders and the maintenance of Federal election records. Under the new law, the FBI has already investigated hundreds of bombings and attempted bombings and photographed tens of thousands of voting records for Justice Department scrutiny.

In 1961, Congress gave the FBI another package of laws to enforce. The targets were airline pirates who hijack airplanes, fugitives who flee to avoid prosecution or prison for any state felony, gamblers and racketeers who travel or send their agents and materials across state lines to further certain unlawful activities.

The racket laws were sought by Attorney General Robert F. Kennedy as needed tools in his coordinated drive against organized crime. These laws, which the FBI, the Postal Inspection Service and the Treasury agents share in enforcing, have also brought the FBI directly into the war on organized gambling as the principal source of profits financing all syndicate crime. By early 1962, the FBI had already smashed several high-powered gambling operations, and the Justice Department announced 2,300 other gambling investigations were underway.

In making its cases against all manner of crime, the FBI uses not only the dogged detective work of its agents but the investigative tools developed over nearly four decades. These are the same tools made available to help local law enforcement—the FBI Laboratory and its Identification Division. Since the FBI Laboratory was established in 1932, it has developed scientific crime detection to such a point that law enforcement officials across the country have become increasingly aware of the mute but telling evidence hidden in a scrap of charred paper or a fragment of shattered glass.

In the 1960 kidnap-murder of wealthy Colorado industrialist Adolph Coors III, the Laboratory not only furnished firm clues to link a known suspect to the killing but also established Mr. Coors' identity —and how he died—when some skeletal remains and clothing were found seven months after his disappearance. Hairs found in the clothing were matched against hairs taken from Mr. Coors' hairbrush, and examination of his jacket proved he had been shot in the back at close range. The suspect, Joseph Corbett, Jr., was caught in Canada after a two-nation manhunt and sentenced to life imprisonment on the basis of evidence furnished Colorado by the FBI.

The FBI Laboratory technicians use reference files as well as microscopes to work their magic. Their National Fraudulent Check File contains more than 80,000 photographs of checks and signatures on fraudulent checks sent in by law enforcement agencies trying to identify bad-check artists. More than half the checks submitted for comparison are positively identified with others in the file. The National Automobile Altered Numbers File frequently leads to the identity of car theft rings. The National Automotive Paint Standards File, containing samples of paint used by various auto makers, often discloses the make and model of a hit-and-run car from flecks of paint found on the victim's clothing. The National Typewriter Standards File, which was checked in the Coors case to identify the typewriter used for the ransom note, carries sample type from all makes and models.

Other reference files contain notes used to demand cash during bank robberies, anonymous letters, animals hairs, textile fibers, paper watermarks, heel prints and tire threads. Any or all of them may be used to establish innocence or point to guilt.

The FBI's Identification Division, with the largest collection of fingerprints in the world, serves as the Nation's repository for fingerprint identifying data. At the start of 1962, almost 162,000,000 sets of fingerprints had been collected and the total was growing at the rate of well over 15,000 every working day.

The Identification Division aids all law enforcement not only by providing instant background on the newly arrested and locating fugitives arrested elsewhere, but also by establishing the guilty party through identification of latent prints found at crime scenes. Its Disaster Squad, a specially trained crew of fingerprint experts, helps identify victims of air, rail, and auto accidents as well as those killed by fire, flood and explosion.

The FBI's agents, its laboratory technicians, its fingerprint experts and the rest of the FBI organization represent a combined force of some 14,000 employees—working together and with all law enforcement in an increasingly coordinated assault on organized crime.

As FBI Director Hoover surveyed the problem at the start of 1962, he summed it up this way:

"In the final analysis, the awesome specter of organized crime is not impregnable. Law enforcement is doing its job well. With the full support of an aroused citizenry, the rulers of the lawless hordes can be routed and our society rid of their ilk. The battle is joined."

PATTERN FOR ESPIONAGE

On a November afternoon in 1954, an American with graying hair and a brush mustache got out of a taxicab on a New York street corner for his long-awaited rendezvous with a Russian spy.

He didn't know who he would meet or if he would meet anyone. He was there to carry out a mission that had its origin months earlier beside the Tomb of the Unknown Soldier in East Berlin . . .

Summer rain was falling lightly on Germany's memorial to its war dead when an American Army colonel with graying hair and a brush mustache arrived to keep his luncheon date with a Soviet Air Force officer. Through his official contacts, the colonel had met many Soviet officers. It wasn't unusual for Americans to join the Soviets on social occasions. The two officers had just sat down to lunch in the Soviet's quarters when a newcomer in civilian clothes joined them.

The talk was casual until the Soviet officer excused himself to brew some coffee. The Russian civilian poured himself a glass of wine while the colonel looked at his watch. His host, he reflected, was certainly taking a long time to brew that coffee.

"I understand you're about to retire," the Russian began. "You're going to live in Leavenworth?"

The colonel nodded, wondering how this man happened to know he was going to settle down in Leavenworth. The colonel remembered mentioning it once to another Soviet officer at a cocktail party, but he was sure he had said nothing about his future plans during this lunch.

"Are you planning to come to New York at all?" the man asked.

"I might in the fall," the colonel replied.

The Russian helped himself to another glass of wine and sketched out a map of downtown Manhattan. He put a dot on the northeast corner of 86th Street and Madison Avenue and said he hoped to get back to New York himself.

Pointing at the dot on the map, he said he would meet the colonel there at 4 P.M. on October 15 or 25; November 5, 15, or 25; January 1; February 1 or March 1. Then, as the colonel listened with growing curiosity, the civilian said he probably wouldn't meet the colonel himself but someone else would. The colonel was beginning to think the man was befuddled with wine.

"You will know him at once," the Russian went on. "He will say to you: 'Seems to me that I have met you at Spechstrasse, Colonel. What is the number of your house there?' You should then reply, 'Oh yes, I have lived there at Spechstrasse 19'."

The colonel was finally getting the pitch. He didn't know anything about espionage himself, but he could recognize a code signal when it was thrust in his face. Obviously, the luncheon had been set up for this approach. For some reason the Soviets apparently figured he would spy for them, The colonel wondered what kind of information they thought he could supply. The answer wasn't long in coming.

"When you come to New York," said the Russian, "you might bring along some books, pamphlets and maps from the school with you."

Fort Leavenworth was the key, the colonel realized. The school there was the Army Command and General Staff School where senior officers were briefed on new tactics and strategy of war.

"I'll be retired," the colonel protested. "I won't be having anything to do with the school."

"Perhaps you can get some material anyhow," the Russian encouraged him.

"Well, I'll have to think it over," the colonel temporized.

The Russian, apparently to help him make up his mind, asked him if he needed any money. The colonel said he didn't, but thanks anyhow. As if on signal, his Soviet Air Force host came back in the room with the coffee and the colonel got out of there as fast as he could.

The colonel's report went swiftly to FBI officials in Washington because a New York street corner would be in their bailiwick. The colonel was ready to cooperate in any way they wished, but this was a job for an agent trained in counter-espionage. The secrets of Fort Leavenworth had to be preserved at any cost.

The colonel had assured the FBI that his play-acting had been good enough to convince the Soviets he might go along with the plot, but FBI officials wanted to make sure of Soviet intentions before they countered with their first move.

On October 15, 1954—the first date given the colonel for a possible rendezvous—a team of FBI agents watched the northeast corner of 86th Street and Madison Avenue. The agents immediately spotted some familiar faces. Officers attached to the Soviet delegation at the United Nations crossed the street, glanced around casually and lingered a few minutes before strolling away.

It was the go-ahead signal for the FBI. The colonel had been taken seriously since the Soviet officers had acted as though they expected him to appear. No one officer, however, looked like he was there to keep the date. Obviously, the Soviets had two goals in view. They wanted to know if the colonel planned to show up and they were checking the area for possible coverage by counter-intelligence agents. If the Soviets wanted a meeting, they would get one—but not with the colonel in retirement at Leavenworth.

FBI officials studied a picture of the colonel. They had exactly ten days to find a substitute colonel, since the next meeting date was October 25. The Soviets would have either a picture or a full description of the real colonel, so the FBI had to produce a look-alike.

The colonel was five feet ten inches tall, weighed about 180 pounds. His chin was round, his complexion ruddy and his hairline receding. His brown hair was graying and he sported a brush mustache of the "Colonel Blimp" variety.

In its New York office, the FBI found a potential look-alike. Agent Jack Goodwin was an inch taller, two pounds lighter and ten years younger than the colonel, but he also had a receding hairline, a rounded chin and a ruddy complexion. He was clean-shaven but make-up could take care of that.

While a professional make-up artist studied Goodwin to determine whether his skill alone could create an older man able to pass inspection in broad daylight, FBI agents in Kansas City pumped the real colonel.

They had to know everything about his background, his family's background, his assignments in Germany and every other biographical detail which Goodwin might need to convince the Soviets that he was the real colonel. The agents also noticed the kind of clothes the colonel fancied and his most characteristic mannerisms. The colonel, they reported, tended to wear loose-fitting, tweedy clothing, chain-smoked, and had a habit of tugging at his mustache. The clothing tip would help, the FBI officials concluded, and Goodwin could smoke if he was careful not to set fire to the brush on his upper lip, but he had to forego the mustache tugging.

On October 25, when the make-up artist settled down to create a new man, Goodwin fervently wished his opposite number had been clean-shaven. The false mustache, held in place with spirit gum, was applied hair by hair to make it look more natural. The agent's brown hair was touched up to appear he was rapidly going gray. Then, the artist got to work with paint and pencil.

When he finally let Goodwin look at himself in a mirror, the agent saw an unfamiliar face and the agents supervising the transformation pronounced themselves satisfied. From the shadows under the eyes to the age lines under the chin, Goodwin looked like the real colonel.

The agent slipped into a loose-fitting tweed sports coat and headed for the Madison Avenue corner. He knew he was not alone as he waited on the corner. Somewhere in the vicinity, he was aware, his fellow FBI agents were watching the corner. Closer at hand, two men seemed to be looking him over carefully but neither approached him.

After waiting a half hour, he took off to get rid of the mustache and the age lines. He reflected with a grin that if he went home with that brush, his wife would probably divorce him.

He went through the same performance on November 5, the next date given the real colonel in East Berlin. This time, no Soviet agents were spotted in the vicinity and nobody came near him. His upper lip was getting raw from his sessions with the spirit gum but he wasn't discouraged. After all, there would be other meeting dates and the Soviet in Berlin had probably forgotten that the Soviet United Nations Delegation would be celebrating the Russian's October Revolution on November 5.

On November 15, he was smiling as he paid off his taxicab at the corner of 86th Street and Madison Avenue. He had a hunch this would be the day. By this time, he was getting used to the corner as it looked at 4 p.m.—the mothers taking their babies for an afternoon ride, the shoppers with their bundles, the impervious crowd seen on any New York street corner any time.

Goodwin saw a man checking his watch as he waited on the corner. From the cut of his dark-blue overcoat and the shape of his dark-gray hat, the man looked foreign. Goodwin was sure he hadn't seen him before. The agent saw the man dart a look in his direction but make no move to approach him.

To help the foreigner make up his mind, the agent paced in front of him. From the corner of his eye, he caught another hard look from the watcher on the corner.

Standing no more than five feet from the other man, Goodwin elaborately checked his own watch. The square-jawed man with the pouting lips still made no move. Goodwin lighted a cigarette cautiously, remembering the disguise on his upper lip, and paced once more in front of the other man as if he was growing increasingly impatient at being kept waiting.

At that moment, the other man pushed his way through the crowd waiting on the corner for the light to change and mumbled something in the agent's ear.

"Pardon me?" the agent said, turning to face the other man.

"Seems to me that I have met you at Spechstrasse," the square-jawed man said with a marked Russian accent. "Colonel, what is the number of your house there?"

"Oh yes," replied the agent, "I have lived there at Spechstrasse 19."

Both men smiled as they shook hands. The rendezvous arranged three months earlier in East Berlin had finally come to pass on this New York street corner.

The stranger was introducing himself to the "colonel" as "Schultz" but FBI agents taking pictures of the scene from nearby vantage points knew him by another name. This was Colonel Maksim Martynov, a member of the Soviet representation to the United Nations Military Staff Committee. The FBI already knew that Martynov had reportedly once been an officer of the MVD, the Russian secret police. He had made several trips to the United States, but this time, he had been in the country less than two weeks when he kept the date on the street corner. It was possible Soviet intelligence agents had delayed the rendezvous until Martynov arrived.

Martynov, in the role of "Schultz," proposed that the "colonel" go for a ride with him. The "colonel" countered with a suggestion that they take a walk through Central Park. The agent wanted to stay where his fellow agents could observe the action and he didn't intend to let "Schultz" take him some place where others might be around to probe further into his identity.

As they started into the park, the agent wanted to make sure the Russian the real colonel had met in East Berlin wasn't lurking somewhere in the background.

"Am I going to meet our mutual friend from Berlin?" he asked expectantly.

"No, but I'm a friend of his, carrying out his mission for him," the Russian replied.

Just to be doubly sure, the Russian said he'd like to see the "colonel's" identification. The "colonel" obligingly handed over an Army officer's identity card. It had the birth date and identifying detail of the real colonel but the picture was of Goodwin after a session with the make-up artist.

Once in the park, the strollers walked along the reservoir and "Schultz" got down to business.

"What is the general course at Fort Leavenworth?" he began.

"I've heard there are many intensive courses of instruction, some probably analyzing lessons of the Korean War," the "colonel" replied vaguely.

The Russian nodded and plied him with more questions. He wanted to know the number of students, how long the courses lasted, who were the higher-ranking officers attending the school, the identity of the instructors and what they taught.

The agent had been given a briefing on Fort Leavenworth before he went to his first street corner meeting. He knew what could and couldn't be said about the Army's command school. With a show of producing something special, he handed "Schultz" a guide map of Fort Leavenworth which "Schultz" pocketed carefully.

"I'd like to get more specific information about what I've asked you," the Russian finally said. "Are you willing to help me?"

"Well, it would be a difficult job," the "colonel" replied, "but it might be possible."

The Russian nodded with satisfaction and reached into his overcoat pocket. "I know you've had heavy expenses in coming to New York for this meeting," he said and handed over a roll of bills.

Without looking at it, the agent stuffed it in his pocket. He half-expected the Russian to ask him for a receipt, which would be standard practice for Soviet intelligence and he was ready for it. He had practiced writing the colonel's signature for just such an emergency but it didn't come up. Apparently, the Russians figured they had him without the added pressure of a receipt to hold over his head later. Before they parted, they arranged another meeting for January 15—same time, same place.

With the usual precautions of the espionage apparatus, "Schultz" gave him alternative instructions in case he was unable to meet the "colonel" on the January date. The "colonel," said "Schultz," should appear on the first Saturday of each succeeding month at a Fifth Avenue book store. If "Schultz" himself didn't appear, another Soviet would take his place. For recognition purposes, the "colonel" should carry a red and blue pencil sharpened at both ends in his left hand and a street guide of Manhattan and the Bronx in his right coat pocket. The "colonel" was to browse through the scientific and medical section of books until a man approached him and asked: "Are you interested in theory?" The "colonel's" reply was to be: "I am interested in elementary theory."

When the Russian was sure the "colonel" had his instructions down pat, he said good-by. The rendezvous had consumed 35 minutes and netted the FBI agent $250, the size of the roll "Schultz" gave him for expenses.

The FBI was fairly sure that the elaborate future instructions were unnecessary, that Martynov himself would show up for the January 15 meeting. The agent's fast acceptance of the money would tend to convince the Russian that the retired colonel was interested in selling information. Martynov had given him two months to get it.

If this had been a case involving ordinary people, the FBI would have begun laying the groundwork then to develop further evidence of espionage. But Martynov was no ordinary person. Like so many of his fellow Russians at the United Nations and at Soviet establishments in the United States, Martynov was more versed in espionage than diplomacy but like the others, he had diplomatic immunity. He couldn't be brought into an American court unless his immunity was waived by his government and that would never happen.

The FBI took the only course open, as it has done many more times than the American people realize. It cleared with the State Department to get formal approval of what it planned to do.

On January 15, 1955, Jack Goodwin faced the make-up artist again. He was getting to the point where he could almost smoke naturally through the brush on his upper lip, but he wasn't liking it any better. Again, the artist aged him and sent him on his way.

Martynov, alias "Schultz," was already there when the "colonel" paid off his taxicab at 4:01 P.M. FBI officials had been right about Martynov's personal eagerness to deal. The agent noticed the Russian glance at the briefcase he was carrying as the two men shook hands.

"Let's take a walk," the Russian said.

The "colonel" turned toward the park but the Russian shook his head. He insisted that they walk up Madison Avenue. His insistence was just enough to put the agent on his guard. Martynov might have a car parked on one of those side streets and the agent wasn't about to be forced into any Soviet car. They finally compromised on a nearby hotel.

"I'll buy you a dinner," the Russian said jovially, his eyes roaming to the briefcase in the "colonel's" hand.

Since the Russian seemed so interested in the briefcase, the "colonel" decided to encourage him.

"I got some of the information you wanted," he said, swinging his briefcase.

When they entered the cocktail lounge of the hotel, the "colonel" led the way to a table in the far corner. It would be spotted immediately by anyone entering the bar and it was some distance away from the nearest occupied table—a man talking to an overblown blonde near the door.

The "colonel" put his briefcase on the empty chair beside him and both men ordered a drink. As soon as the waiter left, the Russian leaned over and cautioned the "colonel" to speak in a low voice.

"I've got everything you asked for," the "colonel" said in a half-whisper. "You want to take notes?"

"You just give me what's in the briefcase," the Russian replied.

As the "colonel" talked, the Russian looked uneasily around the bar.

"I don't like this bar," he whispered. "I know another place where we can go."

Again, the Russian's insistence worried the agent. Either Martynov was anxious to get his hands on the briefcase or he had some confederates in the vicinity who wanted to question the "colonel." The agent was ready to end the masquerade. Reaching for his briefcase, he put it on the table in front of him.

At the bar, two men slipped off their stools and headed for the table in the corner.

"We are agents of the FBI," said the man in the lead. "Don't move."

Martynov paled and said nothing, while the "colonel" roared with protest.

"Identify yourself," said the first agent to the "colonel."

The "colonel" gave his name and introduced "my friend, Mr. Schultz."

Martynov was regaining his composure.

"What's this all about?" he asked. "I just stopped here for a drink." He pulled his credentials from his inside suit pocket and handed them to the second agent.

"Colonel Maksim G. Martynov, Counsellor USSR," the agent read. As Martynov reached for his credentials, the agent told him, "Mr. Martynov, you and this man have been caught in an act of espionage. You are in serious trouble."

Martynov said nothing. Instead, he snapped his fingers to attract a waiter's attention and threw two dollars on the table. Without waiting for change, he picked up his hat and stalked out of the bar. He knew, as well as the agents, that they couldn't stop him. He had diplomatic immunity.

Just in case any Russians were watching the performance, the agents ordered the "colonel" to get up. Each took him by an arm and escorted him from the lounge as though he were in custody.

As soon as he was sure no Russians were within earshot, Agent Jack Goodwin sighed with relief.

"Boy," he said, "will I ever be glad to get rid of this mustache for good."

On February 21, 1955, the State Department formally declared Col. Maksim G. Martynov persona non grata because of his espionage activities. If it had been an American diplomat in Russia, the whole world would have heard about it. Here, there were no blazing headlines, no calculated fanfare. The State Department simply issued a terse announcement that a Russian had abused his status as a guest of this country and he would have to go home.

Martynov left the country five days later but his departure was no invitation to the FBI to let down its guard. Sooner or later, the FBI knew, another Russian would try another gambit to ferret out the secrets of Fort Leavenworth. And FBI agents would use another gambit to stop him.

Part II ★★

THE COMMON DEFENSE

2 ★★★

State Department's Office of Security

It's a fact of life in diplomatic circles that peace or war may hinge on who reads a single piece of paper. Because this is so, the problem of security for pieces of paper is as old as diplomacy itself and as new as tomorrow's headlines.

Benjamin Franklin was aware of his security problems when he went to Paris during the American Revolution. Warned that the French capital was full of spies, his security maneuver was to announce that he would so conduct himself that reports of spies could do no harm. This, it developed, was a wise precaution because a trusted confidant of the American mission to France turned out to be in the pay of the British.

And today, William O. Boswell, director of the State Department's Office of Security, is so concerned about his responsibilities that he keeps his office blinds drawn even on the sunniest day in Washington. Boswell isn't averse to sunshine, but he knows from experience that an agent equipped with a telescope could read his lips or a long-range camera could photograph the papers on his desk.

Basically, security is the protection of "sensitive" information, whether spoken or written. Since a major aspect of our international relations depends on preserving this security, the mission of the Office of Security is a particularly delicate one. It starts and ends with people.

Boswell's force has to make sure that the people entrusted with "sensitive" information are worthy of trust, that the system used to transmit information—whether by code and courier across oceans or from floor to floor in the State Department—is spy-proof, that the information is equally safe when it's locked up at night and when it's locked in somebody's head. The last is the toughest of all. As Boswell puts it, "You can build walls around pieces of paper, but you can't build walls around people's minds." Training people to keep their mouths shut is a key role of the Office of Security.

The rudiments of security for the nation's secrets were practiced from its birth. As early as 1790, American diplomats were sending messages in code and special couriers carried diplomatic pouches between Washington and overseas posts. Safes and fireproofing to preserve secret documents and qualification tests to insure the trustworthiness of those handling the documents were introduced as security measures.

It took the twentieth century, however, with its international stresses, its hot and cold wars, to propel the State Department into establishing a security force. In 1916, Secretary of State Robert Lansing created a Bureau of Secret Intelligence headed by a Chief Special Agent. It was such a hush-hush outfit that the Chief Special Agent drew his operating funds from a confidential account and even paid his agents by personal check.

The Chief Special Agent's job was to advise the Secretary of State on matters of intelligence and security. By 1921, his staff amounted to 25 men.

One of the first problems of these special agents involved passports and visas. Beginning in 1914, European nations began demanding proof of identity. The United States had previously issued passports on request but most people didn't bother to get them. With the outbreak of World War I, United States missions abroad were authorized to issue emergency passports but by the end of 1918, Congress passed a law requiring every departing American to have a passport from the State Department and every alien to show a passport from his homeland and a visa from one of our consular offices before he could enter this country.

The Chief Special Agent's force started sorting out American Communists seeking passports for trips to Moscow and Soviet agents using fraudulent passports. Through the 1920's and 1930's, the State Department investigators uncovered passport frauds world-wide in scope and involving chains of subversive agents on four continents. The investigators pinned down the Soviet use of American passports taken from American volunteers in the Spanish civil war, exposed several elaborate passport frauds to supply traveling Communists and thwarted at least two Nazi espionage plots centering on the use of American passports.

With the outbreak of World War II, the Chief Special Agent's office was expanded to cope with the problem of interning and exchanging diplomatic officials of enemy powers and screening Americans—or those claiming American citizenship—after they were expatriated from enemy controlled areas.

Meanwhile, the Chief Special Agent's force had been secretly inquiring into the backgrounds of prospective State Department employees since the basic security of American diplomacy rested with those carrying it out. Because the Chief Special Agent at the time had been in the Postal Inspection Service before joining the State Department, he naturally called on the postal inspectors to assist in the nation-wide field work of checking on the loyalty of prospective State Department employees.

All these investigations—passports, personnel and other elements of security—had been done via a confidential relationship between the Chief Special Agent and the Secretary of State. In 1945, however, Secretary of State Edward R. Stettinius, Jr., asked the Federal Bureau of Investigation to study the department's system of safeguarding its documents and clearing its personnel for security.

Then, Congress and the President made it clear that all Federal employees had to meet standards of loyalty and suitability and employees in "sensitive" positions had to be fully investigated. Since virtually all State Department positions were rated "sensitive," a mammoth job was faced by its investigators.

Out of the FBI recommendations, the new laws and executive orders emerged an outfit to handle the physical security of buildings and documents, the security of department employees, the coordination of intelligence data and all State Department investigations. The Office of Security was established in 1948.

It never was a large force and it still isn't. Nevertheless, its duties range from investigating prospective State Department employees and reinvestigating them as they go up the career ladder to guarding foreign dignitaries, uncovering passport and visa frauds and protecting our 300 missions overseas against spies, saboteurs and traitors. The office also makes overseas checks for other agencies and briefs approximately 6,000 government employees a year on security before they go abroad.

Its special agents assigned to investigations, its headquarters staff, its overseas security officers and technicians hunting for concealed eavesdropping devices number 235 men. The force is spread so thin that two security officers are responsible for all American outposts in Africa south of the Sahara and two special agents at Denver handle all personnel and passport investigations in a wide strip of states from Canada to the Mexican border.

Because the force is small, it has to be flexible. Thus, a special agent might be investigating a prospective diplomat's college record one day and setting up a security cordon around a visiting Premier Khrushchev the next day.

The cold war years have produced problems and introduced techniques undreamed of in the days when special agents first moved into the State Department. Among these are the electronic devices that have replaced human eavesdroppers in our overseas missions. Since 1949, the State Department's security force has uncovered more than 125 hidden microphones and similar devices planted in American embassies. One of them was concealed in a handsome wooden replica of the great seal presented to the American Ambassador at Moscow as a sample of Russian handicraft. It looked like a solid chunk of carved wood but a technician from the Office of Security found the two parts had been fitted together. Mounted inside was a self-contained listening device activated by remote control—no batteries, no wires, no need for repairs. The seal had been hung behind the Ambassador's desk, but since the Ambassador assumed his place was "bugged," the Russians presumably learned little before the device was exposed.

What worries the Office of Security is the devices it hasn't found. As the electronics industry produces more eavesdropping gimmicks, the job of the "sweepers"—as the technicians are called—grows increasingly more difficult. Overseas, the nationals of a country usually build the embassies for the Americans. That gives foreign intelligence operatives plenty of time to hide their microphones behind steel reinforcing rods where the usual metal detector would be useless. As the building progresses, the foreign agents can check their devices and make necessary changes to be sure they work when the Americans move in.

Faced with that problem, the Office of Security last year got money from Congress to invent new equipment to detect the "bugs" planted to betray us. The Office of Security is currently looking for electronics engineers also authorized by Congress to use the new gear.

Another postwar phenomenon faced by the security force is the frequent presence of foreign dignitaries. In the old days, the visit of a chief of state was a newsworthy rarity. Now, premiers and prime ministers, kings and queens are arriving regularly to consult with the President or visit the United Nations. The security force probably got its severest test in protecting foreign dignitaries in 1960 when Khrushchev of the Soviet Union, Nasser of the United Arab Republic, Castro of Cuba and assorted other controversial figures converged on the United Nations at the same time. For that event, a fourth of New York's "finest" was assigned to protective duties but the responsibility for advance planning and final decisions rested with the State Department's Office of Security.

Sometimes, the security agents have to make quick decisions or draft whatever local manpower is available. When Khrushchev arrived in Los Angeles and announced he wanted to see Disneyland, the State Department officers checked with the local force, found his safety couldn't be guaranteed on such short notice and turned thumbs down on the venture. Elsewhere on Khrushchev's cross-country jaunt, he turned up in Corn Rapids, Iowa, and all the pictures taken of him on a farm there showed a shirt-sleeved, barrel-chested figure at close range. Some snide remarks were made later about a breakdown in security. Actually, the barrel-chested man was no threat at all but one of the local residents hastily deputized by the sheriff for guard duty.

Despite the unexpected, despite the unpopularity of some of the visitors, no chief of state protected by the State Department's security force has ever been injured on these shores. The Office of Security, however, would feel safer if Congress passes the law it requested to give its agents the power to arrest potential assassins when no local police are around to take them into custody.

In addition to protecting foreign visitors, special agents go overseas with the Secretary of State and other top brass attending international conferences. Their job is to make sure private conversations are not overheard and no stranger gets a look at private papers.

At home, one of the principal jobs of the special agents is assuring the loyalty and suitability of employees now in the State Department and those coming on duty. If anything in a man's past makes him subject to blackmail, the department wants to know about it before he learns anything that would make him worth blackmailing. The agents also have to find out if he talks too much or drinks too much or associates with the wrong people.

During the early 1950's, when the President set up security standards for all Federal employees, every State Department employee was reinvestigated. Simultaneously, the program was launched to investigate every incoming employee.

In 1960, the Office of Security started sending its investigators along with the teams recruiting clerical and mechanical help throughout the country. By personal interviews, the special agents weed out about 15 per cent of the applicants as unsuitable. They also go over the job application forms with the prospective employees to spot omissions that could cost hundreds of investigative hours later.

Typical of this on-the-spot weeding out process was the case of an applicant for a housekeeping job. During the investigator's interview, the applicant was led to admit he had just escaped from a mental hospital.

The clerical and housekeeping applicants are given a routine background check but for the potential foreign service officers, the investigators not only do personal interviews but check deeply into every phase of their lives. The agents know the prospective career officers are all potential ambassadors and assistant secretaries of State.

One such candidate had passed his written and oral examinations with flying colors and came highly recommended. A special agent checking his home neighborhood asked if he lived alone. Neighbors said the man lived with his wife, which came as a surprise to the investigator because on all the forms the man had listed himself as single. Further investigation disclosed that the "wife" was married all right, but to another man who was then overseas. The candidate for the foreign service would have been a natural for blackmail.

Reports on the thousands of personnel investigations a year flow into the Washington headquarters to be evaluated for loyalty and suitability by professionals in the Office of Security. They also re-evaluate reports on employees investigated anew before they move into particularly sensitive jobs.

On the basis of these continuing investigations, Boswell says: "There is no reason whatsoever to believe there is a Communist or disloyal employee in the State Department."

As the investigative arm of the State Department, the Office of Security protects American passports and visas just as it protects American secrets. The special agents are especially alert to the rings providing false documents in wholesale lots to force open America's doors. These rings often cross national borders and involve local employees in overseas missions as well as foreign government officials.

Two counterfeit visa rings were exposed in Cuba where would-be immigrants formed long lines daily outside the American embassy in Havana before it closed up. One ring was directed by a Cuban-American in Miami who had a courier service running to Havana to supply forged visas. The other ring was operated through runners who went up and down the lines of visa-seeking Cubans outside the

American embassy and offered to expedite their visas for a price.

Some of the victims didn't even know the visas were counterfeit. That's how the scheme came to light. A girl who had gotten her visa by paying a runner came to the embassy to ask for an extension of time. When a check of records showed she had never been given a visa, special agents were called in to track down the ringleaders. They found a former local employee had duplicated the visa stamp and was doing a land-office business in forged visas.

An international ring dealing in stolen and altered passports was exposed in Palermo, Italy, after a two-year investigation extending from Rome and Paris to New Jersey and upstate New York. The ring operated by stealing and otherwise "collecting" passports from American tourists all over Italy. The passports were taken to Palermo where the original photograph was removed, the photograph of the intended user was substituted and doctored with a false United States seal.

The State Department's investigators developed contacts with a New Jersey colony where immigrants from a town near Palermo usually reported after arrival. By getting names there, the agents traced recent arrivals and backtracked through them to the gang. While the passport ring was in operation, more than 200 passports were stolen and sold at $1,200 a passport.

A Somali clerk at the American consulate in Aden was pinpointed as the culprit in a visa fraud by special agents half a world away. Acting on a tip that the clerk was taking bribes to "expedite" visas, special agents got a list of recent visa recipients and started looking for them across the United States. In a general store in Lodi, Calif., they located a leader of Yemeni affairs who convinced his people to tell the truth. Through them, the agents confirmed the bribes. It developed that the immigrants would have gotten their visas just as quickly without paying off the clerk because he never approached them until he was sure the visa was about to be issued.

State Department agents have also broken Chinese frauds centering on false identity, Beirut frauds involving false documents and Mexican frauds consisting of fictitious letters to prove the immigrants would not become public charges.

While the special agents labor to keep out those who don't belong here, they work just as hard to help Americans who do belong here but can't prove it. An illiterate seaman got drunk, missed his ship in an African port and had nothing to show he was really American. He wasn't sure where he was born. Special agents located relatives for him and proved his story.

An elderly resident of the Philippines claimed he was born in the United States but couldn't even produce a birth certificate. The only clue he could offer was a faint recollection that he had been jailed someplace in California in 1912. A special agent checked jail records and found he had lived in an orphanage as a child before being farmed out. By tracing his whole family history, agents discovered where he was born and cleared the way for the old man to come home.

Overseas, the department's security officers are responsible for making sure that the 300 posts and their documents are safe from prying and spying. Since many of the employees are nationals of the host country, the security officers must make sure they are located where they cannot see or hear classified information. This is as much for their protection as for ours.

Sometimes, particularly behind the Iron Curtain, the local employees are subjected to pressures which are hard to resist even if they want desperately to be loyal to their American employers. So, it's the job of the security officers to run the show in such a way that they aren't exposed to pressure. What they don't know, they can't tell.

Among the other responsibilities of the Office of Security is its role as the clearinghouse for intelligence information reaching the State Department. It collects, evaluates and passes on to key officials vital data dealing with espionage, subversive activities and violations of internal security laws. At the same time, it turns over to other interested agencies what it uncovers about the latest techniques in electronic espionage.

In the final analysis, however, the special agents at home and the security officers overseas are concerned most about people. It's up to the special agents to make sure that security risks don't sit at State Department desks. And it's up to the security officers to make sure that America's safety is not endangered by a forgotten scrap of paper or a careless remark at the wrong time in the wrong place.

A DIPLOMAT NAMED SCARBECK

In the year 1961, when one false move could trigger atomic destruction, an American diplomat for the first time in our history betrayed American secrets to the agents of an Iron Curtain power.

He sold out his country not for pay or love of communism but for a woman—a skinny Polish girl with bedroom eyes and a throaty voice. He might have gotten away with it, too, if a State Department security officer hadn't started puzzling over a series of curious coincidences.

The trail of those coincidences led from the back streets of Warsaw to a sunny terrace on the Rhine, from a bare room in Frankfurt, Germany, to the massive headquarters of the State Department in Washington, D.C. It all began in the capital of Poland.

The Warsaw of early 1961 wasn't a happy post for American diplomats and their families. It was not only that the life was barren or that most diplomatic families had to live in the enforced intimacy of one block of apartments. It was also the strain of being forever careful—careful around the embassy because the local employees had been placed there by the Polish government, careful on the street because Polish intelligence agents kept Western diplomats under constant surveillance, even careful at home because of hidden microphones and Polish maids reporting back to Polish intelligence.

Every American foreign service officer before assignment to Warsaw or any other Iron Curtain capital went through a briefing in Washington on the classic hazards of diplomatic life in the Soviet orbit. He was specifically warned against women sent out by the Communists to bait the trap for blackmail, the most dangerous kind of blackmail—silence in exchange for secrets. The foreign service officers always grinned when briefers cited Russian efforts to tempt grizzled old Marine sergeants at the American Embassy in Moscow by assigning the pick of the Soviet blondes to do their laundry. The Marines didn't take the bait but the Russians never stopped trying.

Before the briefing ended, the foreign service officers were told what to do if they ever found themselves in a compromising situation. They could extricate themselves by reporting it immediately. They would be transferred to another post before the foreign agents could follow through on their blackmail threats. Every foreign service officer en route to an Iron Curtain post signed an acknowledgement that he had received the security briefing.

One of those who signed was Irvin C. Scarbeck, on his way to Warsaw as Second Secretary of the American Embassy.

At 41, the stocky, bespectacled Scarbeck had a flawless record. After Army service, he had stayed in Germany to work in the Office of Military Government. He had been a staff officer for the High Commissioner of Germany until 1952 when he joined the State Department. His personal life was also above reproach. His first marriage had ended in an annulment despite the birth of a child, but it had been an amicable parting, based on his ambition for a foreign service career and his wife's preference for life in America. While in Germany, he had married a Berlin girl and the couple now had three children—a five-year-old daughter and three-year-old twin sons.

When the Scarbecks went to Warsaw in December of 1958, Scarbeck—"Doc" to his friends—was assigned mainly to the housekeeping chores involved in operating a large mission overseas, problems of staff, food and housing. Ambassador Jacob Beam encouraged his officers to read the dispatches passing between the Embassy and the State Department, to keep abreast of Polish and world affairs in their enforced isolation, but Scarbeck's duties didn't require it and he showed little interest in the confidential dispatches on the reading file.

Ambassador Beam also encouraged his men and their families to take "morale leave," to get away for awhile from the strain of Warsaw, but early in 1961 Scarbeck wasn't going anywhere. His friends would see him working late at the embassy in his shirtsleeves, his shock of graying sandy hair bent over a pile of paper work.

A hard worker, his fellow diplomats called him. In fact, they noticed, he was working so hard that he didn't even join his family on a trip to visit Mrs. Scarbeck's mother in Dusseldorf, Germany.

Victor Dikeos, the embassy's ascetic-looking security officer, noticed it too. He and his wife were friendly with the Scarbecks—the extroverted, hail-fellow-well-met "Doc" and his devoted Karen, whose ready smile seemed to overlook the hardships of life in Warsaw. Dikeos wondered why Scarbeck had remained in Warsaw when he could have joined his family on the Dusseldorf trip. It seemed highly unlikely that the Scarbecks weren't getting along, but he filed a question away in his mental storehouse.

It wasn't his job to pry into the private lives of embassy personnel. In fact, his bosses in the State Department's Office of Security would forbid it. They wanted their security officers on friendly terms with the embassy employees so they would freely report any unusual incidents. Besides, Dikeos had enough to do without that—keeping an eye on the Polish staff, spotting hidden microphones planted by Polish intelligence, safeguarding the embassy's secrets.

In early April, 1961, an American consular officer did report an unusual incident to Dikeos. Scarbeck had expressed interest in getting a German visa for a Polish girl.

At that time, West Germany had no diplomatic relations with Poland so the American consul acted for West Germany in issuing visas. The consular official told Dikeos that Scarbeck's right-hand man had shepherded the Polish girl through the visa office and had let it be known Scarbeck wanted the visa request expedited so the girl could hurry to the bedside of her dying brother in Frankfurt. The girl had displayed a telegram from her brother along with her Polish passport.

It wasn't Scarbeck's interest that puzzled the consular office. As a matter of courtesy, foreign service officers often helped out the natives on urgent matters.

"What I can't figure out," said the consular officer, "is why the Poles would ever give a passport to a healthy young girl to leave Poland on any pretext."

Dikeos had been in Warsaw only since October, but he knew what the consular officer meant. The Poles were quite willing to see the last of their old and ailing but they consistently blocked any move by their young people to flee to the West. The future of Poland depended on keeping its strong workers.

As the consular officer talked, something clicked in Dikeos' mind—the first of the curious coincidences. That day's leave roster showed that Scarbeck had put in for two weeks' leave in Frankfurt. That's where the Polish girl said she was going.

Dikeos recalled hearing that Mrs. Scarbeck and the children were still in Dusseldorf. Maybe, he speculated, "Doc" was planning to pick up his family in Dusseldorf and go on to Frankfurt with them. He casually put the question to an embassy official who lived near the Scarbecks.

"Mrs. Scarbeck?" asked the embassy official. "I understand she's on her way back here."

Either the embassy official was feeling talkative or he suspected that the security officer's interest in Scarbeck was more than casual, but he volunteered something that shook Dikeos.

"How come 'Doc' is showing a sudden interest in the reading file?" the chatty official asked. "I was kidding him about it just the other day."

The reading file of dispatches between Warsaw and Washington, the confidential and secret information that Scarbeck had ignored so long.

Back in his office, Dikeos examined the pieces of his mental jigsaw puzzle . . . a Polish passport for a healthy girl . . . a sudden interest in secret dispatches . . . Scarbeck's trip to Frankfurt when his wife was just returning from Dusseldorf, only a two-hour drive from Frankfurt . . . the girl's intention to go to Frankfurt. All coincidence or something else?

"It's too much," muttered Dikeos. "I've got to find out what Scarbeck does in Frankfurt."

That night, he sent two cryptic telegrams in code—one to Kenneth Knauf, security officer at the American Embassy in West Germany, and the other to William O. Boswell, chief of the State Department's Office of Security in Washington. He wanted Knauf to help him violate the department's standing rule against prying into the personal affairs of foreign service officers and he wanted Washington to approve it.

In the sprawling State Department headquarters, Charles W. Lyons looked up in surprise as his chief strode into his office with a yellow sheet of paper in his hand. Usually, if Boswell wanted something, he summoned Lyons to his office.

As soon as Lyons scanned the decoded telegram marked "Secret" and "priority," meaning decode immediately, the veteran investigator understood his chief's urgency. Dikeos had put all his fears into three short paragraphs.

For an hour, the two men discussed the telegram. Lyons, an FBI agent for 13 years before he joined the security arm of the State Department, tried to put himself in Dikeos' position. Having served overseas in five embassies himself, he knew how frustrated he would feel if he got a reply demanding further justification of the unusual request—particularly if Scarbeck were leaving immediately for Frankfurt.

"We're not doing Scarbeck an injustice," Lyons argued. "If he doesn't do anything seriously wrong in Frankfurt, neither he nor anyone else need ever know he was watched and if he is doing something wrong, this is the best way to find out."

Boswell finally stood up.

"Play it the way you see it," he said.

The two men in Washington didn't care for the coincidences, either. Before Lyons went home that night, he typed out detailed wires to be coded and sent to Dikeos in Warsaw and to Knauf at the American Embassy in Bonn, Germany.

He instructed Dikeos to advise him and Knauf when Scarbeck planned to leave and how he would travel. He told Knauf to use his contacts with West German police to keep tabs on Scarbeck. Lyons knew Knauf would get the picture—a friendly chat with a police official, a confidential request for help on a little problem within the family, nothing official and no record to be kept.

On April 10, Dikeos triggered the action with another cryptic cable. Scarbeck would be leaving Warsaw at midnight on April 12, driving a 1952 Cadillac. He would enter West Germany through the Waidhous checkpoint. On April 13, Dikeos cabled that Scarbeck had left as scheduled after reserving a room at the transit billet in Frankfurt. By noon of that day Knauf had arranged to get a room with a view of the apartment reserved for Scarbeck in the block of efficiencies provided by the American government for officials on leave or travelling to new posts.

Although both Knauf and Scarbeck were in the foreign service, they had never met. At least Knauf, a worrier by nature, didn't have to fret about Scarbeck recognizing him and wondering what he was doing in housing for transients. Knauf was as different from Dikeos, his opposite number in Warsaw, as two men could be. Where Dikeos was dark-eyed, lean and intense, Knauf was stocky, patient and stolid, a kindly man of Milwaukee German background.

It was late on the night of April 13 when Scarbeck checked in at the transit billet and Knauf saw him enter his room. Watching him leave in the morning, Knauf realized he needed help from his German police friends. He couldn't keep up with Scarbeck, however discreetly, by staying in a hotel room while Scarbeck roamed around Frankfurt. Knauf gave the German police a description of Scarbeck and his car—1952 Cadillac with oval CD (corps diplomatique) tags at front and back, a PL (for Poland) plate at the back, license number WZ (for Warsaw)-01-16.

On the morning of April 15, Knauf saw Scarbeck leave his room and ambled out behind him to be sure the police had spotted him. He saw Scarbeck pull away from the curb and an unmarked German car slowly turn the corner behind the Cadillac. Satisfied, Knauf reentered the transit billet to await the results of the surveillance. As he went through the outside door a girl brushed past him, but he paid no attention to her.

A short time later, the German police called to report they had lost their quarry. It wasn't unexpected since this was to be a loose surveillance, nothing to attract Scarbeck's attention. But the German police had a story to tell.

When Scarbeck pulled away from his parking spot, the German police inspector reported, he made two right turns and stopped at a corner down the block from the transit billet. There, a girl got in the car—a young woman, very slim with short dark hair and sunken cheeks. She was wearing a black and red scotch plaid jacket and skirt.

Knauf remembered the girl who had brushed by him at the door. She would have had just enough time to walk to the far corner as Scarbeck circled the block. Was it possible that Scarbeck had smuggled the girl into his government housing? If so, who was she?

He flashed the word to Washington. In the security office, Charles Lyons had a hunch who the girl might be. He cabled Knauf to have his German friends check immigration records for the arrival of Urszula Discher, the Polish girl who had gotten a German visa with Scarbeck's help. Lyons knew the Germans required a picture with every visa. The police might be able to recognize the girl from the visa photograph.

If the girl in the car was Urszula Discher, Lyons realized his problem had suddenly become more serious. Her presence with Scarbeck would mean that Scarbeck's interest in her visa was definitely more than a casual courtesy, that the rendezvous in Frankfurt was prearranged.

In Frankfurt, Knauf asked for the immigration check. He also requested a walkie-talkie so he could advise police by radio when Scarbeck left his room. He wanted to watch Scarbeck's room after he left, instead of following him outside as he had done before.

On the morning of April 16, Knauf saw Scarbeck leave and used his walkie-talking to alert the German police. Then he kept his eye on Scarbeck's door. He didn't have long to wait. After a few minutes, the door slowly opened and a girl slipped out—a thin, almost emaciated girl in a red and black scotch plaid suit. From his window, Knauf watched the girl click down the street on high heels toward the corner where the German police had seen Scarbeck pick up a girl the day before.

That day, the police didn't lose the Cadillac. They saw the girl get in Scarbeck's car and followed as the car took the ferry across the Rhine and drove through the vineyards to Rudesheim. From a discreet distance, the police snapped pictures of the couple lunching on the terrace of a hotel overlooking the Rhine. The day was fine and the

Rudesheimer wine delicious. The couple lingered on the terrace, sipping the wine, apparently engrossed in conversation.

After lunch, they drove further along the Rhine, past the Lorelei rocks where sirens of legend lured warriors to their doom. As the police mentioned later to Knauf in some embarrassment, Scarbeck and the girl "exchanged tendernesses" every time they had to stop at a railroad crossing to wait for a train to pass. Since there were many such crossings, the trip took far into the evening. When they returned to the billet, the police watched them enter separately. There was no question now that the girl was sharing Scarbeck's apartment.

While Scarbeck and the girl were enjoying their idyll beside the Rhine, the police had been busy. They had identified the immigration picture of Urszula Discher as the girl in the scotch plaid suit.

When Knauf cabled the identification to Washington, Lyons and Boswell knew they had to take the Scarbeck story to Secretary of State Dean Rusk. The implications went beyond a mild indiscretion, a sexual adventure. Since the relationship between Scarbeck and the Discher woman obviously pre-dated Frankfurt, Polish intelligence agents must know about the affair. That would have made her even more valuable to Polish intelligence, so valuable they would never have let her leave the country. And yet, they had given her a passport.

"There's only one explanation," Boswell concluded as the security chief went over the case with Lyons. "There had to be a quid pro quo. The passport was in payment for something."

Lyons agreed.

"Either she's an agent on assignment or the Poles discovered the relationship and forced her to cooperate without Scarbeck knowing anything about it," he said.

"The other possibility," Boswell pointed out gloomily, "is that Polish Intelligence gave her the passport to pay Scarbeck for services rendered."

Boswell had already made up his mind what he would recommend when he took his story to the Secretary of State. He wanted Scarbeck to be allowed to finish his leave and return to Warsaw. "In all fairness to Scarbeck," Boswell argued, "we shouldn't bring him back here without tangible evidence. If he denied involvement with Polish intelligence, we wouldn't have enough to remove him from the service. He would go on with a cloud of unresolved doubt hanging over his head." Boswell pointed out that Scarbeck's tour of duty in Warsaw was due to end in June and he could be watched until then. He reported that Dikeos in Warsaw had now confirmed Scarbeck's sudden, unusual interest in the reading file of secret dispatches. The file room supervisor dated Scarbeck's interest in the file from January.

To prevent any possible theft of secret dispatches, Boswell proposed that the Warsaw reading file be "desensitized"—cleared of all secret documents—before Scarbeck's return to Warsaw. If the Secretary of State approved, he would advise Ambassador Beam and Dikeos would enlist the cooperation of the file room supervisor and the code room clerk in the Warsaw embassy. They had to be in on this, no one else.

Secretary of State Rusk gave Boswell a free hand to continue with the case as he saw fit. Scarbeck was to be permitted to finish his leave and complete his tour of duty in Warsaw under appropriate safeguards.

In Warsaw, Ambassador Beam gave Dikeos his full support. A warm, understanding person, the Ambassador himself told the file room supervisor and the code room clerk what was expected of them and how to react to Scarbeck's requests without arousing his suspicion. Dikeos, meanwhile, removed the secret items from the reading file and set up periodic checks during the day to determine if anything was slipped out and later returned. He arranged to keep a count of the sheets used to reproduce documents so he would know immediately if Scarbeck used the embassy's own facilities to copy its secret papers.

He was now ready for Scarbeck, but Scarbeck was not ready to return. Scarbeck wired the embassy and his wife that he had had trouble getting all his shopping done at the Frankfurt post exchange and would need another week's leave.

In Frankfurt, Knauf's worries were piling up. The German police sensed from Scarbeck's driving, from the sudden U-turns and backtracking, that he suspected he was being followed. Knauf requested a looser surveillance but it wasn't loose enough.

On the morning of April 21, Scarbeck with the girl in his car, suddenly parked and got out. Approaching the car behind him, he accused the driver of following him.

"I'm an American diplomat from the embassy in Warsaw," he began. "This lady in the car is a poor Polish orphan with whom I have fallen in love. I want to marry her."

The driver, a policeman, listened to this outpouring in some astonishment and had nothing to say. Knauf, when he heard about it, wasn't astonished. Obviously, Scarbeck thought the police wanted to know what a Polish girl was doing in West Germany. Scarbeck had told his tale of love so the Germans would lose interest in her.

Knauf took advantage of Scarbeck's theory as best he could. He told the police to make their surveillance more discreet so Scarbeck would figure his explanation had satisfied the police. Apparently, however, Scarbeck wanted to make doubly sure he wasn't followed. With a German police officer named Fritz Cordes, he visited the special branch headquarters of the police.

Cordes told his colleagues that Scarbeck was a friend of his who had complained of being followed. Scarbeck had taken down the license plates of some following cars and Cordes asked the special branch to trace the plates. The special branch officer said he knew nothing about it and suggested that Scarbeck lodge his complaint with the American consulate.

When Knauf was advised of this development, he promptly wired Washington that a new figure, Fritz Cordes, had been brought into the picture. It didn't take long to unravel that one. Cordes, according to the records, had worked as a chauffeur for the Office of the High Commissioner of Germany while Scarbeck was there as a staff officer.

Scarbeck and the Discher girl were still living together in the Government billet when Knauf dispatched a frantic cable to Washington. William Magistretti, deputy chief of mission at Warsaw and one of Scarbeck's bosses, had just checked in at the same billet with his wife. To Knauf, already worried by Scarbeck's moves to end surveillance, this was the last straw. It had the comic implications of the boss's wife catching an employee in a love nest, but it wasn't funny to Knauf. If Scarbeck spotted the Magistrettis before they spotted him, he would be sure to move out with his girl friend and the surveillance would have to start all over again.

In Washington, Lyons, a Boston-Irishman with a ready wit, saw the humor of the situation but, like Knauf, he was in no mood for jokes.

"Suggest Magistretti look for other quarters," Lyons cabled Knauf.

The Magistrettis moved and Scarbeck stayed.

Just before Scarbeck was due to return to Warsaw, the German police reported that Scarbeck was trying to get a room for the girl in the low-rent district of Frankfurt. Obviously, she wasn't going back to Warsaw.

To Boswell and Lyons in Washington, this was a significant development. They had already established through the German police that the brother near death in Frankfurt—the girl's alleged reason for leaving Warsaw—was non-existent. The telegram she had shown the visa office was phony, simply a ruse to get out of Poland and stay out.

Her plan to remain in Frankfurt made it less likely that she had accompanied Scarbeck on an assignment for Polish Intelligence. In that case, why had the Poles given her a passport? Boswell and Lyons were sure a deal had been made but by whom and in exchange for what?

By now, Lyons had reviewed all the dispatches that might have appeared on the reading file in the Warsaw embassy from January when Scarbeck first showed an interest until mid-April when he left for Frankfurt. If Scarbeck had turned over much of that material, Lyons realized, the damage was enormous but he had a second concern. The Poles certainly kept track of the messages sent in code from Warsaw. If they had gotten many of the decoded messages from the reading file, they could match them against the coded ones and move a big step forward in breaking the code. That would force altering the code throughout the world at a cost of millions of dollars and inestimable damage to this country in its dealings with Iron Curtain powers.

On May 3, Scarbeck left the girl in Frankfurt and returned to Warsaw. As far as Dikeos could discover, Scarbeck never went near the file. Dikeos noticed that Scarbeck held many whispered talks with two Polish employees in his office, but Dikeos knew he couldn't ask them what the conversations were about. Nor could he follow Scarbeck when he left the embassy because the Poles would be following him as well as Scarbeck.

As nothing significant developed, Dikeos' tension grew. He worried that the file room supervisor or the code room clerk might give the show away, that Scarbeck might notice the desensitized file, that he might be meeting the Poles where Dikeos couldn't follow him, that he might conceivably defect to the Poles, particularly if he was aware of the security officer's interest. Dikeos' wife remarked that he was losing weight. His already lean face was becoming gaunt, and June, the end of Scarbeck's stay in Warsaw, was drawing near.

In Washington, Boswell and Lyons shared Dikeos' concern. It had now become a question of timing. Convinced that there was nothing to be gained and much to be lost by waiting longer, they had a routine message sent to Scarbeck through the usual personnel channels.

Scarbeck was to execute his orders for transfer to Naples, Italy, after the usual week's consultation in Washington and three months of home leave with his family. An addition to the message took it out of the routine, but not far enough out to rouse Scarbeck's suspicions. En route to the United States, Scarbeck was to stop by Bonn, Germany, for three days' consultation with the foreign buildings regional officer. Since Scarbeck was in charge of the American buildings in Warsaw, it would be normal for the regional buildings officer to want a consultation.

By remote control, Lyons in Washington worked out the split-second timing of the Scarbeck plan. Scarbeck couldn't be ordered to go directly to Frankfurt because he knew the foreign buildings officer was in Bonn and a Frankfurt order would be just enough to arouse the suspicion that had to be avoided at all costs.

Lyons' goal as he outlined it to his chief was simultaneous, separate, surprise interviews with three people in Frankfurt—Scarbeck, Urszula Discher and Cordes, the German policeman. A few more people had to be cut in on pieces of the plan, but that couldn't be helped. It had to go like clock work or it wouldn't go at all.

The Washington officials were still hoping that Scarbeck had some acceptable explanation for the string of curious coincidences—particularly the Polish willingness to give a passport to his paramour. In detailed instructions to Knauf, Lyons emphasized that he wasn't out to elicit a confession but to learn the truth. The State Department's goal was to find out what damage, if any, had been done to the United States; what, if any, secret information had been turned over to the Soviet satellite. Knauf was to go at once to Frankfurt to arrange for the showdown.

Together, Lyons and Boswell went over the possibilities. If Scarbeck, facing Knauf, simply turned on his heel and walked out, Knauf would have to let him go. He had no authority to hold him. The security officers tried to plan for all eventualities.

They hoped they were ready for anything early in June when the Scarbecks and their three children left Warsaw for Mrs. Scarbeck's family home in Dusseldorf. Scarbeck had suggested to his wife that she would probably prefer to visit with her mother rather than spend three days waiting for him in Bonn.

On June 4, Scarbeck left his family in Dusseldorf and went straight to Urszula Discher in Frankfurt. The German police saw Scarbeck leave the Discher woman's room before dawn on June 5 and catch the 5 A.M. train for Bonn. He entered the embassy right on schedule at 9 A.M.

The embassy's administrative officer was full of apologies. The foreign buildings officer had been called to Frankfurt but he was still anxious to have his talk with Mr. Scarbeck.

"Mr. Farber here has volunteered to drive you to Frankfurt," the administrative officer added.

James Polk Farber, Knauf's young assistant, said afterwards that the next two hours were the toughest of his life. As he drove, he casually asked Scarbeck what Warsaw was like. They compared Polish wines and German wines. Farber studiously avoided any reference to Polish women.

At the consulate in Frankfurt, Farber opened the door of the room where Knauf was waiting, ushered Scarbeck in and briskly performed the introductions. Then, he excused himself and went next door where two direct lines had been installed—one to the German national police, the other to the Frankfurt police. Over the first telephone, Farber gave the signal for the Discher woman to be picked up by the national police, theoretically for questioning about her visa. Over the second telephone, Farber asked waiting Frankfurt police to bring in Cordes.

In the next room, a recording device was beginning to turn in a closet. No one thought then that the tape would ever be played in a courtroom. It was there to get an exact record, in case Scarbeck disclosed anything of interest to security agents.

The tape recorded more than words. The consulate annex where Knauf and Scarbeck talked was a converted apartment house on a busy thoroughfare. The honking of truck horns and the putt-putt of motor scooters were recorded along with the shrill voices of children at play and, once, as the hour grew late, the sound of a bird singing.

Knauf, facing Scarbeck, was painfully aware that all the surveillance, all the cables and diplomatic pouches from Washington and Warsaw, all the months of planning had narrowed down to this moment in the bare room. If he failed—and the sound of his failure would be clearly recorded on the tape—the American government would never know for sure whether the Scarbeck case was simply an illicit love affair or a dangerous threat to foreign policy.

A lawyer by training, a kindly man by preference, Knauf began by mentioning that he had information Scarbeck might be involved in a black market in Polish currency. He did have the information but he brought it up only to give Scarbeck a plausible reason why a security officer might be interested in him.

Scarbeck, after a bit of stalling, admitted he had fooled around a bit with Polish currency. By now, Scarbeck, always the extrovert, was calling Knauf "Ken." Cautiously, Knauf moved a step further. He asked Scarbeck if he knew Urszula Discher. Scarbeck couldn't deny that he had told his right-hand man to say he was interested in getting her a German visa.

Knauf asked Scarbeck if he had had an affair with the girl, if he had lived with her in Frankfurt. After some more stalling, Scarbeck admitted that, too. Obviously, he had concluded that whoever trailed him in Frankfurt had gotten the word back to Knauf.

Knauf wanted to know where Scarbeck first met the girl. Scarbeck said she had called the embassy one night early in September, 1959, to ask for a job and the Marine guard had put the call through to Scarbeck. Attracted by the girl's throaty voice, Scarbeck made a date to meet her later that night. One date led to another and in April, 1960, the girl moved out of the store where she was living and into an apartment rented by Scarbeck. After that, he was with her almost every night. He would leave the embassy to have dinner with his family and go back to his office, pleading he had work to do. After working a few hours, he would go to the girl's apartment, where he usually remained until about 3 A.M. He had been living for a year on three hours' sleep a night.

In answer to Knauf's next question, Scarbeck admitted he had helped the girl get her visa to visit Germany. Now Knauf was ready to lower the boom. He asked Scarbeck how the girl got her passport. As Scarbeck began fencing with him, Knauf quietly pointed out that the Poles would never release a healthy young woman, particularly when they knew she was having illicit relations with an American diplomat.

"It was all very short and sweet," Scarbeck said abruptly. "I was given the treatment. It was right out of the book."

Then he told the story of the night of December 23, 1960, when Polish intelligence agents raided Urszula's apartment and found him in bed with her. The first thing he saw was a camera as the door was flung open.

After that, he said, the Poles threatened to tell his wife and the embassy about the affair if he didn't cooperate. He claimed they also threatened to put the girl in jail where the soldiers could have their will of her. But he insisted that he gave the Polish agents nothing of importance.

"If someone says he knows I have passed secret documents," Scarbeck said, "someone's trying to frame me."

Knauf persisted. He reminded Scarbeck that he had already admitted the Poles helped him get his mistress out of Warsaw.

"What did you do, Doc? Fool them?" Knauf asked gently. "I don't think you did sell out. What did you do to avoid selling out? It's your move, Doc."

Outside, the children were shouting as Scarbeck told the patient man across the table, "I'm getting angry."

"Getting angry isn't going to solve your problem," Knauf returned. "You're boxed in a little bit."

"You're wrong," Scarbeck retorted. "I'm boxed in a lot."

Again, Knauf reminded him that he must have given the Poles something of value in exchange for the Discher woman's passport. "You took documents out . . . they photographed them . . . you brought them back," Knauf told Scarbeck.

The diplomat sighed.

"Yes," he said, "a secret document."

It had taken three and a half hours of questioning, but Scarbeck had finally admitted what all the security men had feared most—that secrets had been exchanged for a passport. The document Scarbeck admitted taking out of the embassy to be photographed was Ambassador Beam's own appraisal of United States policy toward Poland during the past four years.

Once committed, Scarbeck admitted passing on information from other documents—one an estimate of the effectiveness of the Polish armed forces as prepared by United States military attaches and the other a secret report on a new Polish airfield near the border of Czechoslovakia.

Scarbeck insisted he had given the Poles nothing affecting American security, but the security agents took a different view. The information Scarbeck admitted passing would tell the Poles what the Americans knew about their military strength, how effective American intelligence sources were and the American ambassador's own plans to keep Poland amenable to Western influence.

While the questioning went on, Farber manning the direct lines in the next room took a call from the Presidium where the Discher girl was being questioned—and not talking. Another American security officer, who had taken over from German intelligence, proposed that Scarbeck talk with her. Scarbeck, sobbing into the phone, told his mistress to tell the truth.

At police headquarters, Scarbeck's friend Cordes was airing everything he knew, which did not include Scarbeck's involvement with the Polish agents. He admitted sending the phony telegram about the dying brother, admitted helping Scarbeck with other arrangements because he understood the diplomat was in love with the girl and hoped to marry her. He said he had given his help because Scarbeck had done favors for him in the old days, including getting milk for his baby.

In the bare room with the spinning tape, Scarbeck became a compulsive talker. At one point, he described his paramour as foul-mouthed and uncouth. At another, he told how much she loved him.

"I am to her father, mother, sister, brother, wall, rock, strength," he boasted.

Knauf halted the flow of words long enough to put in a call to Washington. He couldn't say much on the open line but he got the message across to Boswell.

"Our boy has made a full confession to the worst possibility," he reported. "What do I do next?"

"Get him right over here, and you come with him."

On October 3, 1961, Scarbeck went to trial in Washington. Dikeos came from Warsaw for the trial, bringing the corroborative evidence he had been collecting ever since Scarbeck talked. The Discher woman came from Frankfurt to testify as a government witness. Karen Scarbeck was there, too, at her husband's side.

During the three-week trial, the jury listened to the tape playing out Scarbeck's own story of love and betrayal. On October 27, 1961, the jury of 11 men and one woman convicted the American diplomat on three counts of passing classified documents to agents of Communist Poland and the judge gave him the maximum sentence—30 years in prison. Scarbeck's attorney promptly announced that he would appeal the conviction.

Karen Scarbeck, who had listened with lowered head as her husband's mistress detailed their nights of love, said she would stand by him. The United States offered asylum to the Discher woman but she turned down the offer and returned to Warsaw. All Scarbeck had done to get her out of there—including the betrayal of his country for a passport—had been in vain.

3 ★★★

The Army Criminal Investigation Division

Ever since General George Washington, Army commanders have worried about crime in the military and how to cope with it. It took nearly two centuries to find the answers, but today the Army has 1,100 criminal investigators assigned to the prevention and detection of crime in the military from Germany to Japan.

They are bolstered by a training school of their own, three criminal laboratories and a central repository of crime files packed with more than 200,000 cases. They are equipped with all the modern gadgets from lie detectors to two-way mirrors and hidden microphones. Their duties range from solving murders to protecting soldiers from being swindled.

Just as a local police department's uniformed men deal with minor crimes and leave the tough ones to headquarters detectives, so today's uniformed military policemen cope with lesser offenses and the Army's military police Criminal Investigation Division concentrates on cases demanding the skills of trained investigators.

Where the Army's modern criminal investigators carry out their missions in unmarked cars with two-way radios, the Army's earliest crime fighters performed their chores on horseback. They were organized as the Provost Corps in 1778 when General Washington was brooding about his ragamuffin army.

"Purity of morals being the only sure foundation of publick happiness in any Country and highly conducive to order, subordination and success in an Army," he wrote, "it will be well worthy of the Emulation of Officers of every rank and Class to encourage it both by the Influence of Example and the penalties of Authority . . .

"The frequent Robberies which have lately prevailed in the Vicinity of Camp are truly alarming and demand the most vigilant Exertions to detect the perpetrators and bring them to the severest punishment."

His Provost Corps was to enforce rules and orders and apprehend marauders, drunkards, rioters and stragglers. The corps was discontinued after the war, re-established during the War of 1812 and discontinued immediately afterwards.

During the Civil War, a Provost Marshal General was appointed mainly to administer draft laws but his subordinates throughout the country were charged with catching up with deserters and spies, reporting treasonable practices and recovering stolen government property. They were helped by partially disabled soldiers in a Veteran Reserve Corps. Again, their role was eliminated at war's end.

When the American Expeditionary Force went overseas in World War I, the Corps of Military Police was activated in France, but it wasn't until the latter days of World War I that the top brass realized a police force needs detectives as well as uniformed men to deal with crime.

The idea of establishing a detective force within the military was first put on paper on May 11, 1918, when the Provost Marshal General of the AEF ordered the creation of a Division of Criminal Investigation.

It was his intention, according to Army historians, to "inaugurate within the department of the Provost Marshal General a force of detectives whose special duty it would be to conduct inquiries into cases of crime or suspected crime reported to it through official channels, similar to the detective departments of police administration in civil affairs."

But intention was one thing, performance another. There was no time to train operatives or search through the Army for experienced investigators from civilian life. As an Army historian delicately put it, the investigations of these World War I operatives were characterized by "marked individuality." In other words, they devised their own investigative techniques without training, orders or official recognition.

Shortly after the Armistice, general orders were issued definitely establishing a Criminal Investigation Division under the Provost Marshal General and the operation was put on a firmer foundation. It had to be. The Army was facing two problems unique in its history. It had to occupy conquered foreign territory and get its soldiers home from overseas. Just as the Army was to recognize nearly three decades later, idle soldiers waiting for transportation home and nationals in former enemy territory could create crime problems that taxed the abilities of even trained investigators.

Early in 1919, the Provost Marshal General announced the organization of seven Criminal Investigation Companies. Later, more companies were organized to cover the American Embarkation Center as well as Belgium, Italy and Germany. The Army's ranks were combed for men with some previous training to man these companies. The result was a collection of lawyers, newspaper reporters, "private eyes," inspectors and special agents. At its peak in post-World War I Europe, the Criminal Investigation Division numbered 67 officers and 767 men spread from Scotland to Germany.

There were problems. Commanding officers weren't sure just how to use their military detectives. Orders had to be issued that the operatives were concerned solely with crime and were not to deal with vice, collect debts or cope with non-criminal controversies. Nevertheless, the hastily gathered collection of citizen-soldier investigators became recognized as an effective factor in maintaining the good repute of the Army.

With the fold-up of occupation duties and the demobilization of the Army, the Criminal Investigation Division virtually disappeared until another war came along.

Just before the United States declared war in 1941, the Military Police Corps was activated again but it wasn't until the end of 1943 that the Provost Marshal General was assigned supervision over criminal investigation within the military establishment. The high command had discovered that the Army's criminal investigations had to be coordinated with other Federal agencies, with civilian police and among the Army commands at home and overseas.

Before the war ended and at its end, plenty of coordination was required. When the Federal Bureau of Narcotics complained that military personnel were getting involved in the use and sale of narcotics, the Provost Marshal General dispatched a confidential letter to commanding generals. Criminal investigators throughout the service worked with narcotics agents to break up the dope traffic.

Then, the Bureau of Customs began reporting that soldiers were mailing home and smuggling stolen government property and dangerous war trophies. By 1945, the problem had become so acute that Army investigators installed "inspectoscopes" at ports of entry. This X-ray device enabled military teams to view the contents of soldier packages without opening them and the round-up of stolen property and explosive trophies finally began.

Meanwhile, the Army's criminal investigators had their hands full with the run of crime to be expected of a cross-section of the civilian population suddenly in uniform. During the last year of the war, they made 50,000 investigations and recovered more than $2,000,000 worth of stolen government property in the United States alone.

This time, at war's end, the Criminal Investigation Division didn't collapse with demobilization. In many ways, its mission became even tougher. Some soldiers with time on their hands and a burning desire for a fast buck went in for smuggling, blackmarketing and even jewel theft. Soldiers became the victims as well as the perpetrators of crime. Occupation forces in Europe and the Far East needed the Army's brand of detectives more than ever before.

In May, 1948, an Army staff sergeant was beaten to death with an iron bar in a railroad station at Kassel, Germany. The motive was obviously robbery since his money and gold watch were missing. After months of futile investigation, Army investigators came upon an ex-convict who, while in jail, had been told by a fellow prisoner of seeing a German with a gold watch and some American dollars near the Kassel station on the night of the murder. From this skimpy tip, the Army criminal investigators developed the true identity of the killer who had gone under an assumed name, traced him across Germany and finally got a full confession. The German slayer had simply seen the soldier's watch glitter in the train station and killed to get it.

Twenty-four hours after the murder of the staff sergeant, the Army investigators had to solve another killing. This time, it was one of their men. In the burned out shambles of a car, Army investigators at Munich, Germany, found the charred remains of an agent from their own detachment and a German police sergeant. They had been taking a German prisoner to jail at the time of the slaying. The prisoner had disappeared but the police of Europe working together in the manhunt located him in Liege, Belgium, as he was trying to make his way to Spain. The evidence developed at the scene and in the CID's German laboratory was so complete that the prisoner promptly confessed.

Whenever there's any suspicion that soldiers may be involved in crimes, the police promptly call in the CID. The police of Bremerhaven, Germany, did that one January morning in 1950 after a bank was robbed. The Army investigators identified the two soldier bank robbers but also proved conclusively that the crime was masterminded by the German owner of a repair garage. Only a German, they showed, would know that a large payroll was to be delivered at the bank on a certain morning and only a German would know that the bank opened at 8 A.M. The American soldier who got his buddy into the hold-up with him, it developed, was trying to pay off his repair bill at the garage by robbing a bank.

In this country, another Federal enforcement agency—the FBI, Secret Service, Post Office or the Treasury's lawmen—may take over the case but overseas the Army handles its own criminal investigations.

Now firmly established as the Army's detective force, the Criminal Investigation Division is manned by warrant officers and enlisted specialists selected from the ranks of the Military Police Corps for special training as criminal investigators. Unlike the investigative arms of the Navy and Air Force, the Army's CID is decentralized in its world-wide operations. The Provost Marshal General of the Army is responsible for over-all staff supervision and the selection, training and assignment of criminal investigators but once they get in the field, they take their orders from their immediate commanders. Unlike the other services, they do not deal with espionage, subversion and treason. Those are responsibilities of another Army outfit—the Counter-Intelligence Corps.

As an elite group of investigators, they do not deal with offenses punishable by less than a year's confinement or minor traffic accidents. Their mission is major crime and any form of misconduct that requires highly developed investigative techniques.

Since they are responsible for the prevention as well as the detection of crime, they are detailed to make crime prevention surveys aimed at minimizing the desire to commit crime by eliminating the opportunity. Investigators may go undercover to find out the extent of gambling, the narcotics traffic, prostitution or the "fencing" of stolen goods in the vicinity of the Army post.

Or the crime prevention survey may center on local businessman exploiting soldiers and luring them into debt. The Army doesn't want its men robbing and stealing to pay off creditors nor does it want fast-talking merchants to take advantage of young servicemen on their own for the first time.

Once the investigators find out the crime potential, they look into ways and means of insulating the soldiers from influences for bad. They assess the cooperation of civil authorities, reputable business establishments and civic organizations and turn over their findings to military authorities for action.

Another type of survey performed by the CID deals with the physical security of the Army establishment. The investigators evaluate the adequacy of existing safeguards to prevent theft or sabotage and recommend ways to reduce the hazards.

Backing up the men in the field are the scientific investigators in the Army Criminal Investigation laboratories. The CID looks to them for the answers provided by the mute evidence—handwriting, fingerprints, a spent bullet, a smear of paint, a handful of dust.

The Army's men against crime have come a long way since General Washington put his first military policeman on horseback.

THE BLACK MARKETEERS

Capt. Bill Wright, commander of an Army Criminal Investigation Detachment, worked his way through his fifth root beer float and tried to look as if he were enjoying it.

"When we get out of this," he told his companion in a soft Virginia drawl, "remind me never to have another root beer float."

The two men—the dark-haired young captain with the deceptively relaxed air and his operations officer—were staked out in the snack bar of an Army Post Exchange at Frankfurt, Germany. From where they sat, they had a clear view of the exchange manager's office through a glass partition. In a field behind the post exchange, the rest of Capt. Wright's team watched the exchange's loading platform through binoculars.

In their loose summer sports shirts, Capt. Wright and his companion looked like all the other Americans crowding into the snack bar on a summer Saturday. Out in his car, the captain had left a shabby jacket of German tailoring. No telling where the trail might lead this day.

A week before, an informant had slipped up the back steps of Capt. Wright's office with a tip. A big shipment of cigarettes was due to leave Frankfurt's largest post exchange in a few days for parts unknown. The way the informant had heard it, about 75 cases of cigarettes with 50 cartons to the case were to be diverted to the black market.

In any other country at any other time, the tip might have been handled routinely, but this was the Germany of 1948 and the cigarette black market was far from routine.

Wright knew without being told why the German police had readily loaned him a detective, why the chief of the Criminal Investigation Division at the Army's European headquarters had supplied a German-speaking ace investigator, why the tip had been relayed promptly to the Provost Marshal for Europe. They weren't just interested in one truckload of cigarettes. They hoped it would lead them to the ringleader of a conspiracy that was becoming increasingly more dangerous.

The informant had said the cigarettes would be moved either July 30 or 31. It was now July 31 and nothing had happened.

"This black market in cigarettes," Wright's operations officer was saying as he idly watched Army wives shopping for groceries and gadgets, "it's big, isn't it?"

Wright nodded, his usually amiable face taking on a somber cast. "It's big and deadly," he said. "Ever since the Germans started using cigarettes instead of money, people have been murdering each other to get them."

The crowded snack bar was no place to air the other danger—that the Russians had begun to show a marked interest in American cigarettes. Just recently, Wright was aware, a truckload of American cigarettes had been seized as the driver tried to slip across the Czech border. He suspected why the Russians wanted the cigarettes—and it wasn't to smoke. American cigarettes had become the medium of exchange in Germany because the money was worthless. Old women bartered their heirlooms for cigarettes to buy food and medicine. Factories and homes were being built with cigarettes instead of money. Anything in Germany could be bought with American cigarettes—including information.

In Russian hands, the cigarettes could be used to pay Germans to spy on the Americans. So, if Americans were involved in the black market traffic in cigarettes—and Wright's informant indicated they were—they were engaged in more than making a fast buck. Whether they realized it or not, they were putting cigarettes in the wrong hands.

Wright's mission—to get the ringleader of the gang—was his first big assignment since taking over as detachment commander. He had gotten to Europe in time for the last desperate days of the Battle of the Bulge. In one day, he had moved up from platoon leader to company commander as his fellow officers were killed and wounded. The challenge of staying alive had prompted him to look for other challenges when the war ended. He had found his challenge in criminal investigation.

He was just getting up to relieve one of the investigators behind the post exchange when a member of his team drifted into the snack bar and sat down at his table.

"They're loading up an Army truck out back," the investigator reported. "It's all cigarettes."

Wright pushed back his chair with a grimace in the direction of the root beer float. "Tell the men to get going," he said.

As the big Army truck rumbled away from the Post Exchange, Wright noticed a youth seated beside the driver but his attention was riveted on a car leading the truck onto the highway. He recognized the man at the wheel of the lead car—James Powell, area supervisor for the ten Post Exchanges in the Frankfurt complex. If he was the ringleader, the investigator realized, there was more to this than one Post Exchange.

The investigators were using the leap frog method of trailing the truck. For awhile, Wright's American car followed the truck. Then, he slowed down to let a jeep with two of his investigators pass him. A small foreign car with the German detective and the German-speaking American investigator passed both and pulled ahead of the truck. As the miles went by, they reshuffled their cars into different formations. On the outskirts of Hoechst, the car leading the truck pulled to the side and Wright saw the driver wave the truck by and turn back toward Frankfurt.

"Powell was there to get the truck through the road blocks," Wright speculated. "He could say it was making a delivery to the PX at Hoechst. If the truck is heading for a black market depot, it should soon be there."

Wright had maneuvered into the lead of his procession with the truck about 100 yards ahead when he braked sharply. An ox-drawn wagon piled high with hay had pulled out of a side road as soon as the truck passed and was now moving slowly across the highway with an old German farmer trudging beside it. The load of hay effectively blocked Wright's view of the road ahead.

"If we lose him now, we're dead," the captain muttered, frantically blowing his horn. "We'll never know where that load of cigarettes is going and we won't have a thing to use on Powell."

The highway was finally clear, too clear. The truck had vanished and the village of Zeilsheim with its honeycomb of streets lay directly ahead. Zeilsheim had been converted into a camp for displaced persons. As the captain knew, the stateless from all over Europe with no place to go and nothing to lose were surviving on crumbs from the black market. The truck could be holed up anywhere in this village.

Wright sped down the main street of Zeilsheim, scanning the side streets as he passed. And then he saw it—the green tail gate of the Army truck disappearing through the iron gates of a driveway. Waving his procession to a halt, he gave his orders. He and his operations officer would stick around in case the cigarettes were transferred to another car and moved out again. The others were to pick up the truck driver and the youth with him on the road back to Frankfurt.

The truck remained inside the gates only a few minutes, just time to unload. When the driver backed his truck out of the driveway, Wright shot a glance at the front seat. The driver was alone.

Strolling by the gates, the only opening in the high stone wall, Wright could see a courtyard, a small house, the edge of a barn. The truck driver's companion was nowhere in sight.

The investigator lounged against a telephone pole at the end of the street, waiting for something to happen. In his shabby German jacket, there was nothing to make him stand out on this street of the idle. Few of the displaced persons had jobs and they, too, were sunning themselves on the summer afternoon. Only the children were busy, chasing each other across the cobblestone street.

After two hours, Wright signalled his companion. The cigarettes obviously weren't going to move for a while and he wanted to get back to Frankfurt to hear what the truck driver had to say.

The truck driver, he found, had little to tell. He had been hired from a local labor service organization and the youth in the car with him had shown him where to go.

"Who was he?" Wright asked.

The driver shrugged. "I never saw him before but I heard one of the men calling him Mendelson."

Wright and his operations officer left to pick up Powell, the post exchange supervisor who had led the truck as far as Hoechst.

"We're investigating PX activities and we've found some matters we'd like to discuss with you," Wright said, identifying himself. "Would you mind coming with us?"

Powell, heavy-set, friendly, radiating the confidence of an efficient businessman, said he'd be glad to oblige.

At the Criminal Investigation Division office, Capt. Wright showed him to a room and left him there. He still hadn't asked Powell a question.

A few minutes later, Wright crossed the room and went out the other door. With him was the truck driver from the Zeilsheim trip. Without appearing to glance in Powell's direction, Wright caught the widened eyes, the reddening face of the Post Exchange official.

Powell was on his feet when Wright re-entered the room alone ten minutes later.

"Hey, I want to know what I'm here for."

"We think you can tell us," the investigator drawled.

The sight of the truck driver had thrown Powell off balance but he still wasn't ready to explain why a truckload of American cigarettes from a Post Exchange had wound up in a displaced persons camp.

Wright told him that the truck driver had talked, that Powell had been followed all day. Powell wasn't impressed by the truck driver's supposed revelations, apparently realizing how little the driver knew. As for being trailed, he wanted to know what was wrong with driving down the highway on a summer Saturday.

Now over his initial shock, Powell was wary and Wright knew it. There was nothing left but a shot in the dark—the name mentioned by the truck driver.

"We've got Mendelson, too," he told Powell. "Mendelson says he works for you."

"He doesn't work for me," Powell protested. "He works for Fred Parker."

As soon as he blurted out the name, he sat back with an appalled expression on his face. Watching him, Wright guessed the reason. He had surprised Powell into naming the ringleader of the conspiracy. Fred Parker, as chief of merchandise control for the ten Post Exchanges in the Frankfurt complex, was in a much better position than Powell to mastermind an operation of this size.

"Unless you want to take all the blame yourself," Wright told the sweating businessman, "you'd be wise to tell us how this thing works."

Powell agreed. "Parker got me into this," he said. "He gave me enough coupons to cover 75 cases of cigarettes."

Wright knew the cigarettes had to be covered by coupons. Since the cigarettes were rationed, anybody buying a carton had to turn in a coupon to get it and every Post Exchange had to produce coupons to account for all the cigarettes sold.

Powell said he didn't know where Parker got the coupons to conceal the black market operations, but he could explain how a truckload of cigarettes could be shipped out without attracting suspicion.

That, he said, was done with transfer slips. Routinely, if one post exchange ran short, it would ask another Post Exchange for a supply. In the black market operation, transfer slips showing the movement of goods from one post exchange to another were used to conceal the diversion of huge shipments to the black market.

As Powell explained the operation in business terms, he said nothing to indicate awareness that his black market traffic was inviting murder or what the Americans feared more—a tool for espionage. As far as the other Post Exchanges in the Frankfurt complex were concerned, Powell said he had heard they were involved but he didn't know for sure. Parker, who got the biggest share of the profits, would know a lot more.

Wright was sure of it. Parker could tell him where the coupons came from, the ready supply of coupons to mask the black market conspiracy. And Parker could tell him where to find Mendelson—the link between the American ringleader and the black market, the man who had collected the money for this transaction. Mendelson had to have the money, close to $9,000, Powell had said. The truck driver didn't have it and neither did Powell.

It was nearing midnight when Wright finally traced Parker to his girl friend's apartment. Parker, tall and raw-boned with the look of a farmer, listened expressionlessly as Wright tried the direct approach.

"We've confiscated a load of cigarettes," Wright told him abruptly. "We've got your boy Mendelson and we know where he got his orders. Powell says you're the boss. If you don't mind, we'd like to search your apartment."

The name of Mendelson worked its magic again. Parker must have known what the investigators would find in his apartment, but he agreed to take them there. In Parker's apartment, the investigators uncovered a cache of cigarette coupons, thousands of dollars worth of military payment certificates and American greenbacks and some interesting letters from friends reporting they had deposited substantial sums for Parker in various American banks. Wright was now convinced he had the ringleader wanted so urgently by American authorities.

Confronted with what the investigators had, believing they had a lot more, Parker reluctantly admitted black market deals arranged through all the Post Exchanges in the Frankfurt area. Like Powell before him, Parker wasn't going to take the blame for anybody else. He brought another man into the conspiracy—the security officer of the Post Exchange system, the man responsible for preventing exactly what had happened.

As Parker explained it, when a customer turned in his ration coupon for a carton of cigarettes, the coupon would be pasted on a sheet at the post exchange. As soon as the sheet had 50 coupons on it, it was sent to Parker as chief of merchandise control to be credited against the next load of cigarettes. The security officer, Parker and a Post Exchange manager were supposed to witness the burning of the used coupons. Since all three were in on the conspiracy, the coupons went unburned and Parker parcelled them out to Post Exchange managers to account for the cigarettes flowing into the black market.

From Parker's admissions and the letters found in his apartment, the investigators could figure the conspiracy had netted at least $100,000 in a year of operation.

Wright now had the scheme, but he knew Parker was shrewd. As soon as Parker got around to thinking things over, he would deny he had said anything and claim the investigators had invaded his apartment without his permission. Wright had to have more evidence, specifically Mendelson and the money, and he had no idea where to find Mendelson. Parker thought Mendelson had been captured. Actually, Parker was the only one who would know Mendelson's whereabouts.

Routinely, Wright began asking Parker for the addresses of various employees. He included Mendelson's name in the middle of the list and Parker supplied Mendelson's address without a moment's hesitation.

It was getting on towards morning when the German detective teamed with the German-speaking American investigator brought in Mendelson and Wright ran into his first real roadblock since the hay wagon. Mendelson didn't have the money.

Wright eyed the German youth dubiously. Here was a German variation of the dead-end kid, a street-wise product of years of war and privation.

"It's the truth," Mendelson insisted. "They said they didn't have the money yet. They promised to give it to me in three installments beginning Monday."

Wright was getting groggy. It had been nearly 24 hours now since his stint with the root beer floats in the Post Exchange snack bar. His team was beginning to round up the Post Exchange managers and the little CID office was getting crowded.

He had planned to raid the displaced persons camp to get back the cigarettes but he couldn't do that until he got the money and by then the cigarettes would probably be gone. He had to get the $9,000—not only because it belonged to the Post Exchange—but more importantly to use as evidence against Parker.

Wright, after a little talk with Mendelson, conferred with his German-speaking American investigator, Master Sgt. Karl Von Klaus. Blond and square-jawed, Sgt. Von Klaus was the product of a Prussian military school, a German general's son. In the days of Hitler's rise to power, father and son had participated in the plot to assassinate him. The senior Von Klaus was caught and executed but his son fled to America, became a naturalized citizen and joined the Army. He was the ace investigator loaned to Wright by the headquarters command and he was about to get his severest test.

"Mendelson has agreed to go back into the DP camp to collect the money," Wright told the sergeant, "but I don't trust him. If he goes alone, we'll never see him again and he's sure to tip off the black market crowd. We want you to go with him, Karl."

He didn't have to tell Von Klaus the risk he would run. The sergeant knew as well as he did that men were being murdered in the cigarette trade. One word from Mendelson and the sergeant would never get out of the camp alive. If the exposure of the black market operation in Frankfurt should leak back to the Zeilsheim camp, the black marketeers would be waiting for him. Somehow, Wright knew, he had to keep the round-up secret until the money was collected—despite the three-day absence of nearly a dozen men from their families and the Post Exchanges.

Wright had to clear with three generals but by Sunday night, he had moved his crowd of "guests" to an old house outside of Frankfurt. The men were allowed to call their homes, but as Wright pointed out, they wouldn't want to worry their wives. They agreed to say simply that they had been called away for a few days.

All the men except Parker were reacting with the resigned cheerfulness of a group stranded in a blizzard. As more Post Exchange managers and finally the security officer were brought to the old house, they greeted them with a cheer.

"So they got you, too!"

Watching from the doorway as a non-stop card game entered its third day, Wright thought about Sergt. Von Klaus on his final trip to the DP camp. So far, Mendelson had behaved, but each day made the risk of a leak progressively greater.

Wright's mind strayed to the wife and baby waiting for Von Klaus to come home. He pictured the house behind the stone wall in Zeilsheim and the desperate men in the DP camp. Looking at his watch for the tenth time in as many minutes, Wright wished there had been some other way to do this but he had to get the evidence against Parker, all the money.

He heard a car pull up and Von Klaus strode toward him with a brown paper package in his hand. The blond German and the dark-haired Virginian grinned at each other.

"That's the last of it," the sergeant reported. "The men were gone but an old woman gave this to Mendelson."

The ordeal of waiting in secret was past. Now the men could be formally charged with misappropriating Post Exchange property. They could never be charged with the crimes their greed for a fast buck had produced, nor the invitation to espionage if the cigarettes fell into the wrong hands.

Wright didn't know it as he herded the men into waiting cars, but he had one more job to do. As the pre-trial maneuvering stretched on for months, three of the accused men restricted to the Frankfurt base disappeared. One of them was Parker, the ringleader. Parker, Wright knew, had tried to persuade Mendelson not to talk. Mendelson had a remarkable memory for dates and places. When the investigators caught up with Parker's attempt to silence Mendelson, Parker pulled out.

Through Parker's girl friend, Wright traced the three who had decamped to Paris. He got one of them in a Paris nightclub on New Year's Eve, but Parker and a Post Exchange manager had flown back to America.

All the others had been tried and found guilty before Parker and the man who fled with him could be brought back for trial. They had fought extradition to the Supreme Court and lost. Wright had been rotated home by then but he was brought back to testify.

Looking at the phlegmatic face of the mastermind of the conspiracy, Capt. Wright reflected how close he had come to getting away with it. If that hay wagon had blocked the highway to Zeilsheim a few seconds longer, he might never have gotten the lever to force Parker's hand —a German dead-end kid named Mendelson.

4 ★★★

Office of Naval Intelligence

A young Assistant Secretary of the Navy with the imagination to look beyond these shores to the potential ravages of spies and saboteurs fathered the investigative arm of the Navy. His name was Franklin D. Roosevelt.

Today, hundreds of special agents trained in the latest investigative techniques serve the naval establishment at home and overseas from the Marianas to the Mediterranean. Their duties are firmly established by executive orders and naval regulations—to investigate espionage, sabotage, fraud, security violations and the gamut of crime.

It wasn't always thus, although the Navy is as old as the country and its Office of Naval Intelligence has existed since 1882. During the Spanish-American War, it is known that naval intelligence officers investigated the activities of Spanish agents, but ONI in those days was more concerned with assessing enemy strength than hunting enemy agents.

The outbreak of World War I in Europe presented problems for the Navy that it had never encountered before, and men like Franklin D. Roosevelt were quick to recognize it. The Central European Powers had been building a spy network over the centuries. Our potential allies also had long-standing intelligence services. If this country entered the war, it had to be in a position to exchange information with our friends and counter the espionage of our enemies.

As Roosevelt's boss, Secretary of the Navy Josephus Daniels, told a Senate investigation after it was all over: "It was well known in this country that the Germans had established a wonderful spy system through which Berlin was being informed of the activities in every branch of industry in the country. It is probable that there was no manufacturing establishment here that did not have at least one paid agent of the German government who kept that government informed of everything that was going on. There is no doubt that even in the departments at Washington, German agents were at work at all times. It was supposed that bases of some sort for the supplying of gasoline and supplies by German submarines were being secretly established in different points along the coasts of Mexico, Central and South America. Before the United States entered the war, Germans were allowed to enter this country freely."

The threat posed by these unfriendly visitors and their American sympathizers worried enough people in the naval establishment to spur the creation of a naval undercover office in New York where investigators served on a volunteer basis. ONI's investigative work really started there, in 1915. That was the year ONI's Security Division was born.

By 1916, naval officials took their problem to Congress. The chief of naval operations asked for expansion of ONI, contending that if it had the means, its usefulness to the whole country could be greatly increased. And Secretary of the Navy Daniels testified that "this year, I know, we have had to call on other departments to make investigations of a military character because the Navy Department had no money to make them."

Two months before the United States declared war on Germany in 1917, the Navy Secretary's senior officers presented him with a plan entitled "Steps to be taken to meet a possible condition of war with the Central European Powers." Among its provisions for war readiness was this investigative role for ONI:

"Organize a comprehensive system of intelligence service covering the whole theater of war in accordance with the plans of ONI. Place under surveillance all citizens of the Central Powers in the Navy or in government employ in naval establishments and remove them from positions in which they may do possible harm."

The declaration of war was the go-ahead signal for ONI's Security Division. For the first time, merchant ships were being used to convoy American troops overseas. Were the merchant seamen loyal? The ONI investigators had to find out. They had to rout out Germans intent on fomenting strikes at naval munitions plants, guard against sabotage to shipping, investigate cases referred by the mail censorship bureau and the cable censor, track down suspicious characters in the vicinity of naval piers and warehouses, investigate fires at naval wharves, protect shipyards and munitions factories, and hunt enemy agents.

To get the job done, ONI's Washington headquarters expanded tremendously, its personnel was reorganized and its activities were extended to every state in the union and all points of the globe, as ONI added security missions to its long-time intelligence functions. By the armistice, its Security Division was a smoothly operating outfit.

But after World War I, the Navy's investigative arm withered. Franklin D. Roosevelt had left the Navy Department. The world had been made safe for democracy and the naval establishment was virtually mothballed. All that was left of ONI's Security Division was a skeleton force in the naval districts. It formed the knowledgeable nucleus, however, for a new generation of investigators when Hitler began making noises in Europe and the naval establishment came out of mothballs.

ONI's investigative role had not been forgotten by its old friend. Three months before war broke out again in Europe in 1939, President Roosevelt issued an executive memorandum recognizing the Security Division as a functioning entity of ONI responsible for investigating espionage, counterespionage and sabotage.

Just as ONI's undercover agents were the first American investigators into Latin America in search of German spies before this country entered World War I, the ONI was the first to deal with Japanese espionage before the FBI took over in World War II. At that time, the Navy was the only American agency with any degree of knowledge about Japan.

From the beginning of World War II, the rapidly expanding corps of investigators literally covered the waterfront. They checked on the backgrounds of naval civilian personnel in jobs involving the national security, investigated suspected cases of espionage and subversive activities, guarded against sabotage, uncovered fraud in the buying or selling of naval materials, traced security leaks and did the Navy's detective work on crime.

Security was their mission and protecting the naval establishment their goal. Not all threats to security, they found, need be related directly to enemy efforts.

In a routine investigation of employees at a naval powder factory they found one who had twice been convicted as an arsonist. His mere presence in a powder factory was as much a threat to security as if he had been a trained enemy agent.

Another background investigation, also routine, turned up a Navy

Yard employee who had been dishonorably discharged from all three services, had been twice committed to mental institutions and had been discharged from his last job for conspiring with a bandit ring to hold up his employer. His job at the Navy Yard was guard duty on the main gate and, of course, he had been given a gun. He, too, was a threat to the Navy's security.

It took the combined efforts of special agents in three naval districts to solve the case of a mysterious fire aboard a Navy plane. Arson was suspected and the sailors on guard duty at the time were all asked to take lie detector tests. Only one refused—the one who had turned in the alarm. Special agents, intent on getting a closer look at his background, talked first to neighbors around his home. All of them, including a private investigator, described him as adult, trustworthy and a clear thinker. A request for further investigation went to the naval district where the family had previously lived. Again, no evidence of wrong doing showed up. The investigation was relayed to the naval district where the sailor had lived as a teen-ager. There, it developed that he had set a neighbor's sofa on fire, stolen five cars, including one which he burned up, and had been suspected of setting fire to a barn. When the sailor was faced with his earlier misdeeds, he admitted he had intentionally dropped a lighted cigarette into a wastebasket on the plane. Another security risk was eliminated.

The Navy doesn't talk about its activities in counterespionage, but in connection with its internal security responsibilities (sabotage, espionage and subversion), ONI is a member of the Interdepartmental Intelligence Conference. The other members are the FBI, the Army's Counter Intelligence Corps and the Air Force Office of Special Investigations.

In the postwar years, the role of ONI's centrally-directed Security Division has been limited to investigations requiring professional techniques in these fields: espionage, sabotage and subversive activities; fraud against the government, major violations of the Uniform Code of Military Justice, personnel investigations, security investigations dealing with the compromise or leakage of secret information and "special investigations as required by the naval establishment, comprising those cases containing unusual circumstances or aspects of sensitivity which may require unusual techniques and the exercise of a high degree of discretion."

To carry out these missions, ONI's Security Division is manned by college graduates, some with degrees in law and accountancy. Among its specialists are pilots, photographers, experts in electronics and linguists. It is staffed by naval officers with previous intelligence experience, backed up by civilian specialists who lend continuity to the operation.

They do for the naval establishment what police do for the cities and a dozen Federal law enforcement agencies do for the country. In detecting violations of the Uniform Code of Military Justice, they run the gamut from murder and mutiny to smuggling and trafficking in narcotics. And their investigations take them all over the world.

To solve a shortage in a ship's store at a naval base in Japan, a special agent had to study daily cash register reports for three years to develop a pattern of embezzlement. When he confronted the logical suspect with the pattern, he got a full admission of three years of looting the till for a total take of $143,000.

A civilian travelling on a Navy supply ship disappeared between Karachi, Pakistan, and the British colony of Aden at the tip of the Arabian Peninsula. An ONI agent joined the ship at Aden to investigate suspected murder. He found bloodstains but no body and no weapon. After interviewing 175 persons and giving 40 polygraph (lie detector) tests, he developed the missing man's gambling partners as the most likely suspects. By the time he left the ship at Naples, he had narrowed the list to one member of the crew. In New York, when the FBI took over the case and confronted the crew member with the facts gathered by the ONI agent, the guilty man admitted the slaying.

In California, ONI agents tracked down a mass murderer who had made a hobby of feeding bichloride of mercury to sailors as a hangover remedy. In Naples, Italian police wrote off the death of a young sailor as accidental drowning, but ONI agents, suspecting murder, traced the sailor's movements on the fatal night and learned he had been seen with a merchant seaman. Out of all the merchant seamen in the busy port, ONI agents found their man.

Like their brother investigators in civilian life, the Navy's special agents are shot at, threatened and knifed. An agent on an investigation in "moonshine" country was mistaken for a revenuer and shot. Two agents met by a suspect wielding a loaded, double-barrelled shotgun did some fast-talking to get it away from him. An agent on a routine background investigation was chased by a band of youths brandishing switch-blade knives. Another agent was confronted by a group of armed men who demanded to know the source of certain information he had developed against them. He stood his ground and managed to get away without betraying his source.

Their exploits and adventures have never been made public because

ONI insists on anonymity. As a matter of policy, ONI has consistently shied away from publicity. Typical of the Navy's reluctance to talk about its intelligence operations is the fact that they are not even mentioned in the official manual covering all the Federal agencies. The intelligence missions of its sister services appear in the U. S. Government Organization Manual but not ONI's.

Only now has ONI's director agreed to allow a glimpse behind the scenes at the operations of the Navy's investigators.

THE CASE OF THE LONELY SAILOR

The February wind blew chill through the gully but the Japanese farmer was grinning as he pushed his cart along the narrow path. Only the day before, he had seen Americans from the nearby naval base dump a load of gravel near the main road. What the Americans discarded, he could use.

The weeds grown tall beside the path bent in the wind and the farmer paused for a closer look. For a moment, he thought he had seen a dark object as the withered grass swayed away from the wind. This could be more salvage for his farm.

Pushing his way through the weeds, the farmer stopped short. He was staring down at the body of a dead man.

Within an hour, two special agents from the Office of Naval Intelligence had joined Japanese police at the scene. Later—tonight or tomorrow—the Japanese would make a formal request for a joint investigation, but the agents wouldn't wait for the formalities. A sailor had been killed and from the look of the body, the trail was already cold.

Special Agent Bill Anderson knelt beside the body to read the name on the identification bracelet: Apprentice Seaman Ted Maxwell. He noticed a tattoo above the wrist: "Mom" and "Dad."

"Poor kid," he thought, gently lowering the hand to the frozen ground.

Special Agent Leonard Brock showed him a sailor hat he had found a few feet away from the body. The name stencilled in the hat was not Maxwell.

The agents searched further—Anderson, a broad-shouldered Texan towering above the tall weeds; Brock, his stocky partner, looking in vain for a weapon. They found no further clues, but they knew they could discount robbery as a motive. In Maxwell's wallet, they had found a military pay certificate worth a dollar, a 1,000 yen note and an American dollar bill.

A Japanese doctor performed the autopsy. Maxwell, said the doctor, had suffered his initial injury on January 20, but he didn't die until January 24—11 days before the Japanese farmer found the body. The dark bruise across his cheek could have come from a kick. The immediate cause of death was a single sharp blow with a blunt instrument on the top of his skull.

Studying the autopsy report, Anderson felt a chill more penetrating than the February wind.

"If the doctor is right," he told Brock, "that boy lay out there in the weeds for four days, alive. And the gate to the base was less than 100 yards away."

The doctor, the agents learned, was right on one score. Maxwell was last seen on the evening of January 20, 1959. He failed to muster at 8 A.M. the next day. The doctor had reported Maxwell's last meal indicated tomatoes, a flour compound, peas and strawberries. The bill of fare at the base for the evening meal of January 20 included spaghetti creole, accounting for the tomatoes and flour; peas and blueberry pie. The doctor had confused strawberry and blueberry seeds, but that was all.

The agents ran out their only lead, the sailor hat. The name of Frazier was stencilled on it.

"I missed it from my locker a couple of days before January 20," Seaman Roy Frazier told the agents. "I reported it."

Frazier, it developed, had reported the loss of the hat and he hadn't been off the base that night. Several seamen said they saw him sleeping in his bunk. Some one else must have worn Frazier's sailor cap.

The agents began interviewing every sailor in Maxwell's dormitory. Always, they began the same way, advising the sailors of their rights under the Uniform Code of Military Justice. The sailors didn't have to answer questions.

In their questioning, the agents had two goals: to find out all they could about young Maxwell and to reconstruct the night of January 20.

Maxwell, they learned, was a quiet boy, friendly but homesick. He had been in Japan less than three weeks when he disappeared. He talked mostly about his family in Iowa and how he wished he had more education. He was planning to take some courses at the base. His only buddy was Seaman Gordon who had served on the same base with him in California.

"We were over at the Enlisted Men's Club that night, playing shuffleboard," Gordon told the agents. "I left him there and hit the sack. Later on, he came in and woke me up. He wanted me to go over the fence with him to the Green House."

On their way in from Kobe, the agents had noticed the Green House, a small bar near the main gate of the base. If a sailor didn't have his liberty card, he could get off the base by jumping the back fence. A short walk down the narrow dirt path through the gully would lead him to the main road and the Green House.

"Did you go over the fence with him?" Anderson asked Maxwell's buddy.

"No, but I loaned him a dollar military pay certificate," Gordon replied. "He said he didn't have any money."

From other sailors in Maxwell's dormitory, the agents learned that one had loaned Maxwell a 1,000 yen note and another had seen an American dollar bill which Maxwell was futilely trying to change. Several sailors said Maxwell had tried to persuade them to go over the fence with him because he had never done it before and wasn't sure of the way. They thought it was close to 11 P.M. when Maxwell called out, "If any of you fellows are coming with me, you better hurry up, 'cause I'm leaving." There were no takers and Maxwell went out the door alone.

In a minute, the sailors told the agents, Maxwell was back again, saying he had forgotten his sailor hat. They saw him grab a hat off his bunk and go out. The next day, Gordon found Maxwell's hat on his bunk. The mystery of the hat was solved. Somehow, Frazier's hat had wound up on Maxwell's bunk and Maxwell had taken it by mistake.

Anderson tugged at his square jaw as he ticked off what the agents had learned so far. Brock, watching him, grinned. He had told his partner that he would never make a good poker player, that the hand straying unconsciously to his jaw was a dead giveaway something was bothering him.

"We've accounted for all the money we found in his pocket," Anderson said. "We know that's all he had to start out with. If he'd reached the Green House, he'd have spent at least some of it. He never got to the Green House."

The agents went over the timetable they had drawn up from what the sailors told them. Maxwell left the dormitory between 10:30 and 11 P.M. with the expressed intention of going over the fence near the unused Gate 7. It would have taken him about 15 minutes to walk from the barracks to the fence and from the fence halfway up the gully to where his body was found. Therefore, he must have been attacked between 10:45 and 11:15 P.M.

But who attacked him? He hadn't been in Japan long enough to get mixed up with any Japanese civilians. The men in his dormitory insisted he had no enemies. None of them had gone over the fence with him. The agents had accounted for them all. Wherever the answer lay, the agents concluded, it wasn't among the men in Maxwell's dormitory.

"I don't think it was somebody he knew," Anderson theorized to his partner. "It's quite likely he just happened to be in the wrong place at the wrong time."

The agents were constantly exchanging developments with the Japanese police. On February 17—two weeks and 200 interviews after Maxwell's body was found—a Japanese detective came up with a report. A civilian guard patrolling the outside of the base on a bicycle had seen two silhouettes near Gate 7 on the night of January 20. As he came closer, he saw the men start into the gully. He was sure he had the right night because it was his first time on that section of the patrol. He fixed the time at about 10:55 P.M.

"One of them could have been Maxwell," Brock pointed out.

Anderson shook his head.

"I don't think so," he said. "I think Maxwell was alone when he went over that fence. No, we've got to find two men."

The memory of the Iowa boy lying in the weeds haunted him. He visualized Maxwell, going off alone to forget his homesickness, tracked down and killed by two strangers. Why, he asked himself, tugging hard on his jaw, why?

The agents started making the rounds of the next dormitory. For the 200th time, Agent Anderson heard himself going through the same routine—advising the sailor of his rights, asking the first question: "Do you have any information concerning the circumstances surrounding Maxwell's death?"

"I didn't kill anybody," said the sailor.

Anderson looked up sharply from his notes. He hadn't gotten an answer like that before.

"Nobody said you did," he responded, and went on with his questioning.

He studied the sailor—James Franklin, thin-faced, wiry, older than the others. This must be his second or third hitch. The sailor acknowledged he was on the restricted list, confined to the base for engaging in black market activities with the Japanese.

"Do you ever go over the fence, Franklin?"

"Lots of times," Franklin drawled. "I went that way with a buddy last night, but I didn't go out January 20, if that's what you're talking about."

"Are you sure about January 20?"

The agent saw Franklin open his mouth to say "yes" and hesitate.

"Well, maybe I did," Franklin finally said with a shrug. "A buddy, Jack Delaney, was waiting outside for us in a taxi. I think it was that night. George Willis and I went over the fence together. Then we all rode into Kobe together."

Anderson sought out George Willis while his partner questioned the other sailor. Delaney said he had met Franklin with a taxi and driven into Kobe with him but he fixed the date as February 1, not January 20. Willis said he and Franklin had gone on liberty together a number of times but always through the main gate.

"The only time I ever went over the fence with Franklin was last night," Willis assured Anderson. "That's the first time I ever did such a thing."

The agents went back to Franklin.

"There are some things we'd like to get straightened out," Anderson told the sailor. "Would you be willing to take a polygraph test?"

Franklin bit at his thumbnail. The agent noticed the nails were already bitten down to the quick.

"Sure," Franklin finally said. "I ain't got nothing to hide."

On February 20, exactly a month after Maxwell's disappearance, Franklin was taken to the Naval Intelligence Unit at Kobe. As he had done before, Franklin freely admitted going over the fence but denied any knowledge of Maxwell's death. The agents showed him a picture of the fence and the gully and asked him to point out how he made his way to the main road. Franklin traced a path through the heavy underbrush—not the obvious track through the gully.

He watched with a defiant half grin as the agents attached the equipment which would test his physical reaction to their questions. The polygraph expert, keeping his voice to a monotone, began with routine questions that Franklin could answer truthfully. This would show his normal reactions. Then the expert began inserting the questions suggested by Anderson.

"Do you know who caused Maxwell's death?"

"No."

"Did you hit Maxwell in the head?"

"No."

"Did you have a fight with Maxwell?"

"No."

"Did you change your way of going to the road after the 20th of January?"

"No."

"Did you see the white hat lying in the path?"

"No."

"Have you told me the truth on this examination?"

"Yes."

Franklin was shown the chart of his reactions. Anderson explained to him that these jagged lines indicated where truth had stopped.

"Could I have a sandwich?" Franklin asked. "Then I'll tell you the truth. I'll give you a statement."

Franklin was left to his sandwich and his thoughts. A half hour later, he was ready to go on. He said he wanted the agents to know it was all an accident.

"I left the barracks at 2210 hours and went to the main gate to see if the coast was clear for leaving the base by going over the fence," Franklin began his statement.

He told of hiding by the water tower until the Japanese security guard walked past, of climbing the fence and starting into the woods.

"When I started walking down the bank, a man yelled at me, 'Hey, what are you doing, jumping the fence?' I said, 'None of your damn business.' I could see this man was a sailor because he had a white hat on and a blue foul-weather jacket. He started towards me and I started towards him. He struck the first blow, hitting me in the face. Then I struck him somewhere in the face and several blows were exchanged.

"Then the man tripped on something and fell over backwards flat on his back. I told him to get up and when he didn't, I started kicking him in the head. He just lay there and groaned. I walked to the main road and caught a taxi into Kobe. I went to some bars.

"After that night, when I went over the fence, I didn't go by that path. I don't know why. On January 23, I knew Maxwell was missing. When I went over the fence that night, I deliberately avoided the spot because I realized that he may have been seriously injured in the fight and could still be laying where the fight occurred. At no time did I have any desire to go to the area where the fight had occurred and see if Maxwell was there.

"I am sorry that this has ended the way it has and that the fight resulted in Maxwell's death. However, had I known at the time, even though I was drinking, that Maxwell had been seriously injured, I would have sought medical aid for him. I did not realize it until it was too late and too many days had passed."

Franklin signed the statement and agreed to reenact the fight as he had described it in the statement.

Watching the reenactment the next day, Anderson pulled hard at his jaw. After Franklin was escorted back to his barracks, Anderson walked alone over the same route. He stood again at the spot where he had first seen the sailor's body, his eyes searching the ground for clues he knew weren't there.

"It doesn't make sense," he said aloud.

He had thought so much about Maxwell, he felt that he knew the young sailor. Maxwell was lonely. He would have welcomed a buddy on his first trek to the Green House. There was no motive for him to pick a fight. He wasn't the fighting kind.

Franklin was different. From what the agents had learned, Franklin was belligerent when he drank and he had been drinking on the night of January 20. And Franklin had been in trouble before. He couldn't afford to get caught. The Japanese had turned up a hostess in a Kobe bar who remembered Franklin hiding upstairs whenever a military policeman entered the bar. The hostess knew Franklin well, called him "Pinsuke"—Blockhead. Suppose Franklin thought for some reason that Maxwell was as much of a threat to his safety as the military policeman in the Kobe bar.

Anderson thought about what the doctor had reported—a single sharp blow with a blunt instrument. There had been no blunt instrument in Franklin's statement. And what about the second figure seen by the Japanese guard as he patrolled on the night of January 20? According to Franklin's statement, he had been alone.

Walking the narrow track to the main road, Anderson made up his mind. He wasn't yet ready to write off Maxwell's death as accidental.

Franklin acted surprised when Anderson had him brought into Kobe again for questioning.

"I already told you everything I know," Franklin protested.

"You did go back to where the fight took place, didn't you?" Anderson began quietly. "You knew Maxwell was still there or you wouldn't have started going through the underbrush."

Franklin bit down hard on his thumbnail. The agent waited. As the silence lengthened, Franklin shifted uneasily in the straight chair.

"I went back," he said finally. "The next night. I didn't touch him or anything, just bent over him to see if he was still living. He was, because he groaned once or twice. Then I went away."

"Did anybody but you know about the fight?"

"Nobody but Willis. When I met him in the bar later that night, I told him I'd gotten in a fight with a sailor. On January 23, when we were in the Enlisted Men's Club, Willis asked me if the sailor that was missing and the sailor I had the fight with were the same. I said they probably were. Willis asked me if I hurt him and I said I probably did. I asked Willis not to tell anybody about the fight and he said he wouldn't."

Anderson thought back to his interview with Willis—the sailor who would never do such a thing as go over the fence. Willis would have to be interviewed again.

Willis, chubby where Franklin was thin, stared at Anderson out of watery blue eyes and denied he knew anything about Franklin's fight with a sailor. After a coffee break, Willis agreed to take a polygraph test.

Most of the questions were routine, but the needle skidded crazily on the chart as Willis answered one question: "Did you see the fight?"

Every successful murder investigation has a turning point—a timely tip from an informer, an unexpected admission, a hunch that pays off. Anderson decided to play a hunch.

Slipping from the room where Willis was being questioned, Anderson sat down beside Franklin in the corridor and handed him a cigarette.

"Why didn't you tell me Willis was with you at that fight?" the agent asked conversationally.

"Well, I couldn't see any use involving a buddy," Franklin replied with a shrug.

Anderson's hunch had paid off. He had accounted for the second man and the investigation was wide open again.

He finished his cigarette and went back to the room where Willis was now giving a statement. Convinced by the other agents that Franklin had admitted telling him about the fight when they met in the Kobe bar, Willis confirmed it. Listening with a grim smile, Anderson decided not to interrupt. Time enough to talk to Willis again after Franklin had put on paper what he had said in the hallway —that Willis was in on the fight.

The next day, Franklin gave his third statement. This time, he put

Willis on the scene as a witness. Otherwise, his story was unchanged.

Now Anderson was ready for Willis, but as the agent confessed later to Brock, he wasn't ready for all the chubby sailor admitted once he was convinced that Franklin had made him a witness.

His story started like Franklin's. He told of a man approaching them, of blows exchanged. He admitted joining in the kicks after Maxwell went down. He told of going to Kobe after the fight and making the rounds of the bars—including one where all the girls wore bathing suits. And then Willis added something new.

"Franklin and I were having drinks two nights later," he said, "when Franklin told me the guy we had the fight with was still alive. I said, 'What do you think we ought to do?' and he said, 'We have to finish him off. How good are you at swinging?'"

"I said I was pretty damn good. I told him I'd take care of it after I had a couple more drinks."

Willis took a gulp of coffee and went on with his statement in the hushed room. Anderson wondered whether the other agents felt the same chill, but he was the one who had seen the body. By now, he had a feeling what was coming—the blunt instrument.

"I went back to the barracks," Willis continued in the same matter-of-fact voice, "and looked in the gear locker for a short piece of pipe. I stuck it in the front of my trousers under my jumper and went over the fence the same as before. When I got to the man, I looked at him to see if he was still alive. He was quivering like he had a bad chill. Then I swung and hit him on the top of the head as hard as I could with the piece of pipe."

Willis' voice trailed off. The sailor taking the statement looked up inquiringly, his pencil still poised over the pad. It seemed to give Willis an idea.

"I wish to state," he added, "that before I hit him, I asked the Lord to forgive me for what I was about to do. Afterwards, I put the pipe back in the gear locker and went back to Franklin at the club. I told him we didn't have anything to worry about now. Franklin just nodded."

When Willis was taken away to join Franklin in the brig, Anderson studied the statement. One point still bothered him. He didn't believe the Maxwell boy in his loneliness had picked a fight with two possible friends. Franklin was brought back for his fourth interview.

"Willis has given us the whole story," Anderson told him. "We'd like another statement from you so any differences between the two of you can be resolved. We know what Willis did afterwards."

Franklin started out as he had before, but Anderson stopped him.

"Now you're not telling the truth, Franklin," he said. "You know Maxwell didn't start that fight. Give us the real story."

Franklin asked permission to smoke. As the agent nodded, Franklin lit up and took two quick puffs.

"All right," he said, "this is the truth. After we went over the fence, we saw a man standing in the gully with his back to us. I said, 'Damn, they've posted a security guard here. We're going to have to slip up behind him and knock him out.' I found a piece of wood and went up behind him and hit him in the head. He staggered but he didn't fall, so I hit him again several times. Then he fell over on his back. We both kicked him. Then we dragged him into the gully where he wouldn't be seen from the road. I picked up my stick and threw it up on the bank on the way to the Green House."

Anderson had it all now. Maxwell had died simply because he had stopped to puzzle out which way to go on his first trip through the dark woods.

He knew it would be hopeless to look for the stick, although the agents would try. The Japanese woodpickers constantly cleared the woods of anything they could find. The pipe had already been recovered and sent to the Army's crime laboratory in Japan to check for fibers from Willis' Navy jumper. Tomorrow, the two sailors would go through a reconstruction of the crime in the presence of Navy photographers.

Anderson had only one more job to do—his final report to the authorities. It wasn't up to him to sit in judgment. His report would be factual, objective; but it would include the seven statements made by Franklin and Willis—the lies, the distortions and, finally, the truth.

5 ★★★

Air Force Office of Special Investigations

Down the hill from the United States Capitol squats a dingy old building—one of the war-time "temporary" structures still defacing the view from the Capitol to the Washington Monument.

Inside the building, some doors are barred with steel and hung with "off-limits" signs. Within those rooms are rows and rows of locked file cabinets—a repository of thousands of stories of crime and corruption, of fraud and intrigue, of innocence proved and guilt exposed. For this nondescript structure houses the nerve center for the world-wide operations of OSI, the Air Force Office of Special Investigations.

Its mission: to provide fast and efficient criminal detection, counterintelligence and special investigative services to Air Force commanders throughout the world.

The proximity of OSI headquarters to the Capitol has a certain historical significance. Fifteen years ago, before OSI was established, investigating Senators uncovered a scandal that rocked the Air Force. Maj. Gen. Bennett E. Meyers was exposed as the behind-the-scenes owner of a firm getting profitable war contracts while the general was deputy chief of Air Force purchasing.

The Air Force had been a separate branch of the armed forces for only two months when the sordid story of the general's peccadilloes emerged on Capitol Hill. Secretary of the Air Force Stuart Symington publicly resolved to create an independent, centrally-directed investigative service. After this, the Air Force would keep its own house clean.

From its inception in August, 1948, the youngest of the military investigative services was patterned after the FBI. Like the FBI, less than half a dozen blocks down the Mall from the OSI headquarters, OSI copes with both espionage and crime. Like the FBI, the OSI's far-flung units are controlled from Washington. And as the FBI serves as the investigative arm of the Justice Department, OSI serves the same function for the Air Force.

The creation of a "little FBI" within the Air Force was no accident. The man borrowed to launch OSI was Joseph F. Carroll, who had risen from FBI agent to assistant to the FBI director. The first OSI director is now Lt. Gen. Carroll, who was picked to head the Pentagon's Joint Defense Intelligence Agency when it was created last year. Maj. Gen. John M. Breit, now OSI director, also serves as Air Force deputy inspector general for security.

Gen. Breit controls all OSI operations in this country, Puerto Rico, Iceland, Labrador, the Azores and Bermuda. He also supplies investigators and specialized assistance to overseas commands from Europe to the Pacific. Although in some overseas areas, OSI operates under theater commanders, OSI agents throughout the world can by-pass military channels and deal directly with each other.

Thus, when the wife of an airman complained she was no longer getting allotment checks and knew nothing about any divorce, OSI agents in ten American and three Japanese cities were drawn into the investigation. Before they were through, they had established that the airman had been married five times, had intercepted his third wife's letter of protest to his commander and forged a reply and had doctored a divorce decree to clear the way for his marriage to a Japanese girl. In his spare time, OSI agents learned, he had also stolen military pay certificates and issued bad checks. The combined investigation stretching halfway across the world netted a 15-year prison sentence for the bigamous airman.

Because the OSI operates on an international scale, it works closely with New Scotland Yard, MI-5 of British Military Intelligence, the French *Sûreté* Nationale, the Royal Canadian Mounted Police and local police from Singapore to Syria.

One such joint investigation dealt a cripping blow to the narcotics traffic in the Far East. It started in February, 1959, when an Army investigator in Japan relayed an informer's tip to the OSI that an airman nicknamed "Skip" was flying narcotics from Hong Kong to Tokyo. A name had been given, too, but it proved wrong. Using the nickname as a handle, OSI agents combed records and interviewed hundreds of airmen till they pinpointed a "Skip" serving as a C-47 radio operator on the international run. On his next return from Hong Kong, he walked into a welcoming committee of OSI agents with $900,000 worth of morphine and heroin. Caught with the goods, he agreed to cooperate with the OSI, Japanese, Hong Kong and Korean authorities. As a result, three dope traffickers were arrested in Korea, four in Hong Kong and four in Japan, including the suspected "narcotics king" of Japan whose arrest culminated an eight-year investigation by Japanese authorities.

Working with Washington police, OSI agents broke a murder case at Bolling Air Force base, across the Anacostia River from the Capitol. A cab driver was found dying on the base, shot with a .38 caliber revolver as the autopsy disclosed. The Army furnished mine detectors in the land search for the death weapon and the Navy contributed diving equipment for a river search but the gun couldn't be found. Meanwhile, Washington police and OSI agents working in teams set out to interview 5,000 airmen and civilians on the base at the time of the murder. Each was asked the same questions: Did he own a revolver, had he ever seen anyone on the base with a revolver, where was he on the night of the murder? The pairs of interrogators had worked their way through 3,700 interviews when three young airmen who had already been interviewed said they wanted to change their stories. They had seen an airman with a gun but were afraid to tell the truth until they talked it over. The airman they named had been among the 3,700 interviewed and, of course, had denied all. When he was recalled, the OSI agent facing him still didn't have the death gun, but he had a blue revolver and a nickel-plated one of the caliber and shape the FBI laboratory reported had done the killing.

The agent picked up one of the two revolvers and told the airman: "You know you had a gun and this was it."

The airman regarded the gun coldly and showed no reaction. The agent picked up the other gun.

"All right," he said, "we were kidding. Here's the gun you killed him with."

At that, the suspect went to pieces. He confessed his motive for killing was robbery—$7. He had hidden the death weapon on his grandmother's farm in Pennsylvania. Washington detectives and OSI agents flew to the Pennsylvania community in an Air Force plane, accompanied state police on a search for the gun and came back to Washington with a completed murder case.

Like the FBI agents on whom they are patterned, OSI agents go through an intensive training course in the latest investigative techniques. Because their work is global, many of them get special training in 17 foreign languages ranging from the Tagalog of the Philippines to Moroccan Arabic. Although a number of them were civilian investigators before they joined the Air Force, all have to go through the ten-week basic training course which runs the gamut from marksmanship to military law, from ballistics to the ways and means of international communism.

They also have to know how to apply their technical training to the case at hand. An agent solved the theft of hundreds of dollars worth of meat from a base hospital by getting a veterinary to match the tissues of a loin of pork with pork chops taken by a suspect. He had translated what he learned about the evidence of tool marks to the cut of a knife through a loin of pork.

Another agent solved a series of burglaries at a visiting officers quarters with a combination of anthracene powder and native imagination. A thief had been extracting money from wallets while officers just back from overseas were taking their showers. When the commanding officer demanded action, OSI agents set a trap for the burglar. On the fourth day of the vigil, an agent crouching under a bed saw a man enter the room, use his handkerchief to flip open the wallet on the bureau and extract the marked money planted there. As the agent gave chase, the burglar fled to the nearest bathroom, flushed the toilet and calmly awaited his pursuer. The evidence of the theft was gone—or so the burglar thought. The agent handed his quarry over to other OSI men and ordered the water shut off in the visiting officers' quarters. Then, he raised the nearest manhole cover and prepared to go fishing. Orders went out to start flushing toilets. As the water flowed by, the agent fished out two marked ten dollar bills—still bearing traces of anthracene powder, invisible except under ultraviolet light. More anthracene powder was found on the suspect's hands and on the handkerchief he had used to avoid fingerprints. But the money fished out of the drain was the clincher.

The use of another technique broke the murder of a Wiesbaden prostitute. She was last seen with a man in an Air Force raincoat. From descriptions of witnesses, an agent with artist's training drew a composite portrait of the suspect. Wiesbaden hotels were checked for the names of every airman registered on the night of the murder and the sketch was circulated to all their units. The agent-artist's concept was close enough to lead to the identification of an airman who had left Europe the day after the murder. When he was traced to Florida, he admitted the fatal stabbing.

Since all investigative functions of the Air Force are merged in the OSI, crime-solving is only one of many duties. Another major one is personnel security investigations—clearing Air Force and civilian personnel for access to secret information. At Bolling Air Force Base alone, which covers Washington and nearby Virginia and Maryland, 750,000 investigative reports were turned out in less than four years and the bulk of them were for security clearances. The Bolling operation, still the biggest in OSI, was set up by another ex-FBI man, Col. Kirby Gillette, who established the Counter Intelligence Corps for General Eisenhower's London headquarters during the war and is now chief of planning and policy for OSI.

Another OSI responsibility traces directly back to the Meyers case —the investigation of frauds against the government or other violations of the public trust in connection with Air Force property. It could be an airman who plays tricks with travel vouchers or pay allotments or it could be an Air Force officer who finagles with contractors to line his own pockets. In one case, an Air Force lieutenant assigned to selling surplus government property seemed to be living beyond his means. An analysis of his accounts showed he had disposed of property once worth more than $6,000,000 for less than $55,000 and of that amount had actually collected under $10,000. As a result of the OSI investigation, the lieutenant and the contractors who had bribed him all drew sizable prison terms. In another case, OSI agents pinpointed 51 firms which had gotten together to rig bids for Air Force construction contracts overseas. Through their collusion, they took turns getting the contracts and the Government lost money on the deals. The OSI investigation not only led to barring those contractors from doing business with the government, but also prompted an overhaul of Air Force contract requirements.

OSI agents shy away from being labelled as "cloak-and-dagger" operatives but it's their job to track down any signs of subversion, treason, sedition, espionage or sabotage within their bailiwick. One of their investigations uncovered a Polish spy just as he got into position to carry out his mission. It developed that he had been trained for two years in the techniques of espionage by Polish and Soviet intelligence officers. His training included courses in the organization and leadership of espionage cells, secret means of communication through microfilm and codes and the psychology of people and nations. When his teachers thought he was ready, he slipped into West Germany and made his way to the United States. There, according to plan, he enlisted in the Air Force and prepared to embark on his mission of espionage. The OSI caught up with him before he could do any damage.

In the spring of 1957, an Air Force captain tossed a rolled-up newspaper through the iron fence around the Soviet Embassy in Washington. The OSI isn't saying how it got the newspaper, but rolled up inside it was a note saying the captain had valuable military information to sell. His asking price was $27,500. The note was to serve as an introduction to those who would contact him in New York. The note served as an introduction all right—but not for the Russians. Armed with the note, OSI agents were admitted to the captain's hotel room where he offered to sell diagrams and information dealing with atomic weapons. The data was subsequently recovered from a public locker in New York's Pennsylvania Station and the Air Force captain was sentenced to serve ten years at hard labor. He was ready to betray his country to pay off gambling debts.

In addition to hunting foreign spies and domestic traitors, the OSI serves as the central clearing house in the Air Force for counter-intelligence data amassed by its own agents throughout the world as well as from its sister services, the FBI, the Central Intelligence Agency and other sources. The information is studied, compared, analysed and finally sent out to Air Force commanders.

The "little FBI" isn't so little any more. Today, it has more than 1,200 agents throughout the world engaged in keeping the Air Force clean and the nation safe. Among the plaudits that have come its way was one from the man whose method of operation has been duplicated in the development of OSI. On its tenth anniversary, FBI Director J. Edgar Hoover wrote that the OSI has "made monumental contributions to the welfare of our nation, and I am sure I speak for all Americans in this expression of deepest appreciation."

ACROSS THE BARBED WIRE

The German tried to light a cigarette and dropped it. He fumbled for a handkerchief and mopped his face.

"Forgive me," he told the man across the desk. "I know I must speak of this. You Americans have been good to me . . ."

The American agent handed him a cigarette, flicked a lighter and waited. From the way the man acted—his furtive glances at the door—it had obviously taken all his courage to enter the German headquarters of the Air Force Office of Special Investigations.

The German drew gratefully on the cigarette as the agent studied him. His face was thin and drawn, his hair graying. His suit hung on him as though it had been bought years ago when he was much heavier. When he began talking, his words came slowly.

His name, he said, was Fritz Broch. He had been a college professor until the Communists came in and tried to tell him what to teach. Then he had made his way to the Western Zone. His wife and daughter had stayed behind in Dresden until he could find work and make a home for them in the West.

It had taken many months but in the spring of 1958, he had finally found a steady job—as an interpreter-translator on an American Air Force base.

"I spent my first week's pay on a locket for my little girl," he said. "Then I went to Dresden to tell my wife that at last we could be together."

Broch talked faster and faster. "I put my key in the door of our Dresden apartment but the key didn't turn. I knocked and knocked and nobody came. I knew something was terribly wrong. A man suddenly came up beside me, a big man I'd never seen before. He told me my wife and daughter had been arrested on political charges. I couldn't believe him. My wife never did anything political.

"They let me see my wife and daughter at the jail for just a few minutes. My little girl was crying but when I gave her the locket she stopped. My wife told me she was going to be tried for talking against the regime. She had simply told a neighbor she hoped I would get a job soon so she could join me."

Broch said he was taken to a room at the jail where an East German, who called himself Karl, told him his wife and daughter would be freed if he cooperated. Karl outlined the conditions. Mrs. Broch and the child could not leave East Germany but they would be set up in an apartment where they would be amply supplied with food and clothing and Broch could visit them whenever he came to Dresden.

Karl said the Communist intelligence service was aware that Broch had just gotten work at the American Air Force base. His family would be safe if he gave the Soviets the information they wanted on Air Force activities. He would also get 1,000 Deutsche Mark each month for his services.

"I signed," Broch sighed. "I thought I had no choice. Now, they have me and I can't go through with it."

The American agent kept his face expressionless but his mind was racing. Only a week earlier, Western intelligence agents had scored a major breakthrough. They had proved to the satisfaction of the intelligence community—agents of the Western allies—that the Communists were using radio commercials to send messages to their contacts in the West. The local agents had decoded the commercials enough to determine that certain words meant the contacts were to deliver or pick up messages at certain locations. They didn't know, of course, who the contacts were or where the espionage "drops" were located. If Broch was telling the truth, he might be the means to unveil an espionage network.

"Did Karl tell you how you would get your instructions?" the American agent asked.

"He made me memorize the code after I signed the paper," Broch replied. "He said I was to listen to the Dresden radio station at eight and ten every Wednesday and Friday night. I would get my instructions from what the announcer said."

The American agent started making notes. Broch was confirming what the German intelligence agents had figured out.

Broch recited the code. If the announcer said: "Congratulations to the Re-no Wurtschen factory employees who have exceeded the established norms," he would find a message in a cavity of a bridge balustrade in the town where the air base was located. An announcement that "the Dresden school children again worked on the nearby farms" meant a message awaited him in a disconnected drainage pipe at the foot of the wall surrounding the museum in a nearby town. If the announcer said: "Congratulations, comrades, our production is increasing daily," he was to look for the message in a hole near the foundation of the bandstand in a city park some ten miles distant.

"Karl told me to watch out for the announcer saying 'All factory workers again volunteered to work an extra hour each day.' That meant I was to expect someone to contact me personally within the next two days. And he gave me a pair of silver cuff links. When the face is turned a quarter of the way to the right, the face of the links drops off. There's a space inside for microfilm.

"What am I going to do?" Broch shuddered. "This nightmare can't go on."

For an answer, the American agent said: "We will try to help you." He then took Broch into the next room and told him to write down everything he could remember about his interview with Karl. He arranged for Broch to take a lie detector test. He could be telling the truth. He also could be making up a story to get some money out of the Americans. It wouldn't be the first time that gambit had been tried. Or he could be a Communist spy trying to infiltrate American counterespionage.

The agent started a fast check of OSI files and the records of other Western intelligence agencies. Nothing about Broch there. After Broch finished his statement, several agents accompanied him to his room. They searched the room looking for tools of the espionage trade—secret writing paper, copying cameras, devices with hidden compartments. All they found were the silver cuff links.

Apparently, Broch's nightmare was real. The agent had him brought back to his office.

"You asked me what you should do," the agent began. "You want to save your family but you don't want to help the Communists."

Broch shook his head vigorously.

"All right," said the officer. "We want you to cooperate with the Communists."

"Oh, no," Broch groaned. "I can't."

"You can, under our direction. You will, of course, tell no one of this association. You are not to come back to this office under any circumstances. You will be contacted by an American you can trust implicitly. You will tell him what information the Communists want and he will supply it to you. You will deal exclusively with him."

The American looked at Broch's bowed head and his voice gentled. "It's the only way to help your family, Fritz," he said. "You came to us because of divided loyalties. This will make you whole again."

Broch pulled out a cigarette and lit it. The agent noticed his hand no longer trembled.

"All right," Broch said. "I'll do what you want."

"Fine," said the officer. "Now tell me about yourself. How do you spend your time when you're not working?"

Broch looked surprised at the turn the conversation had taken but he relaxed and told about visiting art galleries and going to soccer games. He said his room was so empty without his family that he spent his evenings sitting over a beer or two in a gasthaus.

To Broch, this might have appeared idle conversation, but it was vital to the officer. He had to find a handling agent for Broch. In intelligence circles, a handling agent is the key to success or failure of an operation of this kind. He must be a comrade, a man with similar interests. He must keep the espionage agent busy doing things he enjoys doing so he doesn't spend too much time brooding about what may lie ahead. The handling agent must put all his own desires aside. He can't afford to get sick. He's needed that much. He must play two roles simultaneously—the sympathetic companion and the trained observer. A double agent—as Broch was now to become—couldn't be trusted too far.

As soon as Broch went out the door, the officer summoned Agent Bliss Howard. Still youthful, but an old hand at counterespionage, Howard filled the bill. He had once coached the soccer team at the base. If he didn't know about art, he could find out in a hurry. He spoke good German and he had a child of his own back home. He would understand the depths of Broch's despair.

Howard was to move off the base at once and get in touch with Broch. He would use a cover name. If Broch ever decided to betray the Americans, he couldn't provide Howard's true identity.

Operation Broch was launched.

Howard and Broch were listening to the Dresden radio together a few nights later, when Broch got his first message.

"All factory workers again volunteered to work an extra hour each day," said the announcer.

Broch stared apprehensively at his new friend. "That means the Communists are going to contact me," he said, his voice heavy with dread.

"It's all right," Howard reassured him. "Some of our fellows will be around."

The agent had more in mind than reassurance. He wanted Broch to know he was being watched. If Broch was ever tempted to get out of line, he would be under the impression he was being observed —even if the agents happened to lose him.

The next night, as Broch was coming home, a man took the seat beside him on the bus and after an idle remark about the weather, asked if all factory workers had volunteered to work an extra hour each day. Broch said they had. The stranger asked him if everything was all right. Broch nodded and the stranger left the bus.

"That's all there was to it," Broch reported to Howard later. "Why did they bother?"

"They wanted to make sure you were listening to the broadcasts and would cooperate," Howard explained. "They were just checking."

The next message came a week later. "Congratulations to the Re-No Wurstchen factory employees who have again exceeded the established norms," said the Dresden announcer.

With agents following at a discreet distance, Broch went to the bridge and stuck his hand into a hole in the balustrade. They would report to Howard that Broch put nothing in the hole and took out a note. It was up to the surveilling agents to make sure Broch did only what he was told by the Americans. Later, when the Communists started asking for information, it would be Howard's job to see that Broch had no opportunity to add anything to what Howard provided.

The note in the balustrade did ask for information. Broch was ordered to provide a base officers' roster. There were several copies of the roster in Broch's own office, nothing secret about that. The Communists, obviously, were still testing.

But there were other instructions in the "drop." Broch was to be on the corner of Karlstrasse and Hauptstrasse in front of the apothecary at 10 P.M. the next Sunday. A man would ask him the time. He was to respond that he did not know the time because he had given his watch to his father. The man would say, "Oh, your father's watch is broken?" That would be the signal for the meet.

At last, the Communists were beginning to expose their contacts to Broch. The episode on the bus had been too quick, too casual to do the Americans any good. This time, they would be ready.

OSI agents watched the stranger approach Broch on the corner, saw them speak a minute and turn to enter a nearby tavern. But they had stayed on the corner long enough for the agents to get a picture of the stranger with their telephoto lens.

Inside the tavern, Broch handed over the roster of officers and got his next assignment. He was to find out the length of the runways at the air base and photograph the runways and aircraft parked on the ramp. The stranger handed Broch a Minox camera and three rolls of film. Then he gave Broch what looked like an unopened can of meat. He showed Broch that when the bottom of the can was twisted to the left, the top of the can opened. Broch was to put the films of the air base in the can to carry back to Dresden.

When the stranger left the tavern, agents trailed him to a large apartment building. They checked their picture of the street corner meeting against intelligence files of known and suspected agents and came up with a name to go along with the address. Broch's contact was Meyer Ludwig, who had been posing as a refugee from East Germany.

Score one for the Broch operation.

The photographs the Communists wanted from Broch were made by OSI agents with Broch's camera—just in case the Minox had been doctored by the Communists to identify the pictures. The runway photographs were taken from an angle that revealed little and the light was bad. The Communists wouldn't get much out of that assignment.

Howard watched Broch put the film in the meat can. The German's hands trembled with excitement. He was carrying the equipment of a spy, but he would be seeing his wife and child.

The American told Broch where to meet him when he returned from Dresden. In case Broch was followed when he left East Germany, the Communist agents would learn little. Broch would simply be visiting a friend far from the base.

The address Howard gave Broch was a place known in intelligence circles as a "safe house." Howard himself used a different "safe house" to exchange information with OSI agents There was an anonymity about these rooms. Even prying neighbors would have nothing to suspect. Each segment of the operation took place at a different "safe house" and addresses were changed frequently.

When Broch met Howard at the "safe house" after the Dresden trip, Howard questioned him in detail about every step of his journey—what train he took, what car he sat in, what time he went, when he returned. These were check points to be verified with the agents who had trailed him to the East German border. Any discrepancies between what the agents saw and Broch told could be dealt with at the next session with the lie detector—to determine if Broch simply forgot or purposely lied. The agents couldn't take a chance on trusting Broch too far.

After that trip to Dresden with the meat can stuffed with film, Broch answered questions happily. He had seen his wife and child. Across the border, it developed, Karl wasn't so happy. Within two weeks—via the Dresden broadcast and the letter drop in the park bandstand—Karl instructed Broch to make the runway pictures again. Karl reproached Broch for taking pictures of such poor quality.

Howard grinned when he heard that. "Tell Karl you're not sure you know how to operate a camera. Maybe he'll send you to somebody for instructions in picture taking."

The agent wanted to expose more of Karl's contacts and Karl obliged.

"I'm supposed to meet a man in the art gallery at 6 P.M. Saturday," Broch reported. "I'm to stand near the second picture on the right side, near the main entrance. I'm trying to remember what that picture is. Could it be the Goya?"

"Never mind that for the moment," Howard interposed. "How are you to recognize the contact?"

"He'll be writing on a memo pad. When he drops the pencil, I'm to pick it up. Then, he'll say, 'Thank you. My back makes it hard for me to stoop.'"

OSI agents, watching the performance in the art gallery, saw Broch pick up the pencil. They saw the stranger write something on the memo pad and turn so Broch could see what he had written. When the stranger left the gallery, agents followed him to a building on Hauptstrasse. With the help of discreet questioning by local police, the stranger was identified as Gerhard Marx, a waiter in a restaurant near the air base.

Score two for the Broch operation. The second agent had been tabbed.

Howard, briefed by his fellow agents, wanted to know what Marx had written on the memo pad. Broch said he was to report to a room on Bismarckplatz the next Monday at 8 P.M. The Communists, it seemed, had "safe houses" too, but theirs weren't quite so safe.

On Sunday, Howard took Broch to a soccer game to get his mind off the coming meeting. The next night, Broch knocked at a door on Bismarckplatz. The man who opened the door said Broch was to call him "Frederic." He showed Broch how to copy documents, how to prepare microfilm, how to make reports with invisible ink, how to use microdot equipment to make a message look like imperfections in the paper.

"Frederic" left the room soon after Broch. OSI agents recognized him immediately. This was Helmut Schmidt, a suspected hard-core Communist. Now they had the proof against him. Broch had led agents to the third man in the spy network.

The fourth followed quickly. Broch was eating in a gasthaus when a stranger sat down at his table and offered him a cigarette. After a few puffs, the cigarette went out. Broch looked at it curiously and noticed a piece of paper where tobacco was supposed to be. When the stranger saw that Broch had discovered the bit of paper, he nodded and left the gasthaus. Agents trailed the stranger to a small rooming house and learned his identity. The fourth man uncovered in the Broch operation was Horst Kunz, already suspected by local authorities of engaging in espionage.

Broch delivered the piece of paper to Howard. "It's supposed to have some secret writing on it," he said distastefully. "I wonder what they want me to do now."

As Howard dipped the paper in the writing developer provided by "Frederic," he thought about the misery in Broch's voice.

Howard was beginning to worry about his charge. He couldn't shake Broch out of the moods of black despair which followed every visit to his family in Dresden. Broch was staying away from his work too often and fellow employees were beginning to notice it. Unless he straightened out, he would have to be fired from the interpreter-translator job or the others would suspect he was doing something to earn favored treatment from the Americans. He was spending more and more time in the beer taverns. Only last week, an agent keeping him under surveillance had heard him babbling about OSI and photographs of airplanes. The agent had quickly summoned a local policeman to get him out of the tavern. Worried, Howard began to stay with Broch every evening.

"They want a map of the base and some Air Force training pamphlets," Howard told Broch as the secret writing emerged on the paper. "I'll get something for you tomorrow. Then you can go to Dresden this weekend."

Broch stopped fiddling with the letter opener Karl had given him. The opener had a hollow handle, suitable for concealing microfilm. "I think I'll take my wife some of those chocolates I saw at the PX," Broch said. "She'll like that."

Broch couldn't deliver the chocolates on his trip to Dresden that weekend. Karl told him his wife and daughter were sick and had been taken to the hospital.

"He said they were quarantined and I couldn't see them," Broch reported to Howard. "Do you think they're all right?"

Privately, Howard wasn't sure, but he tried to reassure Broch.

Two months passed before Broch got his next instructions to deliver information to Karl in Dresden. When he reported back to Howard, his face was gray. He had not seen his wife and child.

"I told Karl I was through spying for him," Broch said.

Howard was worried. For the first time Broch had acted on his own initiative. If Karl believed him, he might alert his espionage agents in the West and a year's work would be wasted.

"How did Karl react?" Howard asked quietly.

"At first, he just laughed at me. He said I had to keep working for him or he'd expose me to the local authorities. He even showed me the papers I'd signed. I told him if something had happened to my family, I didn't care what he did. He said if I would do one more important job for him, they would release my family."

"What did he want you to do?"

"He wants me to find out the exact number of aircraft on alert status and mark their location on a map of the base."

"Did you agree?"

Broch shook his head. Then he broke down.

"They're dead," he moaned. "I know they're dead."

Howard walked over to the other man and put a gentle hand on his shoulder. In a year of constant companionship he had come to understand the tortured soul of the little professor, and was full of compassion for him. But he had to make sure Karl did not warn the agents in the West to take cover.

"Of course, we're not going to tell him how many planes are ready," Howard told Broch, "but we can try to find out if your wife and daughter are alive. I've been thinking of a plan."

Now Broch was willing to listen. Howard proposed that he send a message to Karl saying he had the information and would turn it over under two conditions. He would give it to Karl on the East-West Berlin border—not Dresden—and only if his wife and daughter were brought to the rendezvous so he could see they were all right.

"If they agree to that, you'll be safe," Howard pointed out. "You won't go into East Germany at all and you'll know about your family."

Broch wrote the letter. Two days later, the Dresden announcer again broadcast his congratulations to the Re-No Wurtschen factory employees. Karl's message would be at the bridge balustrade.

The message was terse. Karl agreed to meet Broch at a point on the East-West Berlin border Friday at 10 P.M. He promised to bring along Mrs. Broch and the child.

Howard suspected a ruse but he couldn't let the little professor know that. The man was too close to the breaking point already. Besides, there was always the chance the Brochs were still alive—that Karl had purposely toyed with Broch to drive him to the point of desperation where he would be willing to try for even the more carefully guarded information in exchange for a chance to see his family again.

"You won't go empty-handed to this meeting," Howard told Broch. "If you see your wife and child, you'll have something to give Karl. It won't do him much good but he won't know that."

Howard had the feeling that Broch only half heard what he was saying. Obviously, the man was fully absorbed in his own fears and hopes. The agent tried to get on Broch's wave length.

"What I'm about to say is important to your family's safety," Howard began, and had the satisfaction of seeing the other man jerk to attention.

"Show Karl you've got something, but make him come over to our side to get it," Howard directed. "Then, if your wife and child are there, you'll have something to trade for them—Karl himself. You must stay on this side of the border or you won't do your family any good."

Howard parted from Broch with a warning.

"Don't get too close to the barbed wire fence."

In the hours left for planning, Howard toured the area chosen for the rendezvous to map concealment for his forces. Both OSI agents and West Berlin police would be in on this one.

The area, he noticed, was relatively unpopulated—presumably because of a cemetery located just over the border in East Berlin. Marking the border was a rusty, five-strand barbed wire fence, obviously constructed soon after the occupation began and never repaired.

An OSI undercover car, Howard figured, could be concealed in an alley only 25 yards from the meeting place and another could be hidden from view in a tree-shrouded lane emerging from the park bordering the West German side. The park, with its low-branched trees would offer excellent concealment for the American and local agents.

Howard reflected ruefully that the gravestones on the East Berlin side would provide equally useful hiding places for Karl's confederates, but he resolved they wouldn't come close enough to threaten Broch.

As the hour of meeting neared, the fog-shrouded street came slowly to life. The dark forms of OSI agents and local police slipped from shadow to shadow in the dimly-lighted streets to the hiding places chosen by Howard. A dozen pairs of eyes peered into the fog, watching the barbed wire for the first glimpse of Karl.

A barely audible signal was passed to Broch when his protectors were all in position. As Broch approached the border, Karl emerged from the shadows of the cemetery and lost no time getting down to business.

"Do you have the merchandise?"

"Yes, I have it," Broch replied, "but where's my wife and child?"

"They're right behind me," Karl told him. "If you come over here you can see them."

Broch thought he saw figures behind Karl but he couldn't be sure in the fog. Desperately, he tried to remember Howard's instructions.

"You come over here and I'll give you the merchandise," he told Karl.

The other man's voice thickened in anger.

"I don't believe you have anything."

For answer, Broch took the letter opener from his pocket, unscrewed the handle and let Karl see a piece of paper stuck in the cavity. In his eagerness to convince Karl as well as to penetrate the gloom on the East German side, Broch forgot Howard's warning to keep a safe distance from the barbed wire.

As Broch came within arm's reach, Karl lunged at him, grabbed his arm and started dragging him between the rusty strands of barbed wire. From the cemetery on the East Berlin side came the faint click of a pistol being cocked and the sound of hurried footsteps. Karl's reinforcements were approaching.

On the West Berlin side, at Broch's first desperate shout, American and German agents poured from the park, the lane and the alley. One agent made a dive and grabbed Broch's leg but the powerfully built Karl was pulling both the agent and Broch into the wire when other American forces joined the tug of war for Broch.

Karl, faced with the choice of releasing his hold on Broch or being pulled through the barbed wire himself, let go with a shouted curse and backed away into the fog.

On the West German side, Broch was shaking with remembered terror as he looked around for Howard. He had missed the OSI man in the border fracas. As Howard joined the other agents around Broch, the little professor clutched his arm.

"My wife, my child," he said, "did you see them?"

Instead of answering directly, Howard patted Broch on the shoulder and told him, "Go wait for me in my car. I'll be along directly."

Howard had one more job to do and it had to be done fast. He moved swiftly to the nearest local police radio car. The Communist hirelings who had contacted Broch during his year as a double agent had to be rounded up before Karl could alert them to take cover.

As soon as Howard heard the pickup orders issued for Karl's West German ring, he strolled over to his car.

In the back seat sat Broch, tightly clasping the hand of a flaxen-haired woman. His arm was around a little girl with a gold locket around her thin neck.

When Broch saw Howard, the words began to spill out.

"They were behind Karl all the time," Broch babbled, halfway between tears and laughter. "When Karl started tugging at me, their guard pulled out his pistol and rushed to join him. That's when they ran to the fence. They were trying to slip under the wire but they got stuck. Then, a man came along and got them through."

As Howard grinned but said nothing, Mrs. Broch spoke for the first time.

"Bless you," she told the OSI man. "We could never have gotten through the fence without you."

Operation Broch was completed.

Part III ★★★

THE GENERAL WELFARE

6 ★★★

Civil Aeronautics Board

Flying is safer today because squads of anonymous heroes have mushed through snow, scaled mountains and dived into the sea in search of clues to airplane crashes. They're the flying detectives of the Civil Aeronautics Board's Bureau of Safety.

Their job is to reconstruct the "crime" from the fragments of charred wreckage and prevent the "killer" from striking again. Unlike police, who rate themselves lucky if they solve half their major crimes, the CAB's force of Air Safety Investigators has solved 93 per cent of its air carrier cases. They have pinpointed the prime causes so precisely and recommended cures so effectively that the same villain has never had a chance to take another life.

Airplane accidents don't choose a time or a place to happen. That's why the flying detectives are always on call. They can never plan a vacation with any assurance they'll get it. One minute, they may be sitting down to Christmas dinner with the family. The next, they're off to the airport to fly to a holocaust on a hillside.

In a recent 18-month period, here's where the trail of disaster led CAB's Air Safety Investigators:

For a crash deep in the jungles of Honduras, they quickly assembled snake-proof pants, rubber boots, drugs, axes and mosquito netting and proceeded to hack their way into the interior for five days. They had to clear a path for jeeps loaded with motion picture and still camera equipment as well as basic laboratory utensils to get samples of burned skin and charred plane fragments. They had to be right the first time. No one, they knew, would be coming that way again.

While this was going on, a DC-4 plunged 25 feet into a lake on a private estate south of Jacksonville, Florida. Three investigators had to take a self-taught course in skin-diving to complete this mission. Then, they dived to the bottom with acetylene torches to open the plane. They had to go through it with the same painstaking attention to detail that they would give a land crash—where they could breathe normally.

A short time later, a plane crashed into an apparently inaccessible region of the Rockies. The investigators organized mountain burro pack teams and started climbing with their snow shoes, rifles and full camp equipment. They found the plane buried in the snow at 11,900 feet.

Another mountain peak presented another challenge. This time, the scene of the crash couldn't be reached by climbing. CAB investigators hired a helicopter and arranged to land on the peak. They knew it was risky business because the helicopter had never flown so high with such a heavy load of equipment, but they had to take a chance. When the helicopter landed safely, the investigators prepared for their next ordeal. They lowered ropes down the face of the cliff and slid down with their equipment to start the investigation.

In the same period, an airliner crashed in a Florida swamp. This time, the investigators hired a flat-bottomed marsh boat and poled their way to the scene. As the first investigator stepped out on the wing of the crashed plane, he recoiled sharply. At his feet were two water moccasins coiled to strike. The investigators were aware more snakes might be lodged in the half-submerged cabin of the plane, but again they had no choice. Snakes or no snakes, they had to crawl into that cabin to find out what made the plane crash. And they did.

They risk their lives and their health regularly, suffer heart attacks from the strain of mountain climbing and slipped discs from carrying heavy loads to the scene of mass death, but they can't let the hazards stop them. No matter how taxing the job, they must find two answers: Why did the plane crash? How can we prevent another one?

Those were the answers Congress demanded back in 1938 when it passed the Civil Aeronautics Act, the great charter of American civil aviation.

The death of a Senator jolted Congress into action, but by that time it was long overdue. Lindbergh's 1927 solo flight to Paris had given flying a tremendous boost. Little airlines were going into business all over the country, new plane designs were being introduced with reckless haste, and one of the nation's favorites was killed when

Knute Rockne, coach of Notre Dame's invincible football team, died in the 1931 crash of a tri-motor Fokker in a Kansas wheat field.

Then, in 1935, came the headline: "Senator Bronson Cutting killed in plane crash." The chaos in American aviation had finally reached the door of Congress itself and taken one of its own. At last, Congress got down to writing a law to bring order out of this chaos. The law had to be Federal because planes crossed several states on a single flight. The same rules, the same safeguards had to be uniform throughout the country.

The act created the Civil Aeronautics Authority and included accident investigation among its many responsibilities. The same authority was also responsible for licensing pilots and aircraft, issuing airworthiness certificates, writing and enforcing civil air regulations and operating the air traffic control system. The conflict of interests soon became apparent. If the crash investigators found the air traffic control system or some regulation at fault, the authority would be investigating itself.

So, in 1940, President Franklin D. Roosevelt reorganized the Civil Aeronautics Authority and created two separate agencies—the Civil Aeronautics Board as an independent regulatory agency responsible to Congress and the Civil Aeronautics Administration to carry out other terms of the 1938 act.

Nearly 20 years later, the wisdom of separating the agencies was underlined when Congress became alarmed at a series of mid-air collisions—the Grand Canyon disaster, the collision of a commercial plane and an Air Force jet near Las Vegas and the one between another passenger plane and a National Guard jet at Brunswick, Md. CAB investigation of these crashes, particularly the one at Las Vegas, spotlighted the weakness of the aircraft control system, for which the CAA had vainly been seeking funds for five years.

Out of a Congressional investigation, spark-plugged by Senator Mike Monroney, emerged the Federal Aviation Agency with enough funds to strengthen the nation-wide system for controlling air traffic and preventing mid-air collisions. CAB, which had performed the investigative job leading to the new act, remained unchanged. Its investigative role was simply reiterated by Congress. Again, it was charged with finding out what causes accidents and how they can be prevented.

Twenty-two years ago, when the CAB's Bureau of Safety started operating, the techniques for solving airplane crashes were still unknown. Each crash presented a seemingly hopeless mass of twisted, torn, scorched metal and fragmented bodies, sometimes scattered over many miles. This required a kind of detective work that had never been done before.

The 20 investigators who went to work for the Bureau of Safety were all pilots, but it soon became apparent they needed more than the ability to fly a plane. The bureau kept on hiring pilots but ones also expert in other lines. Today, 90 of the bureau's 100 air safety investigators are pilots but they are also trained as meteorologists, metallurgists, engineers and technicians in a dozen different fields.

This concentration of investigative skills is united by the common bond of pilotage. The chief of the accident investigation division, Joseph O. Fluet, had headed the CAB's busiest region—from Maine to Virginia—before he came into the Washington headquarters.

The investigators were still pioneering in the techniques of detecting crash causes when their talents were tested by an apparently inexplicable accident that grieved the nation. Carole Lombard, returning from a war bond tour to join her husband, Clark Gable, in California, died with 21 others in a plane crash near Las Vegas on January 16, 1942. The night was clear, the plane by all the tests known at that time was free of mechanical defects, but it rammed into a mountain 15 minutes after take-off. It shouldn't have been anywhere near that mountain.

The investigators flew the course the pilot should have followed. Then, they flew the course his co-pilot had charted and filed with the dispatcher before take-off. It led them right to the mountain. The co-pilot, they found, had made a navigational error that took him nine degrees off course—enough to smash into the mountain.

Usually, the investigators work by process of elimination unless the cause is immediately obvious. And they're not inclined to trust the obvious. One plane heading overseas dropped part of a wheel on take-off. Everybody saw it and everybody concluded the wheel was at fault. Investigation disclosed, however, that the snubber in the landing gear had snapped off during an earlier flight. Several take-offs later, the wheel gave way. CAB investigators could pin that one on faulty maintenance, not a defective wheel. As a result, that airline jacked up its maintenance crews throughout the world and paid a large cash penalty.

To the CAB investigator, the easy answer is rarely the right one. After a National Airlines plane disintegrated in the air and crashed near Cape Fear, N.C., one rainy night in January, 1960, the press quoted the "experts" as saying a propeller flew off and sliced into the cabin. As a result, these "experts" opined, the compressed air in the cabin rushed out with explosive force, shattering the plane and ejecting a passenger, Julian Frank, whose body was found 18 miles from the main wreckage.

The CAB investigators ignored the glib "experts," kept quiet and went to work. Within three days, they had located all the propeller blades buried in the earth near the four engines. That disposed of the "expert" theory since the offending propeller blade—if there had been one—would have fallen many miles from the rest of the wreckage.

Subsequent investigation identified nitrate on Frank's hand and nitrate on a fragment of the airplane. The investigators also learned that Frank had insured himself for more than a million dollars. When all the facts were in and all other possibilities eliminated, the CAB ruled that the crash was caused by a dynamite explosion. Whether Frank committed suicide or was murdered was not up to the CAB to determine.

Since the causes of most airplane crashes are hidden somewhere in the splinters of debris, the CAB investigators have had to develop methods of scientific detection that would astound Sherlock Holmes. The techniques they were forced to invent, for lack of precedence, have become standard practice in today's international aviation circles. They pioneered in using X-rays to search for metal fatigue, in hunting physical clues through pathological studies, in working out ways to determine the power setting of an engine and the speed of an aircraft at impact. They learned how to trace the course of a fire by studying the temperatures at which various metals melt or warp. They figured out methods to tell the difference between damage caused in flight by fire or explosion and damage incurred between first contact with the ground and final impact.

They also devised their own way to "reconstruct the crime." With patience, persistence and chicken wire, they put the pieces together again. Sometimes, the fragments are so tiny that all they can do is lay them out on the floor within the chalked outlines of the plane. But, other times, they can create a three-dimensional "mock-up" that tells its own story. A "mock-up" led to the killer—this time a human one—in the crash of a plane outbound from Denver, November 1, 1955.

Within an hour after investigators reached the scene, they smelled and tasted nitroglycerine. But that year, many hardy souls in Colorado were carrying dynamite sticks in their cars and luggage to go week-end uranium hunting. The CAB investigators knew that dynamite had destroyed the plane in flight. But whether it had been an accidental explosion in someone's luggage, or was done deliberately, had to be determined.

When they had all the pieces tagged and collected, they began reconstructing them into the shape of an airplane. The pieces of fuselage tacked onto the chicken wire grew smaller and smaller toward the center of the plane until they disappeared entirely at the No. 4 baggage compartment. Having thus located the origin of the explosion, the investigators established that only one suitcase had been loaded in that compartment. It belonged to Mrs. Daisie King, who had been seen off at Denver by her son, John Gilbert Graham.

Graham, in later confessing that he put the explosive device in his mother's bag to collect her insurance, remarked ruefully that he had never heard of the CAB but that even CAB would never have found out if the plane had reached the mountains.

Col. James Peyton, who commanded a B-20 bomber group against Japan before he became a CAB investigator, looked at Graham and shook his head.

"Son," he said, "it wouldn't have made any difference."

The investigative technique nurtured by the CAB and unique as an example of public-private cooperation is the group method which uses the top technical men of the aviation industry under the direction of CAB's own investigators.

The CAB investigator in charge of solving a plane disaster invites the affected plane, engine and propeller manufacturers, the airline, the Air Line Pilots Association and the Federal Aviation Agency to join the investigation. Their representatives are organized into specialized groups, each directed by a CAB investigator.

One group collects, identifies and analyzes the airframe wreckage. A second hunts for clues in the engines and propellers. A third, the "human factors group," arranges for autopsies and studies the break-up of the plane to see if some modification in the cabin design would insure more protection for future passengers. A fourth group traces the last flight of the plane, studies recorded radio contacts between the plane and airports en route, reviews the plane's maintenance record to see how well it was serviced before its final take-off and analyzes the crew's records of training and performance. Another group interviews witnesses along the path of the fatal flight.

Through the CAB investigators in charge, any or all of the teams may arrange for special laboratory tests to isolate suspected causes. They may call on the FBI for fingerprinting and dental charts to help identify the dead because there's always the possibility the answer may lie with a victim. The teams may ask for microscopic examination of body tissues by the Armed Forces Institute of Pathology. They may use the National Bureau of Standards for X-ray analysis of metal, chemical examinations and analyses to show structural fatigue. They may ask the aircraft factory to make flight tests under various conditions to check out similar planes for weakness.

Laboratory tests can clear a pilot's name as well as reveal the cause of a crash. An American Airlines test plane crashed into Bowery Bay as it attempted to land at LaGuardia. After performing an incomplete autopsy, local medical examiners reported the crew must have been drunk. To CAB investigators, it didn't make sense that the crew could have soberly prepared a flight plan and responded correctly to all directions from the control tower if the pilot had been as full of alcohol as the partial autopsy indicated. Detailed laboratory tests proved their point.

It developed that tanks of ethyl alcohol used for de-icing had smashed when the plane hit the bay, and the alcohol had mixed with the water which was inhaled as the men drowned—thus accounting for the high concentration of alcohol in the livers and brains of the pilots.

Sometimes, a non-fatal crash can lead to the solution of an earlier fatal one. In October, 1947, a United Air Lines DC-6 radioed that it was fighting an uncontrollable fire. It progressively disintegrated in the air until it finally crashed in Bryce Canyon. Less than three weeks later, an American Airlines DC-6 also reported an uncontrollable fire, but because it was close to the Gallup, N.M., airport, the plane managed to land safely. Investigators checked what they had learned so far in the Bryce Canyon crash against the later accident and swiftly came up with the answer in the fuel system. All planes of that type were grounded for six months while new wing tank fueling systems were installed to prevent such fires from ever happening again.

That, of course, is the basic objective of these investigators—to find the killer mechanism and devise means to prevent a recurrence. In February, 1952, when Elizabeth, N.J., was terrorized by its third major air disaster in two months, CAB investigators raced to find the answer. Within three weeks, they had it. The evidence proved a malfunction had thrown the No. 3 propeller into unwanted reverse. The pilot, apparently thinking the No. 4 propeller was at fault, switched it off, thereby removing all resistance to the backward drag from No. 3 propeller and swerving the plane uncontrollably. CAB promptly recommended an automatic signal system. Now, if a propeller reverses, the pilot knows instantly which one it is by a corresponding red light flashing on the instrument panel.

The "killer" may remain at the scene of the "crime" or may hide miles away. That's why troops are called in to scour surrounding miles, or helicopters fly low over the path of the last flight to account for every piece of the wreckage. In the 1948 crash of a Northwest Airlines Martin 202 near Winona, Minn., a wing recovered two miles from the crash indicated structural failure. A CAB investigator, inching over the torn edge of the wing with a magnifying glass, pinpointed a hairline fissure in a wing fitting. Similar planes were grounded and CAB investigators painted the wing fittings on each plane with a bluish fluorescent dye to reveal any lack of continuity in the metal. Of the 19 planes grounded, five showed a trace of metal fatigue at the same spot. Martin altered the wing structure to strengthen this point of apparent weakness and the same type of accident has never been repeated.

In this jet age of bigger, faster and higher-flying planes, each carrying more passengers than ever before, CAB investigators are putting the emphasis on tracking down the killers before they strike the first time. That's why even a minor, non-fatal accident may bring out a full squad of investigators. A live crew and a fairly intact plane may provide life-saving answers.

Recently, for instance, a plane carrying 107 persons was making an approach to land at Detroit when the plane grazed a tree about 4,000 feet from the threshold of the runway. It landed safely but the pilot was slated to be grounded for error. CAB investigators promptly moved in to look for less obvious answers. What was the pilot doing to bring him so close to the ground that far from the runway? Why didn't the radar spot him? What was the co-pilot doing? Was there any flaw in flight training methods? The CAB investigators expect to learn as much from this minor incident as from a major accident. And the answers should make the air that much safer for other plane travellers.

The detective work in finding solutions and erasing causes has had this effect on American aviation: in 1938, there were 4.5 passenger fatalities for every 100 million miles flown. By 1961, despite the tremendous increase in air travel and the burgeoning fleets of jets, the rate was down to .29 passenger fatalities. For the tenth consecutive year, United States certificated carriers have averaged less than one fatality for every 100 million miles flown.

Keeping the fatality rate down while the rate of air travel continues to go up is the mission and the goal of the nation's force of flying detectives.

THE CLUE ON THE TAPE

The sun glistened on the wings of the DC-6 as the giant airliner soared high over the Pennsylvania mountains on the last leg of its Los Angeles-New York flight. In the cabin, the 39 passengers glanced idly at the flight log prepared for them by the pilot, Capt. George Warner.

United Air Lines Flight 624, the captain told them, was now flying 17,000 feet above sea level at a speed of 300 miles an hour. The trip would be descending from cruising altitude at 12:36 P.M., Eastern Standard Time, over Sunbury, Pa. Its estimated time of arrival at New York's LaGuardia Airport was 1:15 P.M. The log was dated June 17, 1948.

Earl Carroll, the veteran showman whose "Vanities" boasted the most beautiful girls in the world, handed the flight log to his star, Beryl Wallace.

The log passed from seat to seat—to a Frenchman, a Navy commander, a couple from Jamaica with a child, a mother who had boarded in Chicago with her baby daughter. The flight had been late leaving Chicago and the passengers were interested most in when it would get to New York.

In the cockpit, Capt. Warner was reporting his position to the United Air Lines radio operator at LaGuardia. He estimated he would pass over Allentown at 12.48 P.M. When the operator gave him the airways traffic clearance to cross Allentown at 11,000 feet, Capt. Warner repeated the message in acknowledgment. The time was 12:27 P.M.

Four minutes later, the New York radio operator was startled by a string of shouted words—loud, blurred and unintelligible.

"The trip calling New York, try it again," the radio operator said.

Again, he heard the same shouts. He couldn't make out the words, but he could sense the urgency. He told the voice to switch to Very High Frequency, where there was sure to be less static. Nothing came over VHF and no more on the other channel.

At the same time, Capt. E. E. Bach of United Air Lines Flight 132, flying eight or ten minutes behind Flight 624, heard someone shout "New York." After a long pause, he heard what sounded like "emergency descent."

On the ground, a telephone linesman noticed a plane break through the clouds at about 8,000 feet, coming out of the west very fast. A flight instructor at Sunbury Airport, attracted by the popping noise of the descending plane, wondered why it passed over the field at only 3,000 feet. Usually, the through planes to New York were only starting their descent over Sunbury. A truck driver sitting down to lunch felt his house shake with the vibration of the plane and ran outside. He figured the plane was less than 2,000 feet above him. A farmer came out of his barn to see the plane so low that he could read the lettering on the underside of the wings. A miner heard a roar of motors and instinctively ducked. The plane was no more than 300 feet above him. He saw a thin stream of smoke from an engine as the plane started to climb. Then, it disappeared over the ridge.

A young ex-pilot in the Flying Tigers was driving down the road with his father when he saw the plane approaching, dipping first one wing and then the other. He told his father to stop the car.

"He was coming toward me from the right," the ex-pilot told investigators later. "I started running toward a clearing. I heard a surge of power but I couldn't see him so I ran over the hill. That's when I saw him. I was so scared that I wanted to run, but I couldn't. I wanted to yell to my father to run, but I couldn't because he was coming right toward us.

"My father sort of snapped me out of it and we went back to the road and we started to go down a little path, but I didn't want to because the wreckage was all up through there and it was burning."

In New York at that moment, the United Air Lines radio operator was calling United 624 to relay instruction for its approach to New York. When the radio operator got no response, he tried a different frequency. The time was 12:41 P.M.

Capt. Bach, the pilot who had heard the unidentified voice shouting "emergency descent," listened to New York trying unsuccessfully to reach United 624. As he passed over Sunbury, he saw a column of smoke 12 miles ahead and flew toward it.

Instinctively, he was putting together three facts—the shouted voice, New York's unsuccessful efforts to contact Flight 624, the column of smoke. He looked down on a clearing in the woods—a mass of flames and people running toward it. Circling with wing tilted to obscure the view of his passengers, he called New York.

"We have sighted the wreckage of United 624," he reported.

Minutes later, the phone rang in the office of Joseph O. Fluet, then chief investigator for Region 1 of the Civil Aeronautics Board, based at Flushing near LaGuardia Airport. As always, the veteran investigator had a pencil in his hand and an accident report at his elbow when he picked up the phone.

Within 90 minutes, he was airborne on a special flight to the scene of the crash near Mt. Carmel, Pa., but before he left he issued a string of orders. He told United Air Lines to hold its records of the flight and any radio recordings for CAB investigation, told Air Traffic Control to furnish its records of the flight from Chicago, called the nearest Pennsylvania State Police barracks to rope off the wreckage area and establish a guard as soon as possible. Finally, he called home to tell his wife he wouldn't be home for dinner that night or for some nights to come. His boys would be disappointed. He was showing them how to build a model plane, but they were used to their father's abrupt departures.

As his car neared the scene from the closest airport, Joe Fluet's face creased in a worried frown. He could see people straggling away from the scene with pieces of charred metal in their hands. That's what he dreaded most—the souvenir hunters who took away the vital clues to the mystery he was there to solve. He told police to recover the pieces.

Standing on the rocky hillside, Joe Fluet squared his broad shoulders and looked around him at total disintegration. The plane, he realized, must have rammed the hillside at full force. He had never seen a plane shattered into so many pieces—thousands of them scattered over an area 175 feet wide and 585 feet long, all scorched and smudged because of intense ground fire after the crash. No wonder the souvenir hunters had been tempted. There wasn't a piece there that couldn't be picked up and carried away by hand.

The plane had struck a 66,000 volt transformer and severed power lines. Pieces of the airliner were strewn over a hillside of clay, shale and rock. Most of the trees were gone from the immediate area to clear the way for the power line but on both sides of the clearing, tall trees and thick underbrush concealed bits of the wreckage. Because the plane had cut the power lines, Fluet could fix the time of the crash exactly. The nearby electric station had automatically recorded the power break at 12:41 P.M.

Fluet faced his first and greatest mystery, the one that took longest to solve. The last message from Flight 624—the jumble of words heard in New York, the shout of "emergency descent" heard by Capt. Bach—had been timed at 12:31 P.M. What had happened to the plane in those ten minutes of silence?

He shoved that one away from him until the technicians could establish whether the plane's radio was working properly. As the darkness deepened over the little mining community in the Pennsylvania hills, the first reports from eye-witnesses gave him a dozen more questions to answer.

If the plane's descent was gradual and not a steep dive, why didn't the pilot pull out of it? If he was trying to make an emergency landing, why didn't he land at Sunbury or half a dozen other places in the vicinity instead of heading into the mountains where there was no place to land? What was the significance of that stream of smoke seen by the miner—the usual puff of smoke as a plane applied power or was the plane on fire? If power was available, why didn't the pilot use it to get over the mountain? And, finally, the most insistent question of all—why did a plane flying in broad daylight on a sunny day plough into the side of a mountain?

That midnight in the basement of a local saloon which would be headquarters and home to the investigators for weeks to come, Joe Fluet held his first meeting to plan the investigation. Out of that mass of fragments on the hillside, he and teams of CAB specialists had to find the answers to the crash—find them as fast as possible before the same combination of circumstances produced another disaster. The manhunt was on for the killer before it struck again.

In other investigations, some clue had told Fluet where to put the emphasis in hunting the cause of the crash. This time, he had nothing to go on but a gradual descent and that puzzling ten minutes of silence.

He assigned teams to each phase of the investigation—technicians provided by the aviation industry itself, from the plane and propeller and engine manufacturers, from the Airline Pilots Association, from the Civil Aeronautics Administration (now the Federal Aviation Agency), each team headed by one of the Civil Aeronautics Board's own specialists.

One team would delve into the plane's record, one would interview witnesses along the flight path, one would search for the pieces taken as souvenirs. Another would focus on the plane's structure, its frame and wings. Still another would concentrate on its engines, propellers, fuel system. And a last team would work on its radio, electrical, heating, ventilating and control systems.

From the fragments, Fluet wanted them to be able to tell him if a vital piece snapped off in flight, if the power failed, if the plane was out of control, if the instruments were inaccurate, if the plane caught fire in the air.

Fluet, outwardly easy-going with a twinkle in his eye and the suggestion of a dimple in his chin, always ran a tight-lipped investigation. He didn't want his teams to pick up a pet theory and hold to it, foreclosing any other possible solution. He had learned to keep his mouth shut and his mind open, refusing to permit investigation by guesswork or a conclusion until there was physical evidence to support it. The wrong solution would allow a killer to remain at large.

Physically, Fluet was tough, but he had to be. Almost invariably, planes crashed in the most inaccessible spots—in snake-filled swamps or snow-covered mountains, in deep forests or desert wastes. Like most CAB investigators, he was a pilot himself with more than a dozen years of private flying before he joined the CAB in 1942. He was also an expert mechanic, dating back to childhood when he tinkered with his father's Model T truck. He had learned all about the innards of an airplane as a grease monkey in the Army Air Corps.

Now, he went after clues to the crash at Mt. Carmel with the devotion to detail of an Ellery Queen and the fervor of a policeman on the trail of a mass slayer.

Automatically, he asked for a complete list of the cargo, the mail and the baggage and its original location aboard the plane, a list of the occupations of the 39 passengers, a list of the contents of all personal baggage recovered, a record of the training of the four members of the crew—pilot, co-pilot and the two young stewardesses. He sent the clothing of crew members to the laboratories to be tested and asked New York to hurry up with an interpretation of the jumble of words in the pilot's last message.

At his urgent request, police, church and civic groups were rounding up the souvenirs taken from the scene—the missing pieces of the many-pieced jigsaw puzzle. A priest made an appeal to his parishioners at Sunday services for a particularly wanted piece, and as a result a fuel pump was left on a doorstep at midnight. Helicopters cruised the area to see if the plane clipped any tree tops before it crashed into the transformer. Investigators interviewed hundreds of people over a 25-mile area to find eye-witnesses to the plane's descent. Other teams made a systematic search of the wreckage, studying the area of distribution from the point of impact, spotting and identifying the fragmentary pieces, removing them to a flat area to be screened again and assembled in a uniform pattern. Parts were sent to laboratories to be tested for weakness and performance.

Fluet wanted to know how the plane approached the ground. Noticing a slash in the black earth, he dug down with his fingers and came up with some bits of colored glass. That gave him an answer and a new question. The glass came from the right wingtip light so the plane had its right wing down in a steep bank as it hit the ground, but if it was trying to land, what was it doing in a right bank? Had the controls failed? Had the power failed?

At the midnight conference in the saloon basement, Fluet posed his questions as he absently brushed coal dust from the pillow of his cot. The teams of technicians were coming up with answers but all of them eliminated possible causes. They weren't getting any closer to the real cause.

Heavy machinery had been brought to the hillside to haul out the remains of the engines and propellers embedded deep in the ground. By examining the propeller blades to determine their angle setting, the CAB experts could state positively that the plane was generating full power when it slashed into the ground.

The CAB technicians accounted for all the controls, had them tested and reported back that the pilot could have controlled his plane, could have pulled over the mountain. The cockpit was strewn over the ground but the investigators found the instruments from the dashboard and studied what they reported at the moment of impact. The needles were frozen in position, just as a watch flung against a wall would show what time it was flung. The instruments, reported the technicians, were accurate.

One morning soon after the crash, Fluet sat down to rest on the hillside with a CAB investigator, George Clark. It was Clark's first investigation and Fluet was more willing than usual to share his thoughts.

"I've been thinking maybe something happened to both the pilot and the co-pilot," Fluet said slowly. "Physical incapacitation never caused a crash before that we know of but that doesn't rule it out."

"You mean all the time that plane was gradually getting lower and lower, nobody was at the controls?" Clark asked, his eyes fixed on the investigator in charge.

"Either not at the controls or not able to do anything about it," Fluet explained. "Suppose a bird smashed in the windshield. The force of air rushing through the opening at 300 miles an hour might make it very rough for the pilots to see or talk or even breathe."

Fluet knew how fast the plane had been going. He had picked up the pilot's flight log for passengers. The sheet was charred around the edges but still readable.

As Clark listened eagerly to the expert, Fluet said he would see what could be done about trying to piece the windshield together. He would find out about the possibility of food poisoning, how the pilot and co-pilot spent their 30-hour layover in Chicago between planes. He wondered about those blurred, unintelligible voices.

The bird theory was ruled out first. One of the teams accounted for every fragment of the windshield.

As for the pilot and co-pilot, Capt. Warner's widow said he had slept late, worked in his garden, painted his garage and had a late dinner. Afterwards, he walked to the local newsstand for a paper, visited with the neighbors on the way home and was in bed by 10:15 P.M. He had had nothing to drink all day.

Co-Pilot Richard Schember had helped his wife hang out the laundry, had spent the afternoon at a garage having some work done on his car, had taken his wife and a neighbor to an early movie and was home by 10:30. He, too, had not touched a drink on the day before the flight.

At the Chicago airport, the senior flight dispatcher, the passenger agent, the lead mechanic who handled the flight, the ramp serviceman who checked off the cargo, an airline stenographer who had coffee and cake with the pilot and co-pilot just before take-off reported both men were in good spirits and seemed quite normal. The stenographer who shared their snack suffered no ill effects from the food.

So Fluet scratched off food poisoning. He already had a report from the air line's physician that both men had had physicals within the previous four months and were checked out in good health. He wondered how the captain performed in an emergency and got a report on that from a fellow pilot. Only four months earlier, the pilot said, Capt. Warner had landed a C-54 with no flaps and possibly no brakes on a runway with snow drifts as high as six feet. The emergency landing was well done.

Fluet had gotten around to wondering if both the pilot and co-pilot could have been the simultaneous victims of foul play when New York called with what looked like an important break. Out of that confused, static-ridden jumble of sound, the electronic experts had been able to make a few words come clear in the final broadcast from flight 624. The words, Fluet was told sounded like: "We released the fire extinguisher in the forward cargo pit."

Fluet tried to put himself in the pilot's place. A red light from a fire detector unit would flash on his dashboard. He might look out the window to see if he could spot smoke. The position of the red light in the battery of lights would tell him which compartment was burning. He would turn a knob in the cockpit to flood the burning compartment with the fire extinguisher, carbon dioxide under pressure. The forward cargo pit where the pilot said he released the extinguisher was directly under the cockpit.

"The pilot was up there, we weren't," Fluet reminded Clark. "If he says there was fire in the forward cargo pit, we've got to find evidence of it."

Everything above ground was charred, no way of telling whether it had burned in flight or on the ground in the flash fire after the crash. Fluet ordered a crew to dig. As the shovels got down to six feet, Fluet spotted a lock attached to a piece of cord, obviously torn from a mail bag at impact.

The investigator felt a tug of excitement as he consulted the lists he had gotten on the distribution of mail sacks in the plane. That particular lock had been attached to a mail bag stowed in the forward cargo pit, the baggage compartment where the pilot reported he had released carbon dioxide to put out a fire. The lock and the rope showed no trace of fire.

Staring down at the lock, Fluet reached his first firm conclusion. The fire detector flashing on the pilot's dashboard had given a false alarm. The lock proved there was no fire in the forward cargo pit.

A call to CAB Washington headquarters supported his conclusion. In the six months since January, 1948, he was told, pilots had reported 22 false warnings from fire detectors in fuselage compartments and 285 false warnings from smoke detectors. So the witnesses who had reported seeing no thick smoke or flames from the gradually descending plane had been right. The fire detector had been wrong.

One more possible cause of the disaster had been written off and CAB's investigative teams were rapidly eliminating other causes. They had found nothing to indicate either structural or power failure. The pilot had the power and the controls to pull out of that gradual descent to death. Why didn't he do it? His radio was working. Why didn't he use it during the last 10 minutes of his life?

Fluet went back to that first tentative theory he had voiced to Clark on the hillside—physical incapacitation of the crew. Again, he called Washington.

"Give me everything you've got on the effects of carbon dioxide," he requested.

He was thinking back to the moment weeks earlier when he had picked up the pilot's operating manual near an outstretched hand. An indentation in the back of the book fitted exactly into his own big hand. When he held it there, the book broke open at the page carrying the instructions for actions in case of fire in flight. The pilot could have been holding the book in his hand at the time of the crash, reading the fire instructions which called for the release of carbon dioxide. The instructions also stressed opening the release valves to get fresh air into the cockpit. Had the pilot gotten around to that?

The technicians couldn't be positive about the valves but Fluet was inclining more and more to his theory that carbon dioxide was the unknown villain.

He tried to get laboratory tests to confirm his suspicions but the laboratory reported the impact had been so great there was no body fluid left to test for the presence of carbon dioxide.

The information he got from CAB Washington headquarters was revealing but inconclusive. On May 13—less than five weeks before the Mt. Carmel crash—a crew in a TWA Constellation had been partially incapacitated by carbon dioxide released into a forward cargo compartment. Medical studies of the effect of smoke and noxious gases on flight crews were underway and consideration was being given to instructing all flight crews to use oxygen masks when carbon dioxide was released. Nothing definite had been learned yet, Fluet was told, on how carbon dioxide actually affected crews at various altitudes under various conditions.

Fluet thought he knew but he still had to prove it. Clark eagerly volunteered to be the guinea pig. He exposed himself to a room filled with carbon dioxide at LaGuardia airport.

"You get slap-happy," he reported later. "Your mouth gets thick. You couldn't care less what happens."

Fluet and Clark sat in the cockpit of a DC-6 and tried to re-enact what Capt. Warner and his co-pilot went through. Remembering what he had heard about the gas, Fluet tried to picture how he would act. Carbon dioxide was invisible, odorless. The pilot would think he had plenty of time to do all the instructions called for. Fluet pictured the stewardesses busy in the cabin, thinking nothing of a gradual descent. After all, the flight log to passengers had reported the plane would start descending at Sunbury. There was no sudden pitch or roll to attract the stewardesses away from their duties. When they noticed how close they were to the ground, it would be too late.

"We need more than theory," Fluet said finally. "Let's get Doc Lederer."

It was now late August and the final round of official public hearings by the CAB's Board of Inquiry was coming up. Weeks before, a panel of aviation officials had spent all day listening to the recordings of Capt. Warner's last messages and had disagreed on what they heard. One thought a voice was saying, "There're fumes escaping." But to others, the same words meant "our fuses stick" or "fumes in pit." Fluet was no longer interested in the words. He wanted to know if anything positive could be learned from the inflection of the voices.

The hearings had already started when Fluet sent for Dr. Ludwig

G. Lederer, one of the country's top physiologists, an expert on aviation medicine who had worked with CAB on earlier crashes.

"We won't tell him anything so he won't be influenced," Fluet said to Clark. "We'll play the recording until he can tell us something."

Dr. Lederer emerged sweating and dizzy from nearly four hours in a hotel room, listening to the same words by loud speaker and earphones until they were planted indelibly on his mind. Then, Fluet gave him the earlier testimony of eye-witnesses so he could relate the sounds he had heard to the actions reported in those final ten minutes.

Dr. Lederer described in medical terms what he had heard—the first two words an agitated, almost normal yell, followed by a gasp typical of a spasm at the top of the windpipe, the thick enunciation of the last two words, "emergency descent." And then the significant silence.

He phrased his testimony carefully, but his conclusion was unmistakable. The crew had been overcome by the effects of carbon dioxide. While the passengers chatted in the cabin and the stewardesses bustled about their duties, the plane had gradually descended with no pilot at the wheel.

One more question still had to be answered. The chairman of the board of inquiry cited eye-witness testimony of the plane seeming to come out of its descent and flying for several miles on a weaving course, dipping one wing and then the other before the steep bank as it slashed into the mountain side.

"If a person was recovering or partially under the effects and had been under the effects of carbon dioxide for several minutes, do you feel that they could have flown the aircraft under such conditions?" the chairman asked Dr. Lederer.

"Yes," the doctor replied. "That seems more logical to me than any explanation. Bearing in mind very high concentrations of carbon dioxide and the possibility that you can become momentarily unconscious and then regain consciousness, that is true. However, you will not regain *sudden* consciousness. You will be groggy and you might continue doing what you left off doing without really knowing about it and you could go through some gross movements that could account for that type of flight pattern."

Joe Fluet had found his villain. Later, after more tests to determine how fire extinguishing and fire detector systems could be changed to make certain that the same type of accident could never happen again, the Civil Aeronautics Board made it official. In its final report, the Board concluded:

"The board determines that the probable cause of this accident was the incapacitation of the crew by a concentration of carbon dioxide gas in the cockpit."

Joe Fluet works out of Washington now as the chief of CAB's safety investigation division. When he answers the telephone today with pencil in hand and accident report blank at his elbow, he knows he will have to hunt down another killer. Thanks to the answers he found at Mt. Carmel, carbon dioxide will never again seep into a cockpit to leave pilots slumped over the wheel while their planeload of passengers slowly descends to death.

7 ★★★

Securities and Exchange Commission

A man you don't know calls you up one day to say a stock you never heard of is about to skyrocket. He confides that the company is going to merge with one of the big ones or a new gadget has been invented or a fabulous vein of ore has just been uncovered. He wants to let you in on the ground floor.

If you invest without asking yourself why he's doing you, a stranger, such a big favor, you may join the growing list of suckers whose dreams of a tidy profit turn into a nightmare of lost savings.

To protect the investing public from these telephone swindlers and their stock-manipulating confederates, to make sure the public has an opportunity to know the truth about the stocks it buys, is the responsibility of the Securities and Exchange Commission and its corps of attorneys, accountants, financial analysts and investigators. Working together, they form the investigative arm of the SEC.

Their job was never greater. Today, more people are buying stocks than ever before in American history, more companies are offering their shares to investors for the first time than ever before, more real money is flowing through the stock market than ever before.

The dollar volume of stocks traded in the first half of 1961 alone amounted to almost as much as for the whole of any previous year in SEC history. The aggregate market value of stocks listed on the New York Stock Exchange in 1961 was nearly 20 times its 1932 low point.

All this boiling activity in stocks comes at a time when a growing number of retired people want to increase their fixed incomes to meet rising living costs, when the lively market has led upsophisticated investors into believing they, too, can reap large and quick profits, when $2 stocks of questionable value are being sold out the first day they come on the market.

This atmosphere has naturally attracted the confidence men always on the lookout for suckers. High-pressure promoters driven out of other fields have moved in to parlay baseless tips and rumors into fast profits—for themselves alone. Even the hard-core criminal elements have been attracted. At least one "delegate" to the so-called crime convention at Apalachin, N.Y., was involved in a stock fraud scheme of recent vintage, two men since convicted of murder were in on a Florida fast-money deal and the gambling syndicates are known to be engaged in stock manipulation.

The recent tremendous growth in stock trading, the influx of millions of new investors, the burgeoning evidence of fraud prompted Congress in 1961 to order the SEC to make an over-all study of trading and marketing practices on the national securities exchanges and the over-the-counter market. The goal: to determine whether existing rules are adequate to protect the investing public and what additional safeguards are needed to meet new conditions. Congress set a deadline of January, 1963, for the SEC to complete its investigation and recommend new laws for the protection of the nation's investors.

In May, 1962, when stock prices plummeted and bounced back in hectic sessions, the SEC's special study of market conditions took on added significance as well as assurances from SEC Chairman William L. Cary that his agency was looking into the why's of the stock market dive.

A new generation of investors has come along since Congress plunged into its first stock market investigation after the Wall Street bubble burst in 1929.

On March 29, 1933, less than a month after taking office, President Franklin D. Roosevelt sent a message to Congress urging Federal supervision over the inter-state traffic in investment securities.

"In spite of many state statutes," he wrote, "the public in the past has sustained severe losses through practices neither ethical nor honest on the part of many persons and corporations selling securities."

The President emphasized—as the SEC emphasizes today—that the Federal government cannot and should not guarantee that newly issued securities are sound investments but it can make sure that the public knows the truth about what it buys.

The background of the President's message was fresh in the minds of all who read it. In the post-World War I decade, some $50 billion worth of new securities were floated in the United States and half proved worthless. Many securities dealers abandoned careful counselling of investors in favor of high-pressure salesmanship. Because of the deliberate over-stimulation of investors' appetites, underwriters had to manufacture more securities to meet the demand they had created. Investment bankers forced corporations to accept new capital for expansion purposes—whether they wanted it or not—so new securities might be issued for public consumption. Real estate developments were launched, not to meet actual housing needs, but as an excuse for pouring more securities into the market. The literature describing the businesses into which investors were urged to put their savings was often deliberately misleading, and frequently the stock was issued before either the brokers or their customers got a chance to look at a balance sheet.

As the late Sam Rayburn put it when the first securities bill reached the House floor: "One would have to turn the pages of history back to the days of the South Sea Bubble to find an equivalent fantasy of security selling."

The 1933 Act was basically a disclosure method of dealing with the problem. Theoretically, if people could read they would know whether the stock issue was a safe or speculative investment. New issues of stock had to be registered. If the proposed prospectus was untrue or misleading, it could be kept off the market. A waiting time was provided so brokers and their customers would have a chance to find out about what they were buying, and the act made it a crime to use interstate facilities or the mails to promote and sell securities through fraud.

Congress assigned the job of enforcing its pioneer securities act to the Federal Trade Commission but, within a year, Congress decided enforcement of the new law required a separate agency devoted exclusively to protecting investors. In its 1934 law, as later strengthened, Congress not only established the SEC but broadened the scope of its responsibilities. Brokers and dealers had to register with the SEC, the stock exchanges themselves and what came to be known as the National Association of Securities Dealers were charged with self-policing, trading on margin was curbed and trading practices were to be regulated to prevent the rigging of stock prices. Congress also extended its "disclosure" doctrine of investor protection to securities listed on the national exchanges, requiring periodic reports from the companies to give the shareholders an accounting.

The twin laws, passed within a year of each other, were basically designed to restore the shattered confidence of the investing public and to break the habit patterns of careless handling of customers' money. It couldn't be done overnight.

But squads of young lawyers—many of whom had gotten their law degrees in the wake of the Wall Street debacle—were about to try. In the first tremendous thrust of investigation, they went after the bucket shops—so-called because orders to buy stocks were thrown into a bucket and never executed. Then, registration statements for new issues were examined for misleading claims, the stock market was watched closely for an unexplained upsurge or decline of an isolated stock, the financial standing of securities dealers was checked to be sure they didn't become insolvent—and lose their customers' money along with their own.

In those early days, everybody was investigating in a mass clean-up effort. During its first year in business, the SEC gathered the evidence to recommend prosecution of 36 individuals. By the next year, it recommended 177 prosecutions and by its third year, 1936, it handed the Justice Department evidence against 379 individuals, all but 11 of whom were indicted. That was the peak year in the early clean-up drive and it apparently had the desired effect. Only half that many individuals were recommended for prosecution the following year.

The SEC swiftly developed investigative and enforcement units in its regional offices to delve into potential violations, subject to review and direction by the Division of Trading and Exchanges, which handles the enforcement work of the Commission, and by the Commission itself.

The Division of Trading and Exchanges, however, kept a small trouble-shooting unit to go after the major promoters whose stock swindles were nationwide or whose depredations warranted priority attention. The unit started as a two-man team composed of Edward C. Jaegerman, now Chief Investigative Counsel of the Division, and John T. Callahan, one-time all-American football star with a mental file cabinet of stock swindlers' methods of operation. Once tagged the "rover boys," the team of Jaegerman and Callahan went after the "boiler rooms."

A "boiler room" operator sells unknown and worthless securities by long distance telephone to customers on his sucker lists. Sometimes, he gets himself a Wall Street address and a fancy name with "Morgan" or "Vanderbilt" in it. Sometimes, several boiler rooms may operate simultaneously in scattered areas of the country to promote the same spurious issue.

In its present variation, the "boiler room" is the conduit for unloading the stock after the promoter has manipulated the price to a phony high. To create the illusion of an active over-the-counter market, the promoter places small purchase and sale orders with numerous brokers and dealers at prices set by him. As a result, brokers and dealers will publish quotations for the securities at prices specified in these buy and sell orders. The salesman for the boiler room is then able to include a price in his sales pitch which the investor can verify. When the promoter has gotten rid of all his stock at inflated prices, the market for the stock disappears and the investors can't sell it.

The Jaegerman-Callahan team played a major role in breaking a series of boiler room stock manipulation schemes masterminded by Stanley Ira Younger during 1957 and 1958.

In one of these cases, their investigation led to the indictment of 50 persons in the conspiracy, including Carmine Lombardozzi, one of the "delegates" to the Apalachin "crime convention" of 1957.

The nation-wide investigation by Jaegerman and Callahan disclosed that Younger and his confederates had bought a block of stock at 20 cents a share and unloaded it to investors in some 40 states at prices ranging from $1.20 to $3.75 a share. Through a broker-dealer firm they controlled, they peddled the stock through the mails and via long distance telephone calls, using such tried-and-untrue boiler room pitches as assurances that the stock was about to go up, that investors were sure of profits and safe from losses, that the stock would soon be listed on a national securities exchange and that the company was operating at a fat profit.

Along with "pie in the sky" promises, the Younger crowd engaged in numerous over-the-counter transactions in the stock to give the impression of an active and rising market without changing their actual ownership. In that case alone, Younger drew an eight-year sentence.

He was convicted in several other cases including one neat maneuver where he placed orders with a broker for stock in a non-existent corporation and then sold the stock, using an alias, to other brokers. By this means, he and an associate caused brokers to buy the stock which the Younger group never accepted and for which they never paid.

The Jaegerman-Callahan team also went after the boiler rooms which sought safety in Canada for telephone sales beamed into the United States. The investigators got on the track of one of the Canadian operations because the high-pressure salesmen got lonesome for their girls across the border and wanted them to come to Canada for a long weekend. Callahan and Jaegerman have traced the promoters through a maze of aliases, dummy corporations and rapid change of address.

Enforcement attorneys in the regional offices often double as investigators to find out who was responsible for a victim's misfortunes. Thomas W. Rae, now chief of a newly created Branch of Special Investigations, Trial and Enforcement in the Washington headquarters, was working in the San Francisco regional office when an alert Nevada sheriff reported that some farmers from North Dakota had come to town looking for a mine.

Rae started with the Nevada town, where he found an accountant who had kept some books for a mine promoter named Leslie F. Emigh. The accountant had some cancelled checks from a Salt Lake City bank, which led Rae to the Utah capital. He found checks from Rapid City, S.D., endorsed by a Nevada gambling casino. He was beginning to get the picture.

At the gambling casino, he was directed to a mining drifter who had arranged for the sale of an abandoned mine to Emigh. The drifter said Emigh had workmen shore up the shafts and turn on the creaking machinery. He planted a sample of genuine ore and was ready for visitors from South Dakota, where he had been operating.

In the South Dakota town, Rae got the rest of the story. Emigh had moved into a boarding house and won the confidence of the landlady, who had passed the word of the fabulous mine to all her friends. Farmers, widows, retired railroadmen were promised a return of $10 for every dollar they invested in a mine so spectacular that it would produce gold, silver, manganese and tungsten.

When Emigh took a group of his South Dakota friends to the mine and picked up that sample, they were his. He took them for approximately $175,000. Compared to the million-dollar frauds SEC uncovers, the loss was small, but it represented the life savings of the victims. As for Emigh, he was traced to Arkansas and pleaded "no contest" to the charge brought against him.

The merchandising of individual trust deeds and mortgages under high-yield investment promises, without registration with the SEC and often through grossly untruthful claims, has become an increasingly serious enforcement problem.

In California, the SEC's investigation exposed the highly speculative nature of a scheme which had attracted some $40,000,000 from investors lured by promises of a 10 per cent return on what was represented as a comparatively riskless investment. The collapse of these

"10 percenters" created a major financial scandal and led to the passage of remedial state legislation.

A scheme investigated by the SEC in Florida also involved the sale of deeds of trust with a promised 8 per cent return, but these deeds were non-existent and the only return consisted of small slices of the capital invested. In other words, the first investors in the scheme were paid "dividends" out of money invested by later suckers. When the "dividends" stopped coming, the investors started complaining. Among those indicted in that scheme were two subsequently convicted of murder.

As in the Florida case, complaints from the public represent the largest single source of investigative leads, but investigators and securities analysts tap many other sources to prevent frauds before the public gets hurt.

The Commission's market surveillance staff keeps a close eye on tickertape quotations of securities listed on the New York and American Stock Exchanges, the sales and quotation sheets of the regional exchanges and the bid and asked prices published by the National Daily Quotation Service for about 6,000 unlisted securities.

What they watch for is any unusual or unexplained price variation or market activity. When they spot one, they gather all known information about the security in question to see if the actual or apparent trading is a gimmick to induce investors to buy or sell. If their preliminary investigation leads in that direction, a formal investigation may be ordered.

The investigations conducted by the regional offices take two forms. One is a fast quiz to find evidence of unlawful activity. The other is a formal order of investigation, approved by the Commission itself, which carries with it the right to issue subpoenas and take testimony under oath. It's out of the latter type of investigations that most injunctions and recommended criminal actions flow.

The formal and informal investigations may also stem from surprise inspections of the books and records of broker-dealers. The investigators look at the broker-dealer's financial condition to be sure he's using his own money rather than his customers' to run his business. They review his pricing practices, the safeguards he uses to handle his customers' funds and securities, and how accurately he informs his customers about transactions in their behalf.

What they occasionally find is a broker whose records are so badly mixed up that he doesn't know what he owes his customers or they owe him, a broker who keeps switching his customers' stock holdings to make more profit for himself, one who uses his customers' stock as collateral for his own loans, one who sells unregistered stock or touts worthless stock for his own benefit or joins in a multi-dealer scheme to manipulate a stock or uses forbidden sales techniques.

In 1961, the SEC reacted to its increased enforcement problems by creating a special enforcement wing in the Division of Trading and Exchanges. The action was designed to consolidate in one division all the Commission's investigative and enforcement activities in its headquarters office as well as to coordinate similar activities in its regional offices. Irving M. Pollack, who came to the SEC in 1946 and has since been closely associated with its investigative and enforcement activities—particularly in the development of criminal cases—was put in charge of the new wing.

One of his first moves was to turn loose a task force in Washington itself. There, investors unprotected by any local law, were being victimized by a crew of out-of-town promoters and local salesmen who went into business themselves with neither capital nor experience. In the crackdown, a number of dealers have been put out of business before they could do any more damage.

Nationally, the Commission's stepped-up enforcement program was reflected in 546 anti-fraud and other investigations launched during the year ending in June, 1961. The Commission brought 92 injunction actions to halt violations, a greater number than in any previous year. As for criminal prosecutions, 126 convictions were obtained in 45 cases—the largest number of convictions in any fiscal year since the early days of the Commission.

All these cases and the ones before and since then have been designed to carry out aims expressed nearly three decades ago by President Roosevelt when he called for a law to give impetus to honest dealing in securities and "thereby bring back public confidence."

The public confidence has been brought back. The goal of the SEC's corps of investigators is to make sure that the public confidence is not misplaced.

THE GUTERMA AFFAIR

On Valentine's Day, 1959, Alexander Leonard Guterma stared out of owlish eyes at an official piece of paper. This was no Valentine. The boy wonder of Wall Street, the financial wizard whose legerdemain had bemused and confused much older hands at the game, was looking at a warrant for his arrest.

Late that day, when Guterma surrendered at the courthouse, he puffed hard on his Corona Corona and told reporters it was an outrage.

"This is getting a man for spitting on the sidewalk," he said scornfully.

He was charged with failing to file an "insider's report" on his stock dealings in the F. L. Jacobs Co., an auto parts firm he had parlayed into an octopus of a holding company. The Securities and Exchange Commission law requires any officer, director, or 10 per cent stockholder of a company listed on the stock exchange to report his changes in ownership. If an "insider" starts getting rid of his own stock, the outside investor will think twice before he buys it.

In its role as protector of the investing public, the SEC believes the public has a right to know how an insider rates his own company. But never before had a company officer been arrested on such a charge—particularly a man of Guterma's standing in the financial world.

A pair of tips had triggered the arrest long before the SEC was ready to move against Guterma. It would take a third tip and the combined efforts of some 60 attorneys, investigators and accountants working under the pressure of time to find Guterma's multi-million-dollar motive for a "spitting on the sidewalk" kind of a crime.

It would take even longer to get some idea of how many millions of dollars Guterma looted from investors as he flashed like a meteor across the financial world. Guterma then stood at the peak of his empire of companies, controlling a broadcasting company, a movie studio, a lace-making firm, an auto parts factory and a string of other holdings. On the cabin wall of his private plane hung a picture of his private yacht.

He was known to drop $20,000 on the turn of a single card in a gin rummy game. At his executive suite in New York, liveried butlers passed drinks and fruits to his business associates while they admired his priceless collection of oriental jade. His family was installed on an estate in Greenwich, Conn., while he entertained in his $10,000-a-year Manhattan hotel quarters.

His past was as clouded as his present was spectacular. The crumbs of information he dropped for investigators to follow led from pre-Communist Russia, through pre-war China, through Manila under Japanese occupation to the plush resorts of Florida and Las Vegas and finally, to Wall Street, with side excursions into the financial maze of Tangier and the secret world of Swiss banking.

He claimed he was born of "Russian-Protestant" parentage at Irkutsk, Siberia, in 1915—the son of a general who served in the Imperial Army of Czar Nicholas II. Some disenchanted associates found the story hard to believe. They pointed to the American slang in his picturesque profanity, his knowledge of American baseball, his affinity for East Side delicatessen. They found his slight accent puzzling—more cosmopolitan than Russian.

Whatever his origin, immigration records showed he turned up in Hawaii in 1935 and was ordered deported as a non-citizen. He stowed away on a liner bound for China, where, in the hard schools of Shanghai, Tientsin, Tsingtao and Harbin, he began learning the intricacies of international finance. Just before the war, he migrated to Manila and there married an American girl, the daughter of a dentist in the Philippines. The Japanese gave him a hard time at first and put him in a prison camp until he proved he was not an American. Thereafter, he lived by his wits so successfully that at war's end, he was put on the "blocked list" of the United States and Philippine treasuries. That meant he had to obtain licenses for future operations, but he prospered anyway.

His Manila friends were so impressed by his financial sagacity that they entrusted him with a fund—some say as much as $350,000—when he entered the United States as a non-quota immigrant with his American wife in 1950. He took his nest-egg to Florida and launched his first American project—plantations for growing hemp and ramie, a kind of cotton. The projects didn't exactly flourish and his Manila backers were glad to get out with only a fraction of what they had put in—something like $75,000.

Meantime, Guterma was setting up new corporations and selling stock to capitalize them. He was winning new friends all the time—wealthy and influential men captivated by his apparent flair for making money, his quick wit, his boundless optimism, his fund of racy stories and his daring at the gambling tables. His new friends willingly served on his various boards of directors and their names attracted even cautious investors.

He was now well-launched on his rocket to fortune. He piled one corporation on top of another, issuing more stock all the time. Eventually, he merged the lot into an outfit called the Shawano Development Company. The companies he had set up for his Manila backers and bought off for $75,000 were carried into Shawano at a figure of $1,500,000.

The little investors who bought Shawano at the height of its popularity paid $1.25 a share. Later, the stock was split, 4 to 1. At the time Guterma was handed the warrant for his arrest, it was selling for eight cents a share and investors had lost close to $3,000,000.

But that was much later. Shawano was still riding high when Guterma bid farewell to his Florida cronies and went west. There, he parcelled out Shawano stock for controlling interests in other companies—oil, mercury, uranium, insurance and a honey called Micro-Moisture Controls. As Guterma told it, he was riding on an airplane one day when the man next to him confided that he had patented a photo-electric cell which would be activated when water hit it. The inventor explained it could be used to close windows against the rain when nobody was home or to put up the top of a convertible at the first dew. Guterma bought the inventor's rights, christened his find Micro-Moisture Controls and launched a new stock on its way to a fortune—for him. Millions of shares of the stock were first offered at $1 a share. By the time of Guterma's arrest, it was being bid at half a cent.

His empire building next took him into the hotel business. He turned over huge blocks of Shawano stock to Las Vegas gamblers with hotels under their control. Still climbing, he went to Denver and started a new promotion, the Western Financial Corp. Several million shares of that were in the hands of the public by the time it finally went into bankruptcy, but by then Guterma had disposed of it to a Texas manipulator and moved on to his goal—Wall Street.

The pattern was formed, a pattern so intricate that only Guterma himself knew how it worked—the holding companies, the worthless stock sold over long distance telephones to hapless investors, stock exchanged to gain control of companies, small companies merged into big ones and looted of their assets. In five years, the fast-moving Guterma had reached the big time.

In 1955, he was offered an option to buy United Dye and Chemical Co., then being operated for Lowell Birrell, who had run afoul of the SEC in an oil-selling scandal and had fled to Brazil. Guterma didn't have the money himself but he still had those good friends in Las Vegas. Together, they went into United Dye and Chemical with Guterma as chairman of the board. Then, in an incredibly complex financial transaction, they acquired Bon Ami, the cleansing company, by using the company's own assets to buy it. Guterma became chairman of another board.

Guterma now set his sights on another well-known company—F. L. Jacobs, an auto parts firm. To acquire control, he borrowed from the money lenders, pledging the stock as collateral to get more money to buy more stock.

His appetite for money and power still unappeased, he turned F. L. Jacobs into a holding company at the peak of his pyramid of companies and had it acquire control of the Scranton Corp., a lace-making concern. Turning Scranton into a holding company, too, he had it acquire the Hal Roach Studios, which in turn bought control of the Mutual Broadcasting System. Guess who became president of the radio network? Guterma, of course.

And there he stood late in 1958—balding ruler of an empire of companies, by his own description a "goddam genius."

His empire was experiencing its first tremors. Most of his financial finagling was then still unknown to investigators for the Securities and Exchange Commission but investors in his earlier ventures were beginning to wonder why their stocks declined swiftly, sometimes into total eclipse, as soon as Guterma pulled out. The New York Stock Exchange was asking why the F. L. Jacobs Co. had not filed its annual report to stockholders, due on October 31, and now long overdue. SEC investigators had started looking into Guterma's financial hocus-pocus in Bon Ami and United Dye and Chemical Co., but the schemes were so devious they knew it would take many months to pin them down. The SEC had granted F. L. Jacobs Co. an extension of time for filing its annual report to the SEC, but no report had been filed. Investigators had gotten wind of a little holding company named Comficor that seemed somehow linked to Guterma but it was all very vague.

Guterma was still balancing nicely on the high-wire of Wall Street finance on February 9, 1959, when a tip—the first of three—reached the office of Paul Windels, Jr., New York Regional Administrator for the SEC. The informant said Guterma had pledged F. L. Jacobs stock with the money-lenders and they were selling him out.

The tip seemed unbelievable. SEC investigators didn't know then that Guterma was no stranger to the money-lenders. They asked themselves why a man with more millions than he could count would do business with the money-lenders and why they would be foreclosing on him. In 24 hours, the tip had been confirmed. A lot of Jacobs stock was being dumped on the market.

Windels knew he had to move fast to protect the other stockholders, the little people who had put their nest eggs into Guterma's big company. Windels had two facts: Guterma was selling stock, however indirectly, and not reporting it and the annual report of the Jacobs company still wasn't forthcoming. He suspected there was a lot more to this than appeared on the surface, but it would take time to uncover and he didn't have the time. Two days after he got the first tip, Windels asked the court to stop Guterma from selling Jacobs stock through the money-lenders and to require Guterma to file his overdue reports.

On Friday the 13th—an unlucky day for a man who boasted of his luck—the second tip came. This time, an informant said Guterma and his sidekick, Robert J. Eveleigh, had booked passage for Istanbul, Turkey, on a Sunday plane.

It had a familiar ring. Lowell Birrell, who had owned United Dye and Chemical before Guterma, fled the country when the SEC moved in. A check of reservations showed Guterma was booked for the Sunday flight to Istanbul. Windels would have been even more alarmed if he had known then that Guterma had just acquired a $750,000 stake—a payoff from General Trujillo, dictator of the Dominican Republic, to use Dominican propaganda under the guise of news on Guterma's Mutual Broadcasting System.

Windels took the Istanbul tip to the United States Attorney. Guterma had to be kept in the country until the SEC found out why the money lenders were dumping Jacobs stock, why the annual report of Jacobs' financial condition had not been filed, why Guterma was apparently flouting the SEC's rules designed to protect the investing public. The SEC's case against Guterma was still sketchy but the Birrell flight was still fresh in Windels' mind.

So, on the Saturday of Valentine's Day, an angry Guterma faced the judge in chambers on a charge of failing to file an "insider's" report. With him was Eveleigh, arrested as a material witness. Executive Assistant United States Attorney Jerome J. Londin, who was later to carry the prosecution through a blazing seven-week trial, proposed a bond of $100,000.

Federal Judge Sidney S. Sugarman was skeptical. Perhaps, like Guterma, he considered the charge a "spitting on the sidewalk" type of offense despite Londin's assurance that the Government was investigating large-scale frauds amounting to losses of millions of dollars through Guterma's manipulations. Judge Sugarman fixed bond at $5,000.

That same Saturday, Edward C. Jaegerman, chief of the SEC's Special Investigations Unit, was called to an emergency staff meeting in the Washington headquarters. The top officials of SEC were uneasy because the Commission's reputation could be at stake. Had a mistake been made? Guterma was a big man with an excellent public reputation. He was already claiming he had been framed on that airplane reservation to Turkey, that the SEC was persecuting him. It was true he had violated some SEC rules but that could have been an oversight or negligence on the part of his accountants. Could Jaegerman come up with something in a hurry to prove there was more to this than oversight?

Ed Jaegerman, a man whose mind races so fast that his words tumble over each other, reflected on a tip he had gotten the previous day in New York.

"Guterma has been trying frantically to reach a Montreal number all day," the informer had said, giving the number. "Does that mean anything to you?"

It hadn't then, but it might now. In the Saturday loneliness of the temporary building housing the SEC headquarters, Jaegerman called Montreal and asked a friend to trace the number. The friend reported back that the number was listed to the head of a large brokerage firm. Now more interested than before, Jaegerman traced the broker to his weekend retreat—a remote fishing camp with no telephones. Jaegerman sent word through a village store that he would like to meet the stock broker in New York Monday.

He still had no idea why Guterma had been so anxious to reach the Canadian broker and the broker could always say he was too busy to come to New York—unless he had a story he wanted Jaegerman to hear.

That Monday, the Canadian broker came to New York. He did have a story to tell and Jaegerman listened intently. The broker said he had guaranteed $400,000 in letters of credit to the F. L. Jacobs Co. after Guterma showed him a company resolution authorizing the letters of credit and pledging company stock to back it up. Guterma had told him the letters of credit were just for show and wouldn't be used, but they had been used and the banks were coming to the broker now to collect. Guterma couldn't put up the $400,000 and his frantic calls apparently were to keep the broker from selling the stock pledged as collateral. As Jaegerman totalled it up, 20,000 shares of a Jacobs subsidiary had been put in jeopardy along with 100,000 shares of a second company and full ownership of a third.

Thanks to that third tip, Jaegerman had uncovered evidence indicating that Guterma possibly was looting the assets of his company for personal gain. It was enough to convince the SEC to apply for the appointment of a receiver to save what was left of the company for the stockholders who had put their money into it. It was enough to convince the judge that Guterma was being held on more than a "spitting on the sidewalk" offense. It had gained some time for the investigation, but time was running out. Already Guterma's lawyers were demanding that the Government produce or drop the charges.

The SEC was far from ready to go to prosecution. Guterma's violations of the SEC rules were clear enough. He hadn't filed the reports that tell investors how their company is doing, but why hadn't he done so? Was this just a technical violation, an oversight, or was it a deliberate attempt to conceal wholesale looting of a chunk of American industry?

A task force from Washington was sent to join the SEC task force in New York. The United States Attorney took the unusual step of assigning two more prosecutors, David P. Bicks and Leonard P. Glass, to assist Prosecutor Jerry Londin, and the SEC assigned Investigator Charles B. Green to work exclusively with the prosecutors on around-the-clock development of the evidence. Guterma had fractured some SEC rules. They had to find his motive and find it fast.

The investigators started with the money-lenders. They interviewed and examined the records of nearly a dozen money-lenders, including a Swiss one through its New York agent. Through them, they proved their first charge. Guterma's stock had been sold out by the money-lenders when he failed to pay up his loans and he had not filed an "insider's" report with the SEC.

The money-lenders gave them a clue to something bigger. Guterma, the investigators learned, had negotiated loans with the money-lenders in behalf of the little holding company named Comficor—the one they already knew was linked somehow to Guterma. The investigators found a money-lender who remembered Guterma's saying: "Comficor? That's me."

Checking on Comficor, investigators found its nominal president was actually a low-paid clerk and some of its other officers and directors were minor functionaries in Guterma's office. The stock transactions in Jacobs' holdings appeared in the name of Comficor's dummy president but Guterma called the tune.

Now the investigators had to find out just how much Jacobs stock Comficor owned. If it was more than 10 per cent, Guterma had committed another provable offense. Guterma was Comficor and Comficor had filed no "insider's" report on its buying and selling of Jacobs stock. Canvassing 11 brokerage houses, investigators proved Comficor held more than 10 per cent of the stock but they also proved a curious pattern.

Comficor—acting for Guterma—would place its orders just before the close of the stock market to give the impression of a sudden, last-minute rush to buy Jacobs stock. Brokers called this maneuver "painting the tape," purchasing at a higher price at the close of the market day to insure an upward trend in Jacobs stock. By "painting the tape" through Comficor, Guterma protected his loans. If the stock went down, he would either have to put up more collateral to cover his loan or pay some of it off. If the stock went up, he might be able to get a larger loan on the same stock. The investigators found one instance where he did such a good job of "painting the tape" that a money-lender loaned him an additional $24,000 solely on the rising value of the Jacobs stock.

But where did Comficor get the money to buy the stock? From the money-lenders, of course. The investigators were getting a short course in high finance but they still hadn't found the basic motive for Guterma's failure to live by the SEC rules. They turned to the certified public accountants who were supposed to supply the financial statements required by the New York Stock Exchange and the SEC. Guterma was blaming them for his failure to file the annual report.

The accountants told a story of trying and failing to get the books so they could audit them. They told of repeated assurances that the books would be made available and repeated failures to get anything. At a time when Guterma was assuring the New York Stock Exchange that the accountants were proceeding full steam ahead to produce the final audit, he hadn't even let them in the door.

The investigators paid particular attention to one aspect of the accountants' lament. The accountants said they had tried and failed to locate the stock certificates representing the Jacobs company's ownership of its subsidiaries. They had particularly asked to see the 96,959 shares of the Scranton Corp., the lace-making concern that the Jacobs firm had acquired at a cost of $2,000,000. This was the company now controlling the Hal Roach Studios and the Mutual Broadcasting System. Guterma had said 30 per cent of the net worth of the Jacobs company was its Scranton subsidiary and the accountants couldn't find the shares. All they had been able to glean from Guterma was a vague statement that 40,000 of the Scranton shares were out for transfer with the transfer agent and about 20,000 others were around the office.

The investigators went looking for the Scranton shares. If something had happened to them, 30 per cent of the Jacobs company had disappeared. Starting with the money-lenders again, the investigators found Scranton stock had been pledged by Guterma and Comficor and had ultimately been sold out for unpaid loans. To prove this was Scranton stock issued to the Jacobs company and not to Guterma, the investigators traced the certificate numbers through the brokerage houses. The Scranton securities were listed to the Jacobs company. Guterma and his alter-ego Comficor had gotten more than a million dollars by pledging and losing stock owned by Jacobs.

At last, the investigators had found the motive behind Guterma's failure to file "insider's" reports for himself and Comficor, the reason why he blocked the company's annual financial statement. He didn't dare disclose what he had done. In one year, he had decreased the shareholders' equity in the Jacobs company alone by approximately $3,750,000.

In less than five weeks, the teams of SEC attorneys and investigators and the three prosecutors had untangled the web of deception Guterma had woven with years of practice. They had illustrated, in preparing the first criminal prosecution of this kind in SEC history, why the SEC requires these reports to protect investors against finaglers like Guterma.

On March 16, 1959, Guterma and his sidekick Eveleigh were indicted on charges of defrauding the Government by failing to file reports and of obstructing the lawful functions of the SEC in its protection of the investing public. On the same day, Federal Judge Sugarman—no longer skeptical about the Government's case—ordered the F. L. Jacobs Co. into receivership.

Before Guterma went to trial, his past began to catch up with him as investigators continued probing into the life and good times of the wizard of Wall Street.

The indictments piled up. He and various associates were accused of swindling the Bon Ami company out of more than a third of a million dollars, of defrauding purchasers of United Dye and Chemical Co. stock with false statements, of stealing half a million dollars worth of television time from Bon Ami through such fancy finagling that Bon Ami didn't even know it owned the television time in the first place. He was also indicted with others on charges of acting illegally as an agent for Dictator Trujillo and the Dominican Republic. That was the $750,000 deal he negotiated on a flying trip to Ciudad Trujillo just two weeks before his arrest.

Guterma was still claiming the SEC was persecuting him when he went to trial in the F. L. Jacobs case on December 7, 1959. Fingering his white silk tie and listening with reddening face as the Government's evidence piled up against him, Guterma declined to take the stand in his own defense. On January 28, 1960, the jury convicted him.

In imposing sentence, Judge Lloyd F. MacMahon described him as "a freebooter who raided the seas of a free economy."

Guterma shook his head in disbelief as he heard the sentence—four years and 11 months' imprisonment and a fine of $160,000 (later reduced by the Court of Appeals to $140,000).

"I did not loot the Jacobs company," Guterma told the judge, finally speaking up in his own defense. "I did not bilk its assets. I find myself as a mariner befogged in a sea of Federal regulations."

Investigators were coming out of the fog with more evidence for grand juries. On November 2, 1960—the day Guterma drew an eight-to-24-month sentence in Washington for his deal with the Dominican Republic—a Federal grand jury in New York handed down another 42-count indictment charging Guterma and others with violating other SEC rules in selling the stock of the United Dye and Chemical Co.

A month later, the investigators unveiled the Western phase of Guterma's boom-and-bust career and uncovered the long distance and mail sales campaigns to induce investors to put money into get-rich-quick schemes that never materialized. A grand jury indicted him and others in fraud charges in the sale of Western Financial Corp. stock.

In April, 1961, the investigators finally nailed down the one-horse shay that Guterma had ridden like a space ship on his rise to fortune—the ubiquitous Shawano Development Corp. He and some of his Las Vegas cronies were indicted on charges of selling unregistered stock through false statements and manipulating the price of Shawano to lure investors.

Ed Jaegerman, the quick-witted investigations chief who had solved the mystery of the Montreal calls close to the beginning of the Guterma investigation, was in on the finish. An expert on "boiler rooms"—the barrage of telephones manned by fast-talking promoters—Jaegerman had uncovered the glittery promises used by Guterma's boys to sell Shawano to innocent investors.

Guterma and the investigators had now come full circle. The nine years of his empire-building had been exposed by the investigators in its true light—as a series of ruthless schemes to prey on the public by a man in a hurry.

In the late spring of 1961, Guterma, the inveterate gambler, folded his losing stack of cards. He pleaded guilty to various counts of all the charges outstanding against him. Sentencing was deferred.

There may be no connection but Guterma has been making frequent trips to New York from his cell in Atlanta Penitentiary. Guterma, the financial wizard, freebooter, empire-builder, has become a Government witness against his old buddies.

8 ★★★

Coast Guard

Alexander Hamilton, first Secretary of the Treasury, demanded boats to guard the new nation's coast against smugglers, but it took the intricate maneuvers of another century's smugglers to provide his boats with an intelligence force.

Today, the Coast Guard Intelligence Division—born in the Prohibition era, matured in hot and cold war—plays a unique role among the Federal investigative agencies. Its investigators not only track down the violators of Federal laws enforced by the Coast Guard but also gather military intelligence. For the Coast Guard is attached to the Treasury Department in peacetime but serves with the Navy in war.

Thus, the small corps of Coast Guard Intelligence investigators must be equally adept at tracing a hit-and-run speedboat and routing out potential waterfront saboteurs. Like their fellow Treasury agents, the Coast Guard Intelligence investigators are trained in the arts of detection at the Treasury Law Enforcement Officer Training School. Unlike the other Treasury agents, these investigators are drawn from the enlisted ranks of a military organization—the Coast Guard.

The dual role of the Coast Guard and its predecessors—the Revenue Marine of Hamilton's day and the later Revenue Cutter Service—was first spelled out by Congress in 1799 when French privateers were preying on American shipping. Congress ordained that the "revenue cutters shall, whenever the President of the United States shall so direct, cooperate with the Navy of the United States."

The President has so directed every time the nation has gone to war. The rest of the time, the Coast Guard has performed much the same functions that Alexander Hamilton visualized when he acquired the first ten cutters.

Hamilton wanted his little fleet to break the smuggling pattern of the colonial era. In those days, it had been counted a patriotic duty to evade the duties imposed by the British Parliament on goods shipped to the colonies. Now that the duties were needed to finance the new nation, it was the job of the cutters to make sure ships reaching these shores paid their way.

A century and a half later, a different breed of smugglers not only brought expansion to the Coast Guard but spurred the growth of the Intelligence Division which, until then, had consisted of a lone officer on the commandant's staff at Coast Guard headquarters.

The coming of Prohibition had precipitated a deadly war between the Coast Guard and the rum-runners. But the coasts were long and the smugglers' profits large. The pattern of the smugglers was well-known. Large vessels bringing the supply of whiskey from Europe hovered outside the 12-mile limit until speed boats were dispatched from shore to fetch the liquor.

The operation was directed from clandestine shore radio stations, but since the smugglers were aware that the radio messages could be intercepted, they communicated the time and place of rendezvous between speedboats and supply vessels by way of complex codes. Obviously, if the Coast Guard could break the ever-changing codes in a hurry, it could catch up with the liquor-laden speedboats much more effectively than through a blind search of the coast line.

By the spring of 1927, an enormous number of code messages had accumulated on the desk of the one-man intelligence office at Coast Guard headquarters. The secret communications had been intercepted on both the Atlantic and Pacific coasts and the volume was increasing daily. At that point, an expert cryptanalyst, Mrs. Elizabeth Smith Friedman, was brought into the Coast Guard to solve the hundreds of messages on file. Within two months, she had reduced the mass of coded messages from unknown to known. It was then that the Coast Guard decided to launch an intelligence service based on fast translation of whatever secret messages fell into its hands.

Mrs. Friedman, put in charge of the new cryptanalysis section at Coast Guard headquarters, soon discovered the codes used by some of the West Coast rum-runners were more complex than anything devised in World War I when secret methods of communication had reached their previous highest development.

On the Gulf Coast, she found that a Vancouver, British Columbia, company had established a network of smugglers completely surrounding the country.

In 1933, she became the star witness in the case against this Vancouver company, the most powerful liquor smuggling syndicate then in existence. The ring leaders ashore were charged with conspiracy and the Government had to prove their connection with the actual operations of the smuggling vessels. The only way it could be done was to decipher the coded messages to the vessels originating with the company's New Orleans agents. Col. A. W. W. Woodcock, director of the Bureau of Prohibition, who personally tried the case against the conspirators, later wrote the Secretary of the Treasury that he doubted the case would have been won without Mrs. Friedman's testimony on the meaning of the coded messages.

Many of the messages Mrs. Friedman decoded had been intercepted by the Coast Guard Intelligence Office at Mobile. For by now, the Coast Guard was establishing more and more intelligence units in its war on the rum-runners. An intelligence unit was set up in the Coast Guard's New York office in 1930, followed by a "Western Area Intelligence Office" in San Francisco and the one in Mobile. These offices operated radio monitoring units on board the patrol vessels to intercept the radio traffic of the rum-runners.

The work of the intelligence investigators proved so successful in the war against smugglers that the Coast Guard established a unit in Boston in 1934 and finally—in 1936—created an Intelligence Division at Coast Guard Headquarters in Washington. Until World War II, however, no more than 40 persons were assigned to intelligence duties.

Coast Guard Intelligence, now formally provided for in the Coast Guard regulations and organization manual, drew additional duties and manpower with the coming of war. It was responsible for antisabotage and counterespionage on the waterfront as well as security screening of merchant marine personnel and longshoremen. It became involved in the search for the Nazi saboteurs after a Coast Guardsman spotted them wading ashore with their boxes of dynamite on an isolated Long Island beach. It was charged with investigating Coast Guard military and civilian personnel for internal security and breaches of discipline. The Intelligence Division's wartime force grew to 370, of which 160 were investigators.

Its wartime achievements on the home front were in the field of prevention. In World War I, Black Tom Island in New York harbor, major transfer point for supplies shipped to Europe, had been virtually destroyed by dynamite and German saboteurs were busy on a dozen fronts. But during World War II, there was not a single known instance of foreign-inspired sabotage on vessels or waterfront facilities which the Coast Guard was responsible for safeguarding.

Since World War II, the Intelligence Division, reduced to a peacetime force of 70 investigators, has been mainly concerned with port security, keeping subversive elements out of the Merchant Marine and off the waterfronts, enforcing Coast Guard laws and insuring the internal security of the Coast Guard.

One of the newer laws it has been charged with enforcing is the Federal Motorboat Act of 1958, which gives the Coast Guard broader responsibilities for motorboat safety. One of its tougher cases under this act involved a hit-and-run accident on the West Coast where a speedboat ploughed into a small skiff and went on its way, leaving two injured youngsters floundering in the water.

A boat picked up the children shortly after the accident and took them ashore. While doctors fought to save the girl victim's life, investigators questioned her younger brother but he had only a dim recollection of the speedboat running them down and the subsequent rescue. Investigators combed the waterfront in search of possible witnesses and had fragments of the broken skiff examined for paint smears. They finally narrowed their search to the operators of the craft that had rescued the children. The man and wife in the speedboat both stoutly denied they had struck the skiff, but the investigators had collected enough evidence to prove that the speedboat, which appeared to witnesses ashore to be approaching from the opposite direction, had actually only made a wide circle. The skipper of the speedboat was convicted of operating his craft in a reckless and negligent manner to endanger life, limb and property.

While Coast Guard Intelligence investigators also participate if there is any possibility of a criminal violation when persons are killed or injured aboard larger vessels, it is the duty of the Coast Guard's Office of Merchant Marine Safety to investigate marine casualties and acts of incompetence or misconduct by licensed officers and men of the Merchant Marine.

The Office of Merchant Marine Safety, which now has marine inspection units at 49 sea, lake and river ports, was brought into the Coast Guard in 1942 by executive order during the tremendous increase in World War II merchant shipping. It was logical that the Coast Guard, as the government agency already responsible for rescue work and general enforcement of all laws relating to commerce on navigable waters should also be charged with over-all safety at sea.

Congress agreed and in 1946 made the Office of Merchant Marine Safety a permanent part of the Coast Guard.

The Federal government first moved into the area of regulating ships and the men who operate them in 1871, when it created the Steamboat Inspection Service. At that time, steam as a method of propelling ships was in its infancy and explosion of steam boilers as well as collisions were frequent. Mississippi river traffic was then in its heyday, competition was keen and river captains were known to tie down safety valves to get more steam and thus more speed.

The inspectors of the Steamboat Inspection Service were given authority to investigate all acts of incompetence or misconduct by licensed officers. The public took the responsibility of the inspectors so seriously that when the excursion boat *Eastland* capsized in the Chicago River in 1915 with the loss of 812 lives, the inspectors were indicted and brought into the courtroom in handcuffs. (They were later exonerated.)

The Steamboat Inspection Service was attached to various departments as the years passed, but after the *Morro Castle* burned off the coast of New Jersey in 1934, the loss of 125 lives prompted a Congressional investigation. As a result, the Steamboat Inspection Service was abolished, the Bureau of Marine Inspection and Navigation was established in the Commerce Department, and the Secretary of Commerce was authorized to draft comprehensive rules for the investigation of marine casualties and accidents. It was up to the investigators to determine the cause of accidents, the defects that should be corrected and the officers who should be disciplined for their role in the accident.

When the bureau was brought into the Coast Guard during the war, investigating officers as such were mentioned for the first time. Today, they do for the sea traffic what the air safety investigators do for the air lanes—establish the cause of crashes, recommend the cures.

Out of the marine safety investigations have come new laws, new regulations and new treaties.

When the *Andrea Doria* and the *Stockholm* collided off the East Coast in 1956, Congress ordered an extensive investigation, although both were foreign flag vessels outside territorial waters. This investigation prompted the 1960 International Convention for the Safety of Life at Sea to adopt proposed additions to the international rules of the road dealing with the use of radar by vessels navigating through fog.

The Coast Guard's investigation of the 1947 Texas City disaster, when a French ship exploded in the port area and killed more than 500 people, led to stringent regulations covering the transportation of ammonium nitrate fertilizer—a chemical not previously considered explosive.

Another product of the marine safety investigations is the suspension or revocation of licenses for those responsible for marine casualties. Investigation of the collision of the S.S. *Santa Rosa* and the S.S. *Valchem* off the coast of New Jersey of a foggy night in 1959 prompted the Coast Guard to suspend the license of the *Santa Rosa*'s master for 12 months, on grounds of negligence for not slowing down in fog and failing to stop the engines when he heard the fog signal of the *Valchem* nearby. Another 1959 collision in fog—that of the S.S. *Constitution* and the *Jalanta* near New York City—led to a 12-month suspension for the *Constitution*'s master.

In the smaller ports, the investigators of the Office of Merchant Marine Safety have other duties but in the large ports, a senior investigating officer and a staff are assigned full-time to probing marine casualties.

The Coast Guard, then, has two types of investigators—the men of Coast Guard Intelligence as the law enforcement arm and the officers of Merchant Marine Safety whose primary mission is the protection of Americans who go down to the sea in ships.

WHAT HAPPENED TO THE "STEELHEAD"?

The answer to many a mystery lies in the ocean depths. Ships have disappeared without a trace and phantom ships have sailed on without a crew. The sea, most stubborn keeper of secrets, buries the clues along with the victims.

Investigators who look vainly to the sea for their answers finally turn back to the land in search of evidence. Sometimes they find it and sometimes they don't.

This mystery of the sea began with a broadcast on the afternoon of September 28, 1960.

"This is Dave on the *Steelhead*," the voice said. "*Coho II* just shot me. This has been a good life. Goodbye, boys."

A few seconds later, the message was repeated. The voice sounded weaker and the words came more slowly. Then, silence.

Through the fishing grounds off the West Coast, the ships' radios started chattering. All the skippers were trying to contact the *Steelhead*. No response. Then they tried to reach the *Coho II*. Nothing there, either.

Some of the fishing boats hauled in their lines and headed for where they figured the *Steelhead* might be. Some of them recorded the message in their logs. Some of them plotted the course of the *Steelhead* from where they had last seen it.

A housewife fiddling with her ham radio in Seaside, Calif., heard the broadcast and called the Monterey Life Boat Station. The report from Monterey, the messages from the fishing fleet poured into the headquarters of the Twelfth Coast Guard District. There, the headquarters commander alerted his cutters, the air station, the radio stations. All hands were advised to stand by, warm up engines, guard the radio frequency used by the *Steelhead* for its broadcast. Another message might pinpoint the location of the *Steelhead*. There was no other message.

Reports from the fishing vessels conflicted about the probable locations of the *Steelhead* and the *Coho II*, but the Twelfth Coast Guard District Commander couldn't wait. His orders to planes and cutters were stamped "Operation Immediate."

"Proceed to position 180 true 10 miles from Farallons. Attempt contact *Steelhead* and *Coho*. Conduct investigation."

The search was on for the *Steelhead*, a wooden fishing vessel owned and operated by E. A. Davisson of Oakland, Calif., and the *Coho II*, a steel vessel larger and twice as powerful as the *Steelhead*. Its owner-operator was listed as Ted Bean of Bakersfield, Cal.

At 5:42 P.M., a Coast Guard plane reached the last probable location of the *Steelhead*, about 125 miles southwest of San Francisco. The pilot criss-crossed the area until 9 P.M. and saw nothing but the lights of other fishermen, all looking for their friend Dave of the *Steelhead*.

Whatever had happened to the *Steelhead* had been quick and decisive.

At first daylight, the Coast Guard cutter *Active* joined the search while the Coast Guard cutter *Comanche* scanned the seas with radar

50 miles offshore, hoping to intercept the *Coho II* if it headed south. Eighteen hours had now passed since the last message from the *Steelhead.*

At 8:15 A.M. on September 29, a Coast Guard plane spotted the *Coho II* and radioed headquarters. The cutter *Active* was ordered to head for the *Coho II* while the other cutters continued to look for the *Steelhead.*

Bean was alone on his ship when Coast Guard officers from the cutter *Active* came aboard some 90 minutes later. A stocky man with brown hair graying at the sides, Bean stared wonderingly at the Coast Guard officers out of hazel eyes reflecting the gray-green of the sea. He told them he hadn't seen the *Steelhead* since passing mail to Davisson the previous day. The officers found a shotgun and two rifles aboard the *Coho II.* Taking the guns with them they returned to the cutter *Active* and drifted near the *Coho II.* This was a job for the investigators.

In San Francisco, Marine Inspection Officer C. T. Silk and three FBI agents boarded a cutter bound for the *Coho II.* At the same time, the Marine Inspection Office requested the Coast Guard Intelligence agents to launch an investigation. Crime on the high seas was a job for the FBI. The Coast Guard Intelligence agents were assigned to investigate "a marine casualty." From interviews with friends, from the debris which the fishing boats in the area of the *Steelhead's* disappearance collected, the intelligence agents might come up with some evidence.

Already, the fishing boats were beginning to dock with their finds —an eight-foot skiff, a length of white plywood, a hatch cover that looked as though it had been pierced with a bullet. It was becoming increasingly obvious that the *Steelhead* was gone.

At dawn on September 30, Lt. Silk and the three FBI agents boarded the *Coho II.* Bean, his face creased with the lines of weariness, began by flatly denying he had anything to do with the disappearance of the *Steelhead.* He said he was fishing on September 28 when he heard Davisson on the radio saying he was loaded with fish and was now ready to head back to San Francisco.

Bean told the agents he had radioed Davisson and asked for a meeting so Davisson could take a letter from him and mail it to Bean's wife when he reached shore. As near as he could recall, he said, he came upon the *Steelhead* between 10 and 11 A.M. on September 28 and passed the letter to Davisson in a quart bottle which Davisson picked out of the sea. Davisson waved a farewell and turned northeast toward San Francisco.

"And that's the last I saw of him," Bean concluded, "but I've been doing some thinking. The *Steelhead* was completely loaded with fish, even on the deck. It could have been swamped in a heavy sea."

The agents asked Bean about the firearms found aboard the *Coho II.* Bean said he used the rifles to shoot sharks and the shotgun to scare away the seals attracted to the fishing grounds.

"Why didn't you respond to any of the radio messages after Davisson disappeared?" Lt. Silk asked.

"I don't usually listen to the radio while I'm fishing," Bean responded. "I'm alone on the boat and I've got my hands full keeping up with the work without trying to listen to the radio, too. Besides, I'm hard of hearing."

He volunteered to return from the fishing grounds to clear his name. He said he would go to Oakland where his wife was waiting for him.

While Lt. Silk and the FBI agents headed back for San Francisco, the cutter *Active* remained with the *Coho II.* The fishing vessel was to be kept under constant surveillance until the mystery of the *Steelhead* was solved. Late in the afternoon, Bean radioed the cutter *Active* that he was ready to head for Oakland and planned to fish en route. Lt. Jack Leonard Smith, commanding the *Active,* radioed back that he would trail along.

The two ships sailed together until 2.45 A.M. on October 1, when Bean radioed the *Active* that he was so tired he couldn't think straight. He asked permission to shut down his motors and sleep for a few hours. Lt. Smith radioed back that permission was granted, and the fishing vessel and its escort drifted through the rest of the night.

Meanwhile, in San Francisco, the Coast Guard Intelligence investigators had been busy. They had located a long-time friend and associate of the missing skipper of the *Steelhead.* He, too, had heard Davisson's last message and its slow, weak repetition. Earlier on the day of that message, he recalled, Davisson had called his wife by radio telephone to tell her he was heading home with a load of albacore.

The friend impressed the investigators as a rational man of mature judgment. They listened carefully as the friend told them about Davisson's relationship with Bean. He said the two had disagreed bitterly over forming a fisherman's cooperative. Davisson strongly advocated it to protect the fishermen against foreign fishing interests. Bean, said Davisson's friend, opposed the cooperative.

The investigators promptly reported what Davisson's friend had told them. . .

At 7:45 A.M. on October 1, Lt. Smith and others aboard the cutter *Active* saw the skipper of the *Coho II* preparing to get underway again.

It was now full daylight. Despite a slight overcast and a morning haze, visibility was good. A mile away, another fishing boat was silhouetted against the horizon. The sea was calm with only a slight swell as the *Coho II* and its escort picked up speed.

Shortly after 10 A.M., Lt. Smith received new instructions from Coast Guard headquarters at San Francisco.

"*Coho* proceed to San Francisco directly to assist investigating marine casualty. *Coho* will be met off Pier 45."

Lt. Smith, handing the message to his radio operator, wondered what had been learned ashore to intensify interest in Bean and the *Coho II*. "Tell the *Coho* to make for San Francisco, not Oakland," he said.

The *Coho II* and its escort were now ten miles from the Golden Gate Bridge. In a few minutes, the radio operator reported back to his commanding officer. "I can't get a response from the *Coho,* sir."

Lt. Smith nodded, his eyes fixed on the *Coho II*. The fishing vessel had passed the buoys without turning into the main ship channel. It was speeding ahead on an erratic course for the rocky shore off Point Bonita.

"Pull up alongside the *Coho,*" Lt. Smith ordered.

The *Active* sounded its horn and Lt. Smith shouted commands through the loud speaker. The *Coho II* continued to plow ahead toward the rocks.

A speedboat raced over to the *Coho II* and two Coast Guardsmen swung aboard. They found the *Coho II* on automatic pilot, proceeding at full throttle. A cup of lukewarm tea lay on the table in the galley. One shoe had fallen on the deck near the bow.

The fishing boat was deserted. Bean was gone.

The vessel was shipshape. Bean had obviously cleaned up and changed clothes. His shore-going clothes were gone but his watch and money were still stowed away in a cupboard. An orange life jacket was missing.

The Coast Guardsmen searched further, looking for a note. They found nothing. Lt. Smith, composing his message to shore, thought about the sharks he had seen along the way. . . .

A large reception committee had gathered at Yerba Buena Island to await the arrival of the *Coho II*. On the dock were Coast Guard Intelligence officers, Lt. Silk of the Marine Inspection Office, FBI agents and men from the United States Attorney's office. Close to noon, the Coast Guard's Rescue Coordination Center relayed Lt.

Smith's message from the cutter *Active*. Bean, he reported, had abandoned his vessel at sea.

On the dock, the Coast Guard investigators faced a familiar reality. If the sea had claimed the only possible witness, they had to look landward for the answers to their mystery.

The search was already on for the *Coho's* missing owner. Planes still looking for the *Steelhead* were diverted to the hunt for Bean. Cutters sped out to patrol the entire area from the point where Bean was last seen. That had been at 7:45 A.M., when he started his motors. It was now afternoon.

Other cutters concentrated on the Golden Gate's main ship channel and along the shore line. The Marin County sheriff sent out teams to search the shore from the entrance to San Francisco north to Tennessee Cove. San Francisco police covered the shoreline south for three miles. At nightfall, the searchers were called in. No trace of Bean had been found.

The *Coho II* had been brought to dock and investigators swarmed over it. An expended shotgun shell and a rifle shell were found on the deck and sent to the FBI laboratory along with the guns taken earlier from the *Coho II*.

A diver went underwater to examine the hull of the *Coho II*. He found a long scar on the port side and took paint samples. They were shipped off to the laboratory for comparison with paint samples from the debris of the *Steelhead*.

Investigators combed through the pieces of wreckage picked up by the fishing boats. One piece was revealing. It showed a break due to an impact sharp enough to fracture the wood and leave pieces of cork insulation imbedded in it. The debris indicated that the *Steelhead* collided with or was rammed by another vessel on its port quarter in the vicinity of the refrigerated fish hold.

A collision would account for the quick disappearance of the *Steelhead*, but Davisson had used the word "shot." There was that hole in the hatch cover that could have come from a bullet and those shells found on the deck of the *Coho*.

The investigators were aware of another possible interpretation of "shot." Some mariners used the word in referring to a position fix. Was Davisson one of them?

The answer to that could only come from men who knew Davisson. The investigators started canvassing the docks to find out all they could learn about Davisson and Bean. What the sea wouldn't reveal maybe the fishermen could.

A friend of Davisson was sure the *Steelhead's* skipper didn't mean the *Coho II* was fixing his position, locating his whereabouts, when Davisson broadcast his last message. Davisson meant a weapon, the friend insisted.

The investigators followed up their first lead—the hint of a rift between Bean and Davisson. One fisherman told them Bean and Davisson could have become embroiled in an argument over the fisherman's cooperative. He said Bean had been a changed man since his son fell over the side and was drowned while the *Coho* was berthed at San Diego a few years back.

It was only an opinion and investigators collected the opposite opinion from other fishermen. A friend of Bean said he had not been active in the various cooperatives but had abided by the opinions of the majority. Bean's friend recalled that when the albacore fishermen decided to strike against the canneries during the summer, Bean had brought his ship into port at the request of the other fishermen.

A representative of the newly formed Fisherman's Cooperative Association told investigators that both Davisson and Bean were members and there was no reason for them to quarrel.

The Coast Guard Intelligence investigators were beginning to piece together a picture of the two men out of the conflicting fragments of fact and opinion.

Davisson was the older of the two. At 53, he was regarded as an expert seaman, popular with the fishermen for his organizing efforts in their behalf, a devoted family man. Bean, 42-years-old when he disappeared, was described as a quiet man, sober, industrious, not one to associate much with the other fishermen, also dedicated to his family.

The fishermen all had theories to present to the investigators. One confirmed Bean's statement that he was a little hard of hearing. The fisherman said Bean had been a welder during the war and had been somewhat deafened by the welding machinery. Straying into theory, the fisherman suggested that an experienced welder could make a bomb by using acetylene in a closed container and causing it to explode with an electric spark. The fisherman pointed out that the *Coho II* carried a gas welding ring.

Another fisherman insisted that the only way the *Steelhead* could have disappeared so fast was by some well-placed bullet holes along the waterline or by ramming. The fisherman noted that the steel hull of the *Coho II* could have cut the *Steelhead* in two with no trouble at all.

The *Coho II* definitely had dents in the hull when it was brought into port without its skipper. A boat yard owner said the *Coho*'s hull had been damaged while the ship was towing vessels in early summer but a fisherman said he had been aboard the *Coho II* a month earlier and hadn't noticed any hull damage.

The investigators listened patiently to opinions while they searched for facts. The laboratory technicians would be the last word on the hull damage, the guns, the meaning of the debris. What the investigators sought was some hidden clue in the last known hours of Bean and Davisson.

From a dozen interviews with fishermen who had been at sea when disaster overtook the *Steelhead,* from the logs of some of the skippers, from the time sequence of the Coast Guard search, the investigators tried to piece together a time-table.

About 10:30 A.M. on September 28, a fisherman and his wife told investigators, they had heard a radio conversation between the *Steelhead* and the *Coho.* They remembered Bean saying he had a letter he wanted Davisson to mail to his wife since Davisson was returning to port. Bean, they recalled, asked Davisson for the location of the *Steelhead* so he could rendezvous with him and pass over the letter. That matched Bean's story to Lt. Silk and the FBI agents.

About noon, another fisherman said, Bean told Davisson that he hadn't written the letter yet and the two men talked by radio intermittently until 1 P.M. That didn't match. Bean told Lt. Silk that he had passed the letter to Davisson between 10 A.M. and 11 A.M.

A fisherman who heard the same conversation reported that Bean had said the letter would be ready soon. He described the conversation as "routine, friendly."

At 1 P.M., another fisherman told investigators, Davisson's *Steelhead* passed close to his ship and Davisson waved and said he was heading in. Had the *Coho II* passed the letter and gone on its way? The fisherman had not seen the *Coho II.* Shortly after 3 P.M., all the fishermen reported, they heard the last message from the *Steelhead.* That was all the fishermen could contribute to the time-table for September 28.

On the morning of September 29, the day the *Coho II* was spotted by the Coast Guard plane, a fisherman told investigators, he heard Bean talking to another fishing boat, asking to be filled in on what was going on. Bean, according to the fisherman, didn't sound nervous or excited and claimed to have no knowledge of the *Steelhead's* disappearance.

The rest of that day was clear enough—the officers of the cutter *Active* boarding the *Coho II,* taking custody of the guns and standing by to await the investigators.

On the night of September 30 after Lt. Silk and the FBI agents questioned Bean aboard the *Coho II* and Bean volunteered to return to port, a fisherman recalled that Bean talked with a friend in port, saying he was innocent and asking if his wife was going to meet him.

The Coast Guard message to the cutter *Active* ordering the *Coho II* to dock in San Francisco rather than Oakland came about 10 A.M. on October 1. The message had been transmitted on the Coast Guard frequency, not the frequency which the *Coho* had previously used to send and receive messages. Fishing vessels, however, could tune in on the Coast Guard frequency. Had Bean changed his radio setting and intercepted the message? There was no way of knowing now.

That morning, a fisherman told investigators, the *Coho II* and the cutter *Active* passed within a mile of him on course for the San Francisco lightship. He saw the *Coho II* change course and head for the rocks, saw Coast Guardsmen board the speeding ship. He did not see Bean leave his ship but he was positive that if Bean had used the missing orange life jacket, he would have spotted him.

The investigators had reconstructed the last known hours and come up with exactly nothing.

The investigation had been going on for weeks when a fisherman provided something new. He said when Davisson came on the air with his last message, the fisherman heard what sounded to him like a gunshot. He said he hadn't reported it earlier because no one else had mentioned it. The investigators asked him where he was at the time. He acknowledged he was 100 miles from the scene, but he insisted that he had an excellent receiver aboard his ship.

Fact? Fiction? No one else heard the shot and the other fishermen were much closer to the *Steelhead*. If Davisson's body had been recovered, it might have provided an answer but the sea was keeping its secrets.

The answers provided by the laboratory were no more illuminating. The bow damage on the *Coho II* proved to be dents of long standing. The paint samples taken from the long scar on the port side of the *Coho II* showed no similarity to the paint on the debris of the *Steelhead*.

As for the guns, there was evidence of recent use but accumulated rust and dirt made it impossible to determine just when the guns had been fired, and Bean had told Lt. Silk that he had shot frequently at sharks before the *Steelhead* disappeared. The technicians could not determine when the expended shells found on the deck of the *Coho II* had been fired. The investigators faced another dead-end.

In the investigation of murder, three elements usually dovetail—

motive, means and opportunity. A recently fired gun or the steel hull of a ship could indicate the means. With no ships nearby, the opportunity was there. But what about motive? Was there really a basic disagreement between these two men and even if there was, had the investigators found anything to indicate violence in the nature of either man? Conflicting opinions, yes. Conclusive proof, no.

On February 9, 1961, Lt. Silk as the investigating officer for the Marine Inspection Unit sat down to write his final report. Before him were the records of the scores of interviews conducted by Coast Guard Intelligence agents, the FBI reports, the laboratory findings. His problem: to explain what happened to a ship and two men.

First, the ship. Either it collided with another ship or it was purposely rammed. The debris proved that, but since the technicians had failed to find any evidence that the *Coho II* was involved in a collision, Lt. Silk could only report that an unknown vessel was responsible.

What vessel? A check of the harbors, leads from many sources and records of the Coast Guard all along the West Coast had failed to provide any clue to the identity of the unknown vessel.

Second, Davisson. His final message was puzzling to Lt. Silk. From what the investigators had learned, Davisson had been going to sea for a great many years and was considered a devoted family man. Yet his message failed to ask for assistance, failed to give his position and failed to mention his family. It could be taken to mean an actual shooting, but it was also susceptible to another interpretation—that the *Coho II* had taken a bearing on the *Steelhead*. However the message was interpreted, there was still no evidence to prove what caused Davisson's disappearance. This was another unknown.

And finally, Bean. All of Bean's actions—his change of clothes, his arrangements to unload his fish and meet his wife, the neat appearance of his cabin—indicated that he was preparing to enter port. Lt. Silk thought about the tea cooling in the galley, the shoe lying on the open deck, Bean's own statement that he was too exhausted to think straight. Lt. Silk concluded that while Bean was securing the gear in his dazed state, he fell overboard.

You may not agree with Lt. Silk, but where's the proof for any other conclusion? It could be buried forever in the ocean depths but there's always the chance that the keeper of a boat yard somewhere may remember an unexplained scar on an unknown vessel or that the sea will give up a body with a bullet hole. The unpredictable sea, stubborn adversary though it is, has been known before this to share its secrets with mere man.

9 ★★★

Federal Bureau of Narcotics

A bald, blunt and out-spoken ex-diplomat named Harry J. Anslinger has master-minded this nation's long struggle to put the dope traffickers out of business. (In the summer of 1962 Anslinger announced his retirement. His chief aide, Henry Giordano, replaced him as boss of the Federal Bureau of Narcotics.)

Now past his 70th birthday, he's still Mr. Big in the crusade to dry up the sources of the dream stuff. From an office on Washington's Pennsylvania Avenue, the bureau controls undercover agents from the deserts of Syria to the waterfronts of Marseilles, from San Francisco's Chinatown to New York's Harlem.

The force is small and the bureau keeps it that way. The "prima donnas"—as agents are called—are to be used for the big jobs, smashing the international syndicates and the cross-country conspiracies, routing out the white death before it reaches these shores. Local dope peddlers and addicts, as he sees it, should be the targets of state and city police squads. The bureau will lend manpower and train local agents in the techniques of warring on the narcotics traffic, but he contends the states should have strong enough laws and strict enough judges to deal with local violators. By now, most of them do.

His insistence on bringing only the big-time dope traffickers into the Federal courts makes the record of his agents more significant. With a force of less than 300 agents, the Federal Bureau of Narcotics accounts for less than two per cent of the total of Federal law enforcement officers, but at last count close to 17 per cent of the convicts in Federal prisons had been put there by Federal narcotics agents. Of course, judges and Congress have had considerable to do with the ratio of narcotics violators in the Federal prisons. Thanks to stiff penalties fixed by Congress in 1956 and increasingly stiffer sentences meted out by Federal judges, once a major dope trafficker enters a Federal prison, he stays there a long, long time.

Those harsher sentences have made it tougher for the agents to make their cases. Underworld chieftains still in the narcotics business —and their number is dwindling all the time—have become increasingly cautious in their operations. Even their hirelings shy away from strangers unless they have unimpeachable credentials. But infiltrating the headquarters of the mob is virtually the only way the narcotics agent can build his case against the boss.

Unlike most other law enforcement officers, the Federal narcotics agent doesn't start with a crime or a complainant—no stolen diamonds or counterfeit bills to be traced, no killer to be hunted, no bank robbery to be solved. In the world of narcotics, neither the peddler who sells nor the addict who buys is going to complain and the conspiracy of silence controls. So the agent must penetrate this nether world and live in it until he comes out with a case in his hands.

More often than not, the case develops tentacles stretching across an ocean—at one end, the raw opium dealers, the clandestine heroin factory or the international smugglers; at the other end, the American wholesalers.

One such case was officially called to the attention of President Kennedy by his brother, the Attorney General, in his 1961 year-end report on organized crime. American narcotics agents, working in close collaboration with the Royal Canadian Mounted Police as well as with French and Italian authorities, broke a giant conspiracy which had smuggled $150,000,000 worth of heroin into America over the past ten years. A group of Corsicans manufactured the heroin at a secret laboratory in Southern France. From there, it went to Sicily where it was packaged and hidden in false trunk bottoms to be carried to America, via Canada, by innocent immigrants. Attorney General Kennedy called the New York convictions of 11 defendants "the deepest penetration the Federal government has ever made in the illegal international traffic of drugs."

The international war on the dope traffic, spearheaded from the start by Americans, is a twentieth century phenomenon.

The medical values of narcotics were known as early as 400 B.C. when Hippocrates recommended white poppy juices (opium) for a variety of ills. The unhealthy uses to which narcotics could be put were noticed many centuries later when Spaniards conquering South

America found natives getting hopped-up from chewing coca leaves (cocaine). An eighteenth century Chinese emperor saw what opium smoking was doing to his people and banned it, but the Chinese addicts paid little heed to their Emperor's edict.

In America the arrival of the hypodermic needle just before the Civil War encouraged morphine addiction. Some Civil War veterans who had been given frequent injections to ease the pain of wounds began to rely on the drugs. At the turn of the century drug addiction was spreading, particularly among women and teen-agers.

It was a problem outside the country rather than inside it, however, that prompted the first formal move to do something drastic to curb the use of narcotics. President Theodore Roosevelt was appalled by what he had heard about the ravages of opium smoking in the Philippines, our responsibility since the Spanish-American War. In 1909, he called a conference of nations to talk about the opium problem. The delegates from 13 countries who met at Shanghai's Palace Hotel couldn't commit their governments, but they agreed to urge the gradual suppression of opium smoking, the restriction of morphine to medical needs and the national control of morphine and other opium derivatives. Heroin was one such derivative but the extent of its threat wasn't then recognized.

President Roosevelt wanted the opium traffic controlled by formal treaties, so in 1912 he organized a conference at The Hague. There, the delegates signed the Convention, or treaty, which established narcotics control as a duty under international law. That treaty and its subsequent refinements make it possible today for American agents to work shoulder-to-shoulder with foreign colleagues to stamp out the illicit drug traffic.

To show our good faith to the nations of the world, as well as to cope with increasing drug addiction at home, Congress passed the Harrison Narcotics Act in 1914. Its purpose was to control the narcotics traffic, but since there was nothing specific in the Constitution to deal with this problem, Congress enacted the law under its taxing powers.

Since the law was ostensibly a tax matter, the responsibility for enforcing it was laid at the door of the Treasury's Bureau of Internal Revenue. It was hardly welcomed. Even then, before the days of high-powered syndicates and mobs of smugglers, agents recognized that routing out illegal narcotics was dirty and dangerous work.

When the Bureau of Prohibition was established to enforce the Eighteenth Amendment, narcotics went into the new Treasury bureau along with liquor violations. By that time, tons of morphine were coming into the country, mostly from Northern European factories, and the problem of dope addiction was no longer half a world away. A 1920 medical survey showed one of every 400 Americans was a morphine addict. Drug supplies were being diverted from the channels of commerce into the underworld. An addict could go into a New York hotel and order as much dope as he wanted at $12 an ounce. (Today, the rate is $500 an ounce and he can't just pick up a telephone and order it delivered to his hotel.)

During the lawless Twenties, the Bureau of Prohibition had its hands full with rum-runners, but 50 agents were assigned to concentrate on narcotics—the first specialists in the field. They hadn't been at it long when their problem shifted from the diversion of drugs from manufacturers within the country to smuggling from without. Congress, intent on curbing the flow of drugs from Europe, had passed an import-export law in 1922, allowing the import of only enough opium to supply legitimate medical needs and barring the import of such finished products as morphine and heroin. In 1924 Congress made it clear that no opium could be imported to manufacture heroin —by now recognized as the white killer. What was thus banned became a treasure for the smugglers and an overwhelming problem for Treasury agents already struggling to shut the door against liquor smugglers. The narcotics smugglers were shipping in the forbidden goods in cargo lots, using the gambit of switching boxes in transit.

At that time, Harry J. Anslinger, the American consul at Nassau in the Bahamas, was attracting attention for his gimmick to curb liquor smuggling from Nassau into the United States. He had noticed whiskey ships were clearing Nassau for the high seas and returning empty in a few days. Obviously, they were transferring their cargo at sea or slipping into some hidden cove in the Florida Keys. Through diplomatic negotiations, Anslinger won an agreement that ships leaving Nassau had to specify where they were going and bring back a landing certificate to prove where they had been. Nassau's role as jumping-off port for the liquor smugglers promptly ended, and the Treasury borrowed Anslinger from the State Department to work out similar agreements with Canada, Britain, France and Cuba.

With those diplomatic missions accomplished, Anslinger tried a similar routine on the narcotics traffic. He negotiated treaties with the countries of Northern Europe to require their narcotics manufacturers to produce an American import permit before the stuff could leave home ports. That cut down the cargo lots of narcotics inundating American cities.

Anslinger had come to the Treasury to spend a month. He never left.

About the time of his arrival in Washington in 1925, an international encounter shifted the course of America's war on the dope traffic and catapulted the tough Pennsylvania Dutchman into the job he has held ever since.

Representative Stephen G. Porter of Pennsylvania was sent to Geneva as American delegate to the 1925 narcotics convention. Because the powers wouldn't formalize an agreement to stop the opium monopolies in the Far East, the American Congressman stomped out and resolved to show the world that at least the United States was serious about warring on the dope traffic. Mr. Porter proposed a separate bureau of the Government to deal with narcotics nationally and internationally. With that bureau in business, he figured, the American delegation could recommend to the 1931 narcotics convention that every government should establish a similar enforcement arm. He won on both scores, although it took some doing.

In 1930, Congress established the Bureau of Narcotics within the Treasury Department and in 1931, the foreign powers agreed to match the American set-up with their own special bureaus. Thus was built the national and international framework for combatting the dope traffic as we know it today.

Inevitably, Anslinger was named to command the small force of narcotics specialists and inevitably, he shaped them in his own image —shrewd, fearless, dedicated and unorthodox in their methods.

Although they walk with danger as a constant companion, there's surprisingly little turnover among the Federal narcotics agents. If they survive a year, you can't drive them out of the service with a baseball bat. The force has grown from 100 men to about 300—a conglomerate crew of Americans of Italian descent, Filipinos, Chinese, Arabs, Negroes and even some Cherokee Indians. The Italian-Americans usually look and talk like slick hoods. The Negroes—more in the Narcotics Bureau than anywhere else in Federal law enforcement—can penetrate the underworld without elaborate introductions, because the Harlem crowd can't believe Negroes are employed as Federal agents. The Cherokees shamble through the slums with the emaciated look of addict-peddlers.

Looks alone don't keep these men alive in their wanderings through the underworld. They need endless patience, fast footwork and the ability to lead a double life for as long as two years on a single assignment. When a mob was driven out of New York and shifted its scene of operations to California, an agent drifted into the organization as a cook. For two years, he fed the mobsters fancy Italian fare while they fed him the evidence to knock off the ring. At the end of his stint, he had enough to convict 20 men.

Another agent penetrated the innermost circle of a Chinese tong directing a coast-to-coast narcotics traffic. Once he became a blood brother in the tong, he was given entrée everywhere. With the evidence he collected on his cross-country swing, tong headquarters were raided simultaneously from New York to California and the brotherhood's fangs were drawn.

On occasion, the agents face their biggest ordeal with corrupt local police. In one Southern city, an agent was seized by police as soon as he hit town. He was beaten to find out what he was doing there, but he kept his mouth shut and stayed in jail. Through an intermediary, Anslinger arranged for a defense attorney to extricate him—a lawyer known as a mouthpiece for the mob. The police, figuring the agent had the underworld's blessing, let him alone. A year later, when the agent joined in rounding up the local ring, the desk sergeant who had booked him on the earlier phony charge asked sympathetically: "So they got you, too?"

Most police forces, however, work closely with the Federal narcotics agents at home and overseas. Many of them send their men to the Bureau of Narcotics Training School, established in 1956, and make a practice of maintaining a narcotics squad twice as large as the number of Federal agents operating in their city.

Overseas, the American agents set the traps with their underworld deals and stand aside for the local boys to spring the trap and get the credit. In Syria, a ring led by Mahmoud E. Badawi agreed to deliver a large supply of morphine base to an American undercover agent at a rendezvous in the desert. As the exchange was made in April, 1960, the shooting started and the traffickers fled into the desert. They were rounded up by desert patrols and Damascus authorities were given credit for the biggest case of its kind in their history. That was all right with the Americans. Their goal had been to break up the flow of morphine base to Europe and its ultimate destination—American addicts.

For four months, American agents worked undercover with police of Greece, Lebanon, Turkey and Syria to wipe out one of the major international rings in 1954. The case began when an American narcotics agent penetrated the Beirut headquarters of the gang's chief and got a proposition to buy opium and morphine base, smuggle it into Europe to be converted into heroin and eventually ship the finished product to the United States. The case ended with simultaneous raids throughout the Middle East, a large haul of opium and hashish and the round-up of all the principals of the ring.

The foreign raids are always carefully worked out but sometimes the police get their signals crossed. One time, the American agent was supposed to tip his hat as the signal for the foreign police to move in. He tipped his hat. They politely tipped their hats and the exchange of courtesies frustrated the scheme. Another time, the local chief had set his men to tearing up a street to put them on the scene where the agent was negotiating. They were supposed to rush in when he raised the window shade. Instead, they got so intent on their digging that they didn't look up until the agent hurled a chair out the window.

Agents often follow a circuitous route to reach their main target—the foreign suppliers. From a shivering addict in a Skid Row doorway, the trail led to a peddler, to his wholesaler and finally to Chinese smugglers supplying the whole West Coast. From a trio of Puerto Rican peddlers in New York, the trail led to their supplier, a seaman; to his boss in Connecticut and to the boss' supplier, three notorious brothers in Marseilles. With introductions made in America, an American agent arranged with the Marseilles brothers for a package of heroin to be carried to their New York contact. Simultaneous arrests in New York and Marseilles cleaned up that international combine.

Elements of the Marseilles case illustrate how the Narcotics Bureau uses its "special employees." They aren't called informers. An agent with a hunch that a ring is operating makes buys from small-time peddlers—like the Puerto Ricans in the Marseilles case—until he hits one with the underworld connections he needs. When he makes the arrest for peddling, he attempts to persuade his prisoner to cooperate with him in return for a recommendation of leniency to the prosecutor and the court. If the prisoner agrees to cooperate, he becomes a "special employee" and provides the agent with the necessary introductions to the closed corporation of the narcotics traffickers. The "special employee" remains with the gang and frequently gambles for more than a light sentence or insured protection for his family. Often, his life is at stake and sometimes, he loses the gamble. But sometimes he wins a new life.

The narcotics agents work with only one kind of woman on their long tours of underworld duty—the woman scorned. When the narcotics boss shifts from one mistress to another, his rejected paramour may seek vengeance by telling all she knows to a narcotics agent—and frequently she knows plenty.

Anslinger's boys may use unorthodox methods—like playing "The Last Time I Saw Paris" in a prison cell to persuade a homesick Frenchman to talk—but they bend over backward to prevent a frame. Anslinger wants every fact corroborated by a second or even a third witness every step along the way from the source of the narcotics to its ultimate destination. More than once, that insistence on corroboration has foiled someone intent on getting rid of an enemy by planting narcotics and tipping the agents to come and get it.

To Anslinger's way of thinking, the loosely organized syndicates feeding poison for profit have been dominated for decades by the Mafia, an international band of cutthroats bound together by blood ties and terror. Anslinger supplied a list of 800 Mafia members to the Kefauver Committee in 1951. He still keeps a leather-bound Mafia list in his office but its numbers have been sharply reduced. More than 300 of them, by his count, have gone to prison. Some are dead. Many of those still at large, he is convinced, have shifted out of narcotics and into other fields—including legitimate business—where their talents are less likely to draw a 15-year prison term.

The ultimate success of the Federal narcotics agents, however, can best be measured in terms of the rate of drug addiction throughout the nation. When the Federal Bureau of Narcotics was established three decades ago, one out of every 1,000 Americans was a dope addict. Today, the rate is less than one in 4,000 Americans and more than 60 per cent of them are concentrated in New York and California.

To aid those states, the Narcotics Bureau has expanded its investigative details on the East and West Coasts. To aid all the states, undercover agents today are leading their dangerous double lives wherever men of evil are plotting to ship the white death into America.

THE SMUGGLING AMBASSADOR

The tip on the dope trafficker started moving westward from Lebanon. It gathered a name in Paris and a sense of immediacy. That's when it wound up on a special desk in New York.

The desk was occupied by Martin Pera, group leader of a 12-man special unit known to agents of the Bureau of Narcotics' New York office as "M Squad." All the narcotics intelligence from Paris, Rome and the Middle East was funnelled to "M Squad."

To Pera, swarthy veteran of many narcotics investigations, the tips from Europe had become almost routine—important-looking, demanding a lot of leg-work from his agents, high hopes and no score.

Somehow, Pera decided, this slice of intelligence had a different flavor. He was fascinated by the odd assortment of possible principals —a prosperous French businessman, an unidentified diplomat, an airline purser. Pera was caught by the sense of urgency conveyed by the narcotics agent in Paris and the undercoverman in Lebanon, who had picked up the original tip from a Middle East dope merchant.

The group leader started the wheels of investigation turning from the only lead he had and went back to studying the slim file of cables. Pieced together, they told this much.

A man named Etienne Tarditi, who masqueraded as a Paris businessman to cover his traffic in narcotics, was arranging to buy morphine base in the Middle East, get it converted into heroin at a clandestine laboratory in France and sell it on the American market. Tarditi didn't plan to carry the stuff himself. His courier might be a Spanish or Portuguese-speaking diplomat.

Tarditi had just returned from a three-day flight to New York, apparently stemming from a rendezvous with a Trans World Airlines purser named Charles Bourbonnais. Tarditi had been vacationing with his mistress at Antibes on the French Riviera when an urgent call from Bourbonnais prompted him to rush to Paris. The New York flight followed.

Those scraps of information had taken the overseas agents three months to collect—and the New York trip was the only tangible clue. Had Tarditi already unloaded his heroin supply? It was possible, the boss of "M Squad" acknowledged, but the flight could have been engineered by Bourbonnais for Tarditi to make his own final arrangements for delivery.

"M Squad's" investigation had to start with the flight. Agent James Hunt spent eight hours poring over the airline records and when he finally called in, his voice sparkled with his find.

"Tarditi arranged to travel with a Mr. Rosal on his return flight to Paris," Hunt reported. "The line had put a code reference beside Rosal's name to show he was to get extreme courtesy. I asked why the special treatment and they dug it out for me. He's a diplomat—Mauricio Rosal, Guatemalan Ambassador to Belgium and the Netherlands."

Could this be Tarditi's dope-carrying diplomat? Pera of "M Squad" was aware that it was ticklish business, getting mixed up with international diplomacy, but he knew his fellow agents in the Bureau of Customs were also digging and might come up with something solid. They did.

Customs Agent Mario Couzzi searched through old customs records and discovered that back in 1941, while Rosal was married to the daughter of the President of Honduras, he had represented Honduras on diplomatic missions—and had been caught smuggling essential oils valued at $48,000 as well as $37,000 worth of diamonds. Rosal had managed to extricate himself from that one and the earlier smuggling venture never became generally known. So Rosal was no stranger to smuggling and, more checking developed, he spoke Portuguese as well as Spanish.

With the diplomat of the tip from Lebanon tentatively identified, "M Squad" shifted its attention to Charles Bourbonnais, the airline purser whose call was urgent enough to draw Tarditi away from his Riviera idyll.

Agent Armando Muglia, focusing on Bourbonnais, found he apparently had no regular source of income aside from his airline salary, but he owned a $60,000 home in an exclusive section of Long Island and drove a Lincoln.

On Bourbonnais' next arrival in New York, narcotics agents trailed him from Idlewild Airport to an apartment in Jamaica. The idea was to learn the pattern of his movements, but the agents learned something else.

"He's hinky," commented Muglia.

That meant Bourbonnais acted like a man who thought he might be followed. The agents stayed two cars back and to the side of the Lincoln where Bourbonnais couldn't spot them through his rear view or side mirror. Nevertheless, their target kept ducking into side streets instead of taking a direct course.

Agents in New York and overseas were collecting more information about Tarditi, too. On his latest New York trip, they found, he had duly declared a sample of electronic equipment and stated that he hoped to sell the product in the United States. He appeared to be just another affluent businessman. Except for one thing. Agent Andrew Tartaglino, Paris representative of the Bureau of Narcotics, learned that Tarditi had once served a prison term and still had at least one associate with underworld connections.

Pera of "M Squad" was beginning to believe the tip from Lebanon could lead to something big, but there was nothing to do now but wait for the next move. Nothing to do, that is, but check on Bourbonnais' future schedule, find out where Tarditi and Rosal had stayed on previous New York visits, clear with the State Department on Rosal's diplomatic status and keep the customs agents up-to-date on developments.

On September 3, 1960—less than three weeks after Tarditi's latest New York trip—Tartaglino cabled from Paris:

"E.T. (Tarditi) proceeding to Brussels Friday afternoon to meet M.R. (Rosal). French letting go through. Have nothing definite but suspect they make take off together or separately for New York. Suggest alert and surveillance and, if pass made, suspects be knocked off."

Pera took the cable to his boss, George H. Gaffney, the tense and energetic supervisor of the New York office.

"I'll need more men," Pera said bluntly.

He got what he wanted, his pick of the office. With two days to make all his preparations, he called together his team and a crew of customs agents.

"Figure on working the whole weekend," Pera began briskly.

Then he ticked off the assignments. Teams to get the suspects through the airport, teams to follow them to their hotels, teams to install listening equipment in hotel rooms next to the suspects. The listeners had to be able to understand French. Tarditi was a Frenchman and Rosal, as a multi-lingual diplomat, would surely talk to him in French.

Since the agents didn't know where Rosal and Tarditi would stay this time, they made reservations at each of the five hotels previously patronized by the two men. Reservations for the suspects, rooms next door for the agents.

It was a lost weekend.

After meeting all the flights from Europe, Pera called his men together. "O.K. It's a bust. Let's go home," he said. Same old story, he thought. Get the men all steamed up and nothing happens.

He found another cable on his desk. "E.T. left Paris for Brussels Friday but will return Paris and leave for New York Oct. 2. Therefore any surveillance initiated can be relaxed."

The agents couldn't relax. If the Paris agent were right this time, they had to account for Rosal and Bourbonnais. Muglia called the hotels where Rosal had stayed previously. He hit the right one. Rosal had reserved a room at the Hotel Plaza for October 2. Bourbonnais' schedule showed he would make a Paris-New York flight on October 1.

So Tarditi, Bourbonnais and Rosal would all be in New York over the same weekend.

Another Friday night. Another briefing session. Another trip to the hotels to make sure that agents would get rooms next to the suspects. And, finally, a telegram from Assistant Narcotics Commissioner Wayland Speer in Washington about Rosal.

"I have just obtained clearance from State for our proposed operation. The security officer states that as long as M.R. is simply making in and out trips to New York from Europe and is not en route to his country, he has no diplomatic immunity and we may proceed any way we wish . . . In view of this, we may go ahead but should be sure that there is contraband so as not to blow this case . . . When the time comes, you will have to move on your own responsibility."

The stage was set.

At the last moment, the Paris agent cabled that Tarditi would be arriving on Saturday, October 1, not on October 2. He gave the flight number.

On Saturday afternoon, Agent Francis E. Waters, dressed like a New York cabbie, jockeyed the government's undercover taxi to the head of the line at Idlewild International Airport. "When I give the signal," he told the skycap captain, "have the skycap put our man's luggage in my cab."

Inside the sprawling terminal, narcotics and customs agents were lined up in tandem. They didn't know what Tarditi looked like, but from the time he reached the immigration desk, he would never be out of sight of an agent. They would pass him along from agent to agent, each one identifying him for the next.

Martin Pera emerged from the terminal and paused at Waters' taxicab.

"He's through immigration," he reported. "He told the immigration people that he's staying at the Sherry Netherland. I'm on my way."

The group leader stopped to make a call. Agent Anthony S. Pohl was standing by at headquarters to find out where to install his listening devices. "The Sherry Netherland," said Pera. "I'll meet you there."

At 4:15 P.M. Waters, lounging beside his taxi, spotted an agent following a short, barrel-chested, middle-aged man. Tarditi was emerging from the terminal. But he was carrying his own suitcase.

Waters jumped out of his cab and ran toward his quarry.

"I'll help you with that," he said, reaching for the bag. "My cab's right here."

Tarditi followed him to the government cab. "The Sherry Netherland," he said.

"The Sherry Netherland," Waters repeated in a voice loud enough for nearby agents to hear.

Driving slowly enough for the following agents to catch up with him, Waters studied his passenger in the rear view mirror. Custom-made clothes, almost bald, nothing of the hoodlum look about this one.

Suddenly, his passenger leaned forward.

"I've changed my mind," he said in heavily accented English. "Take me to the Savoy Hilton."

The cab was approaching the Queensboro Bridge. Waters glanced desperately at his side view mirror. Yes, the agents were behind him. He had to let them know about the change of plans.

Traffic was coming from all directions as he approached the bridge. With one hand on the wheel and one eye on the traffic, he scribbled a note. Sticking his arm out the window, he pointed down. That ought to alert them. He dropped the note out the cab window.

He saw an agent hop out of the car behind him and grab the bit of paper. He heard the honking of horns protesting the sudden stop on the bridge. Then, the following car moved out to pass him. Waters caught the signal. Slow down. The other car stepped up its speed. There was much to be done.

In a room at the Sherry Netherland, Pera took a telephone call and turned to Pohl, who had just finished installing his listening device.

"It was a beautiful job," Pera said. "You could hear a whisper in the next room. I'm sorry, but you'll have to take it all out. Tarditi is going to the Savoy Hilton. Let's get out of here."

Wordlessly, Pohl started packing up his equipment.

Tarditi had just registered and gone to his room when Pera entered the lobby of the Savoy Hilton. A worried agent came up to meet him.

"They've put him in the wrong room," the agent reported.

The group leader strode up to the reservation desk. "Where did you put Tarditi?" he asked the clerk, who told him.

"Can I get the room next door?"

"I'm sorry," said the clerk. "It's occupied on both sides."

"Well, dammit, get him out of there," Pera stormed. "Tell him anything. Tell him you need the room for sentimental reasons. A Frenchman would buy that."

The clerk, his tranquillity lost in the other man's urgency, reached for the telephone. Tarditi was moved to the room the agents had reserved for him. While Pohl was installing his listening device in the room next door, other agents were trailing Bourbonnais.

This time, a girl rode with him from the airport. Again, he led the agents on a merry-go-round of side streets, but agents keeping vigil in the room next to Tarditi could report that Bourbonnais didn't contact Tarditi that night.

Now for Rosal. A bleary-eyed pack of agents showed up at the airport before the first flight from Europe at dawn the next day. They didn't know what time he would arrive, only that his hotel reservation was for October 2.

At 7 P.M., a customs officer at the counter reserved for diplomats muttered: "He's coming this way."

The watching agents saw a tall, impeccably dressed man in his late forties striding toward the counter. They saw him pause to fit a cigarette into his holder. By pre-arrangement, his four black suitcases moved swiftly through customs but he answered the few questions with the air of an aristocrat among peasants.

Waters edged over to the black suitcases as a skycap loaded them on his wagon. The agent brushed against the wagon. When he turned away, the bottom of each bag bore a tiny penknife scratch. Now, if there were to be any bag-switching, agents would be able to identify these bags as the ones that Rosal had brought into the country with him.

As Rosal strolled toward the exit, the closest agent heard him tell a fellow passenger that he wouldn't be taking a cab into town. He would be met. The agents couldn't use the government cab this time to keep tabs on their target. They could only stay as close to him as they dared at the terminal exit.

Rosal, looking increasingly impatient, had been waiting for forty minutes, when a stationwagon emerged from the thick airport traffic and edged over to the curb. Rosal was gone.

Agent James M. Ceburre's car was closest. As he twisted the car into the single lane of traffic, an airport limousine blocked him. He sideswiped the limousine and kept going. He couldn't lose the stationwagon.

At the turn into the highway, the stationwagon started speeding. So did Ceburre. He glanced once at his speedometer and whistled. At 80 miles an hour, he couldn't use his car radio to alert headquarters. He figured the other agents had stayed at the airport long enough to make sure that Rosal's four black bags were in the stationwagon, but weren't they ever going to catch up with him?

The young agent felt very much alone as he raced through the night. Tarditi had changed hotels en route. Maybe Rosal would too. Maybe the black bags would change hands before Rosal ever went near the hotel. Ceburre wished the stationwagon wouldn't keep changing lanes. He was halfway into Manhattan before he caught the blinking of headlights behind him. The other agents had caught up.

Fifteen minutes after Rosal checked into Room 944 at the Plaza, agents listening in Room 946 heard the telephone ring. A short conversation.

"He's meeting Tarditi in the lobby at 10 P.M.," Pohl reported to Muglia, now manning a liaison post in a room two floors away.

Agents watched the two men greet each other in the lobby, saw them turn to enter an elevator. Another passenger joined them—Ceburre. They were never to be alone.

Pohl started recording the conversation in the room next door. This was what they had waited for—a meeting of the conspirators.

"How is it?" It was Tarditi's voice.

The agents heard a closet door open and shut. They heard Tarditi ask Rosal how much he was paying for his room. The men talked briefly of their flights, what they had had to eat. No mention of the black bags. In five minutes, the door closed behind Tarditi and Rosal was alone.

In the room next door, Pera reviewed the conversation with a growing feeling of certainty. The opening of the closet door might have meant that Rosal was showing the suitcases to Tarditi. Even more important, the conversation was unnatural for two Latins meeting in a foreign land. There was nothing convivial about it. These men were tense.

The group leader called his boss. "I think this is it," he told Gaffney. For the second night, the agents kept their vigil.

Early the next morning, Pohl had something to report to Muglia at the liaison post. "Rosal just made a reservation to go back tomorrow."

Today or nothing.

Gaffney, now in personal charge of the operation, posted agents at every exit from the hotel. Rosal was the man with the black bags. He was the one to watch.

When Rosal went downstairs for breakfast, Gaffney and Agent Frederick N. Cornetta strolled past Room 944. They knew the door would be open because they had heard the hum of the chambermaid's vacuum cleaner. The black bags were still there.

Cornetta, lingering in the hallway near Rosal's room, heard the elevator door opening and backed around a corner. He heard Tarditi asking for Rosal, heard the maid say Rosal wasn't in.

The agent rode down with Tarditi and, a few minutes later, rode up with Rosal. The agents heard the maid tell Rosal he had just missed a visitor. They heard Rosal call the Savoy Hilton and leave a message for Tarditi. He would be waiting in his room.

The agents could hear Rosal pacing the floor. He sounded edgy. "He could have telephoned," they heard him mutter.

More pacing.

"This stupid guy could let me hear from him."

An hour later, agents in the lobby spotted Tarditi heading for the bank of elevators with a small brown paper bag in his hand.

The agents in Room 946 heard a knock on the door next door, heard Rosal let out a loud "Ah . . ." They caught the sound of a bag being opened, heard money being counted.

"So here you have $26,500," they heard Tarditi say. "You have $16,500 for you, $10,000 for me."

"Very well," said Rosal.

"Now another thing," said Tarditi. "I am going to give you instructions."

In the next room, Pohl was translating the French. He nodded at the other agents. It was coming.

"You will take the suitcases," Tarditi was saying.

"Where to?" Rosal asked.

"I will tell you. They are not going to pick them up here."

"Oh, no?"

"Because, you know, the fellows . . . You will go to the corner of 72nd Street and Lexington Avenue. At 12:30 exactly. I will be standing next to the car. You will stop the taxi. You will take the three suitcases. You will put them in that car. There is somebody that sees you, you do not look at him, he does not look at you."

The agents could hear Rosal's murmured assent as Tarditi went on with his instructions.

"The car is a yellow and orange stationwagon. So now, if by chance, you should see something which would not be normal when you leave here, you would go to Idlewild."

"Oh, there is nothing to fear," said Rosal.

"That I am sure," said Tarditi.

Pohl grabbed the telephone in the room next door. Translating as he talked, he relayed the conversation to Gaffney in the lobby. A dozen narcotics agents, half a dozen customs agents headed for the rendezvous.

Agent Charles J. Leya, Jr., now driving the undercover taxi, began cruising. He spotted Tarditi standing on the corner of 72nd Street and Lexington Avenue. He kept on going until Agent Richard M. Manley hailed him a block away. Then he double-parked where he had a clear view of Tarditi.

The agents saw a man approach Tarditi. So Bourbonnais had turned up.

Tarditi and Bourbonnais waited. In the government taxi, Leya and Manley waited. Around the corner, more agents waited. Rosal was late, but the agents knew he was on his way. Gaffney, with a car full of agents trailing the Rosal taxi from the hotel, reported his progress over the car radio.

At 12:35 P.M., Rosal's taxi reached the corner where Tarditi and Bourbonnais were standing. The agents saw Rosal gesture to the cab driver to open the trunk of his cab. As Tarditi peered into the trunk, the agents got ready to move. This was the moment.

But it wasn't.

The cab driver closed the trunk. Bourbonnais walked away. Tarditi and Rosal got in the back seat of the cab and the driver started off. This wasn't going according to plan—not the plan Tarditi had outlined to Rosal in the hotel room.

Gaffney's car began to follow the cab as it picked up speed. The government taxi stopped for two customs agents and fell in behind the Gaffney car. The agents who had followed Bourbonnais reported over their car radios that Bourbonnais had walked half a block and climbed into a yellow and orange stationwagon driven by an unidentified man. The stationwagon was now heading in the same direction as the Rosal cab on a parallel street.

Now the supervisor had to make his decision. Make the arrests now or risk losing the cars in midtown traffic?

"Close in," said Gaffney.

The Gaffney car blocked the Rosal cab on the right while the government taxi pulled in on the left, forcing the cab to stop. Agents piled out of the cars to put handcuffs on Tarditi and Rosal. Gaffney ordered the cab driver to open up the trunk. If those black bags weren't full of heroin, he had blown the show.

First, a quick glance at the bottom of the bags. Yes, the penknife scratches were there. These were the bags Rosal had brought into the country.

And now to open them.

Gaffney stared at packet after packet of white powder. Heroin.

Rosal looked at the open bags and pointed at his companion.

"They're his," he shouted. "His."

Five blocks away, Agents John R. Griffin and Robert J. Furey in one car and Agent Anthony J. Falanga in the other forced the yellow and orange stationwagon to the curb and arrested the two occupants. Other agents moved in to search the wagon.

At narcotics headquarters, the agents totaled their haul.

In one of the four black bags, the one Rosal planned to carry back to Europe with him, agents found $26,500. This was the money Tarditi had counted in the hotel room—$16,500 for Rosal, $10,000 for Tarditi. Under the front seat of the stationwagon, the agents had found a package. Opened, it revealed more than $41,000. Apparently, this was to be exchanged for the suitcases. In the other three suitcases, the agents counted more than 100 pounds of pure heroin—the largest single seizure in the history of the Bureau of Narcotics. On the American market, by the time the pure heroin was cut and cut again, it would have been worth about $15 million to the American dope traffickers.

The agents questioned the girl they had seen with Bourbonnais, hoping for a lead to the American receivers. She admitted she had met Rosal and Tarditi, but insisted that she thought they were in the tuna fish business. Fearful of becoming a defendant herself, the girl tried to convince Bourbonnais to cooperate with the government agents.

Bourbonnais claimed that his principal role in the conspiracy was to pick up the money paid by the American narcotics syndicate and deliver it to Tarditi's mob in France. The man arrested with Bourbonnais contributed even less. He was Nick Calamaras, late of Sing Sing, the American flunkie who turned over the money to Bourbonnais.

Despite the lack of cooperation, agents followed fragmentary leads to another record haul traced to the same ring—110 pounds of pure heroin cached in a Brooklyn apartment.

On January 11, 1961, the quartet of conspirators—Rosal, Tarditi, Bourbonnais and Calamaras—faced Federal Judge Archie Dawson for sentencing.

"Importing this heroin," observed the judge, "is similar to bringing in suitcases full of tuberculosis germs."

He sentenced Rosal—no longer Guatemalan Ambassador to Belgium and the Netherlands—to 15 years in prison. Calamaras also drew 15 years after the judge noted that he stood mute when he could have identified the American customers. Bourbonnais and Tarditi were each sentenced to serve nine years.

The French *Sûreté*, following the leads developed in the New York round-up, arrested a French stockbroker as financial backer of the ring, a French shirt manufacturer as overseer of the smuggling operation and a Paris underworld figure as contact between the ring and its sources of supply.

The arrests on both sides of the Atlantic brought American narcotics agents and the French *Sûreté* into an even closer alliance. The Middle Eastern dope merchant who launched the Tarditi-Rosal case to get rid of a rival knows just how well the French and American agents are working together.

He's out of business.

10 ★★★

Food and Drug Administration

He may be found posing as a truck driver in the market for "pep pills" or picking his way through the rubble left by a hurricane or racing to find a lethal bottle of medicine before a dose is taken or tracking down a ring bootlegging rotten eggs. He wears a badge but he doesn't carry a gun. He's an inspector for the Food and Drug Administration.

He and his fellow inspectors provide the clues for FDA's other investigators—its "chemical detectives." Working in the laboratories, using all the tools of modern science, these scientists isolate the impure, the counterfeit, the unsafe.

Together, the inspectors in the field and the scientists in the laboratories work to make sure that America's foods are the most wholesome, America's drugs the safest and most effective, America's cosmetics the best in the world.

Their quarries among men are the health quacks, the corner-cutting producers, the food and drug racketeers. Their targets in nature are the bugs and rodents, the chemicals combining to form poison, every element that can create impurity of what was once pure.

Their weapons in the field range from walkie-talkies and binoculars on a surveillance job to ultraviolet light for detecting poisonous chemicals and, sometimes, even geiger counters to check for radiation in food from atomic fallout. In the laboratories, they are constantly devising new ways to detect a fraction of a part per million of a poisonous substance, to prove adulteration or to identify a counterfeit drug.

What they started with more than half a century ago was no more than a shopping bag for the inspectors and only enough scientific know-how to test the most brazen forms of food adulteration. But that was before the days of antibiotics and penicillin, of frozen foods and insecticides, of eye make-up and stay-awake pills.

At the turn of the century, the nation's consumers faced a different set of problems. The preparation of food was moving out of the family kitchen and the village store into factories. Each food processor was a law unto himself. He could put what he chose into his wares and say what he pleased on the label—guided only by his conscience and competition.

Few food processors knew or cared about keeping their factories clean and commercial refrigeration was in its infancy. Many of the manufacturers, neither chemists nor bacteriologists, had no qualms about adding preservatives of unknown toxic effects to keep their food from spoiling.

As for medicine, the soothing sirups for infants were loaded with morphine and opium, women's tonics depended on alcohol for their bracing effects and people were becoming narcotics addicts from innocent-appearing patent medicines.

Most states had some form of pure food law, beginning with Massachusetts in 1784, but the state laws lacked uniformity. What one state banned, another approved. The first Federal food and drug bill was introduced in Congress in 1879, and more than a hundred similar measures went into the Congressional hopper in succeeding decades, but the legislators were unwilling to do more than ban the importation of adulterated food and require inspection of animals for disease before slaughter.

Congress wasn't doing enough and the housewives of America—voteless but not voiceless—were becoming alarmed. Enough of them had grown up in the days when all food was processed at home to recognize the taste, odor and appearance of pure food. They knew that what they were now feeding their children wasn't the same as they had been fed—and it worried them.

Their champion was a raw-boned crusader named Dr. Harvey W. Wiley, who had come from Indiana in 1883 to be chief chemist of the Department of Agriculture. He talked, he wrote and he demonstrated the health menaces inherent in the food of the day. His most effective demonstration was his "poison squad," a group of young chemists who volunteered to be guinea pigs in a year-long experiment.

They ate nothing but food prepared with measured doses of the chemicals then prevalent in processed food—formaldehyde, benzoate of soda, boric acid and salicylates. Dr. Wiley became popularly known as "Old Borax," but those who read newspaper reports on the fare of the "poison squad" were getting daily reminders of what they themselves were consuming.

Food manufacturers and medicine men were loath to give up the laissez-faire pattern of the past and the opposition to Federal control was bitter. Nevertheless, Congress finally responded to the demands of an aroused public. On June 30, 1906, President Theodore Roosevelt, who had fought valiantly himself for more consumer protection, signed the first Federal Food and Drugs Act.

Exactly a year later, after the Agriculture Department's Bureau of Chemistry had raced to devise new chemical and microscopic methods for testing food samples, the first food and drug inspectors were assembled in Washington. There were 28 of them—28 pioneers who had to learn in a hurry how to enforce the new law. One of these recruits was later to become commissioner of the Food and Drug Administration.

The concept of the inspector's duties at that time ranged from snatching samples of suspect products to super-sleuthing. For training purposes, each of the new inspectors was provided with a net shopping bag of the kind then in vogue with housewives. They were lined up two-by-two and marched across Washington's Mall to go on their first mission. What they were to buy as samples was left to their own discretion, but the exercise was presumably to give them experience in collecting records of interstate food shipments.

To test their resourcefulness, one of the officials privately asked his neighborhood grocer to refuse to let an inspector see his interstate records. When the young inspector showed up, the grocer firmly denied him access to the records. The inspector departed, apparently baffled, but behind the store he located a couple of lively boys and —for a modest outlay—induced them to stage a fight. When the store clerks went out the back door to witness the melee, the inspector came in the front door and calmly copied the records.

In the years that followed, the inspectors spread out across the country to the mills, the farms, the factories. They went out in pea-soup fog to supervise the dredging and shucking of oysters. And they started playing their undercover roles.

One of their early undercover assignments broke up a dead horse meat racket then flourishing in New York. A concern on the Hackensack meadows was collecting dead horses from the streets, ostensibly to be used for manufacturing fertilizer, actually to be shipped abroad for human consumption. To get the evidence, the inspectors let their beards grow, dressed in shabby clothes and loitered as scavengers on a nearby dump or infiltrated the plant as employees. Their play-acting was so successful that one of them was promoted to driver of the dead horse van. The factory's proprietors, tipped by local authorities that the Federal men were moving in, departed in the night and the racket was stopped for good.

While the inspectors were roaming the country, sampling and seizing, industry was learning to live with the new law. Labels had to be changed to let the housewives know exactly what preservatives were put into the canned goods. Almost immediately, the housewives stopped buying foods labelled with chemical preservatives they suspected would do them no good. The Bureau of Chemistry sent out its inspectors and scientists to show the processors how food could be preserved without chemicals by using adequate sanitation, refrigeration and the right raw materials. The processors who adopted the new methods prospered, and their competitors fell into line, preferring to abandon dubious preservatives rather than declare them on the labels.

The next quarter century, however, brought a new development —the package age. Crackers moved out of the barrel into sealed cartons. Delicatessen came off the tray into jars and cans. Food was thus better protected against contamination but was now concealed from the housewife. No longer could she look and sniff and pinch to satisfy herself of purity. The labels had to tell her more.

Other protections were needed, too—official standards or "recipes" defining the composition of basic food products, compulsory sanitary inspection of factories, heavier penalties for illegal producers, a ban on inherent poisons in food as well as added ones. The drug field also required stronger safety controls as new medicines began to appear and there was still no Federal law controlling therapeutic devices and cosmetics, despite the potential for disfigurement.

In other words, the inspectors in the field and the chemists in the laboratory were finding dangers they had no authority to control. In some places, particularly the rugged West, inspectors were driven out of orchards at the point of a gun when they tried to persuade farmers to be careful about spraying arsenic on their apples. Progress and man's endless ingenuity for both good and bad had outstripped the pioneer law. Court decisions narrowing the authority of the inspectors had also pinpointed the law's weaknesses.

By now, enforcing the food and drug law had moved out of the

Bureau of Chemistry into a separate law enforcement agency still within the Agriculture Department. The agency's chief, Walter A. Campbell, had been one of the recruits in Dr. Wiley's original force of inspectors and the first chief inspector. On Campbell fell the job of convincing Congress and the nation that the 1906 law no longer offered the protections they needed. President Franklin D. Roosevelt lent his voice to the campaign and every inspector became a missionary for new law. Like Dr. Wiley with his "poison squad," Campbell demonstrated loopholes in the law with a "chamber of horrors"—the more shocking examples of deceptive and dangerous products out of the reach of the inspectors under the old law.

A catastrophe sent one inspector on a race against death and jolted Congress into action.

A small Southern plant had hit upon the idea of putting out the then new miracle drug—sulfanilamide—in liquid form. The plant's chief chemist found the drug would not dissolve in most liquids used for medicine-making, but would form a stable solution with a glycerine-like compound which had recently become available. The experimenter tested his liquid medicine for appearance, flavor and fragrance. He neglected to test it for safety and was unaware that the solvent—a chemical offspring of radiator anti-freeze—was poisonous.

His brain-child, "elixir sulfanilamide," went on the market in September, 1937, and orders poured in from all over the country as nearly 200 salesmen spread the word. On October 11, the American Medical Association received two telegrams from physicians in Tulsa, Okla., reporting six deaths and demanding to know the ingredients of the elixir.

Commissioner Campbell mobilized his entire force for a round-the-clock search for every bottle of the liquid poison. Most of it had been dispensed on doctor's prescription, which meant examining thousands of slips for the names of recipients. Sometimes, the druggist had kept no record of the sales and couldn't remember the customers. Since the drug was also used to combat gonorrhea, some potential victims were loath to admit they had bought it. A woman in East St. Louis first said she had torn up the prescription, but under further questioning, admitted she had tossed the bottle out the window. The inspector found it undamaged on the street below—its pink, sweet-tasting liquid a temptation to any child. In South Carolina, the sister of an "elixir" victim told the inspector she had laid the bottle of medicine on her brother's grave in accord with an ancient custom. On the fresh earth of the grave, the inspector found the remaining "elixir."

It was raining in Georgia when an ill and elderly inspector launched his race against death. His mission was to recover one pint bottle of the stuff traced to a small drugstore. When the druggist handed over the bottle, four ounces of the liquid were gone. A doctor had prescribed it, the druggist said, and a woman had picked it up, but he didn't know her name.

The inspector waited for the doctor to return from his country rounds and got the woman's name but not her address. By questioning villagers, he found she might belong to a family living in the next valley, eight miles over the ridge. With a guide, the inspector went over the ridge—only to find the house uninhabited and the family gone. The inspector was now becoming desperate. Each passing moment brought death closer to the woman with the four ounces of elixir. He canvassed the valley through the night until he found someone who thought the family had moved over the next ridge.

And there he found the woman, still alive. She had been so busy moving that she hadn't had time to take the "elixir." At first, she couldn't remember what she had done with it, but a search turned it up in a paper poke under the bed. She was saved from the death that had already come to 107 men, women and children.

The "elixir" disaster not only awakened Congress but was also responsible for a vital section of the new law—a ban on marketing any new drug product until the manufacturer had convinced the Food and Drug Administration of the drug's safety.

In 1938, five years after FDA started plugging for a new law but, only eight months after the "elixir" deaths, President Roosevelt signed into law the Food, Drug and Cosmetic Act, which is today's cornerstone of protection for the health of American families. It came not a minute too soon. The great majority of medicines prescribed today have come on the market since the 1938 law.

The inspectors and scientists, working in tandem to enforce the broad sweep of the new law, soon found themselves under other auspices. In 1940, FDA moved from the Agriculture Department to the Federal Security Agency and its successor, the Department of Health, Education and Welfare. Operating under the new law, the inspectors had new tools of enforcement to go after mislabelled foods, unclean factories, unsafe cosmetics, medical quackery and the food and drug racketeers putting spurious products on the market.

It took their brothers in the laboratory, however, to break a racket worth millions to the racketeers—the olive-oil swindle. Since many people are willing to pay premium prices for olive oil and the spread between the imported product and the cheap vegetable oils is broad, the get-rich-quick operators are attracted to this business.

When World War II shut off imports, the prices of olive oil zoomed. The crooks, aware that FDA's chemical detectives couldn't analyze the percentage of olive oil below 20 per cent, labelled their product as a blend of other oils with 20 per cent olive oil. They left out the olive oil entirely but FDA couldn't prove it.

After years of research, Dr. Jacob Fitelson, the chief food chemist of FDA's New York district, hit upon an element found in many oils but more prominent in olive oil—squalene. The test was effective enough to prove what the racketeers were doing and the racket was broken, but the FDA had been forced to tip its hand. From court airings of the squalene test, the racketeers now knew the criterion was the amount of squalene in the blends.

The racketeers counterattacked. FDA chemists in New York began noticing something queer about the samples of olive oil blends coming into the laboratories and housewives were complaining. The oils lacked the flavor they should have had, but they met the squalene test, and the FDA chemists were helpless.

But not for long. Dr. Fitelson began all over again. Convinced that the racketeers were now putting squalene into their spurious olive oil, he traced their squalene to its source and developed a method of marking it with a dye so effective that one part dye could be traced in 10,000,000 parts of oil. The olive oil packers who had been terrorized by the racketeers into using the squalene were afraid to talk but, when the case came to court, Dr. Fitelson's dye tests talked for them. The olive oil swindlers were convicted and a racket smashed that had cost the public close to a million dollars.

The olive oil racket involved economic cheating. Another type of investigation by the FDA sleuths involved life itself and one of the cruelest hoaxes ever perpetrated on the American people. Harry M. Hoxsey, an ex-coal miner with an eighth grade education, claimed his medication could cure all forms of cancer without surgery or radiation therapy. Patients flocked to his cancer clinics and his take amounted to over a million dollars a year.

FDA inspectors spent a year establishing the worthlessness of the Hoxsey treatment. They travelled 18,000 miles, interviewed hundreds of patients and families of victims, consulted countless physicians and reviewed piles of hospital records.

They no sooner won their first court battle against Hoxsey in the Court of Appeals than another Hoxsey clinic cropped up in another state and they had to go through it all over again—this time against such odds as Hoxsey-coached victims and a local mob of hecklers who protested any interference with the town's prime attraction.

Then, a doctor picked up the Hoxsey treatment and used one of Hoxsey's old clinics to promote it. In September, 1960, after ten years of continuous investigation and almost constant battling through the courts, the Food and Drug Administration finally won its crusade against the Hoxsey treatment. By court order, the doctor was forced to notify more than 10,000 patients that the treatment was no longer available. By that time, it was estimated that cancer patients had spent over $50 million for the worthless Hoxsey treatment. And many of those who died would have lived if they had been treated properly before the cancer spread.

The food and drug inspectors operate on a priority system, because they have so much ground to cover with a limited force, and violations endangering public health rate top priority. One danger to public health came into sharp focus before dawn on December 20, 1959, when a cattle-loaded truck crashed head-on into a passenger bus outside Tucson, Arizona, killing nine persons and injuring 31 others. The truck driver, it developed, was under the influence of amphetamine drugs—the so-called "pep pills," "bennies" or "co-pilots." Medical and driving safety experts agreed then and in many other cases that a driver who uses amphetamines to stay awake may swerve off the road because he sees a traffic hazard that isn't there or drive into the path of an oncoming vehicle because he doesn't see it.

Food and Drug Commissioner George P. Larrick launched a crackdown against the illegal sale of "bennies" that's still going on. This is one of the most profitable of the drug rackets because they can be bought wholesale for as little as $2 a thousand tablets and sell retail for as much as $1 a dozen. Because truck drivers who try to stay awake on long hauls are the most frequent users, food and drug inspectors usually pose as truck drivers when they go undercover to track down the source of supply. On these missions, they come in direct contact with the underworld and sometimes they have to pay for it. One was blackjacked and suffered a fractured skull. Another was held at gunpoint for hours. Operating undercover, an inspector was offered the job of lookout man for a bandit who bought "bennies" in wholesale lots with the proceeds of his robberies.

The dangers faced by the inspectors have become so acute that successive Secretaries of Health, Education and Welfare have urged Congress to make it a Federal crime to assault or kill an FDA man on the job. That deterrent law already applies to Federal judges and many of the government's law men.

The inspectors also clash regularly with the underworld when they go after another priority program of FDA—the form of economic cheating and health threat known as the incubator reject egg racket. Incubator rejects are eggs removed from hatcheries because they don't hatch. Usually they're in varying stages of decomposition and their shipment for food purposes is illegal. They can be bought from hatcheries at a cost of about seven cents a dozen but by the time they're broken out, frozen and mixed with chemical preservatives, the smell is sufficiently concealed for them to sell to food processors at close to the market price of good eggs.

The profit margin is what attracts the racketeers, who move by night, set up clandestine factories and dummy corporations and deal only in cash.

To get the reject egg racketeers, the inspectors use every modern gadget of detection. In one case, a big-time racketeer was convicted because the inspectors succeeded in marking the crates of reject eggs with invisible writing that showed up only under ultraviolet light. They trailed the reject egg truck through the night from a Maine hatchery to its New Jersey destination, kept it under surveillance, and finally got their man. By the time they closed in, the eggs were in an advanced stage of decomposition, but the invisible marks put on the eggs in Maine showed clearly under ultraviolet light in New Jersey.

Another continuing battle is being waged against the so-called health lecturers and self-styled nutritionists who claim that the American food supply is nutritionally deficient and the only salvation is their product. One of the more brazen of these swindles involved the sale of sea water at $2.50 a pint as a cure for everything from asthma to schizophrenia.

Thousands of "doorbell diagnosticians" are roaming the land. Theirs is the "soft sell." They discuss the family's health problems and wind up by selling a six-month supply of their worthless product. To get them, the inspectors pose as customers, make tape recordings of the spiel and prove in court that the pills peddled by the salesman are misbranded because they fail to give adequate directions for treating the diseases the salesman said they could cure.

The inspectors and the scientists behind them recently knocked off the principals in another kind of racket—the making of counterfeit drugs. Just as the rifling of a gun leaves identifying marks on a bullet discharged from it, the scientists have been able to develop similar "ballistics" tests to identify the punch press of a particular drug manufacturer from the distinctive scratches made on the tablets. This kind of evidence has convicted a counterfeit ring from the manufacturers to the distributors.

The FDA inspectors in the field and laboratory sleuths also have to worry about cure-all gadgets, unsafe cosmetics and unclean factories—still the biggest job in terms of manpower used and cases made. They have to make sure that dangerous drugs are sold only on prescription; that hazardous household chemicals are well enough labelled to warn mothers against leaving them where Junior can take a poisonous drink; that only safe amounts of food additives, color and pesticide residue are present in food, that housewives are not gypped by short weights and unreadable measurements on labels. They also have to monitor both domestic and imported foods to determine the level of radioactivity from atomic fallout, and they're usually on the scene in the wake of disaster to make sure that foods and drugs contaminated by wind and water are destroyed.

The Food and Drug Administration's jurisdiction now covers about $110 billion worth of foods, drugs, cosmetics and hazardous household chemicals marketed each year from 105,000 establishments. In addition to checking them as often as they can, the inspectors must make sure that about 400,000 drug stores and public eating places comply with the laws they enforce. And the job continues to grow as atomic tests increase the danger of radioactive contamination, as many new and more toxic agricultural poisons are devised and as more potent lifesaving drugs with their potentiality for harm if misused come on the market.

To carry out its pack of responsibilities, FDA in 1962 had 637 professionally trained inspectors and 725 scientists—the laboratory sleuths who continue to pioneer in scientific crime detection.

Together, the inspector and the scientist do for the housewife what she cannot do for herself. They travel the hundreds of thousands of miles from her home to the factories where so much of the food she serves is now prepared. They make sure the factory is as clean as her own kitchen, that the raw materials from farm and sea are as good as what she would have chosen herself, that the methods of handling and preparing the food meet her standards, that the medicines she gives her family are both safe and effective.

But the FDA men want her to cooperate in their efforts to protect her family. They want her to read the label before she buys and follow the carefully worded directions on the label before she uses what she buys. For Dr. Wiley's slogan at the turn of the century is Commissioner Larrick's policy today:

"Tell the truth on the label and let the consumers judge for themselves."

THE ORANGE JUICE CONSPIRACY

Food and Drug Inspector Walter B. Moses walked heavily from a Houston courtroom in June, 1959, his shoulders slumped and the sharp words of a Federal judge still echoing in his mind. The gray-haired inspector had spent six months developing evidence that an orange product labelled "Fresh Orange Juice—As Nature Made It—Nothing Added" was substantially adulterated with sugar and water. But the judge refused to stop the juice makers.

The meaning of the adulteration had been explained to the judge by experts. If mothers relied on this product as pure orange juice to provide their babies with the prescribed amount of ascorbic acid and vital minerals, the babies simply weren't getting all they needed.

On the witness stand, Moses had told of his repeated visits to the plant of Cal-Tex Citrus Juice, Inc., of Houston. He said he had made his first inspection in early December, 1958, after competitors reported the Cal-Tex juice was far from pure and a few housewives complained that it didn't taste like real orange juice.

On his first visit, Moses said, he had arrived at the plant late in the afternoon and the work stopped immediately. He was told all the oranges had been squeezed for that day. While he was there, he took samples at the tank where the oranges were first squeezed and at the end of the line where the finished juice went into milk cartons to be shipped out to three national dairies and smaller concerns serving Texas and Louisiana.

The judge was told what the analysis of the two samples revealed. The juice in its original form showed nearly twice as much ascorbic acid or Vitamin C as the juice that went into the milk cartons. Where the authentic juice showed a 50-50 balance between sucrose and simple sugars, the finished product showed 70 per cent sucrose and 30 per cent simple sugars. The analysis indicated that the juice in the milk cartons was roughly 60 per cent pure orange juice and 40 per cent sugar and water.

The inspector testified that he returned to the plant in January, 1959, and collected more samples, including some of the oranges from which the juice was made. This time, he made his call in the morning but the plant again shut down immediately. The samples and the oranges were analyzed and the results turned out the same way. The orange juice was definitely not "as nature made it."

Moses had picked up the schedule of shipments on his January visit and in February an inspector and a chemist were sent to a Missouri repacking point to check a tank-load of orange juice from Cal-Tex. The chemist ran a quick analysis for Vitamin C (ascorbic acid) and found only half the normal content. With that, a Federal judge in Missouri signed an order to seize the tank truck. Ordinarily, the shipper goes into court to deny the government's charges but in this case, the court was notified that the juice was spoiled and would have to be destroyed. The government's charges were not contested and the case was dropped.

When Moses returned to the plant in March, he figured that Cal-Tex had learned its lesson and he would find pure orange juice. This time, he arrived at 7:20 A.M. He could hear the plant operating but he was asked to wait outside until an official arrived. At 8:15 A.M., the inspector started collecting samples as he had before, but the plant was due for a surprise. He didn't stop at one collection. He took another sample every 45 minutes until the plant ran out of oranges and had to shut down in mid-morning.

The analysis of this collection of samples showed the gradual progression from adulterated to pure orange juice. The inspector's first set of samples analyzed the same way as the juice collected on his two earlier visits—part pure juice, part sugar and water. The last samples showed pure orange juice. Obviously, his presence had forced the management to stop adding sugared water to the juice. That's why the plant went through its supply of oranges so early in the day.

It was on the basis of this analysis that the Food and Drug Administration asked for an injunction to stop Cal-Tex from interstate shipment of orange juice labelled pure, but adulterated with sugar and water.

The judge listened to the story told by Moses and the chemical analysis explained by experts. He also heard Gordon E. Van Liew, president of Cal-Tex; his brother Dell Van Liew, vice president, and Arthur R. Becker, secretary-treasurer, flatly deny that any sugar or water was added to their orange juice.

When all the evidence was in, the judge made his decision. He refused to grant the injunction. Pointing out that the company officials testified that the juice was not adulterated, the judge said no evidence was presented to show they were not believable witnesses.

"I have also heard testimony that there is a variation in the components of orange juice," the judge added. "There is a variation in all growing things, as well as in minerals. I cannot find that the government has presented a clear case here."

That was the comment echoing in Walter Moses' ears as he walked out of the Houston courtroom.

"A miscarriage of justice," Moses muttered to himself, "but I've got to prove it."

Moses, tall, gray-haired and gentle-voiced, looked more like a college professor than a food and drug inspector, but he had progressed in the service from a seafood inspector in 1937 to assistant chief of the New Orleans District in 1945. He had been resident inspector at Houston since 1948.

This was one case he wanted to make, not only because it was happening in his home bailiwick, but also because Cal-Tex was now free to keep on putting sugar and water into the product mothers were buying for their babies as pure juice. Moses was a father himself, with six children of his own.

"We can't find out what they're doing with more factory inspections," Moses reported to Chief Inspector B. L. Eggerton of the New Orleans District. "We've got to prove they're buying large quantities of sugar and that it's in the plant. I haven't found it but it must be there someplace."

The chief inspector of his district agreed to furnish a surveillance team to watch the plant. Less than two weeks after the judge refused to stop Cal-Tex, two inspectors reported to Moses in Houston. One of them was Herschel Howell, tall and gangling with a weatherbeaten face and the look of a country boy. The other was E. Pitt Smith, a red-headed Texan who had been a rodeo rider before he joined the Food and Drug Administration.

Howell's first assignment was to see if he could find an apartment for rent with a clear view of the plant. An hour after Moses sent him out, Howell called in.

"Walt, there's a garage apartment for rent just across the alley looking right into the back of the plant," he reported to Moses, who told him to grab it.

"I told the landlady I was looking over some real estate," Howell chuckled.

On July 7, 1959, Howell and Smith started watching the plant through binoculars so high-powered that they could read the red-lettered names on the shirt pockets of the Cal-Tex employees. While one of the inspectors maintained a continuous watch, the other logged what he dictated. Every time a man or a truck moved across the back yard of the plant, the movement went into the log.

The garage apartment was stifling in July, too hot for sleep. The inspectors would leave as soon as they made sure the plant had shut down for the day. At a nearby tourist camp, they reported nightly to Moses and returned to their posts before dawn every morning. They had their binoculars trained on the plant when the first employees arrived at 4 A.M.

Smith's wife, Hazel, came from New Orleans to spend some time with her husband. A lively girl with sparkling gray eyes, Hazel Smith kept the men supplied with cold drinks and watermelon as they stood watch through the sweltering days.

Around the plant, the activity looked normal at first except that the orange peel, which should have flowed out constantly, emerged from the conveyor in a thin trickle for ten or 15 minutes twice a day.

As they became more familiar with the routine of the plant, the trucks coming and going, the loading and unloading, the coffee break, quitting time, the inspectors noticed two things that seemed out of the ordinary. They saw heavy drums wheeled from a tin shed into the plant and empty drums rolled out. And they began recording employees carrying empty buckets into the back sheds and coming out again with full ones.

"Got good look at bucket contents," Howell dictated from his post at the window, "and it appeared frothy or as a white powder."

Both inspectors suspected what the white powder was but they weren't calling it sugar until they were sure. Before that day was over, they were simply describing it as "white stuff." Ten times, they saw an employee blithely swinging the buckets as he crossed the yard into a back shed. A minute later, he would emerge from the shed stooped under the weight of what he was hauling.

They had been watching the plant for a week when they got their first clue to what was inside the big drums. They read the lettering stencilled on a drum being wheeled into the plant: "Corn syrup." Later the same day, they had more to report to Moses. An unmarked, green paneled truck parked in front of one of the back sheds and Cal-Tex employees started unloading drums. Smith was ready with his camera as the first barrel left the truck. The label was in clear view: "Anheuser-Busch Corn Syrup."

At 11:50 A.M. on July 15, Smith was manning the binoculars when he spotted the green paneled truck drive into the yard and park just out of sight behind the north end of the building. He could see employees working at the back end of the truck, unloading. As they came into view, he yelled to his partner.

"Hey, that's sugar they're taking out of the truck."

The employees were staggering into the tin shed under the weight of 100-pound brown paper sacks. Smith could read the labels: "Hershey's Sugar."

The surveillance team decided Moses would want to know this development in a hurry. The apartment had no telephone so Smith ran two blocks to a drug store.

"That white stuff is sugar," he reported. "We just saw them unload 40 bags of it."

As soon as he hung up the telephone, Moses called for a conference with United States Attorney William Butler and his assistant, Robert C. Maley, Jr. The prosecutors were no longer interested in trying again for an injunction.

"That might stop them," the United States Attorney said, "but what we've got here looks like a possible criminal prosecution for shipping misbranded products in interstate commerce."

That was all right with Moses, still smarting under the judge's words of a month earlier. This time, he was determined, he wouldn't fail but it would take a lot of planning.

Two days after Smith saw the sugar unloaded, he and Moses went before the United States Commissioner. On the basis of their affidavits, the Commissioner granted a search warrant.

Now that Moses knew the sugar was there, he would make another factory inspection. A deputy marshal would accompany him to remove the sugar and corn syrup as evidence. Moses got permission from Washington to seize all the adulterated or misbranded orange juice in the plant on the day of inspection, provided a fast analysis for Vitamin C proved the juice was adulterated. He asked the New Orleans chief inspector to send him two more inspectors and a chemist.

While Moses labored over his timetable, his surveillance team continued to sweat it out in the garage apartment. By now, they were taking movies through the slats in the venetian blinds—movies of men carrying buckets of white stuff, rolling barrels of corn syrup into the plant and loading trucks with as many as 65 empty drums at a time.

On Monday, July 20—exactly one month since the judge had refused to grant the injunction against Cal-Tex—Herschel Howell and the Smiths reached the garage apartment at 4 A.M. to begin their daily surveillance. Hazel Smith's gray eyes glowed with anticipation because Moses had given her a role to play in Operation Cal-Tex. Howell was busy with his binoculars and Smith was taking movies of a plant worker trudging across the yard with two buckets of sugar. Moses was installing Chemist E. C. Deal at a motel with his equipment to run the fast check for Vitamin C.

At 9:45 A.M., Moses and Deputy Marshal Neal Mathews met the two inspectors from New Orleans, Oliver H. McKagen and Donald C. Duncan, at a drug store not far from the Cal-Tex plant. All of them were waiting for Hazel Smith.

A few minutes before 10 A.M., she walked in and slid on a stool at the soda fountain. As she sipped her drink, Moses joined her.

"They're running," she whispered.

"See any sugar from the shed?" Moses asked her.

"Yes, several buckets but very little peel is coming out."

"Are any officials there?"

"We saw Art Becker come in."

Moses nodded and left her. Hazel's mission was accomplished. She had given the signal. As she watched the four men stroll out, she gulped her drink so she could get back to her husband. She didn't want to miss the climax.

At 10:02 A.M., Smith saw the two New Orleans inspectors walk past his window to join Moses and the deputy marshal on the corner. Three minutes later, he heard an alarm sounding at the back of the plant—one single buzz, one double buzz. Smith nodded to Howell.

"They must be at the front door," he said.

They were. When Becker, the secretary-treasurer of Cal-Tex, came to the door, Moses handed him the notice of factory inspection and introduced him to Deputy Marshal Mathews, who handed him the search warrant.

"Okay," said Becker and without another word, dashed into the plant laboratory and shut the door. When he didn't reappear, Moses and the deputy marshal followed him into the laboratory. It was empty. They spotted a bathroom door at the end of the room and the marshal started hammering on that. They heard the toilet flush and Moses wondered what evidence was going down the drain. He suspected what it might be later, but he never could prove it.

As soon as Becker emerged, the inspectors went about their routine according to the Moses timetable. McKagen immediately started taking samples at the juice vats. He had to get them to Chemist Deal at the motel in a hurry for the check on Vitamin C. If that was out of balance, they had their proof of adulteration and could seize all the juice in the plant.

Moses, Duncan and the deputy marshal headed directly for the shed in the rear where the surveillance team had watched the buckets of sugar coming out. They found only cases of glass bottles, but Moses noticed a door in the back and opened it. Across a narrow alley, he saw another shed which he had assumed on earlier visits belonged to the property next door. This time, he entered the shed, a windowless old building without lights. Peering into the gloom, Moses saw nothing but boxes stacked to the ceiling.

From his post in the garage apartment, Smith saw Moses emerge empty handed from the shed.

"Omigod," Smith groaned. "He hasn't found the sugar."

Grimly Moses returned to the back shed. The sugar, he was convinced, had to be in here some place. As he started walking down the narrow aisle between the stacked boxes to the darkest corner, he felt something crunch underfoot. Dropping to his hands and knees, he turned his flashlight on the ground. Then he saw it—a thin line of sugar leading to the solid wall of cardboard cases.

With a shout to the others, Moses started tearing down the cases. He discovered that the stack of boxes was only one row thick. His flashlight, probing the cave he made in the cases, focused on a 60-pound bag of sugar leaning against the back wall.

He pulled down more boxes and walked through the corridor he had created. The whole cache of sugar was there, ten more big bags and a 60-pound drum of corn syrup, all hidden behind the row of cases labeled "Fresh Orange Juice—As Nature Made It—Nothing Added." The rest of the drums of corn syrup Howell and Smith had seen unloaded from the green paneled truck were still missing, but a search of the sheds failed to turn them up.

Up in the apartment, the surveillance team relaxed as the inspectors emerged from the shed with sacks of sugar. Then, Hazel Smith let out a squeal.

"Ooh, look at those orange peels coming out!"

The peel that had trickled only sporadically during the weeks of surveillance was now pouring out in a torrential flood. At last, with inspectors swarming over the plant, the orange juice was being prepared as nature made it.

By now, Gordon Van Liew, the company president, had arrived

and Moses exchanged a few words with him. The inspector told Van Liew he had found the sugar.

"We never denied we had it on the premises," Van Liew coolly responded. "We used it to make an orange drink."

"When did you make orange drink?" Moses asked him.

"On July 18, for a Dallas company," Van Liew said. "I have the order form right here."

Moses looked at the name on the letterhead and asked Van Liew where he had bought the sugar. The company president named a local firm.

Switching to corn syrup, Moses questioned Van Liew about the drum found in the sugar cache.

"We ordered that a long time ago for the orange drinks," Van Liew replied.

Moses thought of the deliveries recorded by the surveillance team in the past week but his face was expressionless as he asked the company president where he had bought the corn syrup.

"It was so long ago I don't remember," Van Liew replied with a shrug.

In the garage apartment, the surveillance team watched McKagen walk across the plant yard and deliberately take out his handkerchief to wipe his brow three times. Pitt Smith acknowledged the gesture by shuffling the venetian blinds overlooking the yard. In the detailed instructions to his crew, Moses had included the exchange of signals to make sure the surveillance team was safely away before the inspection ended. From the way he and the deputy marshal had headed straight for the sheds, somebody might get the idea the plant had been under surveillance and suspect the occupants of the garage apartment. Moses was guarding against an ambush.

As soon as he left the plant, Moses went straight to his chemist to find out if the samples McKagen had collected showed less than the normal Vitamin C content of pure orange juice. With that evidence of adulteration, Moses could seize all the juice in the plant. But Chemist Deal shook his head.

"I found more Vitamin C than in the authentic juice," the chemist reported. "They must be adding it some way."

Moses frowned. He hadn't found any ascorbic acid in his search of the plant.

"I wonder if that's what Becker was flushing down the drain when we came into the laboratory," he said thoughtfully, but he knew he couldn't prove it.

The chemist had a message for the inspector. A Cal-Tex employee had telephoned the Food and Drug office while Moses and the others were still at the plant. He had given his home address.

That night, Moses and Duncan paid a call on the Cal-Tex employee, cautiously parking their government car three blocks from his home. "I'm damn tired of seeing these people live so high off sugar and water," the Cal-Tex man began.

He said the sugar hauled from the local warehouse mentioned by Van Liew was no longer sold directly to Cal-Tex but was bought in the name of Transportation Leasing Inc., headed by Verne C. Madison. It was a new name to Moses and he listened intently as the man went on.

"I'll tell you something else about Madison. When you all arrived, somebody pressed the alarm buzzer and Madison grabbed four of the employees and had them hide the big drums of corn syrup at each end of the workbench in the shed. He covered the whole thing with a canvas and piled tools on it so it would all look like one workbench. That's why you didn't find the big drums, but I tell you Madison really sweated a couple of times when you got close."

When Moses reached the tourist camp where the inspectors were staying, his team was celebrating the end of the surveillance. Moses joined in the shouts of laughter as the dignified McKagen tumbled fully clothed into the swimming pool, but his thoughts were back at Cal-Tex. For the others, the job was done. For him, it was just starting.

He thought of the surveillance log kept by Smith and Howell. First, the orange peel. The peel truck should have been filled three to five times a day to account for all the orange juice being shipped. Yet the log showed the plant operated for 14 hours without filling the peel truck once.

Next, the oranges themselves. If Cal-Tex was putting pure juice into the cartons and tank trucks counted by the surveillance team, at least one and sometimes two truckloads of oranges should have reached the plant every day. Yet the team had seen only two truckloads of oranges delivered in two weeks.

The log was indicative, but Moses wanted conclusive proof of every added element in the Cal-Tex juice before he faced a judge again—water, sugar, Vitamin C and corn syrup.

Moses started with the water. From the sanitary engineers of the Houston water division, he learned that the water serving the Cal-Tex plant came from five wells in the Houston Heights area. A chemical analysis of the water from these wells showed seven-tenths of a part per million of fluoride. Since this was far more fluoride than would be found in pure orange juice, Moses figured the percentage of fluoride in the Cal-Tex product could serve as an exact index to how much water was added.

Miss Helen Barry, a chemical detective in the New Orleans office, ran a fluoride analysis of all the samples collected at the Cal-Tex plant from Moses' first visit in December to the climactic inspection in July. The tests on the July samples—one month after the judge had refused to grant the injunction—showed the product was 80 per cent water. The ratio of fluoride in the July samples was almost as high as the percentage found in Houston water right out of the tap.

With the water content proved, Moses started tracking down the sugar buys. At the warehouse mentioned by Van Liew, Moses found that Cal-Tex had bought about a ton of sugar a day until May, 1959. The sugar record for Cal-Tex stopped there—the obvious reason why Van Liew was willing in July to say where the sugar came from. But, from what the Cal-Tex employee had confided, Moses knew what to look for—and found it. Since May, Transportation Leasing Inc. had bought approximately 74 tons of sugar. The record of sales showed two tons of sugar were bought on the very day the judge refused to grant the injunction.

To establish the link between Cal-Tex and Transportation Leasing Inc., Moses sent to Austin, Texas, for the corporation charters of both firms. As the Cal-Tex employee had said, Verne Madison headed Transportation Leasing Inc., but its officers also included the top command of Cal-Tex—the Van Liew brothers and Arthur Becker.

The source of the corn syrup was the next item on Moses' list. The Cal-Tex informant had said the firm started adding corn syrup to its product after the injunction hearing in June and Moses knew what that meant. When the analysts at the injuction hearing demonstrated that the balance between sucrose and simple sugars was out of whack in the Cal-Tex product, the Cal-Tex people figured they could restore the proper ratio with corn syrup. They obviously didn't know that the Food and Drug Administration's chemical wizards had developed a positive test for the glucose in corn syrup and, once FDA's chemists knew Cal-Tex was using corn syrup, it had another method of showing positively that the orange juice was adulterated. But Moses still had to find the source of the corn syrup to prove how much Cal-Tex was buying.

From Anheuser-Busch—the name the surveillance team had spotted on the big drums—Moses got the name of the Houston wholesaler for the firm's corn syrup. He drew a blank, though, when he asked the wholesaler if any sales had been made to Cal-Tex or Transportation

Leasing Inc. After the manager insisted he had no record of sales to either company, Moses requested a look at the cash sales slips starting from the day of the injunction hearing in June.

He noticed there were no cash sales for more than $10 worth of syrup at a time until June 25 when he found a slip for $58 worth of corn syrup—ten 60-pound drums. The next day, he found a $95 cash sale for two 650-pound drums and from then on the individual buys increased—four of the big drums at a time. On July 20, he observed, a ton of sugar was ordered. Moses was sure he knew now who was making those cash buys. July 20 was the day the marshal carted away all the sugar in the Cal-Tex plant. If Cal-Tex had decided to replace the sugar, it wouldn't return to the warehouse Van Liew had mentioned to Moses.

Looking for some way to tie Cal-Tex to the cash buys, Moses interviewed the clerk who handled the transactions.

"I don't know the name of the firm" the clerk said, "but the driver comes in a green-paneled truck. The first time I sold him $191 worth of syrup, he paid me with two $100 bills. I was afraid they might be counterfeit so I took down the license number of the truck if you want that."

A call to the auto license bureau settled it. The license number recorded by the clerk was listed to Transportation Leasing Inc.

Despite the efforts of Cal-Tex to mask its operations, the persistent inspector now had everything he needed but one element—the Vitamin C.

Moses asked a friend in the wholesale drug industry to put the grapevine to work. Did anybody remember selling large quantities of ascorbic acid (Vitamin C) since June 20? The inspector worked from that date because the absence of Vitamin C had also been developed at the futile injunction hearing.

A clerk had been impressed by the size of recent orders for ascorbic acid and pulled out some invoices to show the inspector. The name on the orders rang a bell with Moses. He had seen it last on the letterhead Van Liew had shown him. Van Liew had said he needed the sugar to fill an order for a Dallas orange drink company and here was the same name again. A notation on some of the invoices put this out of the realm of coincidence. Verne Madison, it was noted, had picked up the ascorbic acid crystals himself.

A check with the Dallas company tied the last knot. The firm reported that Cal-Tex had made only one experimental batch of orange drink for the Dallas producers, thus accounting for the order Van Liew had shown Moses. The firm also indignantly denied that it had authorized Madison to buy ascorbic acid in its name. It knew nothing of the transaction.

On April 7, 1960, the Van Liews, Arthur Becker and Verne Madison were convicted of conspiring to sell close to $750,000 worth of sweetened water in place of pure orange juice over an 18-month period. The jury also found the quartet guilty of shipping adulterated and misbranded orange juice in interstate commerce.

The convictions have been appealed but they weren't the last of the Cal-Tex crowd's troubles.

The Federal judge who presided at the trial recalled that the Cal-Tex officials had flatly denied to another judge that they put sugar and water in their orange juice. He ordered the record of the injunction hearing referred to the grand jury for possible indictment on grounds of perjury. Gordon Van Liew was subsequently convicted of lying under oath about the purity of Cal-Tex orange juice.

Meanwhile, Assistant United States Attorney Maley on his own initiative asked for an injunction to stop Cal-Tex from misbranding its orange juice. He said he had received evidence as late as the second week of the conspiracy trial that Cal-Tex was still shipping juice substantially diluted with sugar and water.

The same judge who had refused to grant the injunction nearly a year earlier was now of a different mind about Cal-Tex. He promptly issued a restraining order and set a date for an injunction hearing. When the day came, the Cal-Tex officials gave up. They agreed to the terms of an injunction barring the shipment of watered and sugared orange juice as the pure thing.

This time, a different Inspector Moses walked out of the Houston courtroom. His stride was jaunty and his face wore a contented smile.

11 ★★★

Alcohol and Tobacco Tax Division, Internal Revenue Service

The men who track down the liquor law violators from the backwoods haunts of the moonshiners to the big city stills of the syndicates meet sudden death more often than any other Federal investigators.

Prohibition is long gone but in the less than three decades since its passing, the Alcohol and Tobacco Tax Division of the Internal Revenue Service has lost more agents than any other branch of Federal law enforcement. Since enforcement of liquor laws moved back to the Treasury Department as a tax matter after repeal, 48 of the Division's agents have lost their lives and 2,061 have been injured in line of duty. Working with the "revenooers," ten state officers and five Federal officers from other agencies have also been killed.

The deaths are not forgotten. It's established policy that no case involving murder or assault on an investigator on duty will be "closed" if the perpetrator of the crime remains at large. A Texas liquor violator wanted for the ambush murder of an agent thought it was safe to come home after 20 years. He was promptly captured and brought to justice by agents of the Alcohol and Tobacco Tax Division.

Agents are not the sole victims of the moonshine traffic. The lead used in soldering makeshift pipes for the stills gets into the whiskey with poisonous results. During a few months of 1960 in North Carolina's Winston-Salem area alone, eight persons were killed and 30 hospitalized from the effects of moonshine whiskey.

These killers are not the quaint characters cartooned as rocking on their front porch while home brew bubbles in the still. Instead, they are shrewd law-breakers whose combined multi-million-dollar business makes them the nation's No. 1 tax cheats.

More than 90 per cent of the liquor law violations are found in 11 Southern states, but their hoodlum counterparts are concentrated in the New York-New Jersey-Pennsylvania area, where well-heeled syndicates set up factory-size whiskey plants to beat the Federal liquor taxes.

Since the Federal tax on every gallon of whiskey now amounts to $10.50, there's both the incentive to cheat and a substantial loss to the government everywhere non-tax-paid liquor flows. Naturally, the loss has to be made up by increasing the bill of honest taxpayers.

Both the tax on liquor and the resentment against it are as old as the country itself—even older. Long before America was colonized, whiskey was being distilled in the peat huts of Ireland and the highlands of Scotland to evade British excise taxes. The Irish and the Scotch brought their trade with them to the new country, where the first saloon opened in Boston in 1625. By 1633, the Massachusetts Bay Colony required a permit to sell liquor and Connecticut followed in 1643. From then on, the production of distilled spirits has been controlled in accordance with the needs of the public welfare and the treasury.

The first internal revenue law, passed in 1791, assessed the distilleries along with producers of snuff. The law was no more popular than any of its successors. In four Pennsylvania counties, farmers united in the "whiskey rebellion" and had to be subdued by a large force of militiamen. Nevertheless, the liquor taxes of the period paid one-third of the Revolutionary War debt.

In 1802, Congress abolished internal revenue taxes but renewed them with more teeth in 1813 to cope with the costs of the War of 1812. With that emergency passed, liquor was again freed of taxes and thus it remained until the Civil War brought on another money crisis.

The Act of July 1, 1862 established the Bureau of Internal Revenue and that time it was here to stay. Some segments of the public protested. In 1869, when Marines tried to destroy illicit distilleries in Brooklyn, they were beaten off by a mob. Of course, in those days, there were no income tax laws to divert the attention of the citizenry to other assaults on the private purse.

Moonshining in the South was only beginning to attract official notice. In 1871, General George Armstrong Custer was assigned to rid Kentucky of moonshiners. His campaign in Kentucky was no more successful than the one he led later against Sitting Bull.

During the half-century before the Prohibition Era, illicit production, however, was considered a relatively minor problem and not widespread, except in the remote mountain areas of the South. Treasury agents of the day, the first to be tagged "revenooers," enforced all excise taxes without specializing on liquor. Large-scale illicit liquor production was still unknown.

With the adoption of the 18th Amendment, the liquor traffic became a crime rather than a tax problem. The most lucrative criminal enterprise the world had ever known prospered in an atmosphere of gang warfare and mushrooming underworld syndicates.

The mobs took over the liquor business which, in 1917, had amounted to over 168,000,000 tax gallons. As a result, by the time Prohibition was repealed on December 5, 1933, a highly-organized, strongly-entrenched illicit liquor traffic was operating full-blast.

And that's what the Treasury got when liquor law again centered on taxes. On May 10, 1934, President Roosevelt abolished the Prohibition era unit in the Justice Department and established the Alcohol Tax Unit within the Bureau of Internal Revenue. For the first time, a force of Treasury agents was to specialize on liquor law violations —beginning with the still-operating criminal syndicates.

Within a few years the Alcohol Tax Unit, in close cooperation with state authorities, stripped the liquor syndicates down to only shreds of their Prohibition era power. Working with other Treasury units on an anti-smuggling detail, the investigators also broke two international rings so elaborate that huge tanks had been installed in New Jersey by one of the rings to store the smuggled alcohol when it arrived. It reached port, all right, and was promptly confiscated by the Federal agents. By 1936, the alcohol smuggling syndicates had been forced to cease operations and by 1938, the volume of mash seized at illicit distilleries—regarded as the best criterion to measure the extent of the non-tax-paid liquor traffic—had leveled off to about seven million gallons annually.

World War II put a sizable dent in illicit liquor production because of sugar rationing and other wartime controls, but when sugar was again available, the moonshiners made up for lost time.

In what is known as the "moonshine belt" across the southeastern states, particularly in the mountain areas, the techniques of illicit liquor-making have been handed down from generation to generation. Low income groups provide a steady demand for cheap spirits, "dry" counties create a market for whatever is available and the public has an avowed tolerance for the moonshiners.

The problem had existed before and during Prohibition. With the end of World War II and with the curtain rung down on the Prohibition Era mobsters, the liquor investigators again tackled the Southern moonshiners. They tried to put the moonshiners out of business by chopping up their stills. They used airplanes and walkie-talkies to expedite their efforts to locate and seize the backwoods plants.

The moonshiners fought back. They created camouflages over their stills as effective as the wartime camouflages over gun emplacements. They set up business in small towns next to fish markets to conceal the odor of fermenting mash. They shot it out with Federal agents, beat them up, left them for dead and used all the tricks in the book to ward off pursuit.

One gang of bootleggers operating on the Virginia-North Carolina border devised a lethal scheme to elude capture when they took the liquor to market. They moved a road marker indicating a sharp curve. When an investigator pursued their high-speed car, they negotiated the curve successfully because they knew where it was. The investigator saw the curve too late and his car plunged off the highway.

As many as six agents were murdered in a single year. One was killed and another mortally wounded by Tennessee moonshiners shooting from ambush. Another agent, after watching a still in operation from his hiding place in nearby bushes, emerged and announced his identity. Without a word, the Florida moonshiner responded by shooting the agent in the stomach. The agent dropped to the ground, but before he died, he managed to empty his pistol into the murderer. Several agents, after stopping their car to ask directions to a suspected plantation in Alabama, noticed a distillery cooker in the yard. When the moonshiner ran into the house and slammed the door, one of the agents came up on the front porch to question the man further. He was greeted by a shot gun blast.

As the toll of dead and injured mounted, as destruction of makeshift stills proved no deterrent to the moonshiners, it became obvious that the more orthodox enforcement methods wouldn't work.

Dwight E. Avis, who had become director of the division in 1951 after directing a successful attack against black market liquor operations during the war, ordered his investigators to zero in on the lifeblood of illicit distilling—sugar. Since the repeal of Prohibition, the agents had consistently traced sales of sugar to liquor law violators but it was evident that merely knowing who was buying the sugar did not prevent its illegal use.

So, retail and wholesale sugar dealers, as well as dealers in containers, were urged to refuse to sell large quantities of sugar or jugs to known or suspected moonshiners. The voluntary co-operation of the dealers, reinforced by a law which allows investigators to demand written reports on sugar sales, has been a potent weapon against the moonshiners.

Where investigators used to find thousands of pounds of sugar around the stills in 100-pound bags, now the usual haul is in 25-pound bags and not much of that. The moonshiners have to travel further to get their sugar, too, thus multiplying their chances of capture. In their frantic search for jugs, they have turned to plastic containers and milk bottles. Since they have to pay more for their supplies, they are forced to charge more for their moonshine, which annoys the customers.

Another phase of the stepped-up program was based on the theory that the fear of imprisonment was a greater deterrent than the mere destruction of the distilling apparatus. So, the investigators were told to concentrate on getting the individuals responsible rather than simply searching out and destroying the stills. That put the investigators directly in the line of fire, and four of them paid with their lives in 1957 alone as the flash of the badge brought a blast from the shotgun, but during 1956, 1957, and 1958 arrests for liquor law violations averaged more than 11,000 a year.

In the round-up of violators, the investigators were told to give the priority to the big operators, the principals in the moonshine conspiracies. What was wanted was quality rather than sheer quantity in the roll of liquor law violators put behind bars.

To carry out the "major violators program," each of the nine regions has a squad of special investigators whose principal task is to ferret out the conspiracies. The other investigators, directed from 36 branch offices, focus on the "caught-in-the-act" violations.

When the intensified program was spread from the "moonshine belt" to the East Coast bootleg plants in 1958, one of the first plants to be knocked off was a three-story factory in Reading, Pa., capable of turning out 4,800 gallons a day. When the raiders arrived on June 7, 1958, the entrance, protected by an electrically-operated buzzer signal system, was so heavily barricaded that the investigators had to chop their way into the plant. Several agents were injured as they tried to pursue four of the operators through a secret exit to the roofs of adjoining buildings.

They had enough evidence, however, to round up their quarry later and to prove that the plant was jointly operated by a strongly entrenched coalition of New Jersey and Pennsylvania mobs. Eleven defendants were finally convicted. The Justice Department, in a 1960 report on organized crime and racketeering, called it the largest liquor conspiracy ever uncovered in the area and estimated the tax loss while it was operating at close to four million dollars.

Two months after the Reading haul, the liquor investigators scored a direct hit on a big-time bootlegger who had been operating for 20 years.

On August 15, 1958, they raided a plant in Long Island City where 30,000 gallons of mash were fermenting. The well-financed manufacturing and distributing syndicate was master-minded by John Levigno, a long-time bootlegger who, according to the Justice Department, had cheated the Government out of more than $4,600,000 in liquor taxes during the 30 months that the huge plant was operating.

Levigno was down but not out. On September 26, 1959, before Levigno was brought to trial in the Long Island City case, the liquor investigators raided another Levigno operation. This time, the syndicate he headed had invested $50,000 to equip a distillery on city-owned property in Brooklyn. The plant consisted of three silo-type concrete coal hoppers on the waterfront equipped with a large electric hoist to bring up the raw materials and lower the finished product. The investment was a total loss to Levigno since the raiders moved in before a single drop of whiskey moved out.

The second Levigno haul came in a record year of enforcement against the big-town operators. Of 11 major distilleries seized during the year by investigators of the New York and Philadelphia regions, four were put out of business before any of their whiskey was marketed and five of the others were knocked off within the first few weeks of operation.

Despite these severe financial setbacks and their effect on the organized traffic in the East, the alcohol investigators have learned recently that several front-men of the bootleg mobs are looking for financial angels to launch new ventures in illicit whiskey production.

If they get the money, the bosses will be available to direct the new operations. The principals behind the large-scale bootleg plants of the recent past drew such slim prison terms that they are about to be released, or are already free.

Getting the big-time operators as well as the moonshine rings requires months of undercover work combined with a network of surveillance. Either an agent or a trusted informant has to be on the inside right up to the raid to be sure the principals are caught in the net.

Before the investigators reach that point, however, they've got to locate the operation. It can be in the middle of a city—even right across the street from police headquarters—or it can be deep in the woods.

The techniques for finding the plant—other than winning the confidence of a member of the ring—range from studying utility bills to looking for fresh tire tracks on unused roads.

Distilleries are often found where least expected, including private residences in fashionable neighborhoods. Investigators sometimes confirm their suspicions by checking on whether recent consumption of water, oil, gas or electricity is considerably higher than in the past. A still could be using the water and heating equipment.

Sometimes, smell alone leads investigators to a still. The odor of fermenting mash is ripe, yeasty, akin to the odor of a decaying sawdust pile or rising bread dough. The odor of coke gas outside industrial areas is another giveaway. Coke is a favorite fuel of moonshiners because it provides intense heat with little smoke.

Investigators tramping through the woods in search of clues to hidden stills always pay special attention to the creeks. Moonshiners who operate close to the streams from which they draw the water for their stills usually dump their spent mash elsewhere in the stream. After a time, the spent mash becomes a thick foam adhering to driftwood or floating in eddies.

Before the investigators move into an area, they check in with the local police wherever possible. They don't want to waste money buying information from the same source as the local agents, and they don't want the locals to move in while a Federal undercover agent is building a major case. John D. Lathem, chief of the enforcement branch, estimates that in two out of three cases, the raids climaxing the investigation are a joint venture of the Federal, state and county officers.

Because of the close working relationship between the Federal liquor law enforcers and the local police, it was inevitable that the responsibility for enforcing the National and Federal Firearms Acts would be assigned to this division in 1941.

The two arms control acts were created under the taxing authority, which put them under Treasury jurisdiction. Their underlying objective was to keep such gangster weapons as machine guns and sawed-off shotguns out of criminal hands. The alcohol tax enforcers, in their day-to-day work with local authorities, trace the guns to add to the charges against the criminals.

For instance, six bandits armed with army carbines, sub-machine guns and revolvers held up a Mississippi club and escaped with $50,000 in loot. Through an inter-state alert, the gangsters were arrested near

Memphis, Tenn. The Federal agents took it from there to develop a firearms case. Seven members of the gang were taken into Federal court on charges of conspiring to violate the National and Federal Firearms Acts. Each of them drew a five-year prison term.

Stoy Decker, boss of the Kentucky Teamsters, ran afoul of the Federal agents when tear gas was used in a pen gun for a brutal attack on a truck diver. The agents test-fired the pen gun using a shotgun shell and proved that the device was a firearm as defined in the National Firearms Act. Both Decker and a fellow Teamster were found guilty on this evidence and sentenced to five years in prison.

The Alcohol Tax Unit acquired another duty—and a new name—in 1951, when policing the tobacco taxes was added to its other chores. It became the Alcohol and Tobacco Tax Division then.

The division's enforcement officers, now numbering approximately 900 men, in recent years broke up a cigarette smuggling syndicate, which manufactured over a million counterfeit name-brand cigarettes, and brought to justice a group trying to supply foreign insurrectionists with firearms stolen from a National Guard Armory. But the largest —and most dangerous—phase of their job is still tracking down the liquor outlaws.

An indirect gauge of their success is the more than $5 billion collected annually on legal alcoholic beverages and tobacco products. A more direct gauge is the virtual elimination of the illicit liquor traffic from four-fifths of the United States and the substantial inroads made against the organized bootleg mobs in the big cities of the east.

The Southern moonshiners continue to be a problem. Perhaps they will always be as long as the public in general and judges in particular fail to recognize that bootlegging breeds crime and corruption today just as surely as it did when the mobs came to power in the lawless Prohibition years.

MAN ON A TIGHTROPE

Special Investigator James Earl West of the Treasury Department's Alcohol and Tobacco Tax Division was built like a bull with courage to match. For six months, he balanced on a tightrope where men killed first and asked questions later—if at all.

When the worst of it was over, the fear began—not for himself but for his wife and two sons. Until the gang was safely behind bars, he wouldn't let his older boy answer the front doorbell for fear a gunman would mistake the son for the father.

He had reason to fear. Two fishermen found the body of a curly-haired youth floating in a canal, handcuffed and chained. The youth had been a member of the gang—the only one besides West who could link the principals in the conspiracy.

The investigator didn't know until later that one of the principals was already twice a murderer at the time West drove into his life with a truckload of contraband whiskey.

West's undercover job began in March, 1958, when the moonshine business was booming in North Florida. This was no small operation. Federal and state agents had seized enough stills, chased down enough whiskey trucks to know a multi-million-dollar racket was involved. They suspected the identity of some of the moonshiners but they couldn't prove it. The stills were deserted when they made their raids and the whiskey truck drivers they captured wouldn't talk.

For two years, the Federal men had kept an eye on the suspected kingpin of the operation—a beefy character named William Raiford Parmenter of Jacksonville, Fla. Once convicted of a liquor law violation, he was too shrewd now to go near a still or a loaded whiskey car. Agents couldn't pin a thing on him and they couldn't trace the moonshine to his middleman—the distributor selling untaxed whiskey along Florida's plush Gold Coast. It was West's job to link Parmenter to the seized stills and the captured drivers, to identify his distributor and to get evidence on all the major moonshiners in the area.

West drove his unmarked government truck into Jacksonville toward the end of March. He needed only a few days to acquire a new identity, a cover story and a friend. When he was ready to go, he had a Florida driver's license and Florida tags, both in the name of James Wesley.

The records of a Jacksonville shipyard had been juggled to show James Wesley had been employed as a welder and laid off.

He found his buddy in William Crawford, a hard-drinking friend of bootleggers whom West had cultivated on a previous excursion in the Florida area. To Crawford, James Wesley was simply a small-timer out to make a fast buck on some whiskey hauls. Crawford was willing to string along for a share of the profits.

From Investigator Warren J. McConnell of the Alcohol and Tobacco Tax Division's Jacksonville office, West collected pictures of the suspected violators. Now he would be able to recognize them at sight. McConnell would be his contact when he needed a transaction witnessed or a truck seized, but McConnell and the agents would come only when called because the moonshiners had the local agents spotted. West had to walk his tightrope alone.

He began walking it in early April. With Crawford providing the introduction, he started travelling the country roads to remote farmhouses. He would buy the untaxed whiskey for his supposed customers, drop off Crawford and drive by devious routes to the garage beside McConnell's home. There, the whiskey would be destroyed and the evidence recorded on another violator.

Each buying trip, West hoped, was getting him closer to Parmenter. Crawford frequently stopped by Parmenter's house for a chat, but he always made West wait outside. Crawford did tell him once that Parmenter was asking how West was doing in his small-time bootlegging.

Methodically, West pushed Crawford into more introductions. Late in April, they paid a call on a long-time moonshiner the Jacksonville investigators tagged "Moss Back" because he had been a known violator for years, but was always too foxy for the law to catch up with him.

"Moss Back" was still foxy. He told West he wouldn't go near his cache for less than 225 gallons of the stuff. When West protested that he didn't have that kind of money, "Moss Back" shrugged and told him he could have what he needed if he found somebody to take the rest. It was the setup West had been angling for.

"Say, maybe your friend Parmenter could use the rest of it," he suggested to Crawford as if the idea had just hit him. Crawford agreed to approach Parmenter.

On May 4 at 1 A.M., West stood beside Crawford at the telephone as the friend of bootleggers triggered the action.

"Bill," said Crawford, "we are ready to go."

The stage was set. Now, if West fell off the tightrope, he would land in Parmenter's lap.

They met at a deserted shopping center near Parmenter's home. At the wheel of the baby-blue Lincoln sat a squat man going bald, with narrow pig eyes and creases of fat bulging his neck. Parmenter motioned Crawford to join him in the Lincoln and brusquely told West to wait while he called his whiskey driver to meet them.

"Hey, it might look bad with both of us sitting here if the police come by," West objected. "Suppose I just drive down the road a little way and come back."

At a nod from Parmenter, West sped down the highway to a telephone booth in a trailer camp to give McConnell a fast fill-in on the plans. It was his first near-miss. He had just wheeled his car around when he saw the baby-blue Lincoln approaching. A few seconds sooner and Parmenter would have spotted him coming out of the telephone booth.

At a signal from Parmenter, West fell in behind the Lincoln and, a little further down the road, a green 1952 Hudson joined the procession. When they reached "Moss Back's" house, West met the driver of the Hudson—a good-looking youth with black curly hair and a friendly smile. He said his name was Lew Gene Harvey.

"Moss Back" took the lead as the procession started again. The roads grew progressively narrower until the moonshiner finally halted at a gravel pit deep in the woods and told them to wait there. Parmenter didn't linger.

"I'll just go out to the highway and make sure nothing comes along," he told Harvey. "When you get that whiskey in the Hudson, don't stop anywhere near me. You know where you have to go."

The wily Parmenter was going to keep a safe distance between him and the whiskey—just in case.

While they waited for the moonshiner to come back with the whiskey, West helped Harvey put overload springs on the Hudson to handle the upcoming 225 gallons. Grateful for the help, the youth lost his apparent shyness around strangers and mentioned that he had seven hours of driving ahead of him. From the conversation, West gathered he was headed for the Florida Gold Coast.

When the moonshiner was paid, Harvey turned left for the trip south and West turned right toward Jacksonville and McConnell's garage. It was close to dawn when West reached his rooming house across town from Parmenter's lavish establishment, but he still had hours of work ahead. Before he went to bed, he wrote down every license tag, every name, every fragment of conversation. It was the pattern he was to follow for months to come.

After that episode, Parmenter began to trust the stocky young man who talked little himself but listened in wide-eyed respect as Parmenter bragged about his devious ways of beating the law, the mammoth size of his operations, the loyalty of his boys who kept their mouths shut when the law got their trucks.

Occasionally, Parmenter sent him out to arrange buys. At the moment, Parmenter explained, he didn't have a still of his own working. The Government had seized them all, but the moonshiners would hold their whiskey for him if he provided the sugar. West hauled sugar from Georgia to Parmenter's moonshine friends. And Parmenter grew more expansive.

When a jailed moonshiner's wife came to Parmenter for money, the fat man gave her a handout without complaint, explaining to West, "That boy hauled many a load of whiskey and sugar for me. Why, he brought me more money than you can stack in this room. He was carrying as many as four loads a week to that man down state."

West waited patiently for Parmenter to name the man down state, obviously his distributor, but Parmenter didn't trust him that far yet.

Once Parmenter complained that a sugar producer in Georgia was mad at him but he wasn't worried.

"I've always dealt with him over the phone so he couldn't put a finger on me," Parmenter boasted. "He wouldn't know me if he came in that door."

West listened and Parmenter talked on—about a still where a mule was used to plough over the tracks of the heavy-laden whiskey cars, about another still where he got the whiskey out one step ahead of the agents but lost his equipment, about a sugar cache he had thought well-hidden until the revenuers found it. Mentally, West was repeating over and over again names, dates, places. The fat man was linking himself to the "unknown seizures," where agents had seized the tools of the trade but not the traders.

Harvey, who carried Parmenter's loads south, was also becoming more talkative. The youth had just gotten married and West wished him well. He liked the boy, who showed a certain cleverness himself. Harvey told him how he wore a sailor hat on the road and kept a Navy pea jacket slung over the front seat so if any police started following him they would think he was just a sailor on leave.

"I was going through Vero Beach once with 225 gallons of whiskey," Harvey reminisced, "and the trunk lid flew up. I slammed it shut and knocked a hole in one of the cans and half the whiskey leaked out."

West tucked that item away for future reference. He now knew Harvey went through Vero Beach, Fla., on the way south.

On May 27, Parmenter mentioned that he had lined up 45 five-gallon cans of whiskey and the boy was going south with it in the morning. Later that night, West put in a call.

"Gene Harvey probably will be taking a load south tomorrow," he reported. "He should be going through Vero Beach about 11 A.M."

West spent the next two days hauling sugar from Georgia to Parmenter's moonshiners. When he turned up at Parmenter's restaurant to turn over the sugar money, he found a worried fat man.

"The boy isn't back yet," Parmenter told him. "The law may have gotten him."

Parmenter went off to take a telephone call and returned looking even more worried.

"The boy is coming in on the 10:45 bus," he said tersely. "Something happened. How about picking him up?"

West nodded and left the restaurant. At the first telephone booth, he called McConnell to witness the meeting at the bus station and identify the man. West had already been briefed on the skirmish at Vero Beach. The agents had chased down the truck but the man had jumped out and disappeared into the swamps. The whiskey had been destroyed and the truck stored in a garage without any report being made to city or state police.

Parmenter was waiting at the door of the restaurant when West drove up with Harvey.

"What happened to you?" the fat man asked Harvey.

"Either the Feds or the state cops got your car," the youth said. "I got away."

The next night, Parmenter took West aside.

"I believe that boy stole my car and the whiskey," he confided. "I don't believe the law got it. My man down south says there hasn't been a whiskey car seized in Vero Beach or anywhere down there in weeks. How about coming south with us to find out about this?"

It was what West had been waiting for, a chance to tag the man down south.

The next day, the three of them—Parmenter, West and Harvey—started south in Parmenter's air-conditioned Lincoln. Parmenter had told West to drive, so he would learn the route.

West drove and Parmenter talked. As the Lincoln passed through Stuart, Fla., Parmenter told him he had lost a dump truck there loaded with over 350 gallons of whiskey. Further along, he pointed out where one of his boys wrecked a truck trying to escape police and wound up in the hospital. When he fell silent, West primed the pump by saying he didn't see how he could survive financially with so many losses. The fat man started talking again to show this small-timer how big he was. West closed his eyes momentarily to fix it all in his mind—the town, the car, the name of the driver. It would be many hours before he could get to his notebooks.

On the edge of West Palm Beach, Parmenter told him to stop at the next telephone booth so he could call "Bobby." West assumed "Bobby" was the distributor but he was not to meet him that night. Parmenter told West and Harvey to stay in the car when they pulled into the yard of a large bungalow with a three-car garage. The agent noticed four cars parked in the back and memorized the license tags. When the time came, they would be seized along with "Bobby."

It was past 1 A.M. when Parmenter emerged with a sour look on his face and grunted directions to a hotel near the bay. As soon as they arrived Parmenter sent Harvey out for ice so he could have a word alone with West.

"'Bobby' has checked all his contacts," he said. "There's been no whiskey caught nowhere down here."

When Harvey came back, Parmenter told him to take his shower.

"I wanted him to shower first so I could see if he had any scratches on him," Parmenter explained to West. "If he ran through the swamps like he said, he'd be scratched all over. That boy didn't have a scratch on him."

On the way back to Jacksonville, Parmenter had Harvey show him again where the law stopped him. Then, they cruised the streets around the jail looking for the car. Finally, Parmenter turned to Harvey and his small eyes were narrowed to slits.

"The law didn't get that car and whiskey," he stormed. "Somebody stole it."

The youth paled.

"You don't think I took it, do you?"

"Well, I'll tell you this," Parmenter retorted. "I got too many contacts. I'll find out what happened and when I do . . ."

His voice trailed off into silence. West wished there was some way he could help the boy but there was nothing he could do without jeopardizing himself. The tightrope, he found, was getting narrower all the time.

A few days later, the stocky investigator got the break he had been waiting for. Parmenter wanted him to take a load of whiskey south to "Bobby." Harvey would go along to make the contact and Parmenter had something else in mind.

"You seem intelligent enough to get Harvey to make a slip," Parmenter told him. "See if you can't find out what he did with the car and the whiskey. If you can't get anything out of him, I'm going to take Harvey out in the woods and beat him and leave him there."

"I'll do the best I can to find out," West promised.

On the edge of West Palm Beach, West watched as Harvey dialed a number and said, "The merchandise is ready." Then, Harvey drove to a street beside the bay, left the car and walked down the street with West. A few minutes later, a boy Harvey introduced as "Pony Boy" joined them long enough to get the keys to the whiskey car. Watching him drive off, West wondered if he would get to meet "Bobby" after all. Harvey said only that they would walk to the hotel where they had stayed before.

That night, Harvey dialed the number West had seen him calling before and the agent's spirits lifted. Maybe they would meet "Bobby."

Four blocks from the hotel, West recognized a car he had seen in "Bobby's" back yard and the man at the wheel motioned them into the back seat. "Bobby" had parked as far as possible from the nearest street light but in the dimness, West could see a strapping Negro with a scar across the bridge of his nose. Introducing him, Harvey gave him his full name—George David Lincoln, the man Parmenter said he always cleared with before trusting a new driver with a load.

West figured he passed muster because Lincoln, handing over a bag of money, said he wanted him to come back with another load as soon as possible. As Lincoln started his car, he said he had to get back to his pool room to take care of a man he thought was working with the law.

"How are you going to take care of him?" West asked.

"Bobby" Lincoln smirked.

"I'll get a bunch of the boys from the poolroom and give them each 50 cents to throw a brick at this fellow, and a $1 to anybody that hits him. That way, I won't be bothered by the law no more."

As soon as West returned to Jacksonville, he started the agents checking on Parmenter's distributors. Lincoln, they reported back, reputedly controlled the numbers racket and allied gambling in the Negro areas around Palm Beach, owned a taxicab company, a poolroom and other business enterprises bringing in a monthly income of more than $1,200. He also owned about $45,000 worth of real estate. Like Parmenter, he had once been convicted as a liquor law violator but he was older and smarter now.

West was now making regular runs to West Palm Beach, collecting evidence all the while on more moonshiners as Parmenter had him canvass the stills to fill "Bobby's" orders.

He was getting as wary of the law as Parmenter. If he got caught, he couldn't reveal he was a Federal agent. Parmenter and "Bobby" had too many contacts.

He had already squeaked through one brush with the law. He had laid the jugs flat to prevent them from being seen through the rear window when a cork popped and the whiskey leaked through the truck onto the highway. A state trooper coming from the other direction sent a startled glance toward the truck. West was caught in the slow moving traffic but so was the trooper. Before the trooper could safely make a U-turn, West was four blocks ahead of him. By the time the trooper got close enough to make sure the whiskey smell was coming from his truck, West had ducked into a side street and escaped.

He wasn't safe in Jacksonville, either, where he thought his true identity was a well-guarded secret. His wife had come to town and the two were waiting on the street for a Shrine parade to pass. Years before, West had belonged to the drum and bugle corps of a Shrine temple in Chattanooga. When he saw the banner of his old drum and bugle corps approaching, he started to pull his wife out of the crowd, but not soon enough. One after another, the paraders recognized him and started yelling: "There's Jim Earl West." The Wests melted into the crowd and didn't venture out again until the Shriners left Jacksonville.

The near-misses were getting too close for comfort. West welcomed the relief from strain when he had to go to North Carolina for a week to testify at the trial of some moonshiners he had caught on an earlier undercover foray. But as soon as he returned to Jacksonville, he learned he had paid heavily for that week's respite. Parmenter had been busy.

West sensed something was wrong as soon as he walked into Parmenter's restaurant. Mrs. Parmenter told him her husband wanted to see him at home and her voice was grim as she said it.

Parmenter was in his undershirt when West strolled in on him. Sweat dripped from the creases of fat around his neck and his pig eyes stared coldly at the investigator.

"We've heard some pretty straight things since you've been gone," Parmenter began, "and something sure has happened. We think you're a revenuer."

The sweat was cold on the back of West's neck but he kept his voice light.

"I'm flattered by your compliment," he said with a grin, "thinking I'm smart enough to pull off something like that."

There was no answering grin from the other man.

"I had a city detective check the shipyard and that's all right except you worked there less time than you said you did," Parmenter went on.

"The records would only show the last time I worked there," West replied coolly. "Bill, you get some pretty funny ideas."

It went on for an hour, West kidding him about playing detective, reminding him he'd never failed to deliver a load, telling about his own brush with the law. He knew he had it made when Parmenter said that now he knew "Wesley" was all right, he was going to tell him something.

"You didn't have too much on me till you took down the first load and came back with the money," Parmenter said. "If you had been a Federal man, there wasn't but one thing for me to do. I would have to kill you because if you got up there and told the judge all you know about me now, he would give me natural life."

Parmenter admitted he might have made a mistake and acted sort of hasty when he told all the other bootleggers that "Wesley" was a revenuer.

Now, it was West's turn to get angry. Partly, he was putting on a show for Parmenter's benefit but the anger was genuine enough. He still had some violators he wanted to catch and Parmenter might have spoiled his plans.

"I don't appreciate your saying a thing like that to the fellows," he told Parmenter coldly. "You've got a lot of money but I'm still making payments on my car. Now you've fixed it so I can't buy from anybody."

Parmenter was full of apologies.

"You just wait till I put my shirt on," he said, "and I'll take you around to them and straighten things out."

When they drove off in West's car, Parmenter said he wanted to stop at a filling station to make a call. West noticed him drop a fistful of change into the telephone. Later, when the phone booth was checked, agents learned the only long-distance call that day had been made to the residence of George David Lincoln in West Palm Beach, Fla.

West had his tank filled while he waited for Parmenter. The gas station attendant kicked at a tire and commented: "The government sure puts good tires on its cars."

West grinned at him and replied, "They sure do." The word had gotten around. He realized then that if he hadn't sold Parmenter, his life expectancy would have been shortened considerably.

Parmenter had one more test for him when he got back in the car and they started driving again. He asked West to hold his hand straight out.

"If you're a Federal man, your hand is going to tremble."

West took his right hand off the wheel and stuck it in front of Parmenter's face. The fat man watched it a moment and sat back, apparently satisfied.

"No, it's not trembling," he reported. "You're okay."

In front of a country store, a crowd of men with unfriendly faces surrounded the car. West recognized several of them from previous buys. If Parmenter didn't succeed in convincing this bunch, his tightrope was going to end right there and he knew it.

"I was all wrong about this fellow," Parmenter told the crowd. "I've got a lot of apologizing to do."

One of the men looked up from quieting a dog he called Kate and his snarl was as nasty as the dog's.

"I don't know about that," the man said. "He sure looks like a Federal man to me."

"Someone told me that before," the agent responded airily.

"Well, all I've got to say is if a man caught me like that, I'd burn him up," the moonshiner drawled. "As a matter of fact, I wish they'd make a gun that would spray gasoline and fire at the same time so I could just spray the doors and windows to the man's house that caught me and sit back and watch him burn."

"Frank, you wouldn't burn up a man's family because he caught you, would you?" West asked him.

"I'd burn them all up," the bootlegger replied sourly.

On his next solo trip into the country, West made a point of buying 40 gallons of moonshine from the man with the dog called Kate.

West was back in Parmenter's good graces but the fat man was beginning to suspect everybody else. One day, they were sitting in a booth at Parmenter's restaurant when Parmenter punched him in the arm, and whispered: "Don't say anything. That's an officer over there."

West looked curiously at the stranger sitting at the counter and asked Parmenter how he could tell the man was an officer.

"I can smell them across the room," Parmenter replied grimly.

Jim West, looking at the malevolent grimace of the man across the table, silently thanked his lucky star that he was near the end of his tightrope. By now, his notebooks were full. He had traced the ownership of four stills seized earlier by state and Federal agents. He had helped gather evidence on the purchase of millions of pounds of sugar for the moonshine empire. He could prove liquor violations by 60 people—Parmenter, kingpin of the biggest ring; Bobby Lincoln, the distributor, and scores of independent moonshiners and their helpers. He had the proof that in three years of operation, this crowd of bootleggers had cheated the government out of more than $2,500,000 in liquor taxes alone. He himself had bought 930 gallons of moonshine and hauled thousands of gallons for Parmenter. He had scores of pictures snapped with a miniature camera concealed in his hand.

On the night of September 11, 1958, 45 Federal and state liquor agents gathered in a room of the Federal Post Office building in Jacksonville, Fla., still unaware of their mission. At midnight, they learned why they were there.

Jim West appeared before them and started talking. He showed them pictures of the stills and the men who ran them. He rattled off names and places and license tags of the cars to be seized. He told them what to watch for.

"There's a dog at this fellow's house," he said. "She'll bark when you show up but just call her Kate and she'll simmer down.

He hadn't forgotten the man who had threatened to burn up his family.

Seventeen teams of agents started out that night on the biggest simultaneous moonshine raids in Florida history. Moonshiners woke up to hear arrest warrants being read on their front porches. In West Palm Beach, the agents captured "Bobby" Lincoln and his fleet-footed messenger, "Pony Boy." In a remote farmhouse, they arrested the moonshiner known to investigators as "Moss Back," the man who had unwittingly helped West get to Parmenter.

West himself remained at the Post Office building to identify each prisoner as he was brought in and to question as many of them as possible.

At 1:30 A.M., Special Investigator Lacy R. Livesay, who had made a specialty of Parmenter, brought in the fat man. As Parmenter came down the hall, he spotted West and started to grin, obviously thinking West had been caught, too. When he got closer and saw the pistol on West's belt, the grin disappeared.

"What do you say, Bill?" West greeted him.

Parmenter, red-faced, his eyes narrowed to slits, looked at West as though he had never seen him before.

"How do you know my name so good?" he inquired coldly.

Lew Gene Harvey was arrested too, although he had never managed to appease Parmenter after the whiskey truck disappeared at Vero Beach. Like the others, Harvey was released on bail.

Seven weeks after the raids, the chained body of Lew Gene Harvey with a towel stuffed in his mouth and a .38 caliber bullet in his head floated to the surface of a canal near West Palm Beach.

After his murder became generally known, the word leaked out that the gang would pay $5,000 to dispose of West—the only other witness to the link between "Bobby" Lincoln and Bill Parmenter. That's when West kept his teen-age son from answering the front doorbell.

The murder of Lew Gene Harvey went unsolved for nearly two years. Lincoln and Parmenter had gone to prison on the liquor charges and West was off on another undercover assignment when a new sensation rocked West Palm Beach.

A drunken ex-convict said he had been paid to murder Florida Judge C. E. Chillingsworth and his wife, whose 1955 disappearance had been one of the nation's most baffling mysteries. The killer named his accomplice: George David "Bobby" Lincoln.

In his drunken ramblings, the killer said there had been another murder later. That time, he had helped Lincoln get rid of an informer. It didn't take long to guess the identity of the other victim, and Lincoln made a full confession.

When West read the confession, he thought about the curly-haired boy with the friendly grin and the young bride.

"They must have thought he was working for me," West told a fellow agent. "Actually, Harvey never informed on anybody. It was Parmenter, with all his bragging, who talked himself into prison."

Part IV ★★★★

DOMESTIC TRANQUILITY

12 ★★★

Immigration and Naturalization Service

The Communists had a blueprint for action in America.

If they could control all shipping, all transportation, all communications, they could effectively paralyze the nation when the time came. All they needed were a few key men in the right places. And some Moscow-trained agents, of course, to mastermind the operation.

Their grand design had only one flaw. They couldn't rely on native-born Americans to cripple America. Their key men could be deported to the lands of their birth, if America ever woke up to what they were doing.

This was a job for the Justice Department's Immigration and Naturalization Service, but it had no investigative arm, no centrally directed force to match wits with the Communists. Scattered throughout the country were immigration inspectors looking for aliens who had entered the country illegally or committed a deportable crime after they arrived. These inspectors had a number of other duties, too, checking on requests for visas and naturalization.

A law had gone on the books in 1940 to make certain criminals and members of subversive groups subject to deportation but enforcing it was just another chore for the busy inspectors until 1946 when the Immigration and Naturalization Service created the position of investigator for the first time.

In district offices from coast to coast, men drawn from the ranks of inspectors and examiners were assigned exclusively to conduct investigations. The then Attorney General Tom C. Clark, now a Supreme Court Justice, lost no time telling them what he wanted investigated. He launched his program to deport subversive aliens.

Within a year, the Investigations Section, later expanded to the Investigations Division, was established in the Washington headquarters to spearhead the drive against foreign-born Communists and criminals. A force of 400 investigators, directed from Washington in a team operation, was on the move.

Finally, America was focusing on the flaw in the Communist grand design—the foreign birth of its emissaries.

The investigators had a triple job. They had to find the key men in the Communist underground apparatus. Then, they had to prove their targets were foreign-born, tracing their true identities through a maze of aliases. And, finally, they had to prove to the satisfaction of the courts that these men were actively plotting to overthrow the country of their adoption.

That was perhaps the toughest job of all. On the one hand, the Communists marshalled a battery of high-powered legal talent to combat this threat to their grand design. On the other hand, disillusioned former Communists who could testify to the activities of these key men were afraid. They feared they would lose their jobs if they revealed they had ever been Communists. They knew, too, about some people who had talked—and been found beaten on the docks and in the subways. They were willing to give the investigators what they knew in strictest confidence. But come out in the open? Never.

Despite the handicaps, the immigration investigators made strong enough cases to deport 250 hard-core Communists from the time the drive started in 1947 through 1961. Among them:

John Santo, international organizer for the Transport Workers Union in New York. His mission for the Communist Party was to organize everything on wheels. His real name was Desieriu Hammer, but he had cultivated an Irish brogue to carry out his mission. Mario T. Noto, now assistant commissioner of the Immigration Service in charge of the Investigations Division, spent his nights in the subways, talking to ticket agents and cleaners in search of clues to Santo's party membership. He found them. Santo was deported on August 10, 1949.

J. Peters, a man of many aliases, the real head of the Communist Party's espionage apparatus in this country. He was the shadowy figure in the background when Elizabeth Bentley, according to her later revelations to Congressional committees, served as courier between the Communists who had infiltrated Government agencies in Washington and the spy network functioning from New York. Peters was deported on April 12, 1949. When last heard from, he was the commissar of a ministry in Hungary.

Ferdinand Smith, national secretary of the National Maritime Union. His principal mission was to organize the East Coast waterfront so effectively that all shipping could be halted on command. He was deported to his native Jamaica on August 15, 1951.

John Williamson, national labor secretary of the Communist Party in the United States and one of the 11 top Communists convicted of conspiracy to overthrow the Government. Proof of his Communist role was there, but Williamson insisted he was native-born. He used a gimmick frequently employed by the Communists. He claimed he was born in San Francisco before the fire and his birth record had been destroyed. After a long investigation into his background, investigators finally located his mother in a small town in Scotland. Confronted with the threat that his aged mother would be brought here to testify, Williamson finally admitted he was born in Scotland. He was sent back there on May 4, 1955.

Investigators also struck at the financial arm of the Communist movement in the United States—the International Workers Order, ostensibly a fraternal insurance organization, actually a source of revenue for the party with more than $8 million in assets. The investigators uncovered enough documentary evidence and testimony of witnesses to have the IWO declared a subversive organization.

The test case involved Andrew Dmytryshyn, an official of the Ukrainian Section of the IWO and one of its leading organizers. The Communists fought hard but Dmytryshyn was deported on the ground that he was a member of the IWO, which was in fact a part of the Communist movement. On the basis of the evidence furnished by the immigration investigators, New York State succeeded in winning court approval to disband IWO.

Just as the pattern of post-World War II tensions brought the drive to deport Communists, the growing power of syndicated crime precipitated the drive to rid the country of its foreign-born racketeers.

Immigration inspectors had long been concerned with deporting dope peddlers and procurers. But these were small-fry compared to the racketeers spotlighted by Senator Kefauver's crime hearings, beginning in 1950. Senator Kefauver called on the new force of immigration investigators to do some of his sleuthing for him. Were the men behind organized crime in New York, Detroit, Kansas City, Chicago, Cleveland and Los Angeles of the home-grown variety or had they been spawned by the slums of Europe?

In answering questions for the Kefauver committee, the immigration investigators were building their own file. When the hearings ended, investigators studied 13,000 pages of testimony—a screening process that led to the investigation of 556 individuals as potential deportable criminals. The immediate result: 20 racketeers deported, nine others stripped of citizenship as the prelude to deportation.

In 1952, Attorney General James McGranery formalized the campaign to use deportation as a weapon against organized crime. He launched the "Attorney General's Denaturalization and Deportation Program against Racketeers and Subversives." The program was later transferred to the Immigration Service as the "Top Priority—Racketeer-Subversive Program."

Under the twin programs, 204 of the country's most notorious criminals have been investigated. Twenty-eight have been deported. Nineteen more are under final orders of deportation but cannot be expelled yet because the land of their birth—particularly behind the Iron Curtain—won't provide the needed travel documents or their lawyers are still finding ways to drag their cases through the courts. Nine others have been denaturalized but four of the nine can't be deported under existing laws.

Among the characters who remain in America because their native lands won't take them is Irving Sherman, characterized by FBI Director J. Edgar Hoover as one of the top hoodlums of the underworld. Immigration investigators spent years establishing his true identity and his birth in Ungvar, Hungary, now a part of Soviet Russia. In 1958, Sherman was ordered deported on the ground that he entered the country illegally when he returned from a trip and claimed he was an American citizen. The Soviet government refuses to accept him so Sherman stays here as an unwanted guest.

The magnet of the United States—and the easy money within the reach of criminals—is so strong that many of those who are shipped out try to slip back in again. To balk this maneuver, the investigators have to know the whereabouts of the deported criminals at all times, together with any plans they might devise to leave their native soil.

Salvatore Maneri, a deported Brooklyn racketeer, has been shuffling between the United States and Italy ever since he was first expelled in 1955. Each time, he is apprehended and shipped back. On the last go-round, when he was caught in November, 1960, he was sentenced to serve six months in prison for re-entering after deportation. He was scheduled to be deported in May, 1961, but the Federal Bureau of Narcotics stepped in. Before he could leave the country, he was indicted for violating Federal narcotics laws.

In their fight to remain in the land of milk and money, the criminals alter records, assume the identity of other people and terrify witnesses into silence or lies.

Sebastiano Vermiglio, a Detroit narcotics trafficker, claimed he was American-born and could prove it by his baptismal record in a Chicago church. Investigator Robert J. Devlin learned that the church books had been stolen and mysteriously returned. He suspected that Vermiglio had substituted his name for a Chicago baby born about the time of his birth. His suspicions were confirmed when laboratory technicians reported Vermiglio's name was written with a ball-point pen—not invented until 30 years after Vermiglio's birth.

Paul DeLucia, alias "Paul The Waiter" Ricca, heir to Al Capone's Chicago crime syndicate, was exposed through an altered marriage record and a forgotten bank account listing his true parentage and birthplace. The bank account, dormant for 30 years, was for only $57.44 but it opened the door to immigration investigators.

DeLucia had entered the country in 1920 under the name of Paolo Maglio and had his name legally changed to DeLucia when he was naturalized in 1928. Investigators found that DeLucia had been accused of killing a man in Italy and had fled to avoid prosecution. The true Paolo Maglio was located and disclosed that his travel agent had lost his passport for a period of four months—long enough for DeLucia to use it to gain entry into the United States.

Finally, to prove DeLucia's true identity, investigators found the sister of the man he had been accused of killing. She was hysterical with fear because a "stranger" had visited her ahead of the immigration investigators. She testified under Government protection. In 1957, DeLucia's naturalization was revoked for assuming another man's identity. He was ordered deported, but the Italian Government has refused to recognize him as a citizen of Italy.

In New York, Investigator Mitchell S. Solomon spent two years looking for grounds to revoke the citizenship of Frank Costello, the power behind syndicated crime in America. The investigator finally made it. He proved through a parcel of reluctant witnesses that Costello was actually a bootlegger when he listed his occupation as real estate man on his naturalization papers. The Supreme Court upheld the denaturalization and Costello is now under a final order of deportation. However, the Italian government has refused to take him.

On Saturday, November 15, 1957, a sensational story broke in the New York morning newspapers. Sixty-six men had gathered at a home in Apalachin, New York, for what appeared to be a crime convention. At the Washington headquarters of the immigration investigators, Noto checked the names in the newspaper against his big black book of criminal dossiers and promptly called Michael F. Fargione, assistant regional commissioner for investigations in the service's northeast region. Noto assigned him to find out the citizenship status of every "delegate" to the Apalachin crime convention. He already knew about 75 per cent of the men. Fargione worked through Sunday and by Monday night he had the answers. Among the 66 were seven aliens and 29 naturalized citizens.

By 1961, Russell Bufalino, Vito Genovese and Simon Scozzari of the Apalachin group had been ordered deported. Genovese, head of New York's West Side Gang of dope peddlers, counterfeiters, gamblers and bootleggers, can't depart until 1970. He's otherwise engaged at Atlanta Penitentiary.

Of the others, Mario Presta, who masqueraded for 30 years as American-born Paul Scarcelli—until immigration investigators found the mother of the real Paul Scarcelli—fled to Italy; Sam Monachino crossed the border and renounced his United States citizenship; Joseph Ida returned to his native Italy and gave up his citizenship. Denaturalization proceedings were started against Dominick D'Agostino and Anthony Riela, who entered the country illegally and used another immigrant's history to gain his naturalization papers.

Excluding aliens before they get a foothold in the country has prompted the Investigations Division to develop a close liaison with Mexican and Canadian police as well as to assign a special unit to the waterfronts.

The object of the border programs is to identify the unwanted, to prevent their entry and to learn the identity of those who have succeeded in passing the borders. Police of the neighboring countries and other sources tip off immigration investigators when they hear that any of their home-grown Communists and criminals are planning a trip into the United States. If investigators miss them at the port of entry, they go looking for their unwelcome visitors. They traced one such character to the Santa Anita race track in 1960. He lost not only the race but his freedom. Canada wanted him for forgery.

On the waterfront detail, investigators make friends with dock hands to pick up rumors of alien smuggling operations. One day, investigators watching the arrival of the S.S. *Tekla Torm* from Genoa grew suspicious when they saw a man loitering on the dock hand a card to a crewman off the ship. Under questioning, the loiterer admitted he was there to welcome some stowaways hidden by the crewman for $1,500. The crewman had collected $600 in advance and was to receive the balance when he delivered the stowaways to a man who would identify himself by a card—the ace of spades.

J. Austin Murphy, supervising investigator of all criminal and racketeering cases, located a parcel of stowaways without ever leaving his desk in Washington. He had read that Canadian mounted police had found stowaways aboard a Fabre Line ship at Montreal. Figuring that other ships of the line might also have crewmen willing to smuggle aliens, he checked Lloyds Shipping Register to determine when the line's next ship was docking in the United States. When the line's *St. Tropez* docked at Boston, investigators rounded up five stowaways and eight relatives who had paid to bring them here.

Investigators have to crack down regularly on rings specializing in the importation of immigrants with false documents. One ring sold Puerto Rican birth certificates to Cubans to get them into the country without restriction. Another sold phony letters offering jobs, so Mexicans could prove they had a job waiting for them in the United States. Rings arranging sham marriages have been broken up on both coasts. American girls are paid to go through marriage ceremonies with aliens. The marriages aren't consummated and are quickly dissolved, but before that happens, the grooms have claimed American citizenship through their wives. A Texas town did a thriving business in providing delayed birth certificates to Mexicans who claimed they had been born in the United States, but hadn't gotten around to getting the birth registered until now.

The turning point of that racket came when 37 people claimed citizenship through the delayed birth certificate of one Mexican. Twenty of his children and grandchildren had entered the country before the investigators caught up with the Mexican ancestor.

In matching wits against the unwanted, the investigators have to devise their own gimmicks. One such gimmick was tried on Joseph Stacher, alias "Doc Rosen," wealthy associate of the overlords of crime. Stacher had been denaturalized in 1956 but the investigators lacked grounds for deportation. Noto and Murphy, reviewing the case from all angles, decided to try something new.

Investigation overseas had shown that Stacher's wife occupied luxurious quarters in Rome, his children attended school in Switzerland and Stacher made frequent overseas flights to visit them. Why, reasoned the investigators, couldn't they exclude Stacher on the ground that he had abandoned his domicile in the United States and was just an ordinary immigrant entering without a visa? It was worth a try. When Stacher returned from his next flying trip overseas, he was refused admission pending a hearing. His exclusion was upheld, but he has now launched a court fight to stay here.

For nearly a century, America had opened wide its doors to immigrants. Then, it became selective about the quality of its immigrants. Next, it narrowed the quantity of immigrants from any country. And finally, it shut its doors to Communists who would destroy and criminals who would prey on its citizens.

But many of them entered legally before the doors to America were shut—or illegally after the doors closed. Today, rooting out the unwanted is the full-time job of 800 immigration investigators.

The importance of their role was underlined in 1962 when, for the first time, a man from their ranks was elevated to the top job in the service. Raymond F. Farrell, a career investigator who was chief of investigations for the New York district before he came into the Washington headquarters, was appointed Commissioner of the Immigration and Naturalization Service.

THE FALL OF JOE ADONIS

In the criminal hierarchy, puffy-faced Joe Adonis ranked close to the top. He fattened off Prohibition and stayed fat off gambling. He dabbled in labor shakedowns and used underworld tactics to bolster his ventures into legitimate business. Certain politicians courted him for his money and influence. His "strong-arm" troops could be useful at the polls on election day. His guttural voice was reputedly heard in the high councils of Brooklyn's Murder, Inc. Gangland slayings followed meetings with Adonis, but police never got close to proving his hands were bloody.

With his bodyguards at his side, he could be seen occasionally in the clubs patronized by high society—his round shoulders concealed by custom-tailoring, his graying hair pomaded, his small brown eyes slitted to study the crowd. He always sat with his back to the wall.

For three decades, he had been arrested regularly for a variety of crimes from kidnapping to extortion, but he never saw the inside of a prison until 1951 when New Jersey—faced with the testimony of the

Kefauver Committee—indicted him for conspiracy to violate gambling laws. He thought he could draw a suspended sentence with a plea of no contest but somebody goofed. He was given a two-to-three year prison term. With possibly unintentional humor, the prison made him an ice man. In the underworld, "ice" is the term for police bribes.

For Joe Adonis, it was an annoyance to leave a $100,000 home on the New Jersey Palisades, to do for himself instead of having three servants do for him. But it would be only a temporary inconvenience. His lieutenants could collect the take from his far-flung gambling casinos, his real estate, his auto franchises, his shakedowns. He would be free to resume command by mid-1953 and nobody, he vowed, would ever get him again.

Two men were about to try. Joe Adonis would never have heard of either of them. They were not of his world—not the world of crime he commanded nor the world of law enforcement he knew and despised. They were investigators for the Immigration and Naturalization Service.

Investigator Earl Greenleaf, in the fall of 1952, was turning 40. Before he joined the Immigration Service, he had seen something of the world in the Navy. He had sailed the China seas and served around the Panama Canal. Now he lived modestly with his wife and three children, a quiet man—patient and persistent.

Investigator Martin Peters, sandy-haired, quick of movement and somewhat younger, had flown with the Air Force in World War II. He, too, had three children—two boys and a girl. He liked the freedom of going about an investigation his own way, pitting his wits against reluctant witnesses, parlaying a single fact into the whole truth. For him, an investigation was a flight of stairs, starting from nothing, leading into the unknown.

Greenleaf was the first of the pair to enter the world of Joe Adonis. The Attorney General of the United States had just launched his high priority campaign to deport foreign-born gangsters. The name of Joe Adonis had not appeared on the original list because anybody around New York would say "Joey A" was born in Brooklyn—the tough Gowanus Canal section. Joe himself, however, had given a different version when he appeared before the Kefauver Committee. He had said he was born in Passaic, N.J.

In the New Jersey office of the Immigration and Naturalization Service, Investigator Greenleaf drew what looked like a routine assignment: stop by Passaic and check the birth record of Joseph Doto, alias Joe Adonis, but don't identify yourself as an immigration agent. After ten years in the service, Greenleaf knew what that last meant. This was to be a hush-hush job. If Joe's citizenship should become suspect, the service couldn't tip its hand prematurely.

Greenleaf quickly found what he sought on Page 83 of the Passaic register of births: Joseph Doto, born November 5, 1901, at 36 State Street, Passaic. So Adonis was born in Passaic, after all.

Or was he? This was a delayed birth record. Adonis hadn't gotten around to recording his birth until 1933. To a trained investigator like Greenleaf, a delayed birth record was always suspect—the sort of thing money and influence could buy. And Adonis had both.

Greenleaf paid a call at the Passaic city library and thumbed through a half century of city directories. No family named Doto was listed.

A stroll down State Street seemed indicated. Greenleaf slowed down as he passed No. 36. Had the rich and powerful mobster started life in this little house? It looked old, but was it 50 years old? Behind those shuttered blinds might be the answer he sought, but Greenleaf knew he couldn't ask questions. He would have to find his own answers.

Back at city hall, Greenleaf asked to see the building records for 50 years ago. He was directed to an old vault behind a coal-burning furnace in the basement. The vault had once been locked but the steel door had long since sagged on its hinges. Spilled over the floor were bales of records covered with ashes, coal dust and soot.

With a rueful glance at his neatly pressed fall suit, Greenleaf took off his jacket and burrowed for the plumbing permits. Soot smeared his face, his white shirt got as gray as the records, but he finally uncovered the plumbing permits for 1901. Nothing for 36 State Street in the year Adonis said he was born there. 1902. 1903. 1904. Nothing. In the plumbing records for 1905, he found a permit to install pipes at 36 State Street.

"If those were the original pipes, I've got something," he muttered to himself as he reached for the stack of tax appraisals.

Again, he started with 1901. He could find nothing for 36 State Street, but there was a lot beside 34 State Street appraised at $250, unimproved. In 1905, the value of the lot had jumped to $5,000 improved. That tied in with the plumbing permit to install pipes. The house at 36 State Street had been built in 1905—four years after Adonis claimed he was born there.

"He must have been born in a patch of weeds," the investigator grinned.

Greenleaf, a patient man Adonis had never heard of, had succeeded in proving Adonis was not born at 36 State Street, Passaic, N.J. The delayed birth certificate was as spurious as it looked.

Greenleaf passed the ball to New York. If Adonis had lied about Passaic, Greenleaf pointed out, a search of arrivals from Europe over the past half century might turn up something. It did.

One Michele Dato, according to the old immigration records, had arrived in New York in 1906. He had last resided in Montemarano, Italy, and was destined for his brother-in-law Ferdinando DeVito, in Brooklyn. A Maria Dato arrived in 1909 aboard the S.S. *Montserrat* to join her husband. With her were four sons—Antonio, 10; Ettore, 9; Guiseppe, 6; and Genesio, 4. The State Department was asked to look for the birth records of the four sons in Montemarano, Italy.

The big job still lay ahead—proving that the six-year-old Guiseppe Dato of the S.S. *Montserrat* was the Joe Adonis of the New Jersey Penitentiary and, further, that he was deportable.

Investigator Peters of the New York office got the job. His orders: tear away the veil of secrecy woven over two generations, the veil shrouding the foreign birth of Joe Adonis. Build the picture of an immigrant family and its notorious offspring. Joe says he was American by birth. Prove he wasn't.

Like Greenleaf before him, Peters started with the records. He drew a blank with the 1905 census. No Dato or Doto family there. The next time New York took a census was in 1915 and there should be a Doto this time. There wasn't.

Peters played a hunch. The accepted story was that Joe Adonis had given himself that name because he fancied his handsome face. Maybe, Peters figured, his father had thought of it first. Running his finger down the "A's," he came upon Adone. The names had been anglicized since the days of the S.S. *Montserrat* but the family grouping was there—Michael and Mary Adone, the parents, and four sons, Tony, Albert, Joseph, James. All of them were listed as natives of Italy but Peters knew he'd need more than the census to prove it.

School records next. Peters found young Joseph Adone was a "B" student at P.S. 32 in Brooklyn. Tony didn't do so well, he noted. The important thing was that the boys had gone there together, that their names and those of their parents matched the 1915 census. Peters was moving a step closer to the present.

Hospital records, traffic records, the restaurant license for Joe's one-time speakeasy in Brooklyn, baptismal records, marriage records, Selective Service records. Peters searched them all, following the family through the years.

He found among other items that Joe's marriage license listed his birthplace as Brooklyn but when he registered later for the draft, he said he was born in Passaic. The spurious birth record in Passaic had been created between his marriage and his draft registration.

The veil of secrecy Adonis had woven was getting some holes punched in it but Peters knew he still didn't have the evidence he needed to prove Joe's foreign birth. He had to ask some questions.

Peters was well aware that nobody was going to talk directly about Joe Adonis—not with the enforcers at his command—and nobody was supposed to know the Immigration Service was interested in Joe.

Peters took the problem home with him and slept on it. By morning, he had hit on the approach he would use. Joe's older brother Tony had been naturalized. As an immigration officer, Peters could reasonably ask questions to and about Tony. What was true of Tony, at least in the early years, could be applied to his brother Joe.

A worried Tony, heavy set, not suave like his brother, faced Peters across the table. He was obviously afraid Peters had found something wrong with his naturalization papers and Peters let him think so. Tony talked readily about his early schooling—with his brothers—where his family had lived, where he worked. But when the questions came closer to Joe, he had a stock answer.

"Were any of your brothers in the United States before you arrived in 1909?" Peters asked him.

"I don't remember."

"Was your mother ever in the United States before 1909?"

"I don't remember."

Peters was trying to close the door on any claim that Maria Doto gave birth to Joe during a visit to the United States before her 1909 arrival with her four sons.

Joe's Uncle John was no help either. He gave the impression that Joe's mother shuttled constantly between Italy and the United States in the early years.

Peters was feeling frustrated. By now—on the basis of Greenleaf's discovery in the Passaic city hall basement—the name of Joe Adonis had been added to the Attorney General's program for deporting racketeers.

"And I'm getting nowhere," Peters muttered. "Nowhere at all."

He studied the latest report from headquarters. An agent had called on Adonis in prison, ostensibly to find out if Adonis could have expatriated himself by long absences abroad. Adonis, heatedly denying it, had told investigators that the only time he left the country at all was for a few days in 1947 or 1948 when he went to Cuba. Had Adonis known that the Immigration Service even suspected him of being foreign-born, he would have never admitted a trip outside the country. He would be an alien, entering illegally—that is, if Peters could ever prove he was foreign born.

Peters noted from the report that Miami had been unable to find a record of Adonis' arrival from Cuba in 1947 or 1948. Captains of yachts known to have carried racketeers to Cuba to confer with their old friend Lucky Luciano had been interviewed and plane passenger lists had been searched. Peters sympathized with the Miami agents. They weren't getting any place either.

Maybe, Peters thought, he could help the Miami agents pinpoint Joe's Cuban trip. A columnist had once reported that singer Frank Sinatra and friends had visited Luciano in Cuba. If Sinatra had seen Adonis on that trip, Miami could narrow its search for the record of Adonis' arrival. There was no doubt in Peters' mind that Adonis went to Cuba to see Luciano. Adonis and the exiled overlord of crime were such old friends that Luciano had been best man at Adonis' wedding.

Peters arranged to interview Sinatra at a theatrical agency. He had just started posing his questions when boxer Rocky Graziano stuck his head in the door and Sinatra playfully began sparring with him. As the two men danced around in mock combat, Peters persisted. Why did Sinatra go to Havana? It was cold in Miami. Was he with Luciano? He was introduced to him in a bar. Who was with Luciano at the time? A dozen people were hanging around but Sinatra didn't know any of them.

Obviously, Sinatra was going to be no help. Peters left him to his sparring.

His next stop was a Brooklyn tenement, three flights up to the apartment of Ferdinando DeVito, the brother-in-law whose name was listed by Michele Dato in 1906.

The aged Italian sat in his kitchen with his wife and daughter beside him as Peters questioned him through an interpreter. He said he had come to this country at the turn of the century and his sister Maria's husband had arrived a few years later. Some time after that, he said, Maria came to this country with her three sons. It was her first arrival.

"Ask him if he's sure it was only three sons," Peters told the interpreter.

"Yes," Mr. DeVito insisted. "Anthony, Albert and James."

"Ask him about Joe."

As the interpreter translated, Peters noticed the DeVitos exchange a quick glance.

"Joe was born in Brooklyn."

The old man had tried to be truthful, except for Joe's birth. He knew he had to say Joe was born in this country but he forgot that school records, census records, immigration records would all show James as younger than Joe. If any of the four boys had been born in the United States, it had to be James—not Joe.

The tenement reeked of cabbage as Peters started down the three flights. It was dinner-time but he wasn't hungry. The conspiracy of silence around Joe Adonis was putting a permanent dent in his appetite.

The next day, he switched back to brother Tony and called in the two character witnesses who had vouched for Tony at the time of his naturalization.

From the first witness, Peters learned only why Tony had been so nervous under questioning. The witness admitted he didn't even know Tony, although he had sworn that he and Tony were school chums.

The second witness gave Peters a lift. He was Salvatore Cella, a New York policeman and distant cousin of the Doto family. He told Peters he had gone to P.S. 32 with the Doto boys and lived diagonally across the street from them in Brooklyn. He knew all about the family and—more important—he was willing to talk.

As soon as the policeman left, Peters started ticking off what he had. Two witnesses—Ferdinando DeVito and Salvatore Cella—could testify that Maria Doto came to America for the first time aboard the *Montserrat*. That foreclosed any claim that Maria had borne Joe in this country on an earlier visit. One witness—Cella—could testify that Joe came from Italy with his mother. And one witness—again Cella—could positively link Maria's son Joseph Doto with Joe Adonis.

The veil of secrecy was lifting but Peters knew he couldn't stop now. He still had to find the clincher—positive proof that Joe Adonis knew all along that he was foreign-born. There had to be a record somewhere.

One place remained to be searched—the storehouse of old police records in the basement of Brooklyn police headquarters. In the arrest book of the old 79th Command, Peters found Joseph Adone and later Joseph Doto. The records were so old, so unimportant that they didn't even figure in Doto's dossier at the FBI. No fingerprints tied them conclusively to Joe Adonis.

Hardly glancing at the offenses charged, Peters focused on one item—nationality. The records listed Adone and later Doto as born in Italy. If Peters could establish that Doto himself had given that information, he had it made. Here would be the proof that Joe knowingly lied about his place of birth.

Five arrests in the old records. That meant five arresting officers, five desk lieutenants to record the event. Out of ten policemen, Peters needed only one with a long memory.

The first arrest, February 20, 1919, playing cards for money, indecent language. The arresting officer couldn't remember the arrest. It was just a bunch of boys. Happened every day. The desk lieutenant who had recorded that arrest was dead.

The second arrest. The arresting officer couldn't remember and the name of the desk lieutenant was undecipherable. The third arrest. Only the last name of the arresting officer was recorded and he couldn't be identified. The desk lieutenant didn't recall the incident. The fourth arrest. The arresting officer was dead and the desk lieutenant had long since forgotten this little Prohibition violation. There were so many.

The fifth arrest.

"I'm probably just spinning my wheels," Peters told himself as he rapped on the door of Thomas F. Conley, now a first grade detective assigned to the Brooklyn District Attorney's office. Conley was listed as the arresting officer in a 1922 assault case.

It was 8 o'clock in the morning of January 29, 1953. Conley came to the door in his dressing gown.

"Do you recall making an arrest in 1922 in connection with an assault on a girl?" Peters asked mechanically, expecting nothing.

"Yes," Conley replied. "I arrested Joe Adonis."

Peters stared at the policeman. At that moment, standing in the doorway of a Brooklyn apartment house, Peters sensed that the last shreds of Adonis' carefully nurtured veil of secrecy were about to be torn away.

"Do you recall the circumstances?"

Conley rattled off the details as though it had all happened yesterday: A speeding cab skidding to a stop in front of a garage . . . a man coming out of the garage, helping to carry a struggling woman inside . . . Conley, the rookie, hailing the departing cab to find out what it was all about, being told a man in the cab had beaten the woman all the way from Roseland Dance Hall . . . the rookie cop rapping his night stick on the sidewalk to summon help . . . a sergeant coming along to join him in forcing the garage door . . . the woman lying on the running board of a car with the two men bending over her . . . and Conley, remembering the incident all these years because the beaten woman was afraid to prosecute.

"If you want the exact date," Conley concluded, "I can give you that, too."

He opened the door of his hall closet and showed a stack of little green books. He had preserved every memorandum book of his more than 30 years on the force. Leafing through the pages, he found what he wanted and showed Peters the notation: Joseph Doto, 19, Italy, shoe clerk.

Peters took a deep breath and asked his key question.

"Did you ask him where he was born and he answered Italy?"

"No," Conley replied. "The desk lieutenant asked him his pedigree and I copied the answers down. That is how I have it recorded in my book."

At last, Peters had what he had run down so many blind alleys to find—a witness who had heard Joseph Doto himself say he was born in Italy. It had taken three months but Peters—another man Joe Adonis had never heard of—had ripped away the veil of secrecy in which Adonis had wrapped his past.

It remained for others to provide the still missing links in the chain of evidence leading to the deportation of Joe Adonis—proof of his true birthplace and proof of his illegal entry from Cuba posing as an American citizen.

A few days after Peters' visit with Conley, Miami immigration officers finally found the record of Joseph Doto's arrival from Cuba. He had entered the country as an American citizen on December 9, 1946, with a fellow mobster—Vincent Aiello, alias "Jimmy Blue Eyes." Two days after the Cuban trip was established, the State Department came through. Despite the resistance of hostile local authorities, an American consul had uncovered the birth record of Giuseppe Doto, born Nov. 22, 1902, in Montemarano, Italy.

Inadvertently, Adonis himself contributed to his own downfall. On February 10, 1953, he was brought before New Jersey's Bergen County grand jury to answer questions about racketeering on the waterfront.

Adonis regarded the grand jurors with a contemptuous half-smile. Too vain to put on his horn-rimmed glasses, he squinted at his questioners through a cloud of cigarette smoke and gave his usual answers—slick evasions in a gruff monotone. Then, just before he was excused, there came a question he saw no reason to evade.

"Mr. Doto, just so we have the record straight, when and where were you born?"

"Passaic, New Jersey, November 5, 1901."

The careful Adonis had finally committed a crime in the presence of witnesses. He had lied under oath to the grand jury about his birthplace.

At Adonis' deportation hearing, as Peters had sensed on that January morning in Brooklyn, Officer Conley wrapped it up. He testified that he was introduced to Joe Adonis years after that 1922 arrest and Adonis told him with a grin: "I remember you. You arrested me once a long time ago."

On August 5, 1953, Joe Adonis was ordered deported. Usually, that's just the start of a years-long battle against deportation. But for Joe Adonis, troubles were piling up—all because of the lie he had lived so long, the lie proved by Greenleaf and Peters. Adonis was convicted in New Jersey for lying about his birth to the grand jury. Then, he was convicted in Washington for lying about his birth to the Kefauver committee. Faced with years in prison, Adonis gave up.

On January 3, 1956, a stocky, middle-aged man in a custom-tailored suit entered a first class cabin of the S.S. *Conte Biancamano*. Destination: Italy.

As the ship sailed out of New York harbor, Adonis saw the Statue of Liberty for the last time. Her torch had welcomed an immigrant boy half a century before. Now, her hand was raised in farewell to a gangster.

13 ★★★

Civil Service Commission

Charles Guiteau cost us the life of a President, but his act of assassination did more in two minutes for the cause of clean government than the civil service reformers had managed to do in two decades.

Today, a force of more than 700 investigators in the Civil Service Commission's Bureau of Personnel Investigations carries out the Congressional mandates and Presidential orders that began coming into being after the fatal shooting of President James Garfield in 1881.

The goal of these investigators is to insure that the men and women in the Federal service are not only competent and reliable but of unswerving loyalty to their country. Their mission costs the taxpayers $11 million a year but the men in Congress and the Executive departments figure that's little enough to pay to maintain the taxpayers' faith in their public servants.

The founding fathers, of course, never dreamed of such a cost when they wrote into the Constitution that "the Congress may by law vest the appointment of such inferior officers as they think proper in the President alone, in the courts of law, or in the heads of departments."

In the early days, the Presidents did their own investigating. George Washington set high standards for public officials. Honesty and efficiency were his paramount considerations, although he also took into account the job applicant's pre-Revolutionary devotion to the cause of the colonies. He occasionally gave the preference to officers of the Revolutionary Army, but he chose the principal Federal officers from different regions of the country, staffed field establishments with local residents and sought the opinions of Congress in making local appointments.

Washington's appointment policies were followed for the most part by his first five successors. Progressively, however, they inclined toward rewarding those who had helped them win the Presidency. This system of using government jobs for political pay-offs was becoming solidly established in some of the states, but it was President Andrew Jackson who introduced to the Federal government more openly than any of his predecessors the principle that to the victor belongs the spoils.

For the next 20 years, the spoils system prevailed, unrestrained and unashamed. Every change of Presidents marked the wholesale removal of government employees to make room for the new President's supporters. As a matter of routine, the incoming President and his Cabinet set aside their first month in office to sort out the claims of the hordes of office-seekers demanding their reward.

Abraham Lincoln was so annoyed by the persistent flock of would-be Federal employees that when he was felled by an attack of smallpox he ordered his attendants: "Tell all the office seekers to come at once, for now I have something I can give to all of them."

The problem was not merely the quantity but the poor quality of the Federal job hunters. The patronage demands were often to locate jobs for constituents who couldn't find or hold a job at home. The unemployable and the unfit were joined by the grafters. They were willing to pay $5,000 for a $1,500 job, figuring they could milk the public cow once they took office.

The revolving door of public jobs was whirring so swiftly that by the end of 1870, President Grant asked Congress for a law to govern the manner of making appointments to the Federal service. "The present system," wrote President Grant, "does not secure the best men, and often not even fit men, for public place."

Grant's pleas met with no results until the last day of the session in 1871 when Congress grudgingly attached a rider to an appropriation bill authorizing the President to write rules for the admission of persons into the Federal civil service and to hire suitable persons to conduct inquiries. The President quickly appointed an advisory board for the civil service, which recommended a set of rules to classify all jobs according to the duties to be performed and to appoint applicants by way of competitive examinations.

The "Grant Commission," as it came to be known, died before it really got rolling. Congress, still influenced by patronage-hungry constituents, refused to give the commission any money to carry on.

President Rutherford B. Hayes also drew a blank when he tried to squeeze money out of Congress, although the public demands for civil service reform were getting more vociferous.

When President Garfield was inaugurated in 1881, the usual swarm of office-seekers descended on Washington demanding payment for services rendered in the election. One of them was a peripatetic lawyer, author, evangelist and swindler named Guiteau. He had written a speech in Garfield's behalf which had never been delivered, but he latched onto the idea that he had been a decisive factor in Garfield's election and should be suitably rewarded. He thought the least the new President could do was appoint him Ambassador to Austria, although he was willing to settle for the consulship at Paris. He became such a nuisance with his letters and visits that Secretary of State Blaine pointedly rebuffed him and the White House guards refused to admit him.

Now convinced that the country was doomed without his help, Guiteau decided to save it his own way. On July 2, 1881, Guiteau awaited the President in the old red brick building that was then Washington's railroad station. As the President passed, Guiteau shot him in the back. In the press, Guiteau was portrayed as a disappointed office seeker in search of revenge and the whole sordid story of Federal patronage was suddenly and dramatically brought into perspective.

President Garfield died on September 19, 1881. Less than three months later, Senator George H. Pendleton of Ohio, chairman of the Senate committee on civil service reform, was ready with a bill to regulate and improve the civil service. The bill was favorably reported to the Senate in May, 1882—just a month before Guiteau was hanged as an assassin. The bill cleared Congress and reached the desk of President Chester A. Arthur on January 16, 1883. He signed it the same day.

The act specifically required the new Civil Service Commission to make investigations in the enforcement of its rules, but since no staff of investigators was provided, the Commissioners doubled as investigators themselves.

The early investigations dealt with efforts to get political contributions from Federal employees and political discrimination in appointing and promoting workers. The politicos still hadn't gotten out of the habit of thinking of Federal jobs as a reward for favors.

Without a staff of investigators, the Civil Service Commission couldn't make any personal investigations to determine the character or fitness of the job applicants. The Commissioners had to rely on questionnaires filled out by the job-hunters and vouchers certifying they were of "good moral character."

In 1913, however, Congress for the first time allowed the Commission to hire investigators. To get trained men, the Commission tapped the Postal Inspection Service for four investigators who concentrated mainly on charges of misconduct.

In 1917, President Wilson made the first stab at the type of investigation that occupies most of the time of the Civil Service Commission's sleuths today. He issued an order requiring the commission to investigate the experience, fitness, character, success and adaptability of applicants for the job of postmaster where the incumbent was not to be reappointed. For the first time, the investigators were to look behind the answers on questionnaires and make personal investigations into the background of the job-seekers.

The new kind of investigative work prompted the Commission to establish a separate Division of Investigation and Review in 1920. The following year, the President ordered the Civil Service Commission to investigate postmasters for reappointment as well as for their original appointment.

Law enforcement officers were the next to come under the personal scrutiny of the Civil Service Commission's investigators. When Congress, in 1927, brought all positions in the Bureau of Prohibition into the classified civil service, the Commission decided the prohibition enforcers should be investigated because of the special temptations that came their way. To carry out this chore, the Commission hastily recruited and trained 40 investigators.

In two years, the investigators completed more than 3,000 investigations into the background of Bureau of Prohibition employees. The results were startling. About 40 per cent of those investigated—including many already working for the Bureau of Prohibition—had records which showed them unfit for Federal service.

The Commission, with the blessing of Congress, decided it had better take a look into the background of other law enforcement officers. It doubled its investigative staff and started making personal investigations of customs inspectors and border patrolmen.

By 1939, the Commission's investigative program required investigations of the character and fitness of job applicants wherever practicable. Since its sights were set higher than its funds, however, it could only use its authority to check on the background of those going into key positions.

Up to this time, the question of loyalty to the Government had been recognized as something to consider, but it hadn't played a major part in investigations. Congress and the Commission had been more concerned with cleaning up political favoritism in Federal jobs and rooting out criminal elements and grafters.

Beginning in 1939, however, Congress began worrying about the national security as the European war clouds spread a shadow over this country. The 1939 Hatch Act prohibited Federal employees from being members of any organization advocating the overthrow of the American Government. In 1940, Congress gave the War and Navy Departments the power to fire any employee in the interest of the national security. In 1942, the civil service regulations provided for removal of employees on the basis of a reasonable doubt as to loyalty.

As the number of Federal employees expanded with World War II, the number and types of jobs requiring personal investigation likewise swelled. Investigators had to check on the suitability, loyalty and other qualifications of job applicants for strategic posts in the war program. All candidates for high level positions, all key employees, all civilian employees recruited for the Pearl Harbor Navy Yard and the Panama Canal were investigated before appointment.

The investigative work increased from a peacetime volume of 7,800 investigations in 1939 to 89,000 in 1945. The staff of Civil Service Commission investigators expanded from 80 to a wartime peak of 727. To save travel time and cost, the investigative force was distributed among 125 duty stations across the country.

With the end of the war, all but the most important investigative work ceased. Investigations of character and loyalty were discontinued. The staff was cut back to 83 investigators doing just about what they had done in pre-war days, except for investigating appeals for veterans' preference on Federal jobs and the qualifications of top executives.

The postwar lull in investigations, however, was short-lived. As the Communists, our wartime allies, emerged as a postwar threat to our security, Congressional committees began looking at the Communist threat within America—particularly alleged Communists in the Federal service.

As the accusations flew, the hysteria grew. The loyalty of Federal employees became a talk-piece and a political issue. So, on March 21, 1947, President Truman established the Federal Employees Loyalty Program by executive order. For the first time in the Nation's history, a uniform loyalty program covering all present and future Federal employees was established.

The program required checking the names and fingerprints of all present Federal employees through the FBI files. It prescribed a minimum investigation of all future appointees, including a check of the records of the major investigative and intelligence files in Washington as well as written inquiries to former employers, references, schools and local police. It provided for an investigation by the FBI whenever a question of loyalty was developed. It was an enormous job to launch with 83 civil service investigators.

Although the civil service investigators made some personal investigations when a check of the records indicated derogatory information, the Commission didn't have the funds to conduct full field investigations for critical positions. These are investigations where the investigators go out personally to get all the facts about a person's background and activities.

Congress, meanwhile, was demanding more investigations. Every time it created a new agency or appropriated money, it tacked on a rider that employees couldn't be paid until they were investigated by the FBI. Finally, 20 agencies had such provisos for their employees and the FBI was swamped with investigations that had no connection with its primary jobs of catching criminals and subversives.

In 1952, Congress relieved the FBI of much of this burden and put it on the Civil Service Commission. The following year, the investigative role of the Civil Service Commission was further expanded by executive order. The earlier loyalty program was abolished and a broader security program for government employment was introduced. It was so broad that the number of civil service investigators suddenly jumped from 144 in 1951 to 1,037 in 1953.

Under the program as it operates today, all appointments to the Federal service are subject to investigation. The scope of the investigation depends on the duties to be performed as they relate to the national security. For "non-sensitive" positions—that is, jobs that don't involve access to confidential information or vital installations—the investigation is done through checking records and writing letters. For "sensitive" positions, investigators make a full field investigation to probe the entire life of the potential Federal employee.

The investigations are designed to screen out unsuitable applicants, permit the prompt discharge of unsuitable appointees, deter potential applicants who know their records won't bear investigation and at the same time provide assurance that the Federal work force is of high caliber.

With some 300,000 investigations a year, the job of finding the rotten apples in the barrel requires cooperation of the public along with the efforts of the investigators. And the public apparently accepts its share of the responsibility. In the average check on applicants for non-sensitive jobs, nine inquiries go out and seven responses are received. Considering that the names and addresses are furnished by the applicants themselves and go back over a 10-year period, that's a high degree of public cooperation. In all, about three million Americans annually are helping the government's investigators weed out the misfits.

The job applicants for non-sensitive work are also checked through numerous agencies—the FBI name and fingerprint files, the House Un-American Activities Committee, the military intelligence files if there has been a service connection, the State Department if the individual has travelled or lived abroad, the Immigration and Naturalization Service if the person entered the country as an alien during the ten-year period covered by the investigation and two of the Civil Service Commission's own sources of information, its Security Research File and its Security Investigations Index.

The Index was established after the war years found investigators for a half dozen agencies constantly running into each other—all working on the same cases and going over the same ground. The Index is now packed with more than 7½ million cards showing personnel investigations dating back to 1939. Operation of the Security Index has put an end to criticism that the Federal government conducts duplicating and repetitious investigations without knowing the results of previous inquiries about the same individual.

The Commission's Security Research File was centralized at the Washington headquarters in 1948 to furnish leads and possible sources on loyalty questions. It now contains more than two million cards and is searched about 5,000 times a day.

A key investigative tool, the file is guarded against both idle curiosity and misinformation. Only the established investigative agencies of the Federal government can get information from this file and nothing goes into it until a responsible official determines that an actual question of subversive activity is involved, that information substantially identifying the individual is available and that the information came from a known source.

The sources include the Attorney General's list of subversive organizations, Congressional hearings, the Canadian Commission report on the Atom Spy Ring, the Australian Royal Commission report on espionage, state legislative inquiries, lists of Communist Party members with their addresses, signers of Communist Party election petitions supplied by the states and the Communist Party's own publications.

More than 25 per cent of the cases referred by the Commission's investigators to the FBI originate with material in this security file. In all investigations where a loyalty question arises, the FBI gets the case.

The Commission's security file was routinely checked one day in clearing a handyman at an Army arsenal. A card showed that a man by the same name, not further identified, was mentioned during a House Un-American Activities Committee hearing as one of a dynamite crew of eight Communist Party members creating trouble in the mid-West. A check with the FBI revealed that the same man had been arrested in Ohio for possessing explosives and drew a substantial prison term. With the man's identity firmly established, the Army was promptly notified that it had a dynamiter with Communist Party connections working at the arsenal.

Police records are routinely checked on government employees. About a fourth of the decisions that employees and would-be employees are unfit for Federal service stem from these local arrest records.

Before deciding against the employee, however, the Commission always gives the man a chance to explain the derogatory information turned up through record checks or personal investigation. In one such case, Baltimore police records showed that a man named Aloysius Jeremiah Murphy, born July 19, 1916, had been arrested for a serious crime. Murphy, under questioning, insisted he couldn't have been the man.

Commission investigators went out to prove or disprove his story. They checked his last private employment in Connecticut and found time card records and a foreman to prove conclusively he had been in Connecticut—not Maryland—on the day of the arrest. Investigators checked the arresting officer in Baltimore and identifying information on the police record. The bad Aloysius Jeremiah Murphy in Baltimore had been born on the same date but he definitely wasn't the same man. The good Murphy's government job was saved.

The commission's routine checks for "non-sensitive" jobs now average about 265,000 cases a year. Much of this work is done by women in the vaulted though ancient grandeur of the former Pension Building in downtown Washington.

The full field investigations for "sensitive" jobs, directed from Washington but handled by regional offices throughout the country, usually average more than 25,000 cases a year—sometimes closer to 50,000. They are conducted as a service to 50 Federal agencies who want to fill positions in such strategic areas as weapons system planning, space exploration, rocketry, informational activities overseas, foreign economic assistance and nuclear energy. All the private contractor personnel dealing with the Atomic Energy Commission as well as its own employees must be cleared.

The agencies pay the Civil Service Commission for these investigative services. The head of the agency designates which are the sensitive jobs and the agency itself decides whether or not to hire on the basis of the Commission investigation.

Unlike applicants for non-sensitive jobs, who can go to work while the Commission's checks are underway, those appointed to the sensitive jobs cannot start until the investigation is completed. As a result, time becomes a key factor both for the agency with a job to be done and the individual who can't go to work until cleared.

The normal completion date on a full investigation is 60 days, but the Commission can and does speed it up to meet emergencies.

In January, 1961, the incoming administration had many key jobs to fill, all requiring investigations to make sure of the qualifications of those to be appointed. By using long distance telephone calls to assign investigators and get their reports, the Washington headquarters averaged 10.3 working hours from receiving requests for investigations to compiling the completed reports.

At the same time, the Commission's investigators were giving special priority to the full investigations for sensitive jobs that had to be filled on short notice. In these cases, deadlines ranged from a few days to a few weeks.

No matter how fast the job has to be done, the Commission's investigators have to collect enough facts to insure fair and equitable decisions, to safeguard the national security and to protect individual rights.

THE SECURITY RISK

In a tool plant on Chicago's South Side, an engineer named John Duchet had risen to a position of prestige and responsibility. His plant had just been awarded a government contract to manufacture a secret device and Duchet would have a lot to do with the project.

The government agency awarding the contract routinely asked every key employee at the plant to fill out a "personnel security" questionnaire. Along with the others, John Duchet answered all the questions.

Like all the rest of us, John Duchet had been filling out questionnaires for years. There's a form for everything—for jobs, taxes, credit, insurance, college, the draft, passports. Since more people are honest than dishonest, the questionnaires we fill out may only be checked superficially unless some glaring discrepancy presents itself.

Perhaps John Duchet figured his "personnel security" questionnaire would be handled the same way—just go into a file someplace in the Washington maze and be forgotten. None of his answers had ever been questioned before.

The rising young engineer overlooked one fact as he confidently scrawled the answers: the government no longer takes its security for granted. The Federal agency awarding the contract to Duchet's plant was one known in government parlance as a "highly sensitive" agency. Under the law, private contractors given access to this agency's secrets had to get the same security clearance as the government's own employees.

Routinely, then, Duchet's questionnaire arrived with a batch of others at the Civil Service Commission's Investigations Division one August day in 1959. Routinely, the "highly sensitive" agency requested Civil Service investigators to make a "full field investigation" of John Duchet. That meant checking his life back to his birth with particular emphasis on his adult years. Every answer the engineer had given on his questionnaire would have to be verified if it took a dozen investigators to do it. And the agency wanted the answers in a hurry so it could get the device into production without delay.

Within 72 hours, copies of Duchet's questionnaire were en route to investigators in three cities along with enough information to let each one know what the others were checking. The Duchet file had been given a number to keep track of it among the thousands in various stages of investigation; a supervisor in Washington had been assigned to oversee the case to its finish and a deadline had been set. The investigators would have to come up with their answers within a month, regardless of where the trail led.

From records, from friends, neighbors and fellow workers, the investigators had to find out if Duchet was the kind of man they would trust with their secrets. After all, the Government's security was their security.

The Duchet questionnaire provided this information to be verified:

Born in Gary, Indiana, in 1919, six feet tall, hazel eyes, black hair going gray, Army veteran, single. He had graduated from a Gary high school, received his bachelor of science degree from a midwestern university and later attended an eastern university for two years. His first job was as an assistant engineer in Milwaukee, followed by three years as an engineer with a Gary company. He had held his present job in the Chicago tool plant since 1952.

The answers on the questionnaire presented a straightforward picture of a typical American college man, trained in his profession, taking time out to serve his country, finding the right spot and settling down to a promising career. Every month of his adult life was accounted for—no omissions to arouse the curiosity of investigators.

The Chicago phase of Duchet's life was assigned to Investigator Don Adams. In the South Side tool plant, Adams started with the personnel records and promptly ticked off a couple of items on the Duchet questionnaire. The records showed Duchet had been hired as an engineer in 1952. So far, so good.

Then, Adams picked up the application form Duchet had filled out to get the Chicago job. Frowning, he compared it with the questionnaire. Nothing matched, not even his date of birth.

Since the investigators are informed at the start where the other investigators will be working on a case, they know what will be automatically covered. If answers lead in other directions, they propose "extensions" to get the new leads checked out.

Adams jotted down a note to extend the investigation to Indianapolis to verify Duchet's birth date. Another note extended the investigation to a Southern university to determine whether Duchet had received his degree there, as he claimed on his job application form, or from the midwestern college he had listed on his security questionnaire.

The job application form raised another question. Duchet had reported there that he had served in the Army as a first lieutenant, but his security questionnaire listed the serial number of an enlisted man.

Adams knew military service would be routinely checked from Washington, but he tucked the discrepancy away for future reference when he got around to talking to Duchet's associates.

With growing curiosity, Adams worked his way through the rest of Duchet's file. All but one of the records indicated Duchet was a bachelor, as he had reported on his security questionnaire. The one exception was an insurance form which carried a notation that Duchet did not want his wife covered on his insurance. Duchet's marital status was important only if, for some reason, he had lied about it. It gave Adams another item for his personal interviews.

He had learned all he could from the records. From Duchet's associates he hoped to draw a picture of the man's character, his habits, his reputation. Did Duchet have the integrity, the moral fibre, the emotional stability of a man who could be trusted with Government secrets? Was there anything in his background that would make him vulnerable to blackmail?

Adams' many years of investigation had taught him that no man looks the same to any two witnesses. He took into account that a man might appear different to his boss than to the men who worked under him, that the witnesses' own personalities might affect their opinions. Still, Adams figured, if he interviewed enough witnesses he should get a reliable composite picture. Here's what he got:

The first witness: "He's probably all right but not the type I would care to associate with outside of business. Too egotistical. From what he told me, he was married some time in 1954, but it only lasted a few months. He said I shouldn't tell anyone he had ever been married."

The second witness: "I heard his wife was a ballet artist who traveled all over the world. Somebody told me they're now divorced. I imagine she was on the go all the time and John didn't want to follow her around."

The third witness: "John's father is president emeritus of a large university and the family is quite well off. John was married to a hometown girl, a very talented danseuse, but as I understand it, the marriage was annulled. John has quite a war record, but he doesn't say much about it. He was wounded by machine gun fire from a strafing German fighter plane in North Africa. He showed us the scar."

The fourth witness: "John told me he had seen his former wife's parents on a visit home and they gave him a very pleasant reception, apparently no hard feelings about the break-up. John would like to remarry but his family doesn't want him marrying below their cultural and financial status. That, of course, limits the field."

The fifth witness: "John isn't the sort to talk about his personal affairs, but I did hear he'd been married at one time. He's always very calm and collected, never flies off the handle."

The sixth witness: "I understand he comes from a very wealthy family but his father is dead. John has quite a war record, you know. He told me once that as he lay near death on the battlefield, he vowed he would devote his life to some worthy project if he was spared. When he recovered from his wounds, he went into teaching. Apparently, he didn't stay with it but I don't know why."

The seventh witness: "John is the type to get under your skin, the way he's always talking about himself. If you met him face-to-face, you'd think he was the cleanest-cut chap you ever saw, but he shouts at meetings and threatens to resign if anyone puts any pressure on him. I personally question putting him in a position of trust on security matters. He might divulge secrets just to prove how important he is."

The eighth witness: "While he worked under my supervision, he used to pump me with questions about my job. Later, when he replaced me, I realized he was just getting advance information, but I guess it was just a matter of a fellow looking out for himself in this business."

The ninth witness: "I know nothing about his family except they're supposed to have a lot of political power. I don't think much of him as an engineer. I tried going to him for information, but I gave it up because he never had the answers and always referred me to someone working under him."

The tenth witness: "He's not very informative about his personal affairs. He's very discreet and not a blabbermouth at all."

Adams blinked at that as he went on interviewing Duchet's co-workers. Duchet might not be a blabbermouth, as his friend said, but the information Adams was picking up could only have come from Duchet—his family's money and power, his heroic war record, his ballerina wife. One witness even assured Adams that the break-up of the marriage was in no way Duchet's fault. It was that wife of his who wouldn't stay home.

The investigator was curious about the hints that Duchet might not be such an expert engineer after all. He wondered how those discrepancies in Duchet's educational background were panning out, but they were a job for other investigators in other places. Right now, he had to talk to Duchet's neighbors.

Duchet had lived at the same address since 1953 and four neighbors said they knew him well. They were unanimous in singing his praises—a quiet man, a good neighbor with a heart of gold. Although his office associates believed he had been married in 1954, his neighbors knew him as a single man. The investigator came up with one point of similarity. Like Duchet's co-workers, his neighbors were under the impression that he came from a well-to-do family.

Still puzzling over the marriage, Adams visited an apartment listed by Duchet on his questionnaire as one of his three Chicago addresses but the turnover of tenants in seven years temporarily defeated him. By checking city directories, he traced two former neighbors, both women with good memories.

"I didn't ask him anything about his personal life," the first volunteered. "He just seemed to be trying to impress me. First, he said he was single but wore a wedding ring to keep the girls away because they were all after his money. Then, he said he was married to a wealthy girl who was traveling on the continent before settling down to being a housewife. About six months after that, he told me he was married to a psychiatrist away on a lecture tour."

The other former neighbor also recalled Duchet well.

"He's what I would call an odd ball," she said thoughtfully. "He told me his wife was a school teacher temporarily assigned to an overseas post. He said his father was connected with a big university but I never saw the father. His mother was supposed to be of noble birth, but I met her once and you could tell she wasn't just by talking to her."

Both women gave the same answer to Adams' last question. No, they said, they would not recommend him for a position of trust involving the national security.

At Duchet's earliest address in Chicago, Adams talked to his onetime landlady. She added an item suggested earlier by a witness at the tool plant.

"He told me he was a school teacher before coming to Chicago," she said. "He used to mention his students, but he never said why he gave up teaching or where he taught."

Adams had run out all the Chicago leads. He began his report by calling attention to the discrepancies in birth date, marital status and education and the puzzling reference to a teaching career. He summarized the testimony of the witnesses in their own words—the praise, the criticism and the implication that Duchet distorted the truth to suit his own convenience. He had completed his assignment two days ahead of the deadline.

Meanwhile in Gary, Indiana, Investigator Fred Baker was getting a different version of the life of John Duchet. The plant listed by

Duchet on his security questionnaire confirmed that he had worked there but he hadn't been an engineer as he claimed. He was just a timekeeper.

Baker's interviews with Duchet's high school teachers and neighbors developed the picture of a hard-pressed mother and a father who drank a lot and worked a little, mostly as a mill hand. Although Duchet occasionally returned to Gary and visited the neighbors, they knew nothing of a marriage, particularly to a Gary girl.

Again, Duchet's one-time teaching career was mentioned. A neighbor and one of his former teachers told Baker that Duchet had entered a teachers' college and spent some time as a student teacher but, for some reason, had given up teaching. In Baker's report, he suggested extending the investigation to the Indiana town where Duchet had reportedly attended a teachers' college.

In Milwaukee, the third city on the original assignment, Investigator Paul Carter had also started with the records of the company listed by Duchet on the security questionnaire. Like the other investigators, Carter found Duchet's job application at the Milwaukee plant showed marked differences from what he had put on the security questionnaire, but Carter's attention focused on one item in the company records—Duchet's length of service. On his security questionnaire, Duchet had said he worked eleven months at the Milwaukee plant. The company record showed seven months. For some reason, Duchet had covered up four months.

The company's personnel had changed almost completely in the thirteen years since Duchet had worked there, but Carter found one former supervisor with a hazy recollection of Duchet.

"We had an opening for what we loosely called an assistant engineer," the supervisor recalled. "Duchet applied and we hired him. Help was difficult to get in those days, but it turned out to be a more or less unfortunate choice. He had the appearance of being straightforward but I felt he was a pretty shifty sort of person. He impressed me as a boy who was putting up a big front. He may have changed but my general impression then was that I should not trust him very far."

Carter checked the Milwaukee address listed on Duchet's questionnaire, a residential hotel. Neither the clerks nor the tenants remembered Duchet but the hotel had kept its old registration cards and Duchet's was among them. He had listed his occupation as school teacher.

The three original investigators had finished their assignments on schedule but what they had learned had to be tracked down by half a dozen more investigators—particularly the discrepancies in education and the mystery of Duchet's teaching career.

At the mid-western university where Duchet claimed he had received a bachelor of science degree, the records showed he had started twice but never got beyond the freshman year. A professor who remembered Duchet told the investigator that Duchet struck him as unstable, nervous, easily influenced and no student.

At the eastern university where Duchet claimed he had taken two years of graduate work, no record of his attendance could be found. At the southern university which Duchet had listed as his alma mater on his Chicago job application, the records produced no student named Duchet.

As for the teachers' college mentioned by the two Gary witnesses, Investigator Ralph Doyle ran into a strange reluctance to discuss Duchet. A college official said Duchet had only attended the college for a few weeks and no academic record was available.

When the investigator persisted, the official put on his glasses with a sigh and started reading from a folder of papers which he did not show the investigator.

"Mr. Duchet applied late and he was accepted without the usual preliminary investigation," the official began in an apologetic tone.

One of the letters he read from the folder described Duchet as a menace unsuited to the teaching profession. Another item in the folder reported that Duchet had told fellow students that women in the town were trying to seduce him. Since the women he named happened to be prominent and very respectable, when the word got around Duchet was expelled.

One last item remained to be checked—Duchet's military service. Army records showed Duchet had risen no higher than private first class. He had not been strafed by fighter planes in North Africa. He had never been overseas. In fact, he had been discharged in a hurry because of a disability—flat feet.

As the deadline neared, the reports from all the investigators converged on the desk officer assigned to oversee the Duchet case. Studying the mass of fact, opinion and Duchet fabrication, the desk officer recognized the remaining gaps. Now that Duchet's college career had been disproved, several years of his adult life were a blank. There was also that gap of four months that Duchet had taken pains to cover up by extending the length of service on his Milwaukee job. The school where witnesses had said Duchet was a student teacher had not been located, but there were no open leads remaining, no place to seek information except from Duchet himself.

The desk officer decided to send the case as it was back to the agency requesting the investigation. Further investigation, he reasoned, would create more delay, and if Duchet was a security risk, the sooner the "highly sensitive" agency knew it, the better. He was reasonably sure that the agency, on the basis of the investigative reports, would ask Duchet himself some questions before granting or denying security clearance.

Neither the investigators nor the desk officer at the Civil Service Commission would evaluate the findings, in effect sit in judgment where a man's future might be at stake. That was a matter for the agency which ordered the investigation.

As the desk officer had figured, the Duchet case came back to him. The "highly sensitive" agency had called Duchet in to explain the discrepancies between the answers on the security questionnaire and the facts developed by the investigators. Duchet's replies formed the basis for a new request for investigation.

Duchet had admitted misrepresenting facts on his questionnaire and his other job applications, the Civil Service desk officer was informed. He had admitted he had no college degree, but denied ever telling anyone he was married. As for his teaching career, he said he had taught in a small Indiana school for a few months. The claim of 11 months instead of seven months on the Milwaukee job had been an oversight. Duchet now recalled he had worked during the four months at a factory in Fountain City, Wis.

The desk officer sent out new instructions to the investigator to run out Duchet's revised story of his life.

Investigator Tom Farrell drew the Indiana school assignment. When the school itself produced no record of a teacher named Duchet, the investigator called on townspeople who had had children in the school at the time Duchet said he taught there.

Farrell ran into an irate bunch of people. Although Duchet had passed through town more than a dozen years earlier, everybody remembered him.

At first, Farrell was told, Duchet made a wonderful impression, particularly with the women who admired his imposing size, his convincing talk and his small courtesies. Then, the trouble began. He spread rumors that the good and respectable mothers of his pupils were chasing him. While the matrons were reeling from that blow, their daughters complained that he was chasing them. The angry townspeople protested to the school principal and to state authorities. Duchet departed and no one in the town had ever seen him again, but he hadn't been forgotten.

A past president of the Parent-Teachers Association summed it up for Farrell in one non-stop sentence:

"We all feel that he is a person of low character, absolutely devoid of morals, a slippery character, a despicable person, a liar, mentally unsound, and none of us would recommend him for anything, let alone a position of trust involving our national security."

While Farrell was putting his sizzling comments on paper, Investigator Tom Gordon was checking the factory in Fountain City, Wisconsin, where Duchet said he worked during the four-month gap spotted by the investigators.

"I remember him," the supervisor told Gordon. "A constant source of trouble. One thing that sticks in my mind is the way he had of telling fantastic stories. He was usually late for work and would come up with the most unbelievable excuses. He didn't stay with us long."

The supervisor vaguely recalled that Duchet had lived at a nearby inn while working at the factory. There, Gordon located two long-time women residents who remembered Duchet well, but not fondly.

Duchet, they said, claimed his father, an admiral, had been killed in action in the Pacific and his sister was a famous physician. The owner of the hotel, an elderly widow with some money, was completely taken with Duchet. While Duchet was living there, the owner complained several times that money had been stolen from the cash drawer and she accused everyone but Duchet. Other guests reported their trinkets were missing.

Some time later, these two long-time residents happened to be taking a trip together through Indiana and out of curiosity, decided to pay a call on Duchet's family in Gary. The sister was there. They thought she was a very nice woman but she was a stenographer—not a famous physician. Before they left, they noticed something that shook them. The sister lighted her cigarette with the lighter one of the women recognized as the one she had missed while Duchet was in residence. She knew it was her lighter from its unusual shape, even before she spotted her initials.

When the reports from Farrell and Gordon reached Washington, the desk officer understood why Duchet had omitted mentioning his teaching career and his short stay in Fountain City. The investigators had torn to shreds the pattern of lies, half truths and downright dishonesty in which Duchet had wrapped his past.

If the Civil Service investigators had accepted Duchet's answers as he gave them, his vulnerability to blackmail and his compulsive urge to impress his fellows would never have been uncovered. Having come this far, Duchet could be expected to do anything to protect himself from exposure. As for his desire to be somebody, what would be more likely to impress others than an inside knowledge of the workings of a secret device?

The Civil Service Commission investigators had simply gathered the facts. It was up to their client, the "highly sensitive" government agency, to decide whether, on the basis of these facts, John Duchet could be trusted with information involving the national security.

The answer was "no."

14 ★★★

Internal Revenue's Intelligence Division

A special agent leafs through a book seized in a long-forgotten raid and Al Capone's reign of terror comes to an end. An insurance executive refuses to talk until the Queen Mary docks and "Boss" Tom Pendergast's grip on Kansas City is finally broken. A trash collector preserves the dumpings from one barrel on a street in Reading, Pa., and a gambler is through taking bets. A television set written off as "employee recreation" is traced to the company president's own home and the magnate goes to prison.

These are the breaks of the game—a game played for high stakes by the special agents of the Internal Revenue Service's Intelligence Division against the non-paying taxpayers.

Victory for the agents usually means money for Uncle Sam. It also serves to warn other taxpayers that they can't beat the system of voluntary tax compliance. Other side effects are equally meaningful—a city freed of corruption, a labor union cleansed, a potentate of organized crime behind bars.

Recently, the side effects have been emphasized in Attorney General Robert F. Kennedy's drive against syndicated crime. One of his early moves after taking office was a heart-to-heart talk with H. Alan Long, chief of the Intelligence Division, and his top aides. Mr. Kennedy asked the Internal Revenue officials to give top priority to investigating the tax affairs of major racketeers. If other Federal, state and local officers can't get the racketeers directly for their crimes, Internal

Revenue agents may—and often do—get them for failing to pay taxes on the fruits of those crimes.

Johnny Dio—real name John Dioguardi—knows that now.

Back when former Gov. Thomas E. Dewey was a racket busting prosecutor in New York City, he called Dio "the protected child of crime." A personification of the strong arm shakedown world, the molten-eyed mobster spread terror through New York's garment and trucking industries. Firms either succumbed to his harsh demands for money to insure "labor peace" or found acid spilled over newly manufactured clothes or trucks dumped in the East River.

He was indicted for engineering the acid blinding of labor columnist Victor Riesel, but the case never came to trial because witnesses wouldn't talk—what the judge called "underworld lockjaw." He was slowed down in 1958 with a 15-to-30 year sentence for a labor shakedown, but it was only a temporary setback. On appeal, his conviction was reversed.

Appearing before the Senate Rackets Committee, he was every inch the well-heeled mobster—sleek, sour and silent. Dio had to be stopped, but nobody seemed able to manage it.

Then, the special agents of Internal Revenue moved in. Dio had failed to file a tax return for 1951 and 1952. There was no question that money had flowed to him from any number of sources. The problem was to prove it.

An important witness who had told agents he cashed more than $50,000 worth of checks for Dio disappeared. Two other prospective witnesses were jailed for successfully concealing some key union records. Another man who had reportedly made substantial pay-offs to Dio chose a year in jail for contempt of court rather than tell what he knew.

Finally, after the agents had failed to make any headway with scores of men who shook with fear at the very thought of telling the truth about Dio, they struck paydirt. Two witnesses, who had denied even to the grand jury that they ever paid off Dio, agreed to talk.

One of them testified he paid Dio more than $15,000 to continue operating his dress-making factory on a non-union basis. The other, president of a women's wear trade association, said he gave Dio $5,000 as a start and, at Dio's insistence, put Dio's bodyguard on his payroll. All the bodyguard did to earn the money was pick it up and turn it over to Dio.

The man nobody could get is now serving a four-year term in Atlanta Penitentiary.

The pattern of using income tax laws to nail the men who rate themselves above all law was set three decades ago in Chicago. Bribery and murder had paved the way to fortune for Al Capone, but he paid no taxes, kept no books, bought no property in his own name and conducted his business in cash. Capone's shyness about putting his name on paper was the first frustration faced by Special Agent Frank J. Wilson when he was assigned to go after Capone in 1930.

Wilson, later to become chief of the Secret Service, had been digging for months to find a record—any record—when he chanced to pull open a file drawer of apparently unimportant old papers left behind by a former special agent. Among the papers, he found a book with a lot of figures in it and no identification.

The book was the first break. It had been seized four years earlier in a gambling raid on the Hawthorne Smoke Shop—a Capone operation.

It took Wilson four months of tracking, but he finally found the Capone cashier who had made entries in the book and had disappeared immediately after the raid. The cashier's sworn statement to Wilson in a Miami hotel room on February 18, 1931, was the first evidence directly establishing taxable income for Capone and proving tax evasion.

But it was a long way from that first evidence to the penitentiary for Al Capone. Another cashier had to be located and financed on a trip to South America to keep him from getting murdered before the trial. Capone's net worth had to be established to show he was getting money from somewhere to live so high off the hog. Tracing his expenditures, agents found he paid $12,500 for his custom-built cars, spent $1,000 a week on food and drink for himself and friends, put out $3,000 to rent a hotel banquet room to entertain guests on the night of the Dempsey-Tunney fight in 1927 and bought custom-tailored suits for his henchmen. Those suits fascinated the agents. They were provided with especially heavy pockets to carry guns.

An agent went undercover to live with Capone's mob in Chicago's Lexington Hotel. This agent, whose true identity was kept secret until his death, was Michael J. Malone. It was Malone who learned of Capone's plot to kill Wilson and others working on the tax case, of Capone's attempt to fix the jury and of Capone's last-ditch efforts to terrorize potential witnesses into perjury.

Thanks to Malone's tips, every plot backfired. The imported gunmen left town when their identities became known, the judge switched jury panels on the day of the trial and the witnesses who tried perjury were told in open court why they were lying.

Six of Capone's top lieutenants either preceded or followed him to Federal prisons. Jack (Greasy Thumb) Guzik, Capone's second-in-command who controlled the syndicate's gambling and prostitution, went from indictment to trial so swiftly that the mob didn't even have time to tamper with juries or witnesses. Capone's older brother, Ralph, who handled the bootleg breweries, went to Leavenworth Penitentiary after agents analyzed 8,000 bank sheets to trace Ralph Capone's deposits and withdrawals under six different aliases.

The heirs to the Capone empire failed to profit from the experience of their dethroned bosses. Paul (The Waiter) Ricca, whose real name was Paul DeLucia, was the titular head of the Capone mob after the boss went to prison. He first served time for a million-dollar extortion plot and in 1958 was sentenced to nine years for tax evasion. The sentence was later cut to three years, but Ricca now faces deportation.

Nabbing the much-publicized big boys has one salient effect on other taxpayers who might be tempted to cut corners but do profit from other men's experiences. In Chicago at the height of the Capone investigation, for instance, payments of delinquent taxes spurted by a million dollars in one year. Two taxpayers confided that the Capone investigation scared them into thinking they might be the next to go. One handed over $235,000; the other, $200,000. At the time of their visits, the agents hadn't even looked their way.

Internal Revenue's Intelligence Division started out more as a weapon against corruption within the service than crime without. Early in 1919, Commissioner of Internal Revenue Daniel C. Roper, who later became Secretary of Commerce, began to hear sordid complaints that some of his tax-collecting employees were taking bribes or extorting money from taxpayers. Mr. Roper had previously served as First Assistant Postmaster General and knew the work of the postal inspectors in ferreting out dishonest employees as well as mail fraud. He wanted a similar unit in Internal Revenue, and he wanted to man it with postal inspectors.

On July 1, 1919, six postal inspectors were transferred to the Bureau of Internal Revenue. Their assignment: to investigate serious infractions of the rules by revenue employees and serious violations of revenue laws through collusion, conspiracy, extortion, bribery or any other manipulation aimed at defrauding the government of taxes.

One of the six postal inspectors was Elmer L. Irey, destined to become a formidable figure in American law enforcement. It was Irey who warred on Capone in Chicago and Waxey Gordon, most powerful of the New York racketeers of his day. It was Irey who insisted on including easy-to-trace gold certificates and recording the serial numbers of the ransom money in the Lindbergh baby kidnapping, who threatened to withdraw his agents from the case unless the money could be traced, who was vindicated when Bruno Hauptmann was traced through one of those gold certificates. It was Irey who helped launch the Treasury Law Enforcement Officer Training School as a training ground for all Treasury enforcement units. Irey served the Intelligence Division until 1936 when he became coordinator of all Treasury law enforcement.

From the nucleus of six postal inspectors, the Intelligence Division expanded until it now numbers close to 1,600 special agents. Today, they are hand-picked on college campuses from top students trained in the law, accountancy or both.

As the Intelligence Division grew, its duties shifted. Its original assignment, exposing corrupt employees, became the job of the Internal Revenue Inspection Service, created by order of President Truman in 1952 after a Congressional investigation of tax-fixing in high places. President Truman demanded a vigorous inspection service "to expose and punish wrong doers."

While the Intelligence Division was relieved of inspection duties, it accumulated a string of new tax laws to be enforced. Among them were Social Security, withholding, amusement and all other excise taxes except those on liquor, tobacco and narcotics. After the Kefauver investigation pinpointed gambling as the prime source of revenue for all organized crime, the special agents of the Intelligence Division were assigned another tax law—the occupational and excise tax on gambling.

More and higher taxes carry a built-in incentive to evade. Thus, during the 1961 fiscal year alone, special agents investigated more than 16,500 cases. Director Long reported a sharp increase in the number of criminal cases involving would-be tax cheats.

The cheaters come from the high and the lowly, from gravediggers to steeplejacks, from the ranks of doctor, lawyer, merchant, thief.

A Bronx porter claimed his dog Duchess as a dependent, only he changed the name to Doris and made her a daughter. A sailor, instead of following the classic pattern of a wife in every port, collected a tax refund in every port. A doctor juggled his records, but his tax dodging was proved after agents contacted 1,000 of his patients over a period of years.

The millionaire founder of Zippo cigarette lighters paid for remodeling his daughter's home, refurnishing his own, and another daughter's mortgage and wrote it off on the company books as deductions for "repairs and maintenance," advertising and raw materials. He's the one who deducted his home television set as a business expense for "employee recreation."

The president and top officials of Shopmaster, Inc., the firm making home workshop tools, managed—temporarily—to evade $3 million in taxes with a variety of schemes. A down payment on a home was listed as "a lot of brass pots," remodeling a home was written off as "warehouse repairs," clothing bills were deducted as steel purchases. Key employees who handled the books were persuaded not to talk by getting automobiles at company expense, and clerks were silenced with $100 bills—which they didn't report on their income tax returns, either.

To prove cases like this, agents have to track hundreds of items to their source. As taxpayers get smarter in their cheating, agents have to get smarter at outwitting them. In the old days, taxpayers simply tore up invoices of sales and failed to record them on the books. It was a comparatively simple, though time-consuming matter to check the customers and find out what they paid for merchandise. As taxpayers grew more sophisticated and tax rates jumped, sharp bookkeeping practices were introduced to show increased costs in doing business. Agents had to come up with some new techniques of their own, including infra-red viewing—a method of bringing out the original writing despite erasures and changes in the figures.

Now the agents face a new challenge. More and more companies have introduced automatic data processing. When an agent asks to see the company books, he is led to a stack of punch cards. The Intelligence Division has launched a training course to determine how holes in punch cards can be translated into sources of buying and spending.

The bulk of the tax evasion cases stems from taxpayers who have made their pile and just don't want to give any part of it to the Government. The minority of cases—but usually the toughest—involve the unreported proceeds of a criminal act. The agents not only have to prove the tax evasion but also the crime that produced the money. That's where they run head on into missing records, terrified witnesses who lie or flee and otherwise legitimate businessmen who don't want to get involved. The illegal funds may come from kickbacks by contractors to government officials, pay-offs by employers to union officials, pay-offs to police for freedom from interference, bribery, extortion or the profits of abortionists, gamblers, bootleggers and madams.

Proving corruption of public officials tests the ingenuity as well as the patience of the agents because nobody talks—not the official who takes nor the seeker of favors who gives. The blueprint for investigating venality in public life was drawn years ago in the case of Tom Pendergast, boss of Kansas City for close to 30 years. Pendergast wasn't just above the law. He was the law in Kansas City. He virtually owned every officeholder in the state from United States Senators to the lowliest city hall clerk. All of them owed their jobs to him.

Gambling was his weakness. He lost so heavily that he set up a $9,500,000 state insurance fund to finance himself. It proved his downfall. An agent investigating a Chicago attorney's tax liability discovered that an insurance representative had delivered to the attorney 14 checks from fire insurance companies doing business in Missouri. On the same day, the attorney turned over the law firm's own check for the same amount to the insurance representative.

The insurance official admitted the transaction but refused to identify the person who ultimately got the check until the *Queen Mary,* then on its maiden voyage, docked in New York. A check of the passenger list showed Pendergast was aboard and the agents took it from there. On May 22, 1939, Pendergast pleaded guilty to evading $443,550 in taxes and was sentenced to prison for 15 months. It marked the end of boss rule in Kansas City.

A tax investigation may start because an agent is alerted that a public official is apparently living beyond his means or gambling is operating wide-open in a town or a man who looks poor on his tax returns moves into a seaside mansion. Any of them may claim his sudden wealth is something he's had in the bank for years or his wife's uncle gave her the money.

The agents then check the uncle's financial history to see if he had that kind of money to give. They have checked overseas and found that the alleged benefactor was actually a poor farmer. In some cases, they have traced a man's income and expenses back 40 years to determine if he could have amassed a fortune.

An investigation may be launched or aided by a Congressional hearing. There's usually an agent on hand if the Congressmen are delving into possible crime and corruption.

Bernard Goldfine's tax troubles started in 1958 after the House Legislative Oversight Subcommittee began inquiring into the Boston industrialist's quaint habit of bestowing gifts and favors on high-level public officials. His admitted gift of a vicuna coat led Sherman Adams, President Eisenhower's top aide, to resign his White House post. Goldfine himself, on May 15, 1961, pleaded guilty to evading nearly $800,000 in income taxes for himself and one of his firms. He was sentenced to a year and a day in prison and fined $110,000.

An investigation may spread across the country when an agent in one city comes on a clue that a local fraud may be symptomatic of a nation-wide condition.

Homeowners had been victimized regularly by home improvement salesmen who used high-pressure tactics to fast-talk them into buying shoddy roofing and siding for their homes at inflated prices. An agent launched an industry-wide investigation of the salesmen after a check of one of them disclosed a tax-dodging pattern. In all, 80 cases were investigated in the original drive and four other districts subsequently launched investigations of what Better Business Bureaus call the "suede shoe boys."

Where income tax cases frequently require agents to sift through thousands of records, gambling cases require a different range of investigative techniques. Abe Minker, the gambling kingpin of Reading, Pa., was convicted of gambling tax evasion through the cooperation of a private trash collector, who turned over trash from Minker's barrel to special agents regularly for a three-month period. The gambling evidence was combed out of the rest of the refuse.

A combination of surveillance and legwork broke the largest gambling tax case in the nation at Terre Haute, Ind. Leo Shaffer and Jules Horwick, reputed to be the top football bookies in the country, had fled to Canada when the gambling tax law went into effect and fled back again when Canadian police raided their international bookmaking headquarters. They had collected some cronies and moved to Terre Haute.

Intelligence agents weren't far behind, but this was a tough one. The gamblers arranged for a local colleague to apply for a gambling tax stamp and file a monthly return on his modest earnings. He was their front. The agents needed a search warrant to raid the gambling headquarters in a downtown office building. In order to get it, they had to prove that this was the headquarters not for one small-time gambler but for a big-time syndicate.

The agents maintained a watch over the third floor headquarters. They noticed that only members of the syndicate entered and all of them had keys. They checked hotel registration cards to prove the principals all arrived in Terre Haute at the same time. They checked telephone records and found eight telephones had been installed with a billing of more than 5,000 long distance calls in less than three months. They arranged with postal clerks to get a record of registered mail with money paid and received by the syndicate to settle football bets across the country. The agents thus accumulated enough evidence for a search warrant. The raid produced evidence that the syndicate, in ten weeks of operation, had booked a minimum of $3,263,000 worth of bets.

At 11:30 A.M. on January 14, 1959, special agents throughout the country handed subpoenas to wealthy bettors to appear at the trial. The subpoenas were all served simultaneously to discourage the prospective witnesses from suddenly taking long vacations to keep away from Terre Haute. Their testimony—given reluctantly—helped put six men away for five-year prison terms.

Arresting a bookie is sometimes a hazardous operation as agents learned in Atlanta, Ga., in 1960. As an agent was examining a sheet of baseball bets taken from the prisoner's pocket, the bookie touched his lighted cigarette to the paper. The sheet exploded into flame, searing the agent's hand. The bookie had written his bets on nitrocellulose, commonly known as guncotton.

Tax dodgers facing prison are sometimes as likely as murderers to become fugitives from justice. And they are treated the same way. In December, 1955, the Intelligence Division started issuing "wanted circulars." To date, 72 fugitives have made the "wanted" list and 38 have been accounted for—including a man who was recognized as a tax dodging fugitive when he came into the police station at Pawtucket, R.I., to report a routine traffic accident.

Of the 34 fugitives now on the "wanted" list, the most notorious is Virginia Hill, underworld glamor girl who once told the Kefauver committee her income came from "bets and men." It was at the home "Bugsy" Siegel provided for her that "Bugsy" was mowed down by his rival mobsters. The Intelligence Division knows Virginia's whereabouts, but she's living in Europe and income tax evasion is not an extraditable offense.

Tax cheaters who think they can keep it all might have looked into the clouded crystal ball of Claude Alexander, a magician who was billed on the stage as "Alexander, The Man Who Knows." Alexander filed a return for one year showing a net loss of $77.58. Agents went all over the country totaling up his income from vaudeville and a mail order business featuring crystal balls, horoscopes and assorted mystic paraphernalia. Alexander, the agents found, had a net income of $125,919.32.

The judge, without benefit of crystal ball, fined him $2,500. He also had to pay $75,000 in taxes and penalties. "Alexander, The Man Who Knows" didn't know enough to steer clear of Internal Revenue's special agents.

THE RICHMOND CAPER

Richmond is a prim and proper southern city. It viewed a man like Harry L. Donovan with the tolerance of a maiden aunt. Perhaps Harry was a gambler on the side but he was a local boy, a member of the family, so to speak. If there had to be gambling, it was better to keep it in the family than have some of those out-of-town hoodlums moving in.

The Internal Revenue Service took a different view of Harry Donovan. Their intelligence agents in Richmond were convinced that Donovan, a bootlegger during Prohibition, had followed the pattern of other bootleggers and switched after repeal to another lucrative field of crime—the numbers game.

If Donovan was the man behind the numbers business in Richmond, he owed the Government some money. Under Federal wagering tax laws, a gambler has to pay an annual $50 occupational tax, file a return on his gambling profits and pay a monthly 10 per cent excise tax on his gambling gross.

In 1955, Internal Revenue had brought Donovan into Federal court for income tax evasion, charging he hadn't reported his huge gambling profits or paid income taxes on them. Donovan admitted he had been a gambler at one time but insisted he had quit in 1952 when he started his juke box business. The jury found him guilty but the judge set the conviction aside on a technicality.

Beating the tax rap that had put so many other racketeers in jail enhanced Donovan's stature. He was regarded as untouchable. He boasted to his friends that Internal Revenue could never get him for failing to pay his gambling taxes because he never touched a numbers slip. Certainly, there was no police record connecting him with gambling. In fact, Donovan had no police record at all.

Donovan, then, was riding high in the spring of 1959 when he received a visit from two veteran Internal Revenue special agents in the pine-paneled private office of his business place on Main Street—the Richmond Amusement Sales Co.

The agents—Luther Burton and Douglas Waesche—asked him if he was aware that the Federal law required him to pay an occupational tax and an excise tax on his gambling gross.

Donovan, gray-eyed and still handsome though jowly and going to fat, regarded the agents coolly. He waved at the pictures of race horses lining his office walls. His racing stable, he said, was his interest now. Sure, he knew about the gambling taxes but—as he had told the court in 1955—he had given up the numbers business years ago.

The agents thanked him and departed. They had accomplished their mission—to establish that Donovan knew about the gambling tax law and, if he was still in the numbers business, that he was wilfully avoiding a debt to Uncle Sam.

On September 25, 1959, Burton and Waesche picked up a tip. An anonymous informant supplied the name of a man who worked for Donovan—not in his juke box business. This Donovan employee, according to the informant, was Leo Seay. The agents started watching Seay's home.

Seay turned out to be a ferret-faced ex-bootlegger addicted to sunglasses and a slouch hat. A man of regular habits, Seay left his house about the same time every weekday with a man who drove a red, black and white Dodge. Sometimes, they would go off in the Dodge. Other times, they would use one of the two cars parked behind Seay's home—a blue and white Mercury or a blue Plymouth. By tracing the car registration of the Dodge, the agents established the identity of Seay's companion—George P. Smethie, Jr.

While the agents were watching the Seay home, their targets changed their departure time from 1:45 P.M. to 2:30 P.M. The agents knew what that meant. The numbers on which the poor people bet their dimes and dollars daily are figured on the parimutuel results at the various race tracks. If one track has a later starting time than another, the closing time on taking numbers bets varies too. The time Seay and Smethie started out obviously depended on which track the numbers backer was using that day.

The agents started trailing the two men. They followed them to a dead-end street by the railroad track and saw Seay and Smethie park and wait. As if by clockwork, one car after another turned into the dead-end street. Each driver handed over a brown paper bag to Seay or Smethie, made a U-turn and departed. In a half-hour the performance was repeated a dozen times. Then, Seay and Smethie drove away. The dead-end street was obviously the "drop" or rendezvous point.

The agents cut a hole in a nearby railroad shed and started taking pictures in black and white and color. They were getting on film the faces of the drivers, the color of their cars and the numbers of their license plates.

The faces were those of the pick-up men. In the brown paper bags were the numbers slips they had received from the lowest echelon of the racket—the numbers writers who recorded the bets of the customers and took their money.

But where did Seay and Smethie go with the brown paper bags? Some place, there was a counting house where the day's bets were tallied on an adding machine and the "hits" or winning bets were recorded. The counting house was sure to be well-concealed—far from Donovan, if it was Donovan's operation.

Though Seay and Smethie were experts at avoiding surveillance—driving so slowly that a following car could easily be spotted—the agents managed to follow them from the dead-end street to the main highway and thence north toward Washington, past the city limits. The agents saw Seay and Smethie turn off the highway into an isolated, undeveloped subdivision with many intersecting, unpaved streets. It looked like a ghost town. No houses were in sight from the main highway. The agents couldn't follow them into the subdivision. A strange car would be as out of place as an ice cream truck.

The agents studied a plat of the subdivision and mapped their strategy. Each day, an agent would lie in the woods at a different intersection and wait for the Seay and Smethie car to go by. Which way did the car turn? The following day, the agent moved to the next intersection to watch the next turn. It took nearly a week to progress ten turns and ten blocks, but the agents finally narrowed their search to a dirt track with three houses on a dead-end street.

Burton, Waesche and Special Agent Sidney Macauley, who had been added to the team, dressed in old clothes, tucked some blueprints under their arms and sallied forth as telephone linesmen. At each telephone pole, they studid their blueprints, appeared to make notes and passed on to the next pole—always closer to the three houses.

At the first of the three houses, a woman came running out as their approach was announced by the barking of many dogs. Little beagles yipped at her side and in the fenced yard of the white frame bungalow, a dozen large hounds strained at their chains.

The agents asked the woman if her telephone service was satisfactory and moved on to the next pole. If that was the counting house, they had a big problem—those dogs.

On October 26, 1959, while Waesche was still making his movies in the railroad shed, Burton and Macauley parked half a mile away from the three houses on a street they knew Seay and Smethie didn't use. The agents started creeping through the woods, the dry leaves sounding like firecrackers at every step. They dropped to their hands and knees as they neared the three houses. If the dogs saw them or heard them or smelled them, they would give the show away.

At 3:12 P.M., they saw Seay's blue and white Mercury pull up in front of the white bungalow with the dogs. The agents watched Seay and Smethie carry a bunch of brown paper bags into the house. The dogs didn't let out a single yip. Obviously, the two men were no strangers.

"Right on time," Burton whispered.

They had found the counting house, but they were no closer to Donovan.

In early November, Macauley borrowed a truck, hauled out his old clothes again and parked half a block away from Donovan's juke box establishment on Main Street. He saw Smethie park and go into the Donovan place. He saw others go in and out and duly noted the license numbers of their cars.

And then he saw a familiar face. A member of the Richmond Police Department's vice squad parked a private car, entered the juke box establishment and stayed half an hour.

Macauley was still wondering what the policeman was doing in there, when a stationwagon parked in front of his truck. The driver started across the street toward Donovan's place. Then, as he looked down the street to wait for a break in the traffic, he noticed Macauley lounging in the truck. He deliberately changed direction and walked by the truck, looking thoughtfully at Macauley.

The agent, through his rear view mirror, saw the man go to a telephone pay station on the corner, dial a number, talk a minute and then look idly around as if he were waiting for an answer. Then, the man hung up and went down the street to Donovan's place.

When Macauley checked the license number of the stationwagon with the curious driver, he found it belonged to a detective on the Richmond police force. The detective had obviously called headquarters to check the license tags on the truck.

Macauley wasn't worried about that. The tag had come off a bootlegger's car seized by the Alcohol and Tobacco Tax Division, the "revenooers." But the detective's wariness meant the agents had to find another way to watch Donovan's place. They couldn't just go to a house in the neighborhood and say what they wanted. Donovan had too many friends.

Then, Macauley spotted something. Directly across from Donovan's place, a row house had a room-for-rent sign in the window. He didn't want the owner to know he had been hanging around that neighborhood—just in case the owner turned out to be a friend of Donovan—so he checked the newspapers to see if the room had been advertised. The ad was there.

When he telephoned the number listed in the ad, a woman answered. She thought the room was rented but he could come and look, if he liked.

It was just what he wanted—a second floor front room with a big bay window and a perfect view of Donovan's place. The afternoon sun, slanting through the plate glass windows of the juke box establishment, spotlighted people all the way back to the door of Donovan's private office.

The one-legged landlady looked him over. "What's your line?" she asked.

"I'm an insurance salesman," he told her.

"Well," she said, "I've sort of promised the room to a bus driver and his son. Would you give me $20 a week for this?"

Macauley knew it was much too high. He didn't want to seem anxious, but he had to have that room.

"That's pretty steep," he drawled, "but I know a fellow who wants a room, too. He could come in with me and share the rent."

The landlady nodded. "You bring him in with you Monday," she said. "I'll let you know then."

All that weekend, Macauley and Max Johnson—a special agent imported from Norfolk for this job—worked on creating a new identity. Johnson would be a freight handler on the night shift. That would give him the daytime hours in his room to watch the place across the street. Macauley, who actually had been an insurance man, visited his old firm and picked up the usual literature—blotters, calendars, a standard rate book. The agents went over their suitcases and clothing to remove all identifying name tags. If the landlady prowled—and she was just the type—there would be nothing to reveal their true identities.

On Monday, November 23, 1959, Macauley showed up with Johnson. The landlady looked them over—Macauley, young, good-looking, with a suggestion of a Southern drawl; Johnson, short, stocky, amiable. The landlady said they could have the room.

About a week after they moved in, the landlady asked Macauley if he knew Donovan.

"I haven't been around town long," he said. "Who's Donovan?"

"His place is right across the street," she told him with a note of pride in her voice. "Everybody knows Donovan, the big racketeer. He just loaned me $300."

One night, the landlady was entertaining. Macauley could hear guitar music, hillbilly songs, drunken voices. A guest staggered upstairs and insisted that he join the party. He found the guests arguing over which bootlegger to call for a fresh supply of whisky.

"This bootlegger is one of Donovan's boys," a guest insisted. "He'll deliver fast."

The fifth of whisky was on the table in four minutes.

Johnson and Macauley spent their days at the bay window. Every morning, they saw Smethie go into Donovan's place. Once a week, they spotted the pick-up men who had delivered paper bags by the railroad track. And they watched the parade of policemen. There were police in uniform and out of uniform, in police squad cars and private cars, even on motorcycles.

"Donovan's place looks like city hall," Johnson muttered.

When the sun was at the right slant and they could see as far as Donovan's office, they watched the policemen go directly to the private office.

The agents took out bags of dirty laundry and brought them back filled with camera equipment. They carried in film in their lunch boxes and started taking pictures of Donovan's visitors.

The film evidence was piling up. Seay and Smethie, now joined by a third man identified as Raymond Walker, Jr., had moved their rendezvous point from the railroad track to a downtown industrial street where Waesche was taking his pictures through a pane of one-way glass in an old truck.

The troubles were piling up, too. One day, Seay and Smethie didn't take the highway to the bungalow and had to be tracked down all over again to a new counting house in the city. Then, they switched back to the country but used a circuitous new route. The agents parked on the highway to clock them as they crossed the last intersection before the three houses. And then Seay, Smethie and Walker started going to the counting house at night when they couldn't be seen from the highway.

District Intelligence Chief Alan McBride was now having almost daily conferences with United States Attorney Joseph Bambacus. If the agents delayed their move much longer, the Internal Revenue officer warned, they might have to start all over again. Donovan's boys were getting cagy. Their latest gambit was to park their car at the rendezvous known to the agents but take the actual deliveries of the brown paper bags a block away. Furthermore, the police were beginning to steer clear of Donovan's place.

Prosecutor Bambacus was cautious. Donovan had beaten the Federal agents before. There could be no holes in this investigation—no holes that Donovan could crawl through.

To plug one such hole, Special Agents John R. Murphy and Ellis E. Bean hid inside a paneled truck behind Donovan's place to prove beyond argument that Donovan was actually on the premises when Smethie made his daily visits—presumably to report the previous day's take.

The two agents, sweltering inside the truck, gradually stripped to their shorts. Then, they heard a man shouting that the truck was in his parking place. The handle at the back of the truck rattled. Had they remembered to lock the back doors? If those doors opened, they would literally be caught with their pants down. They heard a mutter and footsteps moving away. They had locked the truck.

While agents hid in trucks, trailed suspects, took more pictures, Prosecutor Bambacus and Intelligence Chief McBride reviewed the evidence. There was the pattern—the pick-up men going to the rendezvous, the brown paper bags taken from the rendezvous to the counthouse, Smethie's daily appearances at Donovan's place, the weekly visits of the pick-up men.

"You still haven't any direct proof that Donovan is behind all this," worried the prosecutor. "We've got to link Donovan to the counthouse."

"Let us assume," said Chief McBride, "that Smethie brings Donovan a record of the previous day's play and hits—probably a piece of adding machine tape. If we raid the counthouse and Donovan's place simultaneously, we might get the numbers slips at the counthouse to match against the tape at Donovan's. Then you'd have your link."

"What makes you think the counthouse would keep the slips once they're tallied?" the prosecutor asked.

"If the pick-up men settle only once a week," Chief McBride explained, "the counthouse is likely to hold the slips as proof until the pick-up men give Donovan what they owe him."

The prosecutor and the intelligence chief got down to planning the raids. They would go to Alexandria, Va., for their search warrants. Donovan had too many friends around Richmond who might speculate about the presence of Internal Revenue agents at the courthouse. The raid would require importing more Federal agents and some deputy United States marshals to serve the warrants. The raiders would gather for a 6 A.M. briefing on Friday, January 22. Smethie's departure from Donovan's place that morning would trigger the raids.

On the morning of January 22, Johnson and Macauley stayed near the bay window of their second-floor room, their eyes fixed on the front door of Donovan's place. Down the street, an agent sat in a truck with a radio telephone. He didn't know Smethie himself. Macauley would give him the signal when Smethie left Donovan's place. On the road to Washington, five minutes away from the counthouse, a squad of agents waited on the highway. Around the corner from Donovan's place, a car loaded with agents parked in a lot behind a supermarket.

At 11:03 A.M., Macauley left his room and strolled down the street. Beside the truck, he stopped and pulled out a handkerchief to blow his nose. Then he walked on. The agent in the truck flipped on his radio and muttered a few words. Smethie had left Donovan's place.

At base headquarters, Chief McBride started barking orders. A squad of agents swung off the highway and drove swiftly to the counthouse. Half of them hit the front door with their search warrant. The others hurtled the fence and made for the back door before the big hounds could be unchained. The little beagles ran away from them.

The agents on the supermarket parking lot pulled into the alley behind Donovan's place and pounded on the back door. Another car drove by the front of Donovan's place, dropped more agents and moved on. Everything was to look normal out front to lessen the chance of a tip-off. Macauley went off to visit Smethie.

The first word reached headquarters from Murphy at the counthouse.

"We've got plenty of stuff," the agent reported. "They have a bedroom fixed up like an office with three adding machines. We've picked up a couple of locked metal boxes, six shopping bags full of numbers slips and a 50-pound dog food sack. That's loaded with slips, too."

At Donovan's place, the agents were having a rough time. All they sought was one piece of adding machine tape. Donovan lounged in his big leather chair, watching the agents with a pleasant smile.

His desk was piled high with papers. The agents went through them all. No tape. Donovan unlocked the drawers of his desk for them. The agents flipped through the papers jamming the drawers. Nothing. They searched through the stacks of papers piled on the window sills. Records, invoices, racing forms, no tape. There were close to 150 pictures of horses crowded on the office walls. The agents looked behind all of them.

In the store proper, they surveyed the mass of juke boxes, parts of juke boxes, wires, records, coin boxes, bills, advertisements. To the agents, it looked as though everything in the place had been tossed up in the air and left where it fell. Doggedly, they searched through the junk, looking for one piece of adding machine tape.

Burton eyed an old gray-painted kitchen cupboard in the corner of Donovan's private office. It seemed out of place in the pine-panelled room. He opened the glass doors of the upper half of the cupboard. Nothing on the three shelves but layers of dust. He opened the wooden doors of the cupboard's lower half. Nothing on those shelves either.

He studied the cupboard more carefully. Why would Donovan keep an old piece of furniture like this in his private office, an empty, unlocked cupboard?

The agent looked closer. Between the bottom shelf of the glass-enclosed section and the top of the wood-enclosed section was a gap of about six inches. Burton turned to Donovan. "Have you got a secret drawer here?" he asked. Donovan shrugged and said he knew nothing about it.

Burton pried up the bottom shelf of the glass-paned section. There was the hidden compartment, the reason for the old cupboard in the private office. He saw it could be opened with battery-operated release catches.

At the moment, though, Burton wasn't interested in how the secret drawer operated. He was still looking for the adding machine tape. It wasn't in the drawer, but there were other things of interest. Money, more than $6,000 in small bills. Christmas cards with postmarks on the envelope from the previous month. A 10-cent spiral notebook with a scrawl of figures on every page.

Burton showed the notebook to Donovan. No longer smiling, Donovan answered in a low gravelly voice: "I can't remember anything about that. I haven't been in that compartment for a long time. It's real old stuff."

Burton pointed out that the Christmas cards were recent, that the notebook was slick and clean. Donovan said nothing. Burton put the notebook on the desk and moved away. He noticed Donovan's hand starting to reach for the little book. Burton picked up the book, took it across the room and dropped it on a table. Donovan started toward the table as if a magnet were pulling him to the book. This time, Burton stuck the notebook in his pocket. Donovan had lied about the secret compartment, had lied about the age of the book, had shown an unusual interest in it. There was something about this book that bore further study.

Burton now picked up a personal telephone directory from Donovan's desk and flipped through the pages.

"That's an old one," Donovan volunteered.

At his first look through, Burton spotted numbers later than December, 1957, when the city changed to a lettered dial system. He could make it even more up to date. The directory showed Smethie's new telephone number, which, Burton knew, had been connected less than two weeks earlier. Some telephone numbers had an arrow beside them.

The agents had failed to find the adding machine tape but they had uncovered two items Donovan valued enough to lie about—the telephone directory and the spiral notebook.

Meanwhile, Macauley, accompanied by an agent imported from Roanoke, was calling on Smethie. Questions and more questions. Smethie didn't know a thing, so he said. About 1 P.M., the telephone rang and Macauley picked it up. It was Smethie's friend Seay.

"Everything okay?" asked Seay.

"Yeah," said Macauley.

Seay said he'd be seeing Smethie and hung up.

The agents exchanged glances. Was it possible that two hours after the raids Seay was still unaware that the numbers empire was crumbling? It was worth a trip to Seay's rendezvous with the pick-up men.

At 2:45 P.M., when the agents descended on the meeting place, Seay was carrying on business as usual. Some of the pick-up men had already made their deliveries. Bags of numbers slips lay on the floor of Seay's blue Plymouth. While the search was on, six familiar cars turned into the street and veered off. The agents saw bags of slips thrown from car windows. One car bumped over the sidewalk and ploughed into the woods.

Seay was no more communicative than Smethie.

"You've got me and the stuff," he said. "What more do you want?"

What the agents wanted—had to have—was a firm link between Donovan, the pick-up men, the counthouse men, the whole operation.

They were sure the link was there—somewhere in the pile of numbers slips from Seay's car, the slips and records and a marked calendar seized at the counthouse, the personal telephone directory and that little spiral notebook from Donovan's office.

The telephone directory was decoded first. The arrows pointing to certain numbers meant they were reversed. These were the numbers of policemen. The rest of the names traced from the numbers read like a who's who of big and small-time crooks.

In one of the locked metal boxes seized at the counthouse, agents found what they figured to be hit slips—carbon copies of figures Smethie delivered nightly to the pick-up men. For each day of January, there were 22 slips so they had to account for 22 pick-up men.

On the wall calendar seized at the counthouse, agents noticed a number written under each date. Obviously, this was a record of the winning number each day. Agents could date the hit slips by consulting the calendar.

To verify the winning numbers, agents checked the Racing Form for a track where the first race was off at 2:30 P.M. and found the New Orleans Fair Grounds. Then they added the pay-offs to arrive at the winning number.

They were now ready for the notebook. On each page, the scrawl showed four lines of figures in three columns. The four lines could represent the first four days of the week since the raid was on Friday. Now the three columns of figures. By subtracting the second column from the first column, they came out with the third column.

So, the first column showed what the pick-up man collected from his customers after deducting his own 30 per cent. The second column represented what he owed the winning customers. The third column was what he owed Donovan.

This was all theory. Now they had to prove it. The agents sat down with the bags of slips seized at the counthouse and added them up on the machines just as the counthouse men had done. They worked every bundle of slips for every day and charted it all out. They figured the winners and double-checked them against the hits they had found recorded in the locked box. They accounted for each of the 22 pick-up men.

The counthouse men, they found, had made some mistakes because they went so fast. But the figures were close enough to prove beyond a reasonable doubt that the numbers in Donovan's little notebook tallied with the slips found at the counthouse and the code names of the pick-up men found on the slips in Seay's car matched the code names on each page of Donovan's notebook.

The calculations had taken them two weeks but they had found the undisputable link between the numbers operation and Donovan. Macauley, who had directed this part of the work, reported his findings to Chief McBride.

"On a two-million-dollar-a-year business," said Macauley, "this little notebook was Donovan's accounts receivable ledger."

The agents still had to prove that this was Donovan's own notebook, written in his own handwriting. It wasn't enough to show that the notebook had come out of a secret drawer in Donovan's private office. Donovan could always claim other people had access to his office. The agents had to get a specimen of Donovan's handwriting—one they could testify they had seen him write.

On March 15, immediately after a Federal grand jury indicted

Donovan on eleven counts of violating the Federal Wagering Tax Statute, Donovan was brought to the United States Marshal's office to be booked and fingerprinted.

Usually, a deputy marshal types out the fingerprint card with its identifying information. This time, by request of the agents, the marshal asked Donovan to fill out the card himself. While agents watched from the hallway, Donovan put on his horn-rimmed glasses and filled out the card.

When a deputy handed the completed card to the agents, they scanned it quickly. The most unusual item in the spiral notebook had been the way Donovan wrote the numeral three. Instead of two semi-circles, his three looked like a quarter-moon. On the fingerprint card, Donovan had used figures for his address, age, height and weight but there wasn't a single three.

"Ask him to date the card," an agent suggested.

Donovan did as he was told. He wrote: "3/15/60."

In the pre-trial maneuvering, Donovan's attorneys demanded a look at the Government's evidence. The spiral notebook was stuck in the middle of the pile, as if the prosecutor attached no special meaning to it. Either Donovan had not briefed his attorneys on the significance of the little notebook or they didn't want to call the Government's attention to it. Donovan's attorneys showed no reaction to the notebook.

The lawyers moved to change the scene of the trial from Richmond. They could argue that the city had been aroused against Donovan by a grand jury report citing "overwhelming evidence of appalling and flagrant disregard for law and order which, we believe, seriously threatens the general welfare of our city and state." The first of a series of investigations of Richmond police was already underway in the wake of the grand jury report.

If Donovan's attorneys hoped to get away from Federal Judge Albert V. Bryan by shifting the trial, they were in for a disappointment. Judge Bryan—since elevated to the Federal Court of Appeals—agreed to move the trial to Newport News, Va., but announced he would try it there himself.

Prosecutor Bambacus subpoenaed a long list of witnesses, among them many of Donovan's writers and pick-up men who had already refused to testify against Donovan. But on the list were ones who would talk. By the size of the list, Prosecutor Bambacus had hidden the willing witnesses.

Donovan was still protesting his innocence when the trial began. He still felt safe. After all, he had beaten the Government's rap before and he was well aware that 56 of the policemen summoned to appear before a special grand jury had refused to talk on grounds of self-incrimination.

As the trial progressed, the only witness who faced any real cross-examination was a pick-up man. He testified that he had worked for Donovan for two years and turned over money to him, but court observers were inclined to feel the pick-up man was pretty much discredited by the hot cross-examination. So far, Donovan's attorneys apparently felt he was the only link to Donovan.

With virtually no cross-examination, Macauley testified to seeing the counthouse men going in and out of Donovan's store. The jury looked at movies taken by Macauley and Waesche. Murphy described what he had found in the raid on the counthouse, including the locked box and the bags of numbers slips. The kitchen cabinet with its secret compartment was brought into the courtroom and Burton showed how he had found $6,005 and the little spiral notebook there. The United States Marshal testified to Donovan's filling out the fingerprint card himself and the card went into the evidence with no objection from the defense attorneys. This was all routine.

Prosecutor Bambacus prepared to lower the boom. A handwriting expert from the office of the Treasury's Examiner of Questioned Documents took the stand. He testified that the fingerprint card and the figures in the little notebook were written by the same man.

The defense attorneys were on their feet. "We object to the fingerprint card," they told the judge.

Judge Bryan overruled them. "You had your chance," he said, "when the marshal was on the stand."

On the afternoon of the third day of the trial, Macauley was recalled to the witness stand. The courtroom was darkened. By the use of an opaque projector, what Macauley described was flashed on a screen for the benefit of the jury. Macauley put a page of the notebook found in Donovan's place and a record of the hit slips found at the counthouse side by side. He showed how the middle column of the notebook tallied with the hit slips.

He told the jury how he used the counthouse calendar to date the hit slips, how he added the numbers slips, how the totals coincided with the figures in the notebook. He was on the stand for three hours.

Prosecutor Bambacus had one last question: "In your opinion, what does this little book mean?"

"This little book," replied Macauley, "represents the type of record a numbers backer must keep. No one else would have such a record. The man who keeps that book is a numbers backer."

Prosecutor Bambacus turned to the defense. "Your witness," he said.

Donovan's attorneys held a quick conference.

"It's late in the day," one of them said. "We request that the trial be recessed until tomorrow morning."

The next morning, 10 o'clock came and went, and rumors raced through the courthouse. The judge was conferring in chambers with the attorneys. Every seat in the courtroom was taken. Everybody wanted to hear how the defense was going to attack the little notebook.

An hour passed before Judge Bryan appeared. One of the defense attorneys rose to his feet. "Your honor," he said, "my client has decided to plead guilty to all counts."

Donovan was sent to Atlanta Penitentiary for four years. The Government also assessed him $183,267.84 in taxes and penalties. His counthouse men were tried and convicted in the state court. As for the police whose conduct had shocked a grand jury and the people of Richmond, 86 policemen admitted visiting Donovan's Main Street establishment.

The Internal Revenue special agents had struck a blow for local law enforcement. No longer complacent, Richmond now expects its police force to police.

15 ★★★

Secret Service

You might spot him in a crowd around the President of the United States. He doesn't seem at all interested in what's going on. He's not even looking at the President.

Actually, he's the most interested man there. His eyes are moving over the crowd, ceaselessly searching for a suspicious movement, an unfriendly face, glaring eyes. He is a Secret Service agent.

Protecting the President from disaster is the prime responsibility of the Secret Service but it is not the only major responsibility nor was it the original one. Ironically, the President who approved creation of the Secret Service was Abraham Lincoln, but he and two other Presidents were to be killed before the Secret Service was assigned to protect the man in the White House.

Decades after the Secret Service was established, a newspaper actually criticized the agency for giving the President a bodyguard on vacation. The Secret Service, observed the newspaper critic, was paid to suppress counterfeiting, not to go gallivanting after the President.

It wasn't until President McKinley was assassinated that Congress faced up to an unpleasant truth. During the 112 years between the signing of the Constitution and the fatal shooting of President McKinley, not a single ruler of England, Germany or Spain had been assassinated and France, Italy and Austria had lost only one each.

There had been attempts on the European rulers, but the would-be assassins had been foiled because the rulers were protected. American sovereigns had no such protection.

As the only general investigative agency in the Federal government at that time, the Secret Service drew the job of protecting President Theodore Roosevelt and his successors. The protection was extended to the President-elect in 1913, to members of the President's family in 1917 and to the Vice President, at his request, in 1951.

Members of the Secret Service are duty-bound to sacrifice their own lives if necessary to protect the White House family and the Vice President.

The first agent killed on Presidential duty was William Craig, who was fatally injured in 1902 when a trolley car in Lenox, Mass., collided with the President's carriage. A bullet aimed at President Franklin Delano Roosevelt grazed the hand of a Secret Service agent and killed Mayor Anton Cermak of Chicago in 1932. A plaque at the entrance of Blair House diagonally across the street from the White House reads:

"In honor of Leslie Coffelt, White House guard who gave his life in the defense of the President of the United States here at Blair House, November 1, 1950."

Pvt. Coffelt was a member of the uniformed White House Police Force which is charged with protecting the White House building and grounds under supervision of the chief of the Secret Service. Two other White House policemen—Corpl. Joseph H. Downs and Donald T. Birdzell—were critically wounded as White House police and Secret Service agents shot it out with two Puerto Rican Nationalists attempting to kill President Truman.

Agents have shared joy and sorrow, adventure and death with their Presidential charges. They had to follow President Wilson when he was courting Mrs. Edith Bolling Galt. They kept the vigil with President Coolidge at his dying son's bedside. When President Roosevelt lapsed into unconsciousness, it was an agent who summoned a doctor to his side. Agents had traveled with him through submarine-infested waters to his wartime conferences at Casablanca, Teheran and Yalta, as they later flew with President-elect Eisenhower to the front lines of the Korean War.

Because this is a free country and its chief executive cannot be surrounded by fixed bayonets, the Secret Service has stressed preventive protection. This ranges from tracking down anonymous threats to making elaborate security arrangements wherever the President goes.

Thousands of crank letters with real or implied threats reach the White House each year. They are channeled to the Protective Research Section of the Secret Service for possible identification through paper, handwriting, ink, typewriter characteristics and geographical location. It's up to agents in the field to trace the author, if they can.

A typical one came from St. Louis, Mo., addressed to "Mr. Eisenhower." It said simply: "I am going to kill you soon." It was signed. Agents found that the purported author of the letter was a middle-aged postal clerk who had just gotten married. His bride, under questioning, recalled that a customer in the store where she worked had been trying to date her for years without success. He had never given her his right name, but the agents found him. The disappointed Romeo admitted he had written the letter to embarrass his rival.

When the President travels, Secret Service agents precede him. If he stays at a hotel, they probably know more than the management about the personnel who will serve the President, the load the elevators will take, the ventilation system, the fire precautions and the nearby guests. When the President rides in a parade, the agents have already been over the route, sealing manholes, clearing rooftops, checking people along the parade line.

The danger then is narrowed to the unforeseen, the unexpected, the suicidal attempt.

Richard P. Pavlick was the suicidal type. His first plan was to crash his bomb-laden car into President-elect Kennedy's car. Then, he decided to make a human bomb of himself, get as close to the President as possible in church and detonate the explosive. The Secret Service got him before he could get the President.

The danger may be real—as it was the day in Key West when an agent saw a large barracuda swimming toward President Truman and inserted himself between the killer fish and the President.

Or the danger may be only potential—as it was when white-robed Berber tribesmen lined President Eisenhower's route into Casablanca and fired their guns.

The agents, ready to fire back, were told the bearded tribesmen were only paying tribute to a visiting sovereign with gun powder, but one of those rifles could have held a bullet.

The agents are never far from the President's side but they cannot become so oppressive that an individualist—as most Presidents are—would rebel. Thus, when President Truman took his early morning walks, an automobile full of agents with telescopic rifles and tommy guns followed, but kept just out of his view to give him a feeling of freedom. And when President Eisenhower golfed at Burning Tree Country Club, some of the golfers strolling nearby had high-powered rifles instead of clubs in their golf bags. Chief James Rowley, who headed the White House detail before he succeeded Chief U. E.

Baughman in September, 1961, feared that a sniper might lurk on the wooded golf course and acted accordingly.

Protecting the President's life is directly related to the national security, the orderly processes of government and, potentially, even the peace of the world.

Protecting the nation's monetary system against forgers and counterfeiters—the first and still a major responsibility of the Secret Service—directly concerns the Nation's economic stability. That's why leaders in war from Napoleon to Hitler have used counterfeiting as a weapon of warfare, a silent saboteur.

It was concern about counterfeiting that prompted President Lincoln to approve creation of the Secret Service. At President Lincoln's last cabinet meeting, Secretary of the Treasury Hugh McCullough told him that counterfeiting of the nation's currency was getting out of control. By the latest count, 6,000 different types of counterfeit American currency were on record. The Treasury had offered rewards for detection of the counterfeits but Secretary McCullough had the uncomfortable feeling that some of those collecting the rewards were counterfeiters themselves. President Lincoln gave Secretary McCullough the go-ahead signal for an organized force to war on the counterfeiters before the people lost all faith in the nation's paper money.

The Secret Service was formally created by Secretary McCullough on July 5, 1865, to suppress counterfeiting. Oddly enough, it could have been killed by a Congressman raising a "point of order" at any time for the next 86 years.

It existed solely on the basis of annual appropriation acts until 1951, when Chief Baughman initiated a bill defining the powers and duties of the Secret Service by law.

The present duties of the 325 Secret Service agents revolve around protecting the President and the Government's financial obligations—from gold and government checks to dollars and savings bonds. In earlier days, for lack of any other Federal investigators to do it, Secret Service agents were assigned chores now delegated to a dozen other government agencies.

Agents of the Secret Service investigated naturalization frauds, opium smuggling, espionage and sabotage, land frauds and monopolies, bribery, crime on the high seas and even the ravages of the fruit fly. They went after the Ku Klux Klan in the 1870's and brought in 1,000 of the hooded terrorists. They foiled an attempt to steal Lincoln's body from its tomb—a plot hatched by accomplices of a jailed counterfeiter to use the body in exchange for their buddy's freedom. They marched with "Coxey's Army" of unemployed to prevent violence. They tangled with the Mafia during World War I, when the dreaded secret society of Sicilian cutthroats turned to counterfeiting.

They exposed the huge land frauds in the Western states, when powerful cattle barons were bribing Civil War veterans to file papers as homesteaders and turn over the land for grazing cattle, mining and lumbering. They stepped on the toes of Congressmen then and later when they went after the "beef trust" in Chicago packing houses. They routed out a Spanish spy-ring operating during the Spanish-American war and exposed a German plot to cripple the British effort to buy war supplies in America before this country entered World War I. On orders from President Coolidge, they investigated one of the noisiest scandals of the Roaring Twenties—Teapot Dome.

In more recent years, the chiefs of the Secret Service have been drawn from career men in the Treasury ranks. In the earlier days, the chiefs ranged from soldiers to private detectives. The first chief was William P. Wood, veteran of the Mexican war, crony of Secretary of War Stanton and keeper of the old Capitol Prison. Wood had a reputation for being both ruthless and unscrupulous but within a year, he and his force of less than 30 men had jailed 200 counterfeiters.

He and his successors set out to build a rugged Secret Service. He issued orders that each man should recognize that his service belonged to the Government 24 hours a day.

A later chief, James J. Brooks, made his contribution to government efficiency by announcing that "leave is not needed by a class of agents who for 12 hours of each day are actively exercising their functions of body and mind in the bracing air and purifying sunshine."

The Secret Service got plenty of exercise—mental and physical—at the turn of the century when a counterfeit $100 bill—the "Monroe Note"—came into circulation. It was so nearly perfect that only an expert could detect the defects and then only under a magnifying glass. The notes were pouring out in such volume that an issue of $26 million had to be recalled. The then chief of the Secret Service was demoted because he couldn't find the maker of the deceptive counterfeits.

His successor, John E. Wilkie, an ace crime reporter, took personal command of the "Monroe Note" mystery. The engravers of the phony bills were traced to a cigar factory in Lancaster, Pa., where, it developed, the cigar manufacturer had also used their talents to counterfeit Internal Revenue stamps for his cigar boxes. After the ring went to prison, the engravers were prosecuted again for making counterfeit money in their prison cells.

As counterfeiting increased, so did the duties of the Secret Service. William H. Moran, who served as chief from 1918 to 1936, saw these additional chores assigned to his force: violations of the War Finance Corporation Act, the World War Adjusted Compensation Act, the Gold Reserve Act of 1934, the Silver Purchase Act, certain sections of the Federal Deposit Insurance Act, the Federal Land Bank Act, the Federal Farm Loan Act, the National Housing Act and the Losses in Shipment Act.

Counterfeiting had grown to a million-dollar business when Frank J. Wilson became chief in 1937. As an Internal Revenue intelligence agent, Chief Wilson had been the moving force in the tax case which landed Al Capone in prison. Chief Wilson's predecessors had been leery of talking publicly about counterfeiting but Chief Wilson figured that if merchants and cashiers knew how to detect counterfeit money, the counterfeiters would lose their outlets. He launched a nationwide "Know Your Money" campaign to make the public counterfeit-conscious.

Counterfeiting began to decline but that couldn't be attributed solely to the publicity campaign. A special squad, operating out of the New York office, was breaking up a number of counterfeit rings. Also, World War II was making the materials for counterfeiting harder to come by and many counterfeiters had diverted their attention to counterfeiting ration stamps. The Secret Service was assigned to get them, too.

With the end of World War II, counterfeits of American money began showing up in Europe. Two Secret Service agents, sent to France to work with the French *Sûreté,* located the counterfeit plant, seized $2 million in counterfeit money and rounded up the ring.

More recently, thieves have cooked up dozens of new ways to latch onto other people's money. In 1954, an employee of the Bureau of Engraving and Printing, where the nation's paper money is printed, substituted two dummy packages for the real thing and stole $160,000 from the bureau's vault. The Secret Service was called in to investigate, and he and his accomplices were caught after a spending spree. Most of the money was recovered, but it was the biggest theft in the bureau's history.

In 1959, Secret Service agents, cooperating with postal inspectors, broke up a ring of check thieves and forgers known as the "Red Fox Gang" operating in Dallas, Texas. The 19-member gang made a practice of adding a "1" to all Government checks for less than $100, thereby increasing their take by $100 on each transaction.

In 1960, a gang of 13 operators credited with forging about $250,000 in savings bonds was rounded up in Newark, N. J. Forgery of stolen government checks and bonds had become so widespread that the Secret Service set up a section to catalogue the writing of interstate forgers in the manner of a fingerprint file.

During the fiscal year ending in June, 1961, Secret Service agents seized more than $2 million in counterfeit bills, a 400 per cent increase over the preceding year. The agents, who always go after the phony money plants to stem the flow of counterfeits, seized $1,632,070 of that total before the money went into circulation.

One of those 1961 cases involved a ring in Springfield, Mo., where nine men were turning out $20 and $100 bills in a plant capable of printing one million dollars' worth of worthless money a week. While they were going strong, they often bragged about the precautions they had taken against being infiltrated by an undercoverman. One of their trusted accomplices turned out to be a Secret Service agent.

When their trial ended in conviction, the Federal judge said of the Secret Service agent what has been said in other words about other agents by Presidents of the United States.

"This agent," the judge told the jury, "is a brave man, exceedingly brave, a dedicated public servant. He has demonstrated more courage than I ever had."

THE GIRL WITH THE COUNTERFEIT CHECKS

The balcony of Washington National Airport appeared deserted on this fall afternoon except for four men talking quietly in a corner. Below, in the airport lobby, the crowds milled around the ticket counters, but on the balcony, even the sound of the public address system announcing arrivals and departures was muted.

The four men reached agreement quickly. At a nod from a fat man puffing hard on his cigar, a brief case and a heavy brown bag changed hands. With the business of the meeting finished, one of the quartet—a darkly handsome man with the slick look of a big-city mobster—stood up and stretched.

Suddenly, the airport lobby swarmed with Secret Service agents. The fat man and his lieutenant made a gesture toward their hip pockets but the agents were too fast for them. Handcuffs were snapped on, the brown bag and the brief case were gathered up and the prisoners were hustled down the back stairs.

As the convoy moved toward waiting cars, the fat man moved closer to the handsome mobster. "Nicky," he muttered, "don't tell them nothin'." Nicky nodded, but he had to turn his head aside to conceal a slight grin. He had already told plenty.

Nicky was an ace undercoverman for the United States Secret Service. . . .

For Nicky, whose real name must remain unrevealed, the case began in a Louisiana motel room on June 24, 1959, when he first saw the picture of the girl with the counterfeit checks. The New Orleans agent briefing him on his mission slid the girl's picture across the table. Nicky studied the girl's face.

"Nature sure played a dirty trick on her," Nicky commented. "She'd be pretty if it weren't for that birthmark around her eye."

"She's got plenty of boy friends, anyhow," the other agent told him. "One is a hood named Justin Arphy Sonnier. Another is Gus, a small time operator. He's the one we figure could introduce you to JoAnn—if you play him right. She could be the key to the counterfeit gang."

In the steamy motel room, the New Orleans agent launched his low-voiced briefing. A gang, he said, started passing counterfeit government checks in Florida on May 1, 1959. Within a week, the trail of phony checks led across four Southern states. Small town merchants, used to cashing government checks for veterans, farmers and the aged, were losing money at the rate of more than $100 a transaction. The checks looked good. They had the picture of the Minute Man on their face and the Treasury seal. The agents knew this was no amateur job.

Nicky didn't have to ask what the Secret Service had been doing for the past seven weeks. After 20 years as an agent, he knew the backbreaking job of questioning the storekeepers who cashed the checks. What did the check passers look like? What did they buy before they cashed the checks? What did they use for identification?

"We finally got a break," said the New Orleans agent. "We got Justin Arphy Sonnier—JoAnn's boy friend. The Sonniers—Arphy and his Uncle Joe—have long criminal records in these parts."

Arphy, he explained, had tried to pass a check in a Baton Rouge supermarket but an alert clerk, recognizing him and the check from a Secret Service warning to storekeepers, had refused to cash the check and signalled the store manager. Arphy, sensing something was wrong, had started out the door with the store manager close enough behind to see him enter a pink Oldsmobile. To state police, called by the store manager, the pink car meant something.

Less than two hours earlier, Arphy had visited state police headquarters to pick up clothes seized by police three months earlier when he and JoAnn were arrested on a marihuana charge. Arphy had put the clothes in a pink Olds.

Acting on the store manager's call, state police had found JoAnn and the pink Olds at a roadside tavern, but Sonnier had slipped out the back way. He'd reached Beaumont, Tex., before he was picked up.

The agent tossed another picture to Nicky. "That's Arphy Sonnier. Ever meet him?"

This was a necessary preliminary. The undercoverman had to be sure he wouldn't be recognized by any member of the gang.

"He's admitted passing the checks," the New Orleans agent said. "He's also admitted this man was with him, but we knew that, too."

The agent passed over another picture.

"That's James Douglas Simmons," the agent explained. "He made the mistake of cashing one of these things in an Atlanta liquor store where the clerk was a former policeman. The clerk made Simmons give him a single fingerprint before he cashed the check. When we got Sonnier, we checked his old record for known associates. The single fingerprint and the handwriting of the check endorsement match Simmons' file."

"You haven't caught up with him?"

"No, and he's still passing checks. We think he's with another buddy of Sonnier. Name's Carl J. Schaaphok. Birmingham wants him for a burglary and some of the check victims have identified him as one of the counterfeit gang."

"Did you get anything from Sonnier on the source of the checks?" Nicky asked.

"Nothing but tall stories," the agent replied. "Says he met a man in a bar who had some checks. Then he says he got them from Simmons. When he told us that he and Simmons got them from an old man in the Kentucky mountains, we gave up and turned him over to state police."

Nicky picked up JoAnn's picture again. "How does she fit into it now?"

The other agent hitched his chair closer. "We hear that Sonnier gave her his remaining checks to destroy, but she decided to get some money out of them. When we heard that, we called Washington. You know the rest."

Nicky thought of the teletype handed him by his boss in New York, the quick call to say good-by to his wife and two sons, the flight to Baton Rouge. He went where he was summoned and he went fast.

He didn't need a blueprint for this assignment now. Get to JoAnn through Gus, buy her counterfeit checks, win her confidence enough to point him in the direction of the plant where the phony checks were produced. Somehow, he had to force the gang out in the open.

The New Orleans agent had one more item—the address of a bar frequented by Gus. He looked at his watch.

"Gus usually comes in the bar about now," he said. "He's a little guy, thin-faced, sandy-haired."

While the New Orleans man went on with his description of Gus, Nicky emptied his pockets: badge, revolver, notebook, pencils with "U. S. Government" stamped on them.

"You'd better keep the gun," the other agent advised him. "If you do meet JoAnn, she may take you to her hangout for the boys to look you over. One informant told us that JoAnn's crowd thought he knew too much about the checks, gave him knockout drops at this tavern and tried to kill him on the road. These boys play rough."

Nicky refused the gun. If he weren't immediately accepted by JoAnn's friends, the gun could get him in more trouble.

He started filling his pockets with new identification. Nicky wasn't his real name but he had cards to prove he was Nicky from New York. And a hoodlum's address book, a treasure he had taken from a prisoner years before. He didn't have to worry about his accent. To a Southerner, it was pure New Yorkese. His dark good looks fitted the Italian ancestry of Nicky. His broad shoulders, half-concealed by his loose sports shirt, could be the shoulders of a strong-arm bandit as easily as a man of the law. Not that he intended to say he was a New York mobster. If he were accepted by the underworld, the code of the underworld prevailed. Don't pry. If anybody started asking questions, he could always growl, "Whatcha want? My fingerprints?"

A few hours later, he was over the first hurdle. He had nursed one beer long enough to get into conversation with Gus. The hints he let drop about his New York connections were enough to prompt Gus to propose a meeting with JoAnn.

It was near midnight when Nicky saw JoAnn for the first time. She was standing in the lighted doorway of an old farmhouse in a shortie nightgown. Sitting in the car while JoAnn and Gus talked in the doorway, Nicky could understand why she managed to attract boy friends despite the dark birthmark around her eye.

As the New Orleans agent had predicted, when JoAnn got dressed she ordered Gus to drive to her favorite tavern. No talk about checks yet. JoAnn's friends had to size him up. For their benefit, Nicky played the big city hoodlum hiding out in a small town.

Nicky was doing some sizing-up himself. JoAnn . . . attractive . . . wise in the ways of the underworld . . . no careless name-dropping . . . smart but maybe greedy.

Finally, JoAnn yawned and told Gus to take her home. They had nearly reached her farmhouse when she mentioned the checks for the first time.

"Are you interested in those things?" she asked Nicky abruptly.

"Not me," Nicky replied. "Checks aren't my line, but some of my people in New York could be interested if you had some samples."

Now she was all business. She would sell the checks she had for $25 apiece. If the New York crowd wanted a big order, she could arrange it.

When the car reached the farmhouse, she went inside with Gus and a light appeared in a ground floor room. Cautiously, Nicky crept along the side of the house to the lighted room. He saw JoAnn take a dress out of the closet, rip the hem and pull out a sheaf of bluish-green paper—the counterfeit government checks. With a grin at Gus, she stuck the checks down the front of her dress.

Nicky ducked back to the car and had a cigarette going before she and Gus reappeared. Still, she said nothing about the checks. To get her started, Nicky began talking about the big order. In wholesale lots, he said, the mob would expect to pay no more than $20 a check. If the New Yorkers liked her samples, they would send a man down with the money to meet her suppliers.

She stopped him there.

"From this point on," she told him firmly, "I'm only meeting you and you're only meeting me."

Nicky wanted to get the men behind JoAnn, but he had to agree to her terms or the deal would end before it began. She promptly pulled out 11 checks and he handed her $275.

Now he had JoAnn. He was reasonably sure that so far she had acted on her own. There hadn't been time for any contacts. In case her crowd vetoed the big deal, he had to find out what he could while he could.

Leafing through the checks, he noticed one made out for $3,000. "How do you pass one this big?" he asked JoAnn.

"You're not so smart," she said scornfully. "You can borrow on it at Las Vegas over a weekend when the banks are closed."

Trying another gambit, he admired the workmanship of the checks. She rejected his implied invitation to say who made them.

"If my crowd agrees to deal, how long would it take to get a big supply?" he asked.

"They're made a long distance from here. It would take five or six days for delivery."

Inwardly, Nicky groaned. The check plant could be in California or even Europe. He couldn't press the question. If she became wary, he'd get no closer to the counterfeit plant than he was right now. There was nothing to do but await developments. He told JoAnn where she could reach him.

She came to his motel to say her connections were ready to make a deal. He told her a man was now coming from New York with $20,000 for 1,000 checks of varying denominations. She said she would drive like mad to pick up the checks.

But other agents, keeping an eye on JoAnn, reported she wasn't going anywhere. While Nicky was puzzling over the delay, a sheriff reported a rumor. The Sonnier mob, he said, was out to hi-jack a New York hoodlum who had $20,000 on him. With Arphy Sonnier in jail, the Sonnier mob meant Arphy's uncle, Joe Sonnier—a man with a criminal record even longer than Arphy's. Nothing was going right.

Nicky decided to force the mob's hand. He told JoAnn the heat was now off in New York and he was going back the next day, deal or no deal.

Her return call came quickly. She wanted to meet him in Lafayette, La. The deal would take place there.

Nicky felt like he had been kicked in the stomach. Lafayette was home grounds for the Sonnier mob. If the sheriff's rumor was straight and JoAnn's crowd was out to get him for the $20,000 she thought he had, it would happen in Lafayette.

"I'll meet you in Lafayette," he told her harshly, "but I'm not running all over the state of Louisiana with $20,000."

She said she would call him back. An hour before he had told her he would leave the next day, she called to beg him to bring the $20,000 to Lafayette. When he refused, she swore at him and hung up.

While his fellow agent watched silently, Nicky packed his gear. There was nothing to say. Nicky had made the small buy from JoAnn and she could be arrested any time. But he had failed to locate the counterfeit plant. He hadn't identified the gang behind JoAnn. He hadn't learned the whereabouts of the missing check passers, Simmons and Schaaphok. He had simply set himself up for a hi-jacking by the Sonnier mob.

He was checking out when the call came.

"Nicky, honey?"

This was a different JoAnn, full of Southern charm. Obviously, she had orders to keep the deal alive. Nicky hung up, grinning.

"She wants me to call her when I get back to New York," he told the other agent. "Finally, they're coming to us."

When Nicky called JoAnn from New York, she promptly put a man on the phone, a man she introduced as Johnny.

Johnny said he was sorry about the run-around in Louisiana but now the deal was set. Nicky told him coldly that the New York crowd was no longer interested. In fact, he said, the New Yorkers didn't even believe there were any more checks.

"I tell you we have them now," Johnny protested. "How about coming back here?"

That was the last thing Nicky wanted. He had to come up with an idea—and fast.

"I ran into this Chinaman when I got back," Nicky began. "He's really loaded. He's on his way to the Philippines and he might be willing to deal. I could get a dollar more a check from him than from the others."

Johnny was eager—and generous. "You're entitled to make a buck," he said grandly.

"The only thing is," Nicky went on, "this Chinaman is leaving in two days and he doesn't fly. I could drive him someplace for a meet, but it would have to be close by."

Johnny called back in an hour to say his friends liked the Chinese deal. They dickered over the meeting place until Johnny himself finally proposed the National Airport in Washington. Why not the Treasury steps, Nicky thought to himself, grinning.

Johnny said he could make a flight arriving at 3:15 P.M. the next day. "You go to Eastern and page Leslie Gray," Johnny directed. "That'll be me. I'm fat. I'm ugly. I'll be wearing a brown suit and smoking a big cigar."

The two plotters laughed.

"Well, anyway," said Nicky, "I'll know JoAnn."

"She won't be coming."

That answered that question, but who would be with Johnny? These thieves wouldn't trust the money to one man. Nicky didn't dare ask if Johnny would have a companion.

As he hung up, Nicky looked at his watch. Twenty-four hours to go. He had to know the true identities of Johnny and whoever might be with him. New Orleans would airmail pictures of all of Arphy Sonnier's buddies. An Atlanta agent—someone who couldn't be spotted by the Louisiana crowd—would have to reach New Orleans in time to get on the plane with Johnny. Signals had to be worked out. If Johnny were traveling alone, the agent tailing him would get off the plane carrying his hat in his right hand. If Johnny had somebody with him, the hat would be in the agent's left hand.

Nicky flew to Washington with his Chinese "customer"—a fellow Secret Service agent.

Together, they surveyed the airport with the special agent in charge of the Washington field office. Where should the rendezvous take place? At 3:15 P.M., the long airport lobby would be full of people. If there were any shooting, it had to be away from the crowd.

They decided to plant the Chinese agent on the balcony over the ticket counters. Nicky had already established that his Chinese friend couldn't be pushed around. He would stay put. They had to come to him.

3:15 P.M. The loud speaker announced the New Orleans plane was now landing. The agents saw their man from Atlanta get off the plane. Hat in left hand. So Johnny had somebody with him.

When Nicky was sure all the agents were at their posts, he strolled over to the Eastern Airlines counter.

"Please page Mr. Leslie Gray," he said.

As soon as the call went over the loud speaker, Nicky saw a fat man with a big cigar approaching. The agent recognized him instantly from the packet of pictures air-mailed from New Orleans. This was Louis Emory Roger. Nicky went up to him.

"Johnny?"

"Nicky?" responded the fat man.

As they shook hands, Nicky recognized a man standing a few steps away—Joe Sonnier himself. He was close enough to hear, not close enough to be linked with Roger if he chose to avoid it. Nicky had to get Sonnier in the act.

Edging past Roger, the agent gripped Sonnier's shoulders in a show of greeting. "And who's our friend?" he asked.

From Sonnier's startled expression, Nicky knew he had guessed right. Sonnier had not planned to be in on the meeting. Now he was.

Nicky said his Chinese friend was waiting upstairs on the balcony —with the money.

"Get the bag," Sonnier ordered the erstwhile Johnny.

While they waited for Johnny, Nicky made conversation deliberately designed to establish Sonnier's connection with the plot.

"How's JoAnn?" he asked.

"She couldn't make the trip," Sonnier grunted.

That tied Sonnier to JoAnn's arrangements. Sonnier, now apparently reconciled to playing the role forced on him by Nicky, took the next step himself.

"We didn't have time to put the perforations in the checks," he volunteered. "We brought along the gadget to punch the holes."

"Our Chinese friend can worry about that," Nicky shrugged. Inwardly, he was jubilant. Now Sonnier couldn't claim he was just along for the ride. He knew about the checks down to the last hole.

Roger—or "Johnny"—rejoined them, carrying a big brown bag. As the trio started up the stairs to the balcony, Nicky paused. Suppose something went wrong on the balcony and the men tried to get away before the bag was opened. Under search and seizure rulings by the courts, the agents couldn't just grab the bag and open it without running a risk that the court would throw out the evidence. He had to see what was in that bag before they reached the balcony.

"Wait a minute," he told his companions. "Let's take a look at the stuff now. Then, I'll just tell the Chinaman it's okay and he'll hand over the money."

Sonnier balked. "Somebody might come along."

"Nobody's in sight now," Nicky retorted, "and we don't know who might be on the balcony."

Sonnier gestured to Roger. While Nicky pretended to keep a lookout, Roger opened the suitcase and withdrew a small canvas bag. With a hasty glance around, he unzipped the bag. Nicky saw a thick bundle of checks wrapped in gauze.

"Okay," said Nicky, trying to keep his voice even. "Let's go."

On the balcony, he led them to the Chinese agent—looking inscrutable as a buddha with his own case planted between his legs.

Nicky directed the seating to make sure that he and the Chinese agent were each close to one of the other men. He had already spotted the bulge in their pockets. In case of trouble, he and the Chinese agent could each grab a man before he reached his gun.

"I've seen the stuff," Nicky told the Chinese "customer." "I can vouch for it."

The Chinese agent nodded and opened his case wide enough to show the others that it was full of greenbacks. Case and bag changed hands. As Sonnier began explaining how to use the gadget to punch holes in the checks, Nicky stood up and stretched.

That was the signal. Before he could sit down, the balcony was alive with Secret Service agents.

Sonnier and Roger didn't have a chance to draw their guns. The handcuffs were on them too fast. On Nicky and the Chinese agent, too. It was there that Sonnier demonstrated how believably Nicky had played his undercover role.

"Don't tell them nothin'," Sonnier whispered to the agent.

Nicky's mission was accomplished. He had engineered the big haul —half a million dollars' worth of counterfeit checks that would never get into circulation. He had lured a ringleader, Joe Sonnier, into the net. And Roger was revealed as a check passer. The shoes he was wearing at the time of his arrest came from a store in Tampa, Fla., one of the victims of the check passers.

Now that Nicky had forced members of the gang into the open, it was time to capitalize on their mistakes. Locate the check plant. Identify the master-mind.

JoAnn's prompt arrest in Louisiana provided the first clues. She didn't name names but notes found in her bag did that for her. On one scrap, she had scribbled, "Howard Harden, Casa Blanca Hotel, Durango, Mexico." On the other, "Canal Club, Gulf Shores—Howard Harden" with a Birmingham (Ala.) telephone number.

In Birmingham, agents promptly reported on Harden. Correct name: Rufus Howard Harden. Reputation: Never breaking the law personally but master-minding almost any type of criminal activity. He had avoided conviction on charges of bank robbery, murder and a Mexican timber swindle. Mexico . . . Harden.

Another clue pointed to Mexico. An informant now revealed that Roger had met Carl Schaaphok, one of the still-missing check passers, at Laredo, Tex., and the pair had gone to Mexico together to collect the bundle of checks delivered to Nicky at the Washington airport.

A Spanish-speaking Secret Service agent was dispatched to Durango. There, he gained the confidence of a boy in a printing plant who told of seeing the owner's sons, Rosalio and Ponciano Salas, working nights on what could be the government checks.

The Salas brothers protested their innocence until the agent, with the Mexican police, fine-combed the Salas plant and found pieces of scrap metal that looked like parts of plates for a Social Security card, a Defense Department pass and a government check.

Then, one of the Salas brothers broke down. He said he was introduced to Harden by a friend known to Mexican police as a hireling for a narcotics smuggler. He said Harden provided a check and the various identification cards to be reproduced in quantity and paid them well. He recognized Schaaphok and Simmons, the missing check passers, from their pictures and told where they could be found.

The roundup that followed produced the artist who had given the checks their professional look, the missing Schaaphok and Simmons, the narcotics hireling—and enough information to identify Harden positively as the master-mind of the operation. Harden had started it all with his brother's government check.

In four and a half months—from the day the first check was passed until Rufus Howard Harden was arrested—Secret Service agents broke up an international gang of counterfeiters, located the plant, rounded up every member of the gang, put the master criminal behind bars and even gave an assist to another service. Information collected during the Mexican phase of the investigation and passed on to the Federal Bureau of Narcotics led to the seizure of two kilograms of pure heroin in Monterey before the narcotics could be smuggled into this country.

By that time, the Secret Service agent known as Nicky was off on another undercover assignment.

16 ★★★

Customs Agency Service

A tip from Antwerp breaks a diamond-smuggling ring in New York. A high-speed chase across Texas puts a long-time dope trafficker in prison for 23 years. A customs port investigator spots two seamen waddling across a pier and makes a half-million dollar heroin haul.

The combination of brains, bravery and an international intelligence network makes the cases for the Customs Agency Service, investigative and enforcement arm of the Treasury Department's Bureau of Customs.

The techniques of the smugglers have changed over the decades. The railroad porter who concealed Canadian furs for the trip over the border has given way to the airline stewardess with a load of heroin tucked into her girdle. The ships slipping into remote coves with their contraband whiskey have been replaced by the solo international traveler with a fortune in diamonds hidden in body cavities. The suitcase with the false bottom has been followed by the automobile with marihuana concealed in wells under the front fenders, stuffed into tires and seat cushions or welded beneath the car body.

The techniques of the agents have had to change, too. Nowadays, the movement of passengers and crews leaving planes at Idlewild International Airport is scanned by closed-circuit television. Customs agents use electronic devices to peer into wrapped packages. They tail suspects on foot with concealed walkie-talkies to keep in touch with cars following at a discreet distance. They're even using airplanes to trail flying smugglers.

Their basic goal is to insure that the country gets the revenue from duties imposed on imported merchandise. But for many decades past, the customs men have been intimately involved in blocking the entry of outlawed narcotics as well as other menaces to the health and safety of the people. And in more recent times, they have also been charged with preventing smuggling out of the country of implements of wars and other strategic materials.

Their major enforcement problems today are the smuggling of narcotic drugs and marihuana, watches, watch movements and diamonds and the unlawful export of goods to Cuba.

The Customs Agency Service as it exists today is the field force of the Customs Bureau's Division of Investigations and Enforcement. It is manned by 240 customs agents across the country, 35 customs representatives overseas and its newest acquisition, 500 customs port investigators.

Historically, the service has had many names, many bosses and many identities. It has been the Secretary of the Treasury's own investigative service. It has been an independent agency and, as it is now, the investigative and enforcement branch of the Customs Bureau. But its prime duty has remained constant—detection and prevention of the smuggling of merchandise into or out of the United States.

The Constitution gave Congress the power to impose and collect taxes and duties and Congress lost no time carrying out the mandate. The second law passed by the new legislators was the tariff act of July 4, 1789. Desperately in need of funds, the new nation called the act "the second Declaration of Independence." The fifth act of Congress provided the officers and the methods for collecting import duties.

All this happened before the Treasury Department was even established, but the founding fathers were in a hurry for revenue and customs duties seemed the most likely source. Even as late as 1910, almost 60 per cent of the costs of government were paid by customs revenues.

In the original acts, no specific provision was made for agents to detect smuggling and other revenue frauds but they moved into the scene more or less through the back door. The September, 1789, act establishing the Treasury Department gave the Secretary of the Treasury authority to superintend collection of the revenue and a 1799 act specified that customs officials should "at all times submit their books, papers and accounts to the inspection of such persons as may be appointed for that purpose."

Successive Secretaries of the Treasury interpreted those two acts as their authority for appointing special agents. At first, a Treasury clerk or Customs House employee was tagged a special agent just long enough to review customs records and report to the Secretary. But in 1846, Secretary Robert J. Walker appointed two special agents specifically to deal with customs matters.

Their numbers rapidly expanded. By 1869, the Treasury's original two special agents had grown to 62. It was then that Treasury Secretary George S. Boutwell, in a last-ditch effort to get more work out of his agents, divided the "sea-coast and frontiers" into 16 special agency districts, appointed a superintendent to oversee each district and required each agent to make a monthly report on his doings. This was the first disciplined organization of the special agents' force.

In 1870, Congress made it official by specifically authorizing the Secretary of the Treasury to appoint 53 special agents not only to examine the records of the customs collectors under the 1799 Tariff Act, but to make themselves generally useful in preventing and detecting revenue frauds. Thereafter, for several decades, the size of the force ranged up and down with the needs of the times and the whims of Congress.

A problem that kept the agents busy then—and still occupies the customs representatives overseas today—was the undervaluation of imported goods to minimize customs duties. In 1879, the special agents force struggled to establish the true market value of fine kid gloves from France and proved that velvets imported from Germany were being systematically undervalued. The products have changed, but not the practice. During the past year, false evaluations spotted by customs agents ranged from automobiles to antibiotics.

In 1882, the biggest case made by the agents was the seizure of a ton of opium as a landing was attempted at San Francisco. The load was valued then at $26,000. It would be worth many times more today, but it couldn't happen. The largest opium seizure made in the United States in the past decade was a 53-pound haul brought ashore by five Chinese crewmen at New Orleans in 1960. They were promptly arrested along with the receivers by customs agents and customs port investigators.

As early as 1890, the supervising special agent of customs, then A. K. Tingle, complained that "nothing pleases smugglers more than increased duties on articles which can be undervalued or smuggled." At the time, he was talking about increased duties on Mexican cattle from $2 to $10 a head which "makes prevention of border smuggling even more difficult." Today, the 100 per cent duty on watch movements from abroad creates a similar invitation to smugglers and challenge to customs agents.

It was also Tingle who called attention to the changes wrought by the coming of steamships and railways. Ports like Galena, Ill., La-Crosse, Wis., and Kennebunkport, Me., he pointed out, were now destitute of foreign trade and no longer needed customs collectors.

The country and its neighbor to the north were growing and so were the customs problems. The opening of rail lines through Manitoba, the Northwest Territory and British Columbia was facilitating over-the-border smuggling of Chinese—then a customs problem. To the east, the coming of the trans-Canadian railway brought habitation at intersection points on both sides of the border and opened new smuggling routes. Many of the fashionable who flocked to summer homes in the increasingly popular Thousand Islands also loaded their lake craft with British woolens and Hudson Bay furs on the Canadian side of the border.

Before the turn of the century, a force of customs agents had started operating in Europe to determine the true value of merchandise and spot merchants conniving to cheat American customs. But they also gathered information on the plans of prospective smugglers, including one hot tip that led to the seizure of $20,000 worth of smuggled jewelry in 1894. Today's customs representatives in foreign ports still perform the twin functions of detecting under-evaluations and collecting intelligence on smuggling operations, but they are now spread across the world from Rome to Singapore.

Today, the customs agents use every detective method available. They pit their wits against some of the wiliest crooks in the world, as well as the roughest. In one Prohibition year alone, four customs officers were shot down by liquor smugglers. On the Texas border, they knew which liquor gangs would put up a fight, but they loaded their guns and went after them, night after night. The latest of many customs men to die in the line of duty was a young officer with a wife and two children who caught three Mexican smugglers on the banks of the Rio Grande in 1957. As he walked them back to town, they had to go through a barbed wire fence. That's when they got him.

An agent clung to the running board of a car as it raced toward Mexico. The smuggler driver tried to shake him by brushing against the side of the bridge. When that didn't work, the driver repeatedly smashed at the agent's face with a tire iron. Finally, the agent, his face streaming with blood, managed to grip the wheel and wreck the car.

Customs agents have to be trained in the techniques of hot pursuit to deal with some of their more unpleasant border-crossers. The training came in handy in 1960 when John J. Vaccaro, a notorious narcotics trafficker out of New Orleans with a record dating back to 1928, tried to escape pursuing customs men on a 63-mile chase across Texas. While pursued and pursuers were travelling at more than 120 miles an hour, a government car was forced off the road and demolished, and several private motorists went into the ditch. When the agents finally caught up with Vaccaro and put on the handcuffs, he fought back with his manacled hands. His prison term of 23 years is the longest ever imposed in a customs case.

In the course of making a case against the ring-leader, the agents may have to convoy smuggled goods a thousand miles. El Paso agents did that in 1961 when they picked up a car with 112 pounds of marihuana coming over the border from Mexico. They persuaded the carriers to cooperate so they could get the ultimate receiver, enlarged the convoy when they seized another marihuana car in New Mexico, and finally wound up on the doorstep of the marihuana wholesaler in Chicago. There was only one hitch. A customs agent was hidden in the trunk of each marihuana car to witness the delivery and one of the agents found himself inside a locked garage. He extricated himself by using his walkie-talkie to direct covering agents to the rescue. Thirteen smugglers were convicted in this case.

A single slim clue can lead to a major haul. A customs representative in Mexico had studied sheafs of airway bills of foreign airlines and determined that hundreds of thousands of watch movements had been shipped into Mexico City and from there to Mexicali, Baja California, during the previous year. Customs agents in that area developed reliable information that the shipments left Mexicali by car for Tia Juana, the take-off point for smuggling into the United States. Now, they knew the pattern but not the smugglers.

On August 30, 1961, a stationwagon driven by a Californian started through customs at San Ysidro, Cal. On the basis of a lookout posted by customs agents, the driver and his car were searched but nothing was found—nothing, that is, until a customs agent climbed up to examine the luggage carrier mounted atop the stationwagon. The agent noticed the paint was chipped on the heads of the screws fixing the luggage carrier in place, and the damage showed no signs of rust. It wasn't much of a clue—just an indication that the luggage carrier had been tampered with at some recent time—but it was enough to have the luggage carrier removed.

In a concealed compartment, masked by the luggage carrier and extending the entire length of the stationwagon's roof, the customs men found 10,200 17-jewel watch movements and 680 watches. The haul was appraised at $90,000, but it was only the start of a continuing investigation. Customs agents at Los Angeles, by January, 1962, had rounded up six more members of the watch movement conspiracy and they're not through with this one yet.

As well-organized as the watch movement conspiracies are the diamond-smuggling rings. Customs agents, acting on information from their opposite numbers in Europe and using the "inspectoscope" to scan suspect packages, have found diamonds air-mailed into the country in toy dogs, sports equipment and false sides of packing cases.

They also have to cope with professional diamond smugglers. An international diamond trafficker, with a record stretching as far afield as Johannesburg, South Africa, arrived at Miami International Airport on a flight from Venezuela in January, 1962. His past record warranted the "special customs treatment" but a personal search indicated nothing amiss. A tube of vaseline found in his luggage, however, was the clue the customs men sought. It could be used to ease a packet into a place it didn't belong. When the agents bluntly told the smuggler they had a good idea where he hid his diamonds, he ejected a plastic tube from a natural body cavity. In the tube were 248 carats of loose cut and polished diamonds, valued at $45,000.

Customs agents work with other Federal investigators to block the entry of animals and food stuffs that endanger life and the nation's own agriculture. Agents in California exposed a ring, master-minded by a lawyer, flying in forbidden parakeets from Mexico. They were banned because of the danger of psittacosis. An agent in Texas spent two years proving a rare breed of French cattle had been smuggled in from Mexico, from which imports are severely limited to prevent the spread of hoof and mouth disease. When the agent's long investigation proved the smuggling, the principal was convicted and the American-born calves were deported along with the alien cows.

Two embargoes that have gone on the books since the cold war have added to the chores of customs agents. One deals with Red China, and the other with Cuba.

Merchandise of Red Chinese origin can't be imported without a license from the Foreign Assets Control Administration. As a result, traders moved into the business of peddling smuggled Chinese art treasures. The arrest of a California art dealer in 1959 led to a New York seizure of $370,000 worth of Chinese art. A Boston ramification of the same investigation revealed a Chinese woman had taken several valuable pieces of art from the Communist mainland to Hong Kong and later brought them into the United States as personal household effects. Customs agents found the forbidden treasures on display at Harvard University and Mount Holyoke College.

The embargo on shipments to Cuba, except for food and medicine, went into effect in November, 1960, and inspired a coterie of get-rich-quick smugglers. Since industrial machinery, trucks and electronic installations in Cuba were mostly of American origin, Cuba could only get needed replacement parts through illegal exports from this country.

Customs investigations revealed that in addition to outright smuggling, foreign merchants set up dummy corporations in Mexico to receive American goods and ship it on to Cuba. In one such case, Fidel Castro himself helped prove the ultimate destination of $400,000 worth of insecticides and fungicides ostensibly bound for Mexico. When customs agents seized millions of pounds of the stuff at Miami and located another shipment at Houston, Castro indignantly told his people the shipments belonged to the Cuban government.

Along with the added duties of enforcing embargoes, the Customs Agency Service acquired a powerful helping hand in 1960 on Congressional recommendation. The men of the old customs port patrol, who had been under the customs collectors, were reorganized, retrained, re-equipped and renamed customs port investigators in the Customs Agency Service. They do the enforcement job by waterfront patrols, in uniform and plainclothes, and by searching airplanes and vessels to tie in with the intelligence gathering and investigative chores of the customs agents.

The customs port investigators have been so effective in their new assignment that the President has asked Congress for 200 more of them at once.

The men who used to patrol the port areas worked regular hours and took their holidays, but not these officers. Two Chinese seamen found that out. When their waddling walk aroused a customs port investigator's suspicion and a search led to the discovery of packages of heroin strapped to their thighs, the seamen sadly confided that they hadn't expected customs men to be out working on Christmas night.

The exploits of the newest arm of the Customs Agency Service range from using judo on a suspect who turned out to be former middleweight boxing champion of Algiers, to forcing an airport door behind which a disheveled stewardess was trying to get rid of heroin concealed in her underclothes before she was searched.

A successful side venture of the customs port investigators has involved clearing the docks of thieves and other marauders. In New

York alone, during 1961, they turned over 100 prisoners to local authorities for offenses discovered during customs searches. Many of the prisoners were found with pistols and knives used to intimidate waterfront workers.

C. A. Emerick, the veteran Deputy Commissioner of Customs in charge of the Division of Investigations and Enforcement, recently called attention to a present threat to be combatted by the new branch of his Customs Agency Service.

"The danger from smuggling and clandestine importation of implements of sabotage and chemical, radiological and bacteriological warfare has never been greater in the history of this nation," he reported. "The primary responsibility for the detection of such threats rests with the customs port investigators whose numbers and efforts provide the only vessel and plane searching and waterfront patrol protection available to the people of this country."

THE GUN RUNNERS

The men who bend and break the law are sure anybody can be bought if the price is right. And the price is right just often enough to make bribery an underworld commonplace.

That's why a gang of gun-smugglers thought Customs Agent Wallace D. Shanley could be bought and, for official reasons, Shanley let them think so.

The time was late March, 1959. Fidel Castro had come to power in Cuba. The ousted Batista forces were plotting for their grand return to Havana. Generalissimo Trujillo of the Dominican Republic had not yet fallen before an assassin's bullet. Intent on preserving his dictatorship and fearful that Castro's influence might spread to his half an island, the Generalissimo was ready to spend millions to arm a legion of Batista exiles to war on Castro. But he had to get the arms.

The obvious place to buy was the United States but there was one hitch—a law. Congress had spelled it out: "The President is authorized to control, in furtherance of world peace and the security and foreign policy of the United States, the export and import of arms, ammunition and implements of war . . ."

Customs Agent Shanley, a ruggedly handsome Texan with steel gray eyes and the lean frame of an athlete, was one of the men enforcing this law.

Working out of the Miami customs office, he and his partner, William B. Lankford, had become so deft at ferretting out and blocking arms shipments that certain Caribbean diplomats padded their expense accounts by claiming they needed funds to bribe the two customs agents. When word of this maneuver leaked back to Shanley and Lankford, they redoubled their efforts to knock off the gun-runners. They also became acutely sensitive on the subject of bribes.

A small-time con man with big ambitions chose that time to try to buy Shanley.

The agent was driving Leonard Trento to the customs office when it happened. The swarthy, heavy-browed little man suddenly squared himself away and pulled out a thick wad of money.

"I want to make a deal," he announced.

"Put that away, Trento," Shanley ordered. "What's the matter with you?"

Then the words came pouring out.

Trento said he had a chance to make a fortune supplying arms to the Dominicans for a proposed invasion of Cuba. He couldn't get an export license, so the guns would have to be smuggled out.

"If I start buying guns, you'll find out about it and I'll lose everything," the little man concluded. "I've got to have you. I can't do this without you."

Shanley cut him off.

"You can't buy me and I don't think you can buy any other customs officer," he said. "Why don't you give it up, Trento? You're not cut out for this gun-smuggling business. These people you're dealing with are going to outsmart you."

As the car pulled into the parking lot beside the customs office, Trento made a last pitch. He peeled three $100 bills from his roll and dropped them on the seat.

"This doesn't have anything to do with a deal," he told Shanley. "It's just because you helped me get home for Christmas last year. Buy something for your wife."

Shanley controlled his rising anger and opened the car door.

"Pick those up and get going," he told Trento. "Actually, I should arrest you for talking like this."

As the tall Texan strode into the customs office, his anger gave way to pity. He had known Trento since before Batista's downfall. Just before Christmas the previous year, he had caught Trento trying to smuggle a load of machine guns to the Batista forces. With Batista out, the charges had been dropped and Trento thought of Shanley as his friend. Shanley thought of Trento as a foolish, impulsive little man with big ideas.

Before Trento had made the bribe offer that day, he had come into the customs office to pick up the suitcases Shanley had seized at the time of the machine gun arrest. Shanley instantly recognized the man with him—a disbarred lawyer named Sidney Neubauer, a pasty-faced, cynical character who had been kidnapped briefly by a Cuban contingent after he bilked them of $30,000 on an arms deal. Neubauer, Shanley noticed, had carefully absented himself before Trento went off with Shanley to pick up the suitcases and make his money pitch.

If Trento was mixed up with characters like Neubauer, Shanley decided, Trento's story had better be reported to the front office at once. Signaling for his partner to join him, Shanley went in to talk to Supervising Customs Agent Joseph A. Fortier.

"I've just been offered a wad of money to help Trento smuggle out a big arms shipment," he began abruptly. "What he says is probably true. It looks like we're in for an era of gun-smuggling financed by the Dominicans."

Shanley and Lankford went over the Trento proposition with the supervising agent. Both insisted they could stop the guns without getting into the ring themselves via the proposed bribery route. Fortier said he would discuss it with Washington.

In the next few weeks, the two agents developed the uncomfortable hunch that they needed more information than they were getting. A check of telephone calls made by Trento and Neubauer from their hotel before they left for New York worried the agents. Several calls had gone to Augusto Ferrando, the Dominican consul general in Miami. Trento had also called Joseph Liquori, a detective in the Miami Police Department assigned to the Dominican consulate.

Liquori, Shanley learned, had accompanied Rafael Trujillo, Jr., on his excursion to the Command and General Staff School at Fort Leavenworth, Kansas, where the free-spending son of the Dominican dictator lived it up in a $100-a-day hotel suite until he got bored and went to Hollywood. Liquori, a husky six-footer with masculine good looks and dark wavy hair, did well in Hollywood himself while

"Ramfis" Trujillo was dating Kim Novak and Zsa Zsa Gabor. When the dictator's son became chief of staff of the Dominican armed forces, the detective returned to more mundane duties. Shanley wondered whether the firm friendship between the two men had extended to gun-smuggling.

Shanley was also learning more about Ferrando, the Dominican consul general. An Italian by birth, Ferrando was no diplomat. He had risen through police ranks to become chief of intelligence in the Dominican Republic with a reputation for liquidating Trujillo's enemies. His reputation as an international killer preceded him to Miami and the State Department withheld diplomatic immunity.

"Looks like Trento has gotten himself some nice playmates," Shanley told his partner Lankford. "I'm beginning to think if Trento approaches me again, we might have to agree to be bribed. It may be the only way we can find out where Liquori and Ferrando fit into this thing."

Lankford nodded slowly. A veteran of some 30 years in the customs service, he had served with the customs patrol of Prohibition days, catching rum-runners. He knew just how tough it was to guard every exit and every entrance against a well-organized band of smugglers without inside information.

The customs agents didn't have long to wait. Late one night, toward the end of April, Trento called Shanley at home. In an excited voice, the would-be gun-smuggler asked for a meeting with the customs agent. Knowing Trento, Shanley could picture what had prompted the call. Trento had probably been with a group of Cuban exiles, pounding the table, vowing oaths to restore Batista, getting himself worked up to the point where he decided all over again he had to have Shanley on his side.

The customs agent faced Trento over a cup of coffee at the international airport the next day. He had to convince Trento that an unbribable customs agent could be had. He had to get Lankford into the act as a witness, and he had to arrange a setup that would guarantee no arms left the country.

"The reason I didn't go for a deal the first time you offered it," Shanley began carefully, "was because we were getting a lot of information about you and your group. I wasn't sure I could deal with the situation the way you wanted it."

Trento nodded eagerly.

"I can't do this alone," Shanley went on. "Bill Lankford knows everything I do. Our minds coordinate. I've tentatively sounded Bill out. He's willing to go along under certain conditions."

"I want to make a deal," Trento replied.

"Well, we're interested in the money but you've got to agree to two absolute rules. We won't have anything to do with buying the arms or getting them here, but once they get here we must have complete control over the storage and movement of the arms. Once we decide to handle it, we handle it all."

Trento frowned.

"You'll have to talk to the big man," he said.

"Who's that?"

"Ferrando."

As the two men parted—Shanley to talk to Lankford, Trento to report to Ferrando—the little man dug into his pocket, palmed a $100 bill and thrust out his hand.

"Don't you ever shake hands?" he asked Shanley, his dark face creasing into a grin.

Shanley shook his head and turned away. He wasn't ready to be bought yet—not by the unpredictable Trento nor by anyone else if he could find out what he needed to know without it. He had already scored once. Ferrando had been identified as the kingpin of the conspiracy.

Two days later, Shanley and Lankford approached the back door of the Dominican consulate—a converted mansion behind an avenue of palms. A young tough wearing dark glasses and a shoulder holster opened the door for them.

"Shanley to see Ferrando," the agent muttered, recognizing the greeter as part of Ferrando's cadre of half a dozen bodyguards.

They were ushered into a small sitting room where Trento introduced them, and a tall, middle-aged man with cold eyes and an impassive face greeted them in a mixture of Spanish and English. This was Ferrando, but at this moment he obviously wasn't the boss in his own sitting room. Seated behind his desk was Col. Juan Abbes Garcia, whom Trento explained in a quick whisper was now chief of Dominican intelligence and Trujillo's direct representative for the gun-smuggling.

"These are the men who can do it for us," Trento began.

Garcia asked the first question.

"How much?"

As Shanley started outlining his conditions, he was grimly aware that he was in Ferrando's home territory. He suspected that his words were being taped and his face was being photographed. If they couldn't get his cooperation one way, they would try another—blackmail. There was nothing he could do about it beyond measuring every word.

"This has got to be done our way," he said, as Trento interpreted. "The stuff will have to be stored where we say. We'll take payment only when it gets out safely."

Again, Garcia wanted to know how much it would cost. Shanley continued to stall. So far, he was learning what he wanted to know without taking any money and he wanted to keep it that way as long as he could get away with it.

The Dominicans let it rest there and Trento happily announced he was off to New York to buy some guns.

Shanley was still wondering where Liquori fitted into the scheme when the detective himself supplied the answer. Shanley was checking into another matter at the airport about a week after the talk with Ferrando when Liquori accosted him. At his first words, Shanley placed him in his proper niche. Liquori was in it all the way.

"The Dominicans are unhappy," Liquori reported. "They think you're dragging your feet on making a deal."

Shanley shrugged.

"I know it's big and attractive," he drawled, "but there are too many guys in this thing. I'm not going to dive in. If Trento gets into trouble, he'll drag us in with him."

"Don't worry about Trento," Liquori assured him. "I can take care of him. Why don't you and Lankford take a retainer from Ferrando —say $200 a month? It wouldn't obligate you to a thing."

Not much, thought Shanley, just put us at their mercy. Aloud, he said he would talk it over with Lankford. Before he left Liquori, he told him just where he stood.

"Obviously," he said, "you and Trento are shooting for something big. You're talking about joining your buddy in the Dominican Republic and Trento expects to be a big man in Cuba. Lankford and I are risking everything we have—our jobs. I'm telling you, if we don't reach an agreement on handling the guns after all this fooling around, we're going to do everything we can to knock you people off."

As Shanley left the airport parking lot after his confab with Liquori, he was satisfied he had laid the detective's suspicions at rest. Apparently, Liquori was ready to believe the Federal agents could be bribed because he, a law enforcement officer himself, was also plotting to break the law.

He figured Liquori would report back promptly to Ferrando and another money pitch would be made. This time, he and Lankford agreed, they had to accept. Liquori would get suspicious if they continued to hold out.

They weren't surprised when Ferrando called to ask them to pay a visit. Liquori had done the expected, and they would do the expected —demand more money than they were offered.

At the consulate, Ferrando got right down to business. Pointing at a calendar on the wall to indicate he was paying for the month of May, he handed Shanley $300.

"That isn't much money for both of us," Lankford promptly objected.

Ferrando shrugged and pulled out another $100. The agents asked for an interpreter to explain their terms. They told him they wanted 20 per cent of the value of any arms shipped. Ferrando nodded with satisfaction. This he could understand.

As the agents left the consulate, Shanley felt as if the money was burning a hole in his pocket. The feeling of revulsion didn't leave him until the agents marked the bills for future identification and turned them in at the customs office to hold for evidence.

Ferrando had elaborately assured the agents that they would be informed the minute a gun shipment reached Miami, and he didn't expect anything for a month. They learned the next day how little they could bank on his promises, when Lankford got a tip from a friend in the air freight office at the airport. The friend thought he might be interested in two shipments that had just arrived.

One shipment consisted of two packages of gun parts consigned by Charles Colle of Union, N.J., to Joseph Liquori. The other, marked machinery and dies, was consigned from Colle to Colle.

Watching from a discreet distance, they saw Trento and Liquori pick up the cases consigned to the policeman. They weren't ready to move yet although Shanley was burning at the apparent attempt to double-cross him.

An hour later, Trento drove up in a rental truck with a stranger—a man with green eyes and kinky hair the color of rust. They saw Trento's companion sign for the six-case shipment and concluded this must be Colle, the gun-dealer from up North.

As soon as the truck was loaded, they followed it out of the airport. Trento dropped the rusty-haired man at a motel and the truck proceeded to cruise aimlessly.

"Either he's trying to get rid of a tail or he's planning a meet," Lankford muttered as the truck rattled up one street and down another through the industrial back streets of Miami.

The truck finally stopped at a corner and the agents saw Liquori get out of a car and come over to talk to Trento. After a few words, the detective moved off and the truck started up again.

Deciding to make their move, Shanley and Lankford pulled up

beside the truck and motioned it to the curb. Neubauer was with Trento on the front seat.

"All right, Trento," said Shanley harshly. "You've had it. You're both under arrest."

Trento and Neubauer both started protesting bitterly. First they said they were going to get all the stuff together and then notify the agents. Then they claimed Liquori had been supposed to clear the shipment. Finally, Trento, incoherent and near tears, said he didn't want Colle to know about his deal with the agents or the gun-dealer would cut him out and take over the arrangement himself. If they arrested him now, Trento lamented, he would be ruined before the big haul.

Lankford played the good guy. He suggested they all have something to eat and talk things over. During lunch, Trento said he was waiting for a shipment of 200,000 rounds of ammunition from California. He told the agents sadly that he had only ordered 100,000 rounds but Colle was forcing him to take twice that much. He complained that Colle scared him with his boasting of big underworld connections, that Colle was trying to push him out of the big deal and had consigned part of this shipment to Liquori so he could involve the policeman in the illegal handling of guns.

"What about our 20 per cent?" Shanley demanded. "You've got $28,000 worth of stuff written down here. That's $5,600 for us."

Trento moaned. First, they threatened to arrest him and now they were asking for $5,600 he didn't have.

Shanley appeared to relent.

"All right, forget that for now," he said. "But you'll have to store these machine guns in my garage. I'm not going to let you have this stuff back. We're going to play it loose so we can still go either way."

Trento had no choice now. He had to agree.

The agents were well pleased. The airport tip had been their biggest break to date. It had served to convince Trento that he couldn't slip guns past them.

Shanley was reporting the latest development to his chief when he was summoned to the telephone. An angry Colle was calling from Shanley's home.

"Shanley, I want my guns," Colle shouted into the telephone. "You've hijacked my merchandise."

"I'll get around to you," Shanley retorted. "You just slow down."

"I'm going to call the police," Colle yelled. "You can't steal a legitimate shipment. You're in trouble."

"Get out of my house," Shanley ordered, and hung up.

He waited a few moments and called his wife. Her voice was shaking with fear and indignation.

"Four men got out of a car and started prowling around the garage," she reported. "Then the red-headed one pushed his way into the house and phoned you. They're still standing around outside. They look like a bunch of gangsters."

"All right, honey," Shanley quieted her down. "Lock the doors. If anything happens, call the police. I'll get there as fast as I can."

Shanley felt like exploding.

"I've got to go," he told his chief hastily. "There's trouble at my house."

As he ran out of the office, he yelled to some agents to get behind him but to keep out of sight until—and unless—he needed them. On his car radio, he contacted Lankford. His partner, closer to the Shanley home, could get there while Shanley was still fighting boulevard traffic.

The next 20 minutes were the longest of his career. He could picture his blue-eyed, blonde wife, a gently raised southern girl who had never seen the kind of characters now prowling around her home. She had watched the guns being stored in the Shanley garage and from her expression, he knew she didn't like the idea. He had told her about the bribery, too, and she didn't care for that any more than he did.

Wondering where their three small children were when Colle forced his way into the house, Shanley suddenly lost his appetite for tracking down gun-runners. All his resentment at the bribery, the necessity to sit around and drink and plot with the gun-smugglers, rose to the surface. He felt like killing Colle.

Lankford met him at his front door, a cool and deliberate Lankford with everything under control.

"Take it easy," Lankford quieted him. "Your wife is safe with a neighbor. The children are all right. I think we can work this out."

His partner quickly filled Shanley in on what had happened. Before Lankford arrived, both Colle and Mrs. Shanley had called the police but Lankford had sent them away by saying this was one of his deals. Lankford had then sat down with the four angry men—Colle, Neubauer, Trento and Liquori. As soon as Colle heard about the deal with the agents, a great light dawned and he told Lankford he had been looking for an arrangement like this since 1952.

Shanley, struggling to simmer down, got Colle's promise that the agents would be notified at once when the munitions mentioned by Trento arrived from the West Coast.

As the quartet walked out the door, Trento whispered to Shanley that he had been forced to tell Colle where the guns were when Colle demanded payment from the Dominicans, and they told him the arms had never reached them.

With the help of the other agents, Lankford and Shanley spent the rest of the night photographing the machine guns and making a list of their serial numbers.

Another tense week passed while they kept a discreet eye on Colle and waited for the shipment from California. Finally, on a Sunday night, Colle reported that the munitions truck had arrived, and he had made arrangements for Trento to receive the shipment the next day.

Now, they weren't going to let Trento out of their sight. They went with him to sign for the shipment and to take possession of 116 crates of ammunition. They had decided to store this stuff in a warehouse where it could be watched. Late that night, the two agents and Trento, trying to maneuver the truck into position to unload it, felt the truck sag. A rear wheel had broken through a cesspool. The agents grimly set to work unloading the crates. When they finally finished, Trento regarded them with a cheerful grin.

"When I saw you two sweaty guys hauling those crates," he said, "I told myself you were all right."

The weary agents just looked at him.

They still had to find out what Ferrando planned to do with the guns and ammunition. They had decided on the gambit he would understand when they went to see him that afternoon. They demanded more money.

This time, Ferrando gave them $1,000 and assured them they would get a lot more when the big deal came through. The agents told him that right now, they were interested in the munitions stored in Miami. Ferrando said he was making arrangements for a banana boat to haul the arms to the Dominican Republic.

Again, the agents marked the bills for identification and turned them in for evidence. By now, their evidence was piling up. They not only had the proof of bribery in the $1,400 but a collection of significant pieces of paper. Every time the agents went near the conspirators, they made a point of figuring out the planned arms shipments on the paper at hand—the back of a motel envelope, a restaurant paper napkin, a lunch counter receipt. Theoretically, they were calculating their 20 per cent profit. Actually, they were identifying dates, places and conversations about guns.

On the afternoon of May 21, Liquori called the customs office and Shanley, in the pattern of a bribed law man, proceeded to bawl him out for calling him at work.

"I had to tell you this," Liquori apologized. "The boat is out. The stuff is leaving tomorrow by plane."

"Meet me at 7 P.M. at the Gem Bar," Shanley said shortly and hung up.

Shanley and his partner went into a worried huddle. Before the night was over, they had to locate the plane, keep control over the arms, appear to act helpful in making the necessary arrangements and, at the same time, make their own arrangements. Those guns couldn't get off the ground.

Liquori and Trento were having a huddle of their own in the darkest corner of the dark bar when the agents slipped into the booth.

"There's one more guy you've got to meet," Liquori began.

Shanley promptly protested. As a bribed customs officer, it would be in character for him to balk at putting himself at the mercy of any more people. As an investigator, he had to meet as many conspirators as he could.

It was finally agreed that Shanley would accompany Liquori while Lankford and Trento went to the airport to size up the problems involved in loading the plane.

"This guy's name is Dominick Bartone," Liquori explained on the way to a downtown hotel. "He's negotiating with Ferrando to sell eleven huge planes to the Dominicans—C-74s. Ferrando decided to put the gun deal together with this one and let the Dominicans see one of the planes."

Shanley reflected that planes were also considered munitions of war and needed export licenses. He wondered how Bartone planned to get around that.

The hotel door was opened by a gorilla of a man, almost as tall as Shanley's six-two and much heavier. His blue-jowled face seemed to wear a perpetual scowl.

"You sure this guy's all right?" Bartone asked Liquori with a nod at Shanley.

The customs agent pulled his badge out of his pocket.

"What'll you pay for it?" Shanley asked coldly.

Bartone turned his back on Shanley, but apparently he accepted his presence because he talked freely to Liquori. Shanley, reading a newspaper with a show of disinterest, learned how Bartone planned to get the plane to the Dominican Republic without an export license. He had instructed the pilot to file a flight plan for Puerto Rico but feign engine trouble en route and land at Ciudad Trujillo.

Once he had that answer, Shanley got into the conversation to show he was trying to exercise caution about the arms loading. When Bartone told him where the plane would load, Shanley protested it was too public for a daylight operation but Bartone assured him that the plane was surrounded by friends of his and Shanley appeared to relax.

As soon as he left Bartone that night, Shanley did some fast checking on the man who had assured him he would soon be able to deliver millions of dollars' worth of guns to the Dominicans. As he suspected, Bartone was strictly a mercenary. He tried to peddle the C-74s to Castro but when that didn't work, he turned to Castro's enemies.

Shanley and Lankford spent the rest of the night supervising the loading of the munitions from Shanley's garage and the warehouse where the truck had smashed into the cesspool. As soon as the agents had everything on a huge van, Shanley went off with Liquori and Bartone to arrange for a forklift to get the crates into the belly of the plane while Lankford stayed with Trento. They were getting so close now that they had to watch everybody.

Shortly before 10 A.M. on May 22, 1959, the agents prepared for their last big scene. As the bribed customs agents, the gun-smugglers looked to them to get their plane off the ground without interference.

Escorting the van through the airport gate, they saw the monstrous plane parked in the center of the vast reaches of concrete in the industrial area of the airport. The agents promptly set up what they told the others was a guard operation. Shanley remained near the plane while Lankford parked his car a few hundred yards distant.

The forklift elevated the first pallet of ammunition into the cargo compartment where Trento and one of his helpers started stowing away the crates. Bartone had gone off for a cup of coffee. Liquori was chatting with Shanley when the customs agent raised his arm to shade his eyes from the sun.

Lankford saw the arm go up and spoke a few words into his radio. Within minutes, half a dozen customs agents and uniformed customs inspectors surrounded the plane.

"Tell them to go away," Liquori whispered to Shanley.

The customs agent felt a twinge of pity as he shook his head.

"Joe, you've been had," he told the detective. "This is it."

Together, Lankford and Shanley went off in search of Bartone. They found him cowering in a hangar.

"Why don't you take care of this?" he gritted. "That's what you're paid for."

Shanley responded by snapping handcuffs on Bartone's hairy wrists.

Later that day, the agents greeted Ferrando as he stepped out of his consulate. His goons wouldn't do him any good this time. With the arrest of Colle in New York, the roundup was complete. All the principals—Ferrando, Bartone, Liquori, Colle, Neubauer and Trento—either pleaded guilty or were convicted.

Shanley wasn't the kind of man to hate anybody but, as he told his blue-eyed wife when it was all over, he couldn't feel any sympathy for men who would believe he could be bribed.

"It was a deep, basic insult," he said.

17 ★★★

Postal Inspection Service

A postage stamp can lead to crime as surely as a pistol in the hands of a hold-up man.

The victim may be a young mother who falls for a "work at home" scheme or a small businessman who gets what looks like a tempting offer to sell his store or a blind man who is led to believe he can become self-supporting with a few hours work a week.

Or the victim may buy a sure cure for cancer, baldness, obesity, flat feet or flat chest. She may be a lonely one in search of love via magic potions or correspondence clubs. He may be a boy who sends away for a toy airplane and gets on a mailing list for obscenity. She may be a wife driven to suicide by "poison pen" letters or blackmail threats. He may be a father wanting a fall-out shelter to guard his family against atomic attack.

Since the government, through the mails, provides the means and the opportunity to swindle and corrupt, it must also provide protection against the swindlers and corrupters. That's one of the many missions of the Postal Inspection Service's 975 men.

They've been protecting the mails under one title or another since long before the nation was born. They hunted highwaymen on the lonely post roads of colonial times, rode west with the covered wagons, launched the "Pony Express," balked the nineteenth century brand of confidence men, warred on the "Black Hand" band of extortionists, fought it out with Prohibition era gangsters raiding post offices and mail trains, and now unravel mail frauds as complex as the mind of man can devise.

They have seen the country grow from a few scattered colonies where a letter was a luxury, long-awaited and possibly never received, to a nation whose postal service is the largest business in the world and enough mail is posted daily to average one piece of mail every day for every American man, woman and child.

Each generation for more than two centuries has created new problems for the postal inspectors to combat, and Congress, once the nation was established, has recognized these problems with new laws. Today, the men of the Postal Inspection Service regularly make more than 250 different types of investigations.

Back in colonial times, the main problem was getting the mail delivered. Colonists came directly to the ships to pick up their mail from England. Letters went astray so often that writers sent duplicate or even triplicate copies, hoping one would reach its destination. Businessmen were known to claim their competitors' mail, intending to destroy it or profit from the information before sending it on to its proper recipient. Even the colonial Governors complained bitterly that their own mail failed to arrive. Money sent through the mail was pilfered regularly.

Benjamin Franklin was assigned to do something about it when he became postmaster at Philadelphia in 1737. He was given the added chore of "regulating the several post offices and bringing the postmaster to account." His mission was to reorganize and speed up the postal system as well as to spot cases of embezzlement—where the early postmasters failed to account for funds entrusted to them. Inspecting the post offices is still a prime function of postal inspectors today.

When Franklin was appointed Postmaster General by the Continental Congress, he created the title of "surveyor of the Post Office"—the predecessor of the postal inspectors. One such surveyor was Noah Webster of dictionary fame, who had plenty of time to reflect on new words as he travelled the post road from New York to Hartford, Conn., tracking mail bandits.

The highwaymen had become the big problem when the mail started travelling overland. As soon as the Post Office surveyors found mail routes to link the colonies, the bandits moved in to ambush the post riders.

Just as Congress was to respond in later years to other misuses of the mails, it passed a law in 1794 to deal with the mail bandits—the death sentence for stealing mail. Before the end of the century, the penalty was reduced to flogging and still later to a term in prison, but the mails still lure the thieves. Of the 10,000 people arrested annually by postal inspectors today, 40 per cent are mail thieves. Their prime target: the 450,000,000 Treasury checks posted annually.

As the nation moved into the nineteenth century, postal "surveyors" gave way to "special agents." Theirs was the job of setting up mail service as well as protecting it in the westward expansion. Thus, they travelled with the homesteaders and gold seekers, finding new routes, shooting it out with the Indians, burying the dead and hunting down the marauders.

The thinly spread force of "special agents" was still concerned mainly with mail looting—inside and outside the post offices—when the post-Civil War era produced a new problem. The transcontinental railway had just been completed and the days of the $5 letters by "Pony Express" were over. Eastern businessmen could now mail their goods west by train, for the mails had at last become comparatively safe, swift and inexpensive. As the honest man turned to the mails, so did the swindlers. Mail routes stretching across the country provided both the means and the opportunity to prey on the public.

And the public was ill-prepared for this assault. Buyers were used to dealing with storekeepers they knew. If anything went wrong, they could run down the street and complain. If it went very wrong, they could go into their own court and sue. Now the people they dealt with might be half a country away. Half the time, they didn't even know the identities of those who had defrauded them—and if they did know, they couldn't sue. Some of the schemes were amateurish by modern standards but others cooked up by bogus bankers and brokers were as sophisticated as today's stock swindles.

Again, Congress responded to the complaints of the public, and postal agents were given a new responsibility. In 1872, Congress passed its first law "to prevent the perversion of the mails to improper purposes." That was the granddaddy of progressively stiffer laws to deal with mail fraud.

About the same time, the public was protesting on another score. From the gutters of Europe, peddlers of obscenity were beginning to arrive on American shores.

Spearheading the public protests was one man, Anthony Comstock. He had started out as an agent for the New York Society for the Prevention of Vice, but since so much of the obscene material was going through the mail, Comstock was commissioned a postal agent. He later became such a fanatic on the subject of vice that his name became a derisive term for that form of fanaticism—"comstockery."

A rugged fighter for what he believed, Comstock haunted the halls of Congress through three days and nights of debate on his obscenity bill. Promoters from New York were also working on the legislators. They wanted to kill the bill and Comstock along with it. On March 3, 1873, Congress passed what came to be known as the Comstock Act, and postal agents were given new weapons in their war against filth in the mails.

For decades, the Comstock Act proved effective in cleaning the mails, but nearly 85 years later Congress again grew concerned about obscenity in the mails, particularly as children became the targets of the smut peddlers. After World War II, the sale of pornography to children exploded into a $500,000,000 a year business. Boys sending away for toys got on mailing lists—the most valuable tool in the kit of the filth peddlers.

Mothers and community groups protested as circulars advertising the wares of the pornographers found their way into neighborhood mail boxes. Postal inspectors uncovered evidence that racketeers were moving in to share the tremendous profits of pornography, but liberal court rulings established virtual sanctuaries for the pornographers. The courts ruled that dealers in obscenity could be prosecuted only where the obscene material was mailed—not where it was delivered.

In 1958, Congress stepped in. A law was passed to permit prosecution at the point of delivery. The smut peddlers were brought out of their big city headquarters to face courts, juries and parents in the communities where children were sent invitations to obscenity. The postal inspectors at last had the legal weapon to carry on the fight launched by Comstock.

The dauntless Comstock had not stopped with his anti-vice campaign. As a special agent, he went after phony stock brokers and suppressed 23 firms. He uncovered lottery schemes, silver and gold mine swindles and counterfeit money sold to suckers as the real thing. In 1882, he wrote a book about his adventures entitled, *Frauds Exposed: or How The People Are Deceived And Robbed And Youth Corrupted.*

"It is better than a play to head off one of these sharpers and bring him to justice," he wrote. "There is a pleasure in stretching a strong arm between them and their victims."

By that time, a force of 90 men was stretching the strong arm. In 1880, Congress had created the title of Chief Post Office Inspector and his men—the surveyors of colonial days, the special agents of the nineteenth century, became known as post office inspectors. Later, the variety of their duties prompted the shorter title of "postal inspector."

Congress had outlawed mail frauds, but they continued to flourish as the criminal cases made by the inspectors worked their way slowly through the courts. The promoters could make fortunes before the courts put them out of business. This was a time when the promoters were preying on a new crop of innocents—the immigrants who believed all they had heard about the fortunes to be made in America. The little money they brought with them went into counterfeit lottery tickets, "gold" bricks and "once in a lifetime" opportunities. In 1889—the year Ellis Island was opened to the flood of immigrants—Congress acted to protect them. The Postmaster General was given the right he still has to issue fraud orders, stamp the swindler's mail "fraudulent" and return it to the sender without waiting for the court to act.

The first decade of the twentieth century saw the mails misused for other purposes and Congress provided more duties for the postal inspectors. They were to keep the mails clear of poisons, pests and infernal machines under a 1909 law. It wasn't until half a century later that Congress was jolted into providing the death penalty where a bomb sent through the mail killed anyone. Ironically, the law long sought by postal authorities stemmed from a bomb not actually sent through the mails, but secreted in an airline passenger's suitcase. John Gilbert Graham's confession that he put 25 sticks of dynamite in his mother's luggage before seeing her off on the fatal flight from Denver on November 1, 1955, presented the horrifying possibility that bombs sent by air mail could also bring multiple deaths in flight. On September 3, 1957, President Eisenhower signed into law the measure to make killing by mail a Federal crime punishable by death or life imprisonment.

Criminals, like honest men, have found it almost impossible to conduct any business—legal or illegal—without using the mails. That's why the package of anti-racketeering bills sought by Attorney General Robert F. Kennedy brought postal inspectors into his drive on organized crime. One of the bills signed into law by President Kennedy in September, 1961, makes it a crime to send through the mails any gambling paraphernalia, from lottery tickets to numbers slips. Another new law forbids the use of the mails to further half a dozen different rackets.

In going after a different type of racketeer, the mail-fraud artist, the postal inspectors need patience as well as courage and all the investigative techniques developed since Congress passed its first mail fraud law some 90 years ago. Even Congress on occasion isn't aware that what looks like a crime calling for new laws actually can be dealt with by the postal inspectors using the tools already in their kit.

In 1958, for instance, several Senators proposed a law to curb a racket which both state and Federal authorities said they were helpless to prevent. Fast-talking salesmen were collecting advance fees from small businessmen on the pretext of selling their business or getting them a loan. The businessmen didn't sell their business or get their loan, but they couldn't sue to recover the fee because the fine print in the contracts gave the promoters an out. Postal authorities assured the Senators they didn't need a new law, that these promoters could be gotten via the mail fraud laws. Thereafter, by learning the spiel of the salesmen and sometimes infiltrating their ranks, the postal inspectors were able to show that the mails were used as part of the scheme to defraud. In less than three years, by mid-1961, postal inspectors had developed enough evidence to get 160 persons indicted in cases where small businessmen had been bilked to the tune of more than $22,000,000.

The "advance fee" racket that so concerned Congress was symptomatic of the rash of rackets sweeping across the country after World War II. More people, more money around and particularly more communications reaching into the most remote hamlet all combined to lure the quick-money boys.

They robbed their victims as surely as though they stuck a gun in their ribs, but they did it by mail and they moved fast. As soon as one community was milked dry, they struck another community half the country away. They were gone before the victims realized they had been taken for their life savings.

In 1957, the Inspection Service declared war on this new breed of promoters. Because of the complexity of the schemes, the appearance of legitimate contracts and the disappearance of the promoters, prosecutors were reluctant to prosecute.

The Chief Postal Inspector organized a group of more than 50 specially qualified inspectors throughout the nation and assigned them exclusively to major fraud investigations. He set up a clearing house in Washington on all schemes of national scope and consolidated the available information on every major promoter. It swiftly became apparent that the swindlers stuck to their own lines. They might change the names of their companies, they might be president of the company under one set-up and secretary-treasurer under another, but they didn't change their pattern of operations.

Finally, a conference was organized in Washington, bringing together legal and medical experts in and out of the Government for a concerted drive on the mail fraud operators. The Justice Department's fraud section was in the act from the beginning, making sure that the cases developed by the postal inspectors would catch up with the promoters wherever they roamed and put them out of business via prison.

In the years since the all-out drive was launched, arrests for mail fraud violations have increased by 137 per cent. Currently, a further step-up has been ordered in the campaign despite the limits of manpower and the time consumed in proving each case.

Modern inventions undreamed of in the days when Congress passed its first fraud laws are being exploited today to prey on those who can least afford the loss—widows with scanty incomes and the disabled who can't take full-time jobs. One such racket involves vending machines for cigarettes, candy and nuts. The victims are induced to buy the machines on the theory that for a few hours' work a week they will collect a tidy income and can sell their vending machine route at a profit any time they choose. A Florida widow's complaint to postal inspectors that the machines were no good and the company wouldn't take them back launched a ten-state investigation that located hundreds of victims and uncovered a million-dollar racket in worthless machines. Other promoters are still operating in this field, despite the success of postal inspectors in getting 90 of them indicted.

One promoter advertised what appeared to be a bona fide offer of home employment. After paying a $2 fee, the victims learned they had to clip and sell newspaper items and would have to spend more money to buy laminating materials to preserve the clippings. The Texas swindler who collected $60,000 on that racket will have plenty of time to read and clip newspapers himself. He drew a five-year prison term for mail fraud.

More costly to the victims were the knitting machine schemes, where young mothers were induced to buy machines costing $300 to $450 on the promise that they would have a ready market for their products. Once the victims were hooked, the patterns were changed frequently to discourage the knitters and the promoters moved on, leaving the victims with worthless machines, no market for their knit goods and no means of paying the finance companies which held their notes. Postal inspectors have virtually eliminated the knit-at-home racket but losses to victims may come close to $40,000,000.

The state of Maryland had no effective law to control savings and loan associations and the fast-money boys moved in. Postal inspectors investigated 19 Maryland savings and loan associations offering fancy returns, free gifts and "insured" operations. The first prosecutions stemming from their investigations spotlighted the inadequacy of Maryland law and led to legislation which they helped draft. Since the law was passed, postal inspectors have joined state authorities in uncovering the misuse of millions of dollars of depositors' funds. Receivers have been appointed for a number of the associations, only to find the cupboard bare and depositors deprived of all their savings.

Swindlers are reaping a rich harvest from other forms of fraud—charity rackets where the principal recipient of charity is the racketeer, song sharks who prey on people seeking a little help to make their compositions salable, promoters who collect fees for phony offers of foreign employment, quacks who make fortunes out of "cure-all" tonics and gadgets. Because medical frauds may delay proper treatment until it's too late, the team of postal inspectors concentrating on the phony "cure-alls" was expanded in 1961.

A new form of fraud is in the offing and postal inspectors are waiting to pounce before it gets rolling. The emphasis on the need for fall-out shelters is expected to attract the brand of promoters who use scare tactics to sell their flimsy wares. At the request of the Justice Department, postal inspectors have launched an all-out investigative program to stop this fraud before it gets rolling.

What can you do to protect yourself against the twentieth century fraud artists and help the postal inspectors protect others? If any promises are made through the mails that run counter to the normal, every-day way of doing things, let your local post office know about it. What's put in writing may sound innocent, but it could be the opening wedge for a glib salesman out to take you for all he can get. Where the mails are used either to solicit business or for your response, a case of mail fraud may be in the making.

For instance, powerful radio stations across the border in Mexico were broadcasting lengthy commercials advertising quack remedies to American listeners. They violated the rules of broadcasting but the Federal Communications Commission couldn't do a thing about it because the stations were out of the country. Postal authorities spotted a way to get at the American promoters via mail fraud laws. Since listeners were invited to send their orders for the advertised remedies to post office boxes in Texas and California, the mails were being used in the scheme. Once postal inspectors started investigating, the FCC monitored the Mexican commercials and supplied batches of the taped broadcasts to postal inspectors. Then the Food and Drug Administration's chemists analyzed the advertised products and reported their value—or lack of it. The Justice Department's fraud section alerted prosecutors throughout the country to work with postal inspectors in stopping American promoters from using Mexican radio to defraud Americans, and several indictments have followed.

The public could take a tip from other government regulatory agencies. They all turn frequently to the postal inspectors just because the mails figure somewhere in most illegal enterprises.

The Securities and Exchange Commission investigators work with postal inspectors because much of the promotion in stock swindles goes through the mail. It took the combined efforts of SEC investigators and postal inspectors over a period of two years to unravel a Texas oil conspiracy promoted by Francis P. Crosby, playboy ex-husband of actress Denise Darcel. The conspiracy was so complex that the judge took eight hours to charge the jury. As the case emerged from the Court of Appeals, the SEC charges were dropped and only mail fraud remained.

The armed forces investigators also turn frequently to postal inspectors to look into obscenity mailed to servicemen and the security aspects of correspondence clubs for men only. During one such investigation, postal inspectors found Soviet agents were writing the club for "pen pals" and getting membership lists of an all-male club. The security threat involved in that operation prompted the postal inspectors to move fast before the club's lists could be used to blackmail men into espionage.

Postal inspectors supply information to Internal Revenue agents whenever the lush profits of mail fraud or pornography might not appear on income tax returns. Postal inspectors wound up their two-year investigation of the pseudo-religious cult known as the "I Am Society" by providing the information for tax agents to collect more than $100,000 in back taxes from the promoters.

President Kennedy himself has reason to be grateful to the Postal Inspection Service. It was a postal inspector in Belmont, N.H., who notified the Secret Service that a local character had made threats against the life of the then President-elect and was probably on his way to Palm Beach to carry them out. When Richard P. Pavlick was taken into custody, the President-elect probably understood what Postmaster General Blair had meant exactly a century earlier when he referred to the postal inspectors as "my eyes, my ears and my hands."

DOLLARS FOR THE CHINESE REDS

Postal Inspector R. Frank Ogden considered himself only an ordinary guy with an oversized bump of curiosity. This ordinary guy, virtually single-handed, exposed a Communist conspiracy funneling millions of dollars a month into Red China to buy American war materials.

Before he was through, he broke three counterfeit rings, dried up a thriving black market in American postal money orders and convinced the American government to change several long-standing policies for handling money matters in the Pacific.

While he was tracking down counterfeiters and Communist agents, both American and Philippine authorities worried plenty about the dogged inspector with the wide Irish grin who seemed so blithely unconcerned about his personal safety. They warned him repeatedly that with millions of dollars at stake, somebody could get hurt in trigger-happy Manila.

"I've got my orders to stop this Communist conspiracy," he would say with stubborn cheerfulness, "and, by golly, I'm going to do it."

The full story of what he exposed was discussed at White House Cabinet sessions as it developed, but it was kept under wraps for more than a decade because of international implications. Now for the first time, Frank Ogden can be given the credit for his one-man war against Communist aggression.

His own bump of curiosity started it all.

That curiosity had always delighted his four children, now grown up with children of their own. They loved his wide-ranging interest in the world around him, the why of everything. He told them stories liberally sprinkled with Hawaiian native words because he had made Hawaii his home.

It was curiosity that led him to wonder why Chinese chop marks suddenly began appearing on the backs of American money orders, and why a certain chop mark only appeared once. Later on, the same curiosity prompted him to lift the lid of a pot of food in Manila with decisive results.

But that was much later. The story of Frank Ogden's solo war against the Chinese Reds actually began in April, 1950, when he was making a routine inspection tour of Hawaiian post offices and turned up some puzzling Chinese symbols on the backs of postal money orders.

From his years in Hawaii, the veteran inspector was aware that Philippine workers on the coffee and pineapple plantations regularly sent money back to their families via postal money orders. Routinely, their wives cashed the money orders at banks or post offices in the Philippines. The money orders Ogden was turning up hadn't followed that route at all. They had never gone into the Philippine postal system or they wouldn't have those Chinese chop marks all over the back.

With the help of a Chinese scholar to translate the chop marks, Ogden traced the path of the errant money orders. They had travelled from Manila to Hong Kong and from there to banks on the American mainland, usually New York. The banks apparently credited the Hong Kong people with the dollars and sent the money orders back to Hawaii for repayment.

Ogden's first report to San Francisco prompted some checking on the mainland. The San Francisco post office reported it was also getting demands for repayment of money orders routed via Hong Kong. In New York, Postal Inspector W. J. Skau checked the banks mentioned by Ogden and found Hong Kong firms in New York alone were being credited with $2,600,000 a month in American money orders and Treasury checks.

Still following the trail of the wandering money orders, Ogden asked all postmasters in Hawaii and Guam to keep a record of the Philippine-bound orders they were asked to repay. In two months, they reported, $1,250,000 worth of money orders had been routed back to them for repayment via Hong Kong and mainland banks.

Ogden had other things to do but at night, sitting on the lanai of his home at Kailua, he studied his growing collection of money orders. He had had photostats made of the chop marks appearing most frequently on the backs of money orders. Because he was curious about a chop mark that appeared only once, he had a picture made of that, too.

His stack of money orders, he noticed, showed destinations throughout the Philippines and yet every one of them got to Hong Kong.

"There's money and organization behind this," he told himself, "and in the Orient, that means Chinese."

By October, he was ready to put on paper a theory that had been needling him since April. In a personal and confidential letter to his immediate boss in San Francisco, he theorized that if the syndicate collecting the money orders was backed by the Red Chinese, the

Communists would be getting millions of dollar credits to buy supplies for their burgeoning war machine. It was just a theory, he wrote apologetically; he had no proof but American intelligence agencies might want to investigate.

As it turned out, it was to be his private war from start to finish. It happened this way: soon after Ogden's confidential report reached the Chief Postal Inspector in Washington, William Y. Chan, a clerk in the San Francisco post office, discovered a group of money orders that looked different from the others. All were allegedly issued at the Army Post Office in Okinawa—APO 239—and all were counterfeit.

Then, a few days after that, Rear Admiral Francis P. Olds, commander of naval forces in the Philippines, radioed Washington requesting that a postal inspector be dispatched to the Philippines. The admiral had been told of wholesale buying of postal money orders by sailors and the Philippine wives of American servicemen. He suspected the money orders were being sold on the black market.

Frank Ogden was inspecting the Guam post office when he got his instructions from Washington to proceed immediately to Manila to investigate possible black marketing and counterfeiting of postal money orders. He wasn't sure where the counterfeiting fitted into his theory of a Communist conspiracy but the black marketing by sailors and Filipinas could fit very neatly.

On November 12, 1950, Ogden reported at the U. S. Naval Station, Cavite, Philippine Islands. As he faced the admiral, he was acutely aware of what the Chinese could do with American dollar credits. To the north, the Chinese Reds were feeding North Koreans the munitions to kill American servicemen.

A quick examination of money orders at the Naval Post Office disclosed that ten seamen were buying an average of $500 worth of money orders every day.

"Either there's a big game going on and these boys are extremely lucky, or they're being paid to buy the money orders for someone else," Ogden told the admiral.

The inspector was pretty sure he knew the answer but he wasn't yet ready to air his theory. He had no proof. Instead, he shifted to the Army Post Office in Manila, where he found that in two months about 46 Filipinas married to American soldiers had bought $533,000 worth of money orders—ostensibly to send to Army husbands overseas.

"Here's a switch," Ogden commented. "These women should be getting money from their husbands. Now, they're reversing the process."

The Filipinas, he was sure, wouldn't talk but the seamen might, particularly after Admiral Olds authorized him to say they wouldn't be court-martialed for their black marketing if they cooperated.

One by one, as a typhoon raged over the naval base at Cavite, the seamen admitted they had had a good thing going before Ogden came along. A Filipino vegetable man driving a yellow jeep, they said, would come on the base with a fistful of Military Payment Certificates, the currency used to buy money orders at the naval post office. He would give them the certificates to buy the money orders and pay them 20 pesos ($10) for every $100 money order they bought. The seamen would make the orders payable to a mother or father back home, but immediately sign them to transfer ownership and give them to the vegetable man.

Ogden persuaded them to point out their benefactor and the next time the vegetable man came on the base, his pass was cancelled.

Within four days, Ogden had accumulated enough proof to cable the Chief Postal Inspector in Washington recommending that Filipinas be barred from buying money orders at military post offices and that sales to servicemen be restricted. It was the first gun fired in Ogden's own war with the Chinese Reds and it hit its mark. Orders carrying out his recommendations were promptly issued by the Secretary of Defense.

Ogden had put a crimp in black marketing of money orders, but he still didn't know how they wound up in Hong Kong or what use was made of the dollar credits. Until he could prove the dollar credits were falling into Communist hands, he knew the American government wouldn't consider such a drastic step as discontinuing its domestic money order system with the Philippines.

The inspector wanted to dig deeper, much deeper, and the Philippine authorities helped him do it. By now, he had been made an officer of both the Philippine Military Intelligence Service and the National Intelligence Coordinating Agency to give him some official status and agents when he needed them. His new colleagues gave him his first positive link to Hong Kong.

Only a month before, he learned, Hong Kong authorities had reported that more than $140,000 in American dollar instruments—money orders, Treasury checks and even greenbacks—had been seized at Hong Kong's Kai Tak airport, as an airline employee tried to smuggle the money bundle off a Manila plane.

Ogden caught the next flight to the British island. As his plane swooped down between the peaks for the breath-taking landing at

Kai Tak, Ogden looked forward eagerly to studying the smuggled money orders as they appeared before being plastered with Hong Kong chop marks.

It wasn't to be that simple, although the Hong Kong customs report on the smuggling incident looked promising. According to the report, the airline employee was caught with 15 envelopes stuffed with American checks and money orders. When two Chinese merchants claimed the envelopes, they insisted the money was payment for merchandise they had shipped to Manila.

"You didn't believe them?" Ogden asked Detective Sub-Inspector Siu Chung Yin, who had been detailed to help him in the British Crown Colony.

"No," the Chinese detective replied. "Neither of them could show a bill of lading to cover any shipment to Manila and neither operates a store, just an office."

Ogden nodded happily. This was fitting nicely into his theory of a Chinese conspiracy. He asked for a look at the smuggled money orders.

"We haven't got them any more," Siu told him apologetically. "The smuggling violated Philippine law, not ours. The judge ordered us to turn the envelopes over to the merchants."

It was a setback but Ogden swallowed his disappointment. He pulled a stack of photostats out of his pockets, the Hong Kong chop marks he had collected in Hawaii.

"We'll call in the owners of the chop marks," promised Siu.

Ogden spent the next four days closeted with Siu in his little office at police headquarters. As the American's own feeling of frustration grew, he developed a strong admiration for the Chinese detective patiently interviewing the Chinese merchants in Cantonese dialect and translating their replies for Ogden in perfect English with a decided Harvard accent.

Small of stature, impeccably dressed, Siu never raised his voice as the merchants blandly and obviously lied. All the merchants told the same story. An overseas Chinese from their old village would visit Hong Kong on his way back to China. If he had a money order to cash, the Chinese merchant would put his chop mark on it as a sort of endorsement since his fellow countryman was unknown in Hong Kong. There was no conspiracy here, just friendly Chinese helping each other.

On the afternoon of the fourth day, Ogden restlessly strode over to the window while a tea coolie shuffled in to serve the inevitable tea and biscuits. The American stared out at the ferries plying between Kowloon on the Chinese mainland and the island of Hong

Kong and at the Chinese junks sailing out of Hong Kong's busy harbor. Lights were beginning to flicker on the ridges behind Kowloon. Beyond those hills, Ogden knew, lay Red China and the answer to the secret these merchants were trying so hard to conceal.

"This isn't getting us anywhere," Ogden blurted out. "By golly, I'm about ready to throw in the sponge and go back to Manila."

Siu shook his head.

"You're looking at this with an Occidental mind," he said. "Being an Oriental, I know how these merchants think. If we can get something to prove to them we actually know what's going on, I'm sure we'll get the truth."

Ogden thumbed through the rest of his photostats until he came to the lone chop mark that had roused his curiosity in Hawaii because it appeared on only one money order. He tossed it across the desk to Siu.

"Mean anything to you?" he asked the Chinese detective.

Siu's usually impassive face broke into a smile.

"This may be our break," he said. "That's Pao Hong Loon, a small-time money-changer, a hanger-on in our underworld. The last time he was arrested, I went rather easy on him. I think we can collect on that debt."

When Pao Hong Loon was brought in, Ogden reflected that shady characters looked the same the world over, the same cringing shoulders, the same furtive glances. Ogden didn't know what the Chinese detective was saying to the money-changer but he figured it must be working because Pao Hong Loon began to talk.

As Siu translated, a grin crept over the American's face. The pattern of conspiracy was emerging.

"He says as far as he knows, an agent in Hong Kong is called from Manila and told that the money envelopes will be hidden on a certain plane," the Chinese detective reported.

"The Chinese agent in Hong Kong contacts an airline employee at Kai Tak to pick up the envelopes when the plane lands. Each envelope bears a single Chinese character which tells the agent where it is to be delivered. When the Chinese merchants get their envelopes, they place their chop marks on the checks and money orders and sell them to the On Lung Bullion Brokers or deposit them in the Dao Heng Bank."

Ogden's curiosity about the lone chop mark had paid off. Pao Hong Loon had given him the lever to use on the Chinese merchants, but Ogden groaned inwardly at the thought of four more days of Chinese doubletalk.

"You'll see," Siu promised him. "It will be different this time."

Siu, it developed, had been right about the Oriental mind. Faced with the facts disclosed by Pao Hong Loon's story, they admitted their role in the conspiracy and, to Ogden's amazement, they did it in perfect English.

With the Chinese detective, Ogden climbed the ladder steps of Hong Kong's back streets to call on the On Lung Bullion Brokers and the Dao Heng Bank. What he sought was the answer that would put the Hong Kong end of the conspiracy on ice—what use they made of the American dollar credits.

Like the merchants, the manager of the On Lung Bullion Brokers side-stepped Siu's questions until he was sure the Chinese detective knew how he had acquired the money orders. Then, he admitted that a combine known as the United Hong Kong Company, Ltd., had been established in New York to act as a collection agency for dollar instruments bought in Hong Kong. The On Lung official glossed over what happened after the dollar instruments were shipped to New York and deposited in a bank for collection. But Ogden gathered the United Hong Kong Company was a front for the Chinese Reds.

When the Communists wanted American equipment, the United Hong Kong Company would place the order and have it shipped to Hong Kong, paying for it with a check drawn on its account at the New York bank. The equipment would then travel by junk from Hong Kong to Red China.

Remembering the junks he had watched sailing down the Pearl River, Ogden wondered how many were carrying American war materials bought with American dollars.

Ogden's last call was at the Dao Heng Bank but he didn't expect much. The place was so small, hardly bigger than a money-changer's alcove. His eyes widened when he saw a battery of Chinese girls calling all over the world for the latest rate of exchange in every currency. He got an idea of the wealth of this hole-in-the-wall establishment when the manager showed him a subterranean vault stacked to the ceiling with millions of dollars' worth of gold bullion.

The American was beyond surprise when he was ushered into the bank's board room, exquisitely furnished in rare Chinese woods and decorated with jade ornaments.

The bank manager explained that his firm maintained its own account in a New York bank. When a so-called merchant, acting for the Communists (although the bank manager didn't say so), placed an order with an American firm, the Dao Heng bank covered the purchase with a cashier's check drawn on its New York account. The money orders smuggled out of Manila, Ogden knew, were bulging that New York bank account.

Flying back to Manila, Ogden reflected that he had unmasked the supply line of the Chinese Reds but he still hadn't located the supply base in the Philippines. That, he decided, would have to wait a bit. His next order of business would have to be the counterfeiters.

From what he had learned in Hong Kong, the counterfeits were no part of the Communist plan. Some of the counterfeit APO 239 money orders, he was told, had come into the Dao Heng Bank and somebody had lost money. Obviously, Filipinos aware of the Chinese quest for American dollars had gone into the counterfeiting business. It amused Ogden to contemplate the indignation of the Communists when they learned they had been tricked with counterfeits, but he had to find the makers before any more counterfeits filtered back to America.

When Ogden told his Philippine contacts what he wanted to do next, they regarded him with worried frowns. This crazy American, they told each other, not only wanted to take on the Communist conspirators but the Manila underworld, too. They agreed to help him but they made him promise to carry a gun, to move out of his hotel into safer quarters in the American embassy compound, to get off the streets by 4 P.M. and under no circumstances to leave the city without an escort. They warned him to be on the lookout for ambush and attempted assassination.

Ogden proceeded to bait a trap for the counterfeiters. He let it be known that he was an affluent American with plenty of pesos he wanted to convert into money orders to get his loot out of Manila. When the trap was sprung on the grounds of the Manila hotel, the Philippine agents closed in too soon to get the counterfeits, which the wily ringleader had passed to a confederate to hold until he was sure the coast was clear. But Ogden and the agents did get the counterfeiters.

The American watched in disappointed silence as the counterfeiters were searched and questioned. No money orders and no information. The counterfeiters were about to be led off to jail when Ogden remembered something that had piqued his curiosity. He had noticed an agent taking a note out of the shoe of one of the prisoners. At his request, the agent translated.

"Mr. Lara," the note said. "Please don't fail to see him at the Boulevard tomorrow December 27, 1950, at 11 A.M. Sharp. Hope everything are all good results. Greg."

Ogden asked to see the prisoner away from the others. It was the first of his many meetings with Luis Llora.

"You want to stay out of jail?" Ogden began.

The young mestizo nodded his head vigorously as soon as Ogden's question was translated.

"Would you like to make some money working for me?" Ogden went on.

Llora looked dubious but the combination of money and the inspector's friendly smile gradually sold him. The Spanish-Filipino and the Irish-American formed an alliance that night that lasted throughout Ogden's stay in the Philippines.

Ogden lost no time making use of his underworld Man Friday. He began with the note that had brought Llora to his attention. The "Greg" of the note, Llora told him, was Gregorio Lopez and the note had to do with counterfeit money orders Lopez was arranging to sell. That's what Ogden suspected when he separated Llora from the others.

Coached and cajoled by Ogden, Llora agreed to accompany a Philippine agent on a visit to Lopez to buy counterfeits. The pair returned two hours later, triumphantly flashing a counterfeit money order and announcing that Greg had 500 to sell. Ogden looked at the sample and groaned. It wasn't drawn on APO 239. This one presumably was issued at Cayuga, New York. Another counterfeit ring had started operating.

Doggedly, Ogden laid another trap. He told Llora and the Philippine agent to go through with the meeting "Greg" had agreed to set up with the maker of the counterfeits where final arrangements were to be made for printing the 500 counterfeits. When the counterfeiter left the rendezvous, Ogden had him followed to his printing plant.

With six Philippine agents, Ogden raided the printing plant. They couldn't find a single counterfeit. Obviously, if the printer was turning out 500 counterfeits, he wasn't doing it on his own printing press. He wasn't even there.

While the search was going on, a Filipino youth came in with a bunch of small enamel pots used by Filipinos to carry food. With his usual curiosity, Ogden lifted the lid of a pot to see what the Filipinos ate. It was empty and so were all the others. Through an interpreter Ogden asked the lad what he was doing with the empty pots. The boy explained he had come to pick up food for the printer and his wife who were working today at the Rizal Memorial Press.

That's all Ogden needed. An hour later, armed with a search warrant, the American and his Philippine crew raided the Rizal Memorial Press. Behind the printing press, they found 485 money orders presumably printed for the Cayuga post office.

"Tell him we want the plates," Ogden said.

The owner of the plant shrugged and pulled a small package from under a pile of paper stock. Opening the bundle, Ogden stared at a photoelectric plate used to print the words "United States Postal Money Order" on the blue paper stock.

Ogden indicated he wanted more. This time, the owner opened a small wooden partition and produced the plate to print the reverse side of the money order. As Ogden continued to insist, the owner went to another hiding place and uncovered the plate used to print the face of the money orders. He claimed that was all he had but Ogden kept his hand out.

"I need one more," Ogden said. "It's probably a small one with the image of the postal money order shield."

The owner of the shop and the printer from the other establishment were still protesting they had no others when the printer's wife walked into the bathroom and came back with the missing plate.

"Now," Ogden said, "let's have the original."

Reaching into his shirt pocket, the printer handed over a $3 money order issued at Cayuga eight months earlier. Satisfied they now had the whole kit, the raiding agents turned to leave but Ogden turned back to the owner of the printing plant.

"Do you have anything else here you shouldn't have?" he asked.

It was a shot in the dark but the owner reacted with a heavy sigh. From a clothes press, he pulled out a photoelectric plate that could be used to print part of the reverse side of a U.S. Military Payment Certificate. He told Ogden it had been given him simply to pull a proof and he didn't have the other parts. This time Ogden believed him.

Military Payment Certificates were no part of Ogden's job but he was knocking them off as he found them. The inspector told his faithful Luis Llora to let it be known in the underworld that he had a buyer for Military Payment Certificates. Within 24 hours, Llora reported back that he had been approached by three Filipinos who had the plates but needed an angel to finance the printing. On New Year's Eve, the three men and their plates were seized in a Manila saloon and Ogden wrote off another counterfeiting ring.

Now the postal inspector was getting restive. He had exposed the black market worrying Admiral Olds, he had uncovered two counterfeiting rings and Llora told him the makers of the APO 239 counterfeits had destroyed the plates after another narrow brush with Ogden and his crew.

On the basis of his Hong Kong excursion, Ogden had recommended to Washington that the postal money order business with the Philippines should be put on an international basis where only pesos could be exchanged for the money orders. Ogden was aware, however, that Washington was waiting for the one answer he had failed to provide: How did the money orders flow from their original recipients to the planes bound for Hong Kong? He knew the beginning of the story and the end, but he still lacked the middle.

He decided to try his luck with the Filipinas buying wholesale lots of money orders ostensibly for their husbands. The Defense Department order barring Filipinas from buying American money orders had gone into effect the day before but the Filipinas didn't know it yet, so Ogden made arrangements to have them detained as they came into the Army Post Office.

Seven women showed up with $17,000 worth of Military Payment Certificates. As Ogden had figured, once the Filipinas knew there was no longer anything to be gained by lying, they told the truth. They said they went regularly to a certain street corner where they were approached by Filipinos who gave them the certificates to buy $1,000 or $2,000 worth of money orders at a time. When they handed over the money orders, they were given a few pesos for their services.

Ogden quickly dispatched two intelligence agents to the street corner with instructions to arrest both the Filipino and the woman if they saw an exchange made. The inspector waited eagerly for their return. He hadn't risked questioning the sailors' vegetable man because it was then too early in the investigation. Now, he had nothing to lose by picking up a Filipino serving the Communists.

A half hour later, one of the intelligence agents returned and his dark eyes burned with anger and embarrassment.

"My partner and I saw an exchange made and moved in to make the arrest but complications developed," the agent reported. "Two detectives from the Manila police force stepped in and refused to let us arrest anybody."

"Where's your partner?" Ogden asked.

The agent looked away and his answer was so muffled that Ogden asked him to repeat it.

"The police arrested him," the agent said. "They sent you a message. They said they'd release him if you'd return the money orders or the pay certificates you got from the women."

Angry and disappointed, Ogden was also curious. He went back to the room where the Filipinas were still being questioned to find out why the detectives would want to make a deal like that. And he got the answer. Of the $17,000 found on the women, $8,000 had been given them by the two detectives.

The postal inspector was feeling as discouraged as he had before the lone chop mark led to the break in Hong Kong. He had timed his questioning of the Filipinas to the one day when they might lead him to a buyer and, in turn, the Manila syndicate supplying the Chinese Reds. Now, that source had dried up and he knew he wouldn't get anything from the two detectives who had gummed up his plans.

As Manila simmered in the January heat, the gray-haired investigator thought wistfully of the breeze that blew constantly over his home in Kailua and yearned for a break. It wasn't long in coming.

On the basis of an anonymous tip, Philippine agents searched a plane departing for Hong Kong and found a package stuffed with $93,000 in money orders, Treasury checks and American currency. For the first time, Ogden could examine the money orders before they were covered with the chop marks of Hong Kong and the bank endorsements of New York. That's what he had hoped to find in Hong Kong, the mute evidence of the Philippine sources.

He noticed that the money orders were drawn on post offices throughout the Philippine Islands. On the back of each of the money orders, he found a handwritten initial. There were five groups of initials, indicating the money orders came from five different sources before they were collected for the trip to Hong Kong. The clearest of all the initials was the letter "M" and it appeared frequently.

While he was still puzzling over that batch, lightning struck again. Another anonymous tip sent agents back to the airport. This time, the take amounted to $78,000 and Ogden found six different groups of initials. From the two seizures, he concluded that 11 syndicates were buying dollar instruments to smuggle to Hong Kong.

Again, Ogden turned to his priceless helper, Luis Llora. He showed him the initials and told him to see if he could identify any of them. Ogden figured if he could get information on one gathering point in Manila, he could pin down the whole Red conspiracy.

This time, Llora didn't come through so fast. The key figures in the conspiracy, he reported, were well hidden.

While he was waiting for Llora to report, Ogden got a tip that a counterfeit plant was operating from a Huk guerrilla stronghold in Bulacan Province. He proposed to go after it by posing as a war correspondent, but this time the Philippine authorities firmly vetoed the idea. Enough Americans had already been killed in Huk territory, they told Ogden, and furthermore they believed, like Llora, that all the plates had been destroyed and Ogden's tip had simply been a ruse to lure him to his death.

Ogden had just proved to his own satisfaction that the Huk tip was a death trap when Llora diverted him. A woman lawyer named Mrs.

Emiliana Saturnino, said Llora, had bought some counterfeit money orders and lost approximately 17,000 pesos ($8,500) on the deal. She had tried to get the seller arrested for swindling but had failed because he was in with the police. Llora thought she might be indignant enough to talk.

It was now April, five months since Ogden had arrived in the Philippines to launch his private war with the Chinese Reds. He knew if one of the initials on the smuggled money orders belonged to Mrs. Saturnino and she admitted it, he could go home soon.

Ogden found Mrs. Saturnino at the small curio and gift shop she owned on a Manila side street. An attractive woman, he thought, with intelligent eyes but perhaps more than a trace of vanity. Ogden summoned up all his Irish blarney for the occasion. He admired the little shop, commented on how unusual it was to find a woman lawyer in Manila, marvelled that she could look so cool on such a hot day.

They smoked companionably, the smiling dark-eyed woman and the friendly American.

"I heard you got swindled and the police wouldn't do anything about it," Ogden commiserated. "That's a darn shame."

The woman nodded angrily.

"I didn't know a thing about it until the money orders came back from Hong Kong," she said, "and then they held me responsible."

"I'm just back from Hong Kong," Ogden ventured. "I heard about the counterfeits there. In fact, I know the whole story. I'm just trying to get all the loose ends tied up."

Afterwards, Ogden wasn't quite sure whether it was the Irish blarney or Mrs. Saturnino's indignation at being swindled or her shrewd awareness that the game was up that prompted her to talk, but talk she did.

Sometime in 1950, she said, she had started dealing in money orders and Treasury checks. All her purchases were financed by Chinese merchants in Manila.

Ogden didn't want to push her too fast but he had to know how the system worked throughout the islands. Mrs. Saturnino obliged.

"A Filipino hangs around a post office," she explained, "and waits for somebody to go in to cash a money order from the States. Then, he offers to pay a premium, usually $25 or $35 more than the legal rate on a $100 money order. Sometimes, a post office clerk will tip him off when a Treasury check arrives so the Filipino will be on hand to buy it from the recipient.

"When the Filipino has all his capital invested in money orders and checks, he goes to the Escolta area of Manila where buyers with more capital pay him a premium for the lot. That's where I come in. My runner canvasses the Escolta buyers and gets everything they have to sell."

Mrs. Saturnino coolly estimated that she bought a daily average of $10,000 to $18,000 in dollar instruments, and her personal profit ranged from $500 to $1,350 daily. At the close of each day's business, she said, a Chinese agent called at the gift shop to collect the bundle and pay her off in pesos.

"Suppose your runner came in with more money orders and checks than you could pay for," asked Ogden, amazed at the size of her daily business. "What would you do then?"

"I would call my syndicate and say I needed some pesos," she replied.

When she saw the look of disbelief on Ogden's face, she dialed a number, spoke a few words in the native Tagalog and hung up. In a few minutes, a man walked into the office, dropped a parcel on the desk and walked out. Mrs. Saturnino opened the parcel and smilingly showed Ogden the contents—25,000 pesos.

Ogden noted that the man hadn't even asked for a receipt for what would be $12,500 in American money. There was one more point he had to prove.

"Do you have a private mark you put on the checks and money orders?" the inspector asked.

"I certainly do," the woman replied with an edge of bitterness in her voice. "The syndicate makes me initial every one of them, in case something comes back. That's how the counterfeit money orders were traced back to me. I'll show you my mark."

Ogden stared down at the letter "M." The initial that had attracted his attention because it appeared so often on the bundle of money orders seized at the airport belonged to Mrs. Saturnino.

Walking out of Mrs. Saturnino's gift shop, Ogden didn't notice the sticky afternoon heat of Manila. Mrs. Saturnino had given him the names of other operators, particularly the ones who had also been stuck with counterfeits, and of course he would interview them, too. But that wasn't why his step was buoyant as he strode down the boulevard. He had the middle of the story now—the indisputable link between the checks and money orders flowing into the Philippines and the checks and money orders siphoned off to the Chinese Communists. Now he could go home.

Before he left Manila, he saw the results of his private war with the Communists.

On the basis of his recommendations, Gen. MacArthur in Tokyo ordered a change in the series of Military Pay Certificates, which would make worthless any certificates then in the hands of people who shouldn't have them. The change caught the Chinese with approximately a million dollars worth of valueless certificates, accumulated to buy money orders at military post offices.

With Ogden's conclusive proof that the money orders were getting into Communist hands, the Postmaster General suspended the long-standing domestic money order system with the Philippines and replaced it with the international system under which the government would get the dollars and the recipients of the money orders would be paid in pesos. That dried up an estimated source of $2,254,000 monthly in dollar credits for the Communists.

The Defense Department decided to follow the lead of other government agencies in stamping its checks to Philippine recipients of pension and retirement benefits "Payable only through the National Bank of the Philippines." Because of the red imprint on the face of the checks, the Filipinos dubbed them "Lip Stick," but the Chinese Reds no doubt called them something else. The Defense Department alone had been good for nearly $912,000 monthly in dollar credits for the Communists. With all Treasury checks now restricted to payment in the Philippines, the Communists lost a potential source of $100,000,000 a year in American dollar credits.

The counterfeit money orders disappeared and no one was inclined to go in that business any more. They couldn't find buyers. With the restrictions on money orders approved on Ogden's recommendation, the black market in legitimate money orders dried up.

Manila finally stopped being a source of dollars for the Chinese Communists—thanks to an ordinary guy named Frank Ogden.

★★★

THE BLESSINGS OF LIBERTY: A Conclusion

The missions of the Federal investigators are often carried out despite roadblocks that would dismay less dedicated men.

The investigators are aware of the occupational hazards when they put on the Federal badge. They know that a criminal might attempt to shoot his way out of capture, that incriminating records may be destroyed, that an attorney can be expected to use every legal maneuver to keep a client from losing his business or going to jail.

It's only later that some Federal investigators discover that they can't go armed against the criminals, that they can't get the records before they're destroyed, that they can't use the facts they know to meet the attorney's maneuvers.

These are some of the obstacles created largely because the demands on the Federal investigators mushroomed faster than Congress has supplied the needed investigative tools. As the history of the Federal investigative agencies demonstrates, the founding fathers and successive legislators and Presidents created new investigative units to meet immediate needs and public demand. But as Congress assigned them additional duties, the tasks of the investigators both multiplied and shifted.

Some investigators who started with what could be regarded as "briefcase" jobs now tangle regularly with underworld characters and fast-moving promoters. Yet some of them lack the authority to carry a gun or serve a warrant. Some are not even covered by the law which makes it a Federal crime to assault most Federal agents performing their official duties.

Although investigators for some regulatory agencies are becoming more and more involved in police work, they are so bound by administrative red tape that they have to get permission from Washington before they can subpoena company records and by that time, the books may be long gone.

Investigators for some agencies have no more power to make an arrest than a citizen without a badge, although at the time an arrest is necessary they may be basically on a law enforcement mission.

Some investigators have to halt their investigations midway and turn their cases over to another agency because that's the way Congress dealt out the laws. On the other hand, some agencies find themselves with such overlapping responsibilities that they must work out cooperative procedures to avoid duplicating each other's investigations.

Most of the investigative agencies are short on manpower. That's one of their principal problems. Frequently, the tasks assigned by the President or Congress have far outstripped the manpower authorized to handle them. So the individual agent either has to do the job of two men or let the trail go cold while he takes a night off.

Court decisions are another major hurdle for the investigator to overcome. Defense attorneys are quick to point out any weakness or vagueness in the law, and the courts sometimes agree with them. On occasion, the courts suggest in their opinions that Congress clarify what it actually meant when it wrote the law. Until Congress acts to repair the defect—and that may be years later, or not at all—the investigators are not permitted to probe where they probed before nor testify to the facts they have accumulated.

Ironically, Congress sometimes has no way of knowing the roadblocks in the path of the investigators. Most investigative agencies are an arm of a larger department. Any requests they make for more manpower, new laws, new methods of meeting newly created problems, must be cleared by the department—and frequently they stop right there. The department heads, usually cabinet officers, have to consider all their agencies, all their demands for more manpower and new laws. The needs of one have to be balanced against the needs of the others—and the investigators who enforce the laws for the department are sometimes the last to be heard.

When an investigative chief appears before the legislators handling appropriations for his agency, he can discuss only what his department head—and the Bureau of the Budget—has approved. Recently, an agency chief appeared before a Senate investigating committee. It was a golden opportunity for him to explain how a new law would help his agents pursue the very type of evil that the Senators were exploring. He didn't seize the opportunity, however, because the request for the new law had not been cleared with higher authorities.

How can Congress help the investigators to carry out the missions assigned by Congress itself? One proposal advanced—and opposed—was the creation of a National Crime Commission to coordinate the efforts of the agencies dealing principally with law enforcement problems. Attorney General Robert F. Kennedy, who favored the idea himself before he found out how much cooperation already existed between the agencies, and how much more was possible without additional law, turned to a system of pooling existing information about known racketeers and targeting in on the most likely violation in each case. He brought into his program some Federal agencies whose investigators had collected intelligence data of no immediate use to their agencies, but valuable as clues to the investigators of other agencies. This coordinated drive demonstrated almost immediately where investigators have been stymied through lack of effective law. The Attorney General managed to win from Congress during the first year of his administration a package of new laws—some of which had been sought unsuccessfully for nearly a decade—but he hasn't gotten them all yet nor can he be the champion for investigative agencies who are only on the fringe of his coordinated drive. So the responsibility again rests on Congress.

Another proposal that encompasses all the Federal investigative agencies is an over-all survey of their duties under Congressional auspices. This proposal was first advanced as a step toward streamlining the agencies, removing some duties and adding others for more effective enforcement. But such an investigation of the investigators could have a much broader significance than merely straightening out the lines of command.

It would give Congress an opportunity to hear from the investigators themselves what new laws and additional manpower would help them to do a better job of protecting the people. It would give the President support for programs he has urged to increase public protection, as reported by the men on the firing line.

And it would give the American people an education. Many of them would learn for the first time the identity of all the Federal investigative agencies they can look to for protection. This education is vital, for the people have a responsibility, too. The Federal investigators need the cooperation of all the people they have taken an oath to serve. This cooperation can take many forms.

If "Junior" sends away for a toy airplane and gets on a mailing list for obscenity, send the material, envelope and all, to the Postal Inspection Service.

If a plane crashes nearby, help keep the souvenir hunters away so the Civil Aeronautics Board's investigators can collect clues to the crash.

If the Secret Service sends out an alert on counterfeit bills and you're a cashier, study the description of the bills and their passers and notify the Secret Service immediately when you spot a phony.

If the Civil Service Commission's investigators write and visit you for information on a prospective Government employee, tell them the facts you know.

If a promoter tries to sell you a stock by telephone but refuses to put any of his high-flown promises in writing, tell it to the Securities and Exchange Commission.

If you recognize the face or description on a "wanted" poster, call the Federal Bureau of Investigation.

In these and many other ways, you can help the man behind the Federal badge to assure you the "blessings of liberty."

Other Agencies

Most agencies of the United States government are required to carry out certain investigative activities. These range from duties performed by small security units checking on personnel to major assignments for large forces of inspectors, examiners, auditors and analysts. The following list spells out the *investigative* functions of elements of the federal government not included elsewhere in this book.

AGENCY FOR INTERNATIONAL DEVELOPMENT

Management-Inspection Staff is the "eyes and ears" of AID in investigating and appraising overseas projects financed with American money or aided by American technicians, to make sure programs are effective in helping the countries involved and contributing to our foreign policy.

AGRICULTURE DEPARTMENT

Agricultural Marketing Service inspects poultry and poultry products, inspects grain and grain merchandising, inspects rosin and turpentine for adulteration or mislabelling, inspects and grades farm products for quality and condition, inspects capacity of hampers used in marketing fresh fruits and vegetables for deceptive or short-weight containers, protects farmers against unfair or fraudulent marketing of their goods in interstate commerce, checks operation of public stockyards and trade practices of meat packers, inspects commodity warehouses and investigates warehousemen for licensing, checks on sale and advertising of agricultural seed.

Agricultural Research Service inspects meat, enforces plant and animal quarantines, inspects facilities for eradicating animal disease and for plant pest control.

Agricultural Stabilization and Conservation Service's Investigation Division makes general investigations for the service and the Commodity Credit Corporation.

Commodity Exchange Authority investigates price manipulation and other unfair practices in trading on commodity futures markets to guard against artificial or distorted prices for wheat, corn, cotton and other raw commodities.

Forest Service investigates incendiarism and trespass in national forests.

Federal Crop Insurance Corporation's Claims Management Division investigates crop insurance indemnity claims.

Foreign Agricultural Service carries on agriculture intelligence to collect information on foreign agricultural competition, production and trade.

Office of Personnel's Investigation Division conducts department-wide inquiries into employee misconduct and wrongdoing.

ATOMIC ENERGY COMMISSION

Compliance Division checks on AEC licensees to make sure they comply with regulations to protect users and the public against radiation hazards; inspects these operations for safety and investigates reports of accidents or unusual circumstances involving radioactive materials or facilities subject to AEC authority.

Inspection Division investigates complaints affecting AEC programs and activities of Commission and contractor employees.

Division of Operational Safety investigates accidents in AEC operations to determine causes, technical defects, extent of losses and corrective action required.

CENTRAL INTELLIGENCE AGENCY

Coordinates the intelligence activities of Government agencies in the interest of national security, advises the National Security Council on these Governmental intelligence operations, correlates and evaluates intelligence related to the national security, presents to the National Security Council "National Intelligence Estimates" covering specific foreign situations or the world situation generally, conducts research in economic and scientific intelligence, monitors foreign broadcasts and collects intelligence abroad.

COMMERCE DEPARTMENT

Bureau of Public Roads' Project Examination Division checks federally-aided state highway programs and investigates alleged irregularities or malpractice in the highway construction program.

Bureau of International Programs' Export Control Investigations Staff makes investigations to prevent the unauthorized diversion, re-export, trans-shipment or smuggling of goods or technical data to areas of the world where the best interests of the United States dictate they should not go.

Maritime Administration's Chief Investigator and Security Officer investigates possible violation of contracts, false statements and foreign discrimination against American ships and makes special investigations dealing with transfer of ships to foreign flags, mortgage and insurance of ships.

COMMISSION ON CIVIL RIGHTS

Investigates sworn complaints that citizens have been deprived of their Constitutional rights because of color, race, religion or national origin and conducts investigations in the fields of voting, education, employment, housing and the administration of justice as they affect the rights of citizens to equal protection of the laws.

FEDERAL AVIATION AGENCY

Flight Standards Service checks airmen, aircraft and equipment in airline and private service to insure high standards of operation; evaluates all new aircraft, engines and equipment for type certification; makes daily checks of navigational facilities along the federal airways and cooperates with the Civil Aeronautics Board on accident investigation.

FEDERAL COMMUNICATIONS COMMISSION

Field Engineering and Monitoring Bureau's "kilocycle cops" suppress unlicensed radio operations, protect air navigation radio aids and police emergency calls by keeping the airways clear of interference, locate such local sources of interference with television reception as faulty electrical apparatus, locate electronic eavesdropping devices, aid search and rescue missions for lost ships and planes by fixing the location from which distress messages are sent, investigate illegal radio transmissions from race tracks, monitor space and track earth satellites and, in wartime, go after clandestine radio stations attempting to send messages to hostile forces.

FEDERAL DEPOSIT INSURANCE CORPORATION

Division of Examinations goes over the books of state banks which are insured by the FDIC but are not members of the Federal Reserve System and investigates new banks and branches applying for deposit insurance to make sure the quality of their assets is adequate to protect depositors.

FEDERAL HOME LOAN BANK BOARD

Division of Examination and Supervision checks all federal savings and loan associations and conducts joint investigations with state authorities of all federally insured state-chartered associations to guard against unlawful or financially unsound practices.

FEDERAL POWER COMMISSION

Investigates water resources and the interstate activities of electric power and natural gas firms dealing with rates, accounts and services and conducts general investigations to make legislative recommendations and to provide a central source of information on the electric power industry.

FEDERAL RESERVE SYSTEM

Division of Examinations goes over the books of state-chartered banks which are members of the Federal Reserve System to insure that the banks comply with banking laws and maintain financial soundness.

FEDERAL TRADE COMMISSION

Bureau of Deceptive Practices investigates false advertising, unfair and deceptive sales techniques and unfair methods of competition directly affecting the public.

Bureau of Wools, Fur and Textiles polices laws requiring honest labelling and selling of these products.

Bureau of Trade Restraints investigates manufacturers' or wholesalers' discrimination toward retailer customers, illegal brokerage practices, mergers which restrain or eliminate competition and other monopolistic practices.

GENERAL ACCOUNTING OFFICE

Investigates all matters dealing with the receipt, disbursement or use of public funds; examines records of Government contractors and recipients of federal loans and grants; makes other investigations ordered by Congress and lends investigators to Congressional committees to assist in their probes.

GENERAL SERVICES ADMINISTRATION

Compliance Division investigates law violations affecting GSA operations such as fraud against the Government, theft of Government property, threats to the physical security of the national stockpile, crimes in Government buildings, conflicts of interest, collusion in bidding, influence peddling, favoritism in procurement and surplus property disposal, employe misconduct, labor law violations and discrimination against minorities by GSA or by Government contractors.

HEALTH, EDUCATION AND WELFARE DEPARTMENT

PUBLIC HEALTH SERVICE

Division of Biologics Standards investigates production and distribution of vaccines, anti-toxins, blood derivatives and other biological products to make sure they meet standards of potency and safety.

Communicable Disease Center, on request of state or local health authorities, investigates outbreaks of infectious diseases to determine the nature of the disease, its source, method of spread and means of control.

Division of Water Supply and Pollution Control, on request, investigates stream pollution to determine what caused it, the extent of actual or potential damage to health and other water uses and means of control.

Division of Air Pollution Control, on request, aids state or local authorities to investigate the nature and source of air pollutants, extent of damage and means of control.

Division of Engineering Services investigates sanitary conditions on interstate planes, trains and buses, including purity of drinking water and food preparation, and investigates outbreaks of food poisoning to determine nature and source.

Division of Foreign Quarantine checks all incoming travelers to the United States to assure proper immunization and to prevent the introduction of infectious diseases from abroad.

BUREAU OF FEDERAL CREDIT UNIONS

Investigates character and fitness of those wanting to organize federal credit unions and evaluates the economic advisability of permitting a group to establish a federal credit union; reviews financial reports and examines each federal credit union annually to check compliance with law, financial soundness, management and service to members.

HOUSING AND HOME FINANCE AGENCY

Compliance Division polices the urban and housing functions of the agency, including the Federal Housing Administration, Public Housing Administration, Federal National Mortgage Association, Urban Renewal Administration and Community Facilities Administration; investigates misuse of FHA insured loans in home improvement rackets; investigates wage violations and collusive bidding on federally-supported construction and checks on misuse of federal authority or funds by local or federal housing personnel.

INTERIOR DEPARTMENT

Bureau of Sports Fisheries and Wildlife investigates violations of federal laws to protect and preserve migratory birds and aids other federal and state agencies in protecting all American species of fish, animals and birds.

Bureau of Commercial Fisheries investigates federal law violations centering on international agreements to conserve fur seals, whales and several species of commercial fish.

Bureau of Mines investigates all fatal accidents, fires, explosions and disasters occurring in the nation's coal mines or in other mines designated by Congress or the Secretary of the Interior and makes safety inspections in all coal mines.

INTERSTATE COMMERCE COMMISSION

Investigates the carriers it regulates—railroads, trucks, buses, oil pipelines, barges and coastal shipping, freight forwarders and express companies—to insure safety of operations, accurate accounts and nondiscriminatory service to shippers and the public.

LABOR DEPARTMENT

Wage and Hour and Public Contracts Divisions investigate violations of federal labor laws directly affecting 28 million employees in 1.1 million establishments and requiring minimum wages, overtime pay and limits on child labor. Investigators also check health and safety provisions for employees working on Government contracts in excess of $10,000.

Bureau of Labor-Management Reports' Office of Compliance and Enforcement investigates all civil violations of the Labor-Management Reporting and Disclosure Act and all criminal complaints arising from the reporting provisions of the Act, union trusteeship, bonding of persons handling labor organization funds or property or trusts in which labor organizations are interested, loans by labor organizations to officers and employees of labor organizations and the payment of court-imposed fines by a labor union for a union official or employee.

NATIONAL AERONAUTICS AND SPACE ADMINISTRATION

Inspections Division carries out program to prevent and detect illegal or unethical conduct by NASA employees or those directly or indirectly associated with NASA.

NATIONAL LABOR RELATIONS BOARD

Through its 34 field offices, investigates charges of unfair labor practices by employers or unions or both involving interference with employees joining or refusing to join a union, discrimination against employees because of union activity, refusal to bargain in good faith, domination of a union by an employer, excess fees required of union members, forcing an employer to pay for work not performed, secondary boycotts and other forms of discrimination, coercion and pressure.

STATE DEPARTMENT

Inspector General, Foreign Assistance, inspects and audits programs being conducted by the Agency for International Development and the Peace Corps and assesses programs under the Agricultural Trade Development and Assistance Act to check on the efficiency and economy of administration and to evaluate the effectiveness of the programs as they affect foreign policy.

TARIFF COMMISSION

Investigates tariffs and foreign trade matters to gauge the impact of imported articles on competing U.S. products, investigates the operation and effects of trade agreements and customs laws and makes special investigations on its own initiative and at the request of the President or Congress.

TREASURY DEPARTMENT

Comptroller of the Currency's examining division goes over the books of national banks to determine their financial condition, soundness of their operations and compliance with laws, examines District of Columbia banks and investigates all applications for national bank charters and national bank branches as well as state banks converting to or merging or consolidating with national banks.

UNITED STATES INFORMATION AGENCY

Research and Analysis Section evaluates effectiveness of overseas information program and gauges areas of curiosity, concern and apprehension abroad as a guide to programming.

Inspection Staff examines programs in the field to determine effective use of personnel, budget and techniques.

VETERANS ADMINISTRATION

Investigation Service checks on allegations and complaints of misconduct or irregularities in VA programs by VA employees or individuals and firms doing business with VA in its medical, pension, loan guarantee, educational, insurance and other programs for veterans.

Index

Abel, Col. Rudolf, 9
Adams, Don, 240-243
Adams, Sherman, 255
Adonis, Joe, 220-229
Agency for International Development, 337
Agriculture Department:
  Bureau of Chemistry, 171, 173
  investigative activities, 337-338
Air Force Office of Special Investigations, 65, 77-94
  counter-espionage activities, 82-94
Air Line Pilots Association, 102, 108
Alcohol and Tobacco Tax Division, Internal Revenue Service, 191-210
  agents, 191, 198
  "major violators program," 195-196
  moonshine business in Florida, 199-210
  National and Federal Firearms Acts, 197-198
  Prohibition Era, 193-194
American Medical Association, 173
American Stock Exchange, 122
Anderson, Bill, 67-76
Anslinger, Harry J., 150, 153-155
Apalachin crime convention, 217-218
Armed Forces Institute of Pathology, 102
Army Counter Intelligence Corps, 52, 65
Army Criminal Investigation Division, 48-61
  black marketeers, 53-61
  duties, 48, 52
  historical development, 48-50
  Provost Marshal General, 49-50, 52
Arthur, Chester A., 232
Atomic Energy Commission, 8, 238, 338
Avis, Dwight E., 194
Bach, Capt. E. E., 105-106
Baker, Fred, 243-244
Bambacus, Joseph, 263-264, 269-271
Barry, Helen, 188
Bartone, Dominick, 306-308
Batista, General, 296, 298
Baughman, U. E., 274-275
Beam, Ambassador Jacob, 34, 40, 46
Bean, Ellis E., 263
Bean, Ted, 141-149
Becker, Arthur R., 181-190
Bentley, Elizabeth, 214-215
Birdzell, Donald T., 273
Birrell, Lowell, 126, 128
Black market in cigarettes, 53-61
Bloch, Fritz, 83-94
Bolling Air Force base, 79, 81
Bon Ami company, 127, 132
Boswell, William O., 25-26, 36-42, 47
Bourbonnais, Charles, 158
Breit, Maj. Gen. John M., 78
British Military Intelligence, 78
Brock, Leonard, 68
Brooks, James J., 276
Bryan, Albert V., 269-271
Bufalino, Russel, 218
Bureau of Commercial Fisheries, 342
Bureau of Customs, 50, 159
Bureau of Federal Credit Unions, 341
Bureau of Mines, 342
Bureau of Prohibition, 233
Bureau of Sports Fisheries and Wildlife, 342
Burton, Luther, 258-259
Butler, William, 183

Calamaras, Nick, 167
Callahan, John T., 119-121
Cal-Tex Citrus Juice, Inc., 179-190
Campbell, Walter A., 173
Capone, Al, 249, 251-252
Carroll, Joseph F., 78
Cary, William L., 117
Castro, Fidel, 29, 295, 296
Ceburre, James M., 163-164
Cella, Salvatore, 226
Central Intelligence Agency, 82, 338
Cermak, Mayor Anton, 273
Chillingsworth, Judge C. E., 210
Chinese communists, 294, 318-332
Civil Aeronautics Administration, 98-99
Civil Aeronautics Board, 97-115
  Air Safety Investigators, 97-98
  Bureau of Safety, 99-100
  Mt. Carmel, Pa. air disaster, 105-115
  techniques of detecting crash causes, 99-102

Civil Service Commission, 8, 230-248
Bureau of Personnel Investigations, 230
Division of Investigation and Review, 233
loyalty investigations, 234-238
reform movement, 232-233
Security Investigations Index, 236
Security Research File, 236
Clark, George, 110-113
Clark, Tom C., 214
Coast Guard, 135-149
historical background, 135-136
Intelligence Division, 135
investigation of *Steelhead* and *Coho II*, 140-149
Office of Merchant Marine Safety, 138-139
Prohibition and rum-runners, 136-137
Coffelt, Leslie, 273
Colle, Charles, 302, 303-305, 308
Comficor, 127, 130-132
Commerce Department, investigative agencies, 139, 338-339
Commission on Civil Rights, 339
Communists, 83-94
deportation of, 213-214
infiltration of American industry, 213
Comptroller of the Currency, 343
Comstock, Anthony, 311-312
Congress and the Federal investigators, 333-336
Conley, Thomas F., 227, 229
Coolidge, Calvin, 273, 276
Cordes, Fritz, 41, 43-44, 46
Cornetta, Frederick, 164
Costello, Frank, 217
Couzzi, Mario, 159
Craig, William, 273
Credit Unions, Bureau of Federal, 341
Crosby, Francis P., 317
Cuba:
embargo on shipments to, 294-295
forged passports from, 30-31
Custer, General George Armstrong, 192
Customs Agency Service, 289-308
Division of Investigations and Enforcement, 290
historical background, 290-291
imports from Red China and Cuba, 294
smuggling, 293-294, 296-308
waterfront patrol protection, 295-296
Cutting, Bronson, 99

Daniels, Josephus, 62-63
Davisson, E. A., 141-149
Dawson, Judge Archie, 167
Decker, Stoy, 198
Delaney, Jack, 71
DeLucia, Paul, 217, 252
Denver airline crash, 102
Devlin, Robert J., 217
Dikeos, Victor, 34-40, 42, 47
Dio, Johnny, 250
Discher, Urszula, 38-47
Dominican Republic, 132-133, 296-308
Donovan, Harry L., 258-271
Downs, Joseph H., 273
Duchet, John, 239-247

Eggerton, B. L., 181
Eisenhower, Dwight D., 81, 255, 273, 274, 313
Elizabeth, N.J. air disasters, 103-104
Emerick, C. A., 296
Emigh, Leslie F., 121
Eveleigh, Robert J., 128

Falanga, Anthony J., 167
Farber, James Polk, 43-44, 46
Fargione, Michael F., 218
Farrell, Raymond F., 220
Federal Aviation Agency, 99, 102, 108, 339
Federal Bureau of Investigation, 3-22
Communist investigations, 8-22
counter-intelligence data, 82
crime reports, 4-5
Disaster Squad, 4, 13
history of, 5-7
kidnappings and bank robberies, 9-12
Laboratory and Identification Division, 12-13
loyalty investigations, 8, 235, 237
National Academy, 4
Federal Bureau of Narcotics, 50, 150-168
duties and responsibilities, 151-157
international dope rings, 155-168
organization, 150-157
smuggling by ambassador, 157-168
Federal Communications Commission, 316, 339
Federal Deposit Insurance Corporation, 339
Federal Employees Loyalty Program, 234-235
Federal Home Loan Bank Board, 339-340
Federal Motorboat Act of 1958, 138
Federal Power Commission, 340
Federal Reserve System, 340
Federal Security Agency, 174
Federal Trade Commission, 118, 340
Ferrando, Augusto, 298-308
Fitelson, Dr. Jacob, 175
Florida, moonshine business, 199-210

Fluet, Joseph O., 100-115
Food and Drug Administration, 169-190, 316
  Hoxsey cancer-cure racket, 175-176
  jurisdiction, 177-179
  orange juice conspiracy, 179-190
  responsibilities, 169-179
Foreign Assets Control Administration, 294-295
Fortier, Joseph A., 298
Frank, Julian, 101
Franklin, James, 71-76
Frazier, Roy, 68
French *Sûreté* Nationale, 78, 167-168
Friedman, Mrs. Elizabeth Smith, 136-137
Furey, Robert J., 166-167

Gaffney, George H., 160, 164-166
Garcia, Col. Juan Abbes, 300-301
Garfield, President James, 230, 232
General Accounting Office, 340
General Services Administration, 340
Genovese, Vito, 218
Germany:
  black market in cigarettes, 53-61
  spy system, 63
Gillette, Kirby, 81
Goldfine, Bernard, 255
Goodwin, Jack, 16-22
Gordon, Waxey, 252
Graham, John Gilbert, 102, 313
Grand Canyon mid-air collision, 99
Grant, President Ulysses S., 231
Greenleaf, Earl, 221-223
Griffin, John R., 166-167
Guiteau, Charles, 230, 232
Guterma affair, 124-134

Hal Roach Studios, 127, 131
Hamilton, Alexander, 135-136
Harden, Rufus Howard, 287-288
Harrison Narcotics Act in 1914, 152
Hauptmann, Bruno, 252-253
Harvey, Lew Gene, 201-210
Hayes, Rutherford B., 232
Health, Education and Welfare Department, 174, 341-342
Hill, Virginia, 257
Hoover, J. Edgar, 5-6, 13-14, 82, 216
Horwick, Jules, 256
House Un-American Activities Committee, 236-237
Housing and Home Finance Agency, 341
Howard, Bliss, 86-94
Howell, Herschel, 181-190
Hoxsey cancer-cure, 175-176

Immigration and Naturalization Service, 213-229
  deportation of foreign-born racketeers, 215-217
  fall of Joe Adonis, 220-229
  investigators, 213-214
Intelligence Division of the Internal Revenue Service, 249-271
Interdepartmental Intelligence Conference, 65
Interior Department, investigative agencies, 342
Internal Revenue Service:
  Alcohol and Tobacco Tax Division, 191-210
  Intelligence Division, 249-271
    investigations of racketeers, 249-252
    numbers racket in Richmond, Va., 258-271
    special agents, 253
    tax evasion cases, 253-254
  postal inspectors and, 317
International Workers Order, 215
Interstate Commerce Commission, 342
Irey, Elmer L., 252-253

Jacobs, F. L., Co., 124-134
Jaegerman, Edward C., 119-121, 129-130, 133
Japan, espionage in World War II, 64
Johnson, Max, 262
Justice Department, 316-317
  Federal Bureau of Investigation, 3-22
  Immigration and Naturalization Service, 213-229

Kefauver Committee, 157, 215-216, 221, 253
Kennedy, John F., 151, 274, 317
Kennedy, Robert F., 12, 151, 249, 313, 335
Khrushchev, Nikita, 28-29
Knauf, Kenneth, 36-41, 43-45
Kunz, Horst, 90

Labor Department, 342
Landford, William B., 297-308
Lansing, Robert, 26
Larrick, George P., 176, 179
Lathem, John D., 197
Lederer, Dr. Ludwig G., 113-114
Levigno, John, 196
Leya, Charles J., Jr., 165-166
Lincoln, Abraham, 231, 272, 275
Lincoln, George David, 205-210
Liquori, Joseph, 298-308
Livesay, Lacy R., 209
Llora, Luis, 325-327, 329-330

Lombard, Carole, 100
Londin, Jerome J., 128, 130
Long, H. Alan, 249
Lopez, Gregorio, 326
Luciano, Lucky, 225
Ludwig, Meyer, 88
Lyons, Charles W., 36-43

MacArthur, General, 331-332
Macauley, Sidney, 260-270
McBride, Alan, 263-265
McConnell, Warren J., 200
McGranery, James, 216
McKagen Oliver H., 184-186
McKinley, President, 272
MacMahon, Judge Lloyd F., 133
Madison, Verne C., 187-190
Mafia, dope traffic dominated by, 157
Magistretti, William, 41
Maley, Robert C., Jr., 183, 190
Maneri, Salvatore, 216
Manley, Richard M., 165-166
Martynov, Colonel Maksim, 18-22
Marx, Gerhard, 89
Maxwell, Ted, 67-76
Meyers, General Bennett E., 77-78
Micro-Moisture Controls, 126
Minker, Abe, 256
Monroney, Senator Mike, 99
Moran, William H., 277
Moses, Walter B., 179-190
Mt. Carmel (Pennsylvania) air disaster, 105-115
Muglia, Armando, 159, 164
Murphy, J. Austin, 219
Murphy, John R., 263, 270
Mutual Broadcasting System, 127-128, 131

Narcotics, Federal Bureau of, 150-168
National Aeronautics and Space Administration, 342
National and Federal Firearms Acts, 197-198
National Association of Securities Dealers, 118
National Bureau of Standards, 102
National Crime Commission, need for, 334-335
National Daily Quotation Service, 122
National Labor Relations Board, 342-343
National Maritime Union, 215
Naval Intelligence, Office of, 62-76
New York Society for the Prevention of Vice, 311
New York Stock Exchange, 116, 122, 131
Newbauer, Sidney, 298-308
Noto, Mario T., 214, 217-218

Office of Military Government, 34
Office of Naval Intelligence, 62-76
  personnel, 65-66
  Security Division, 63-64
Office of Special Investigations, Air Force, 77-94
Ogden, R. Frank, 318-332
Olds, Rear Admiral Francis P., 320-321

Parker, Fred, 57-61
Parmenter, William Raiford, 199-210
Pavlick, Richard P., 274, 317
Pendergast, "Boss" Tom, 249, 254-255
Pendleton, George H., 232
Pentagon's Joint Defense Intelligence Agency, 78
Pera, Martin, 157-168
Personnel Investigations, Bureau of, 230
Peters, J., 214-215
Peters, Martin, 221-229
Peyton, Col. James, 102
Philippine black market in money orders, 318-332
Pohl, Anthony S., 161-165
Polish Intelligence, 33-47, 81
Pollack, Irving M., 123
Porter, Stephen G., 154
Postal Inspection Service, 12, 309-332
  mail fraud, 311, 313-316
  obscene mail, 311-312
  postal inspectors, 313
  "special agents," 311
Powell, James, 55-58
Presta, Mario, 218
Prohibition and rum-runners, 136-137, 152-153, 193-194
Public Health Service, 341

Rae, Thomas W., 121
Rayburn, Sam, 118
Red China, 294, 318-332
Ricca, Paul, 217, 252
Richmond, Va., numbers racket, 258-271
Riesel, Victor, 250
Roger, Louis Emory, 285
Roosevelt, Franklin D., 7-8, 62-64, 99, 117-118, 173-174, 193, 273
Roosevelt, Theodore, 152, 171, 273
Roper, Daniel C., 252
Rosal, Mauricio, Guatemalan Ambassador, 158
Rosenberg case, 9
Rowley, James, 274-275
Royal Canadian Mounted Police, 78, 151
Rusk, Dean, 39-40

Salas brothers, 287-288
Santo, John, 214
Saturnino, Emilana, 330-331
Scarbeck, Irvin C., 33-47
Scarcelli, Paul, 218
Schaaphok, Carl J., 280, 287
Scotland Yard, 78
Scozzari, Simon, 218
Seay, Leo, 259, 267
Secret Service, 272-288
  counterfeiting and, 275-288
  powers and duties, 272-273, 275-277
  Protective Research Section, 273-274
  White House Police Force, 273
Securities and Exchange Commission, 116-134
  brokers and dealers requirements, 118, 122
  Division of Trading and Exchanges, 119, 123
  Guterma affair, 124-134
  Jaegerman-Callahan team, 119-121
  market surveillance staff, 117, 122
  registration requirements, 118
  trust deeds and mortgages, 121-122
  works with postal inspectors, 317
Schember, Richard, 111
Scranton Corp., 127, 131-132
Senate Rackets Committee, 250
Shaffer, Leo, 256
Shanley, Wallace D., 296-308
Shawano Development Company, 125-126, 133
Sherman, Irving, 216
Silt, C. T., 142-149
Simmons, James Douglas, 280
Siu Chung Yin, 322-324
Skau, W. J., 319
Smethie, George P., Jr., 259-267
Smith, E. Pitt, 181-190
Smith, Ferdinand, 215
Smith, Jack Leonard, 143-145
Solomon, Mitchell S., 217
Sonnier, Justin Arphy, 279-280, 283, 285-287
Sonnier, Joseph, 283, 285-287
Soviet espionage, 8-22, 81-94
Speer, Wayland, 161
Stacher, Joseph, 219
State Department:
  Bureau of Secret Intelligence, 26-27
  investigative agencies, 343
  Office of Security, 25-47
    passports and visas, 30
    protection of foreign dignitaries, 28-29
Steelhead, disappearance of, 140-149
Stettinius, Edward R., Jr., 27
Sugarman, Judge Sidney S., 128-129, 132
Symington, Stuart, 77

Tarditi, Etienne, 158-168
Tariff Commission, 343
Tartaglino, Andrew, 159
Tingle, A. K., 291-292
Transport Workers Union, 214
Treasury Department:
  Bureau of Internal Revenue, 152
  Bureau of Prohibition, 152-153
  Coast Guard, 135
  Comptroller of the Currency, 343
  Customs Agency Service, 289-308
  Law Enforcement Officer Training School, 135, 253
Trento, Leonard, 297-308
Trujillo, General Rafael, 128, 133, 296
Trujillo, Rafael, Jr., 298-299
Truman, Harry S., 234, 253, 273, 274

Uniform Code of Military Justice, 65-66
United Dye and Chemical Co., 126-127, 132-133
U.S. Government Organization Manual, 67
United States Information Agency, 343

Vaccaro, John J., 293
Van Liew brothers, 181-190
Vermiglio, Sebastiano, 217
Veterans Administration, 343

Waesche, Douglas, 258-270
Wage and Hour Division, 342
Walker, Raymond, Jr., 263
Warner, Capt. George, 105, 111
Washington, George, 48-49, 230-231
Waters, Francis E., 161-163
West, James Earl, 199-210
West Berlin, 92-94
Western Financial Corp., 126, 133
White House Police Force, 273
Wiley, Dr. Harvey W., 171, 173, 179
Wilkie, John E., 276
Williamson, John, 215
Willis, George, 71, 74-76
Wilson, Frank J., 251, 277
Wilson, Woodrow, 233, 273
Windels, Paul, Jr., 127-128
Woods, William P., 276
Wright, Captain Bill, 53-61

Younger, Stanley Ira, 120

DISCARDED
Goshen Public Library